Contents

Boxes

GLOBAL MONITORING REPORT 2007

Figures

Tables

Foreword

The 2007 *Global Monitoring Report* takes stock of progress toward achieving the Millennium Development Goals and assesses the contributions of developing countries, donor nations, and the international financial institutions as they work toward meeting commitments under the 2002 Monterrey consensus. This fourth annual GMR finds both areas of progress and gaps where far greater effort is required. This year's special topics—achieving gender equality and addressing the problems of fragile states—highlight two particular areas where serious challenges confront the international community.

The GMR presents striking evidence of real progress on the MDG agenda in several areas. Globally, rapid growth is translating into falling levels of extreme poverty: in the five years between 1999 and 2004 global poverty fell by nearly 4 percentage points, lifting an estimated 135 million people out of destitution. Sub-Saharan Africa's performance has also been encouraging over this period; the share of extreme poor fell by nearly 5 percentage points, although the absolute number of poor has not fallen: Sub-Saharan Africa remains the poorest developing region in the world with about two-fifths of its people living on less than US$1 a day.

Significant gains are occurring in human development: globally the primary school completion rate has increased from 78 percent in 2000 to 83 percent in 2005 and the pace of increase has accelerated in all regions (except Latin America and the Caribbean, where levels were already high).

Aid quality and effectiveness are improving: signatories to the 2005 Paris Declaration on aid effectiveness are monitoring progress on harmonization, alignment, and managing for development results. Still, many challenges remain in accelerating the implementation of the Paris Agenda.

Strengthening future performance will require greater attention in two important areas. The first relates to gender equality and the empowerment of women. Second is the condition of fragile states, where nearly 500 million people, or nearly one-fifth of all people in low-income countries, reside.

Gender equality and the empowerment of women are important for basic reasons—fairness, equality of opportunity, and economic well-being. Increasing efficiency and achieving the full potential of men and women alike is a precursor to prosperity. Gender equality is also vital to advancing the other millennium goals—halving poverty, achieving primary education for all, and lowering the under-five mortality rate. Achieving equal opportunity for women will require greater accountability among donors, developing countries, and international institutions such as our own. It will entail moving beyond a general institutional call for attention, toward a concrete strengthening of programs and project implementation. This would in turn allow a focus on outcomes as well as on a longer-term agenda. Such a shift requires improving monitoring systems for tracking progress in gender equality, and evaluating the impact of interventions aimed at attaining equality of opportunity.

Fragile states, with their limited capacity to secure a better life for their citizens, merit special attention because of the enormity of the problems they face. These countries by definition have weak governments and are hard put to deliver basic services to their people. Over one-fourth of extremely poor people in developing countries live in fragile states. These nations face enormous challenges, regarding both how to take action to meet human development needs, and how to stave off a potential downward spiral of conflict, human abuse, and refugee flight. New instruments should be considered to help countries that have turned the corner to quickly stabilize, restore both security and basic services, and bring greater accountability into public service. This will require better coordination and more effective intervention by the international community.

To move both of these crucial agendas forward and to secure faster progress toward meeting the MDGs, international efforts to scale up aid for deserving country programs are vital. We have not made sufficient progress in delivering on the promises of the Monterrey Summit in 2002, or the 2005 Gleneagles commitments to scale up aid to Africa. Current examples of countries that have received significantly scaled-up aid to help finance sound programs to meet the MDGs are few and far between. This is not for lack of opportunity, which abounds at the project-, sector-, and country-levels. Rather, the dearth of successful scaling-up efforts points to the need for the greater "mutual accountability" called for under the Monterrey consensus. First, we need to identify and fund existing opportunities for scaling up based on current knowledge and capacity, such as in the country and sector areas that the World Bank and the UN have identified. Second, we must work together to develop a dynamic strategy for country-based opportunities to sequentially scale up, including with sufficient technical assistance from our two organizations, working together with other development partners. This will require that donor countries fulfill their pledges to strengthen their development strategies and that they put real resources to work to enact these programs.

Deadlines to deliver on promises in 2010, 2015, and 2030 are looming large and, collectively, we need to speed up investments in projects and reform programs that will save lives, create jobs, and promote growth. The responsibility for this lies with donors, our own and other institutions, and recipients alike.

Paul Wolfowitz
President
World Bank

Rodrigo de Rato
Managing Director
International Monetary Fund

Acknowledgments

This report has been prepared jointly by the staff of the World Bank and the International Monetary Fund. There was also consultation and collaboration with other partner institutions including the Organisation for Economic Co-operation and Development and its Development Assistance Committee, several United Nations agencies, the African Development Bank, the Asian Development Bank, the European Bank for Reconstruction and Development, the Inter-American Development Bank, and the Islamic Development Bank. The cooperation and support of staff of these institutions are gratefully acknowledged.

Mark Sundberg was the lead author and manager of the report. The work was carried out under the general guidance of François Bourguignon, Senior Vice-President, and the overall supervision of Alan Gelb, Director, World Bank.

The core team for the report included Peter Fallon (chapter 1); Barbara Bruns (chapter 2); Mayra Buvinic, Elizabeth King, Andrew Morrison, and Nistha Sinha (chapter 3); Punam Chuhan (chapter 4); and Stefano Curto (chapter 5). The Bank core team also included Brendan Fitzpatrick, Julien Gourdon, and Sachin Shahria, who provided research, written inputs, and coordination to the overall report. Other significant contributions were made by Amar Bhattacharya,

Carlos Primo Braga, Kirk Hamilton, Julia Nielson, Bernard Hoekman, Sarah Cliffe, Sima Kanaan, Adam Ross, Giovanni Ruta, and Juan Carlos Guzman.

Many others have made valuable contributions, including the following from the **World Bank**:

Aban Daruwala, Ajay Chhibber, Akihiko Nishio, Alessandro Nicita, Amie Batson, Ana Cristina Torres, Anand Rajaram, Arthur Karlin, Arunima Dhar, Bee Ean Gooi, Bonaventure Mbida-Essama, Brian Levy, Brice Quesnel, Christopher Hall, Claudia Paz Sepulveda, Desmond Bermingham, Dhushyanth Raju, Dianne Garama, Dorte Domeland-Narvaez, Doug Hostland, Eduard Bos, Elizabeth White, Emi Suzuki, Eric Swanson, Robert Francis Rowe, Gauresh Rajadhyaksha, Gary Milante, Gilles Bauche, Gisela Garcia, Hiau Looi Kee, Jessica Lynn Ebbeler, Joseph Naimoli, Joy De Beyer, Kavita Watsa, Louise Cord, Luc-Charles Gacougnolle, Lucia Fort, Martin Ravillion, Mary Hallward-Driemeier, Maureen Lewis, Meera Shekhar, Michael Koch, Monica Das Gupta, Nevin Fahmy, Nina Todorova Budina, Olusoji Adeyi, Pablo Gottret, Patrick Grasso, Prem Sangrula, Rekha Mehra, Rene Bonnel, Reynaldo Martorell, Rifat Hasan, Robert Watson, Robin Horn, Roula Yazigi, Shahrokh Fardoust, Shaohua Chen, Shunalini Sarkar, Soe Lin, Sulekha Patel, Susan Stout, and Waafas Ofosu-Amaah.

Contributors from the **International Monetary Fund** included:

Alun Thomas, Ben Umansky, Carlo Sdralevich, Emmanuel Hife, Marie-Helen Le Manchec, Mark Plant, and Scott Brown.

Contributors from **other institutions** included:

Kazu Sakai, Christopher MacCormac, Manju Senapaty, Patrick Safran (ADB), Philibert Afrika, Ferdinand Bakoup, Maurice Mubila, Penthesilea Lartey (AfDB), Ernesto Castagnino, Marco Ferroni, Max Pulgar-Vidal, Afredo Garcia (IADB), Samuel Fankhauser, James Earwicker (EBRD), Brian Hammond, Patricia O'Neill (OECD-DAC), and Chandrika Bahadur (UNDP).

Guidance received from the Executive Directors of the World Bank and their staff, and the International Monetary Fund during discussions of the draft report is gratefully acknowledged. The report has also benefited from many useful comments and suggestions received from the World Bank and International Monetary Fund management and staff in the course of the preparation and review of the report.

The World Bank's Office of the Publisher managed the editorial services, design, production, and printing of the book—in particular Susan Graham, Denise Bergeron, Aziz Gökdemir, Nancy Lammers, Stephen McGroarty, Randi Park, Santiago Pombo-Bejarano, and Janice Tuten, along with Kirsten Dennison and associates at Precision Graphics, Candace Roberts and associates at Quantum Think, Gerry Quinn, Bruce Ross-Larson, and Michael Treadway, provided excellent help with publishing this book on a very tight schedule.

Finally, acknowledgments are due to Matthew Burke and Maria Del Carmen Cosu of the World Bank Art Program, who helped us find the artwork for the cover.

Abbreviations

AAP	Africa Action Plan	HIPC	heavily indebted poor country/countries
ACP	African, Caribbean, and Pacific countries	HIV	human immunodeficiency virus
ADB	Asian Development Bank	IADB	Inter-American Development Bank
AfDF	African Development Fund		
AsDF	Asian Development Fund	IBRD	International Bank for Reconstruction and Development
AIDS	acquired immunodeficiency syndrome		
		ICS	Investment Climate Surveys
AMC	Advance Market Commitment	IDA	International Development Association (of the World Bank Group)
ART	antiretroviral treatment		
COMPAS	Common Performance Assessment System		
		IFAD	International Fund for Agricultural Development
CPIA	Country Policy and Institutional Assessment		
		IFC	International Finance Corporation (of the World Bank Group)
DAC	Development Assistance Committee (of the OECD)		
DALY	disability-adjusted life year	IFFIm	International Finance Facility for Immunization
DB	Doing Business (surveys)		
DHS	Demographic and Health Survey	IFI	international financial institution
EBRD	European Bank for Reconstruction and Development	IMCI	integrated management of childhood illness
		IMF	International Monetary Fund
EC	European Commission	LIC	low-income country
EFA-FTI	Education for All-Fast Track Initiative	LICUS	low-income countries under stress
EPA	Economic Partnership Agreement	MDB	multilateral development bank
		MDG	Millennium Development Goal
ES	Enterprise Survey	MDRI	Multilateral Debt Relief Initiative
FAO	Food and Agriculture Organization (of the UN)		
		NGO	nongovernmental organization
G-8	Group of Eight	NTM	nontariff measure
GII	Global Integrity Index	ODA	official development assistance
GMR	*Global Monitoring Report*	OECD	Organisation for Economic Co-operation and Development
GNI	gross national income		

OOF	other official flow	TRI	trade restrictiveness index
OTRI	overall trade restrictiveness index	UNDP	United Nations Development Programme
PEFA	Public Expenditure and Financial Accountability	UNESCO	United Nations Education, Scientific and Cultural Organization
PFM	public financial management		
PIU	project implementation unit	UNFPA	United Nations Population Fund
PRSP	Poverty Reduction Strategy Paper	UNICEF	United Nations Children's Fund
R&R	results and resources	USAID	United States Agency for International Development
SDR	special drawing right		
STD	sexually transmitted disease	WHO	World Health Organization
SWAp	sectorwide approach	WSS	water supply and sanitation
TB	tuberculosis	WTO	World Trade Organization

Millennium Development Goals (MDGs)

Goals and Targets from the Millennium Declaration

GOAL 1	ERADICATE EXTREME POVERTY AND HUNGER
TARGET 1	Halve, between 1990 and 2015, the proportion of people whose income is less than $1 a day
TARGET 2	Halve, between 1990 and 2015, the proportion of people who suffer from hunger

GOAL 2	ACHIEVE UNIVERSAL PRIMARY EDUCATION
TARGET 3	Ensure that by 2015, children everywhere, boys and girls alike, will be able to complete a full course of primary schooling

GOAL 3	PROMOTE GENDER EQUALITY AND EMPOWER WOMEN
TARGET 4	Eliminate gender disparity in primary and secondary education, preferably by 2005, and at all levels of education no later than 2015

GOAL 4	REDUCE CHILD MORTALITY
TARGET 5	Reduce by two-thirds, between 1990 and 2015, the under-five mortality rate

GOAL 5	IMPROVE MATERNAL HEALTH
TARGET 6	Reduce by three-quarters, between 1990 and 2015, the maternal mortality ratio

GOAL 6	COMBAT HIV/AIDS, MALARIA, AND OTHER DISEASES
TARGET 7	Have halted by 2015 and begun to reverse the spread of HIV/AIDS
TARGET 8	Have halted by 2015 and begun to reverse the incidence of malaria and other major diseases

GOAL 7	ENSURE ENVIRONMENTAL SUSTAINABILITY
TARGET 9	Integrate the principles of sustainable development into country policies and programs and reverse the loss of environmental resources
TARGET 10	Halve by 2015 the proportion of people without sustainable access to safe drinking water and basic sanitation
TARGET 11	Have achieved a significant improvement by 2020 in the lives of at least 100 million slum dwellers

GOAL 8	DEVELOP A GLOBAL PARTNERSHIP FOR DEVELOPMENT
TARGET 12	Develop further an open, rule-based, predictable, nondiscriminatory trading and financial system (including a commitment to good governance, development, and poverty reduction, nationally and internationally)
TARGET 13	Address the special needs of the least developed countries (including tariff- and quota-free access for exports of the least developed countries; enhanced debt relief for heavily indebted poor countries and cancellation of official bilateral debt; and more generous official development assistance for countries committed to reducing poverty)
TARGET 14	Address the special needs of landlocked countries and small island developing states (through the Programme of Action for the Sustainable Development of Small Island Developing States and the outcome of the 22nd special session of the General Assembly)
TARGET 15	Deal comprehensively with the debt problems of developing countries through national and international measures to make debt sustainable in the long term
TARGET 16	In cooperation with developing countries, develop and implement strategies for decent and productive work for youth
TARGET 17	In cooperation with pharmaceutical companies, provide access to affordable, essential drugs in developing countries
TARGET 18	In cooperation with the private sector, make available the benefits of new technologies, especially information and communication

Source: United Nations. 2000 (September 18). *Millennium Declaration.* A/RES/55/2. New York.
United Nations. 2001 (September 6). *Road Map towards the Implementation of the United Nations Millennium Declaration.* Report of the Secretary General. New York.
Note: The Millennium Development Goals and targets come from the Millennium Declaration signed by 189 countries, including 147 heads of state, in September 2000. The goals and targets are related and should be seen as a whole. They represent a partnership of countries determined, as the Declaration states, "to create an environment—at the national and global levels alike—which is conducive to development and the elimination of poverty."

Report Overview

Introduction

Broad-based global economic growth in 2006, and more generally since 2000, provides grounds for optimism about progress in advancing the Millennium Development Goals (MDGs). For low-income countries, real per capita income growth in Sub-Saharan Africa and South Asia has been stronger in the period since 2000 than at any time since the 1960s, and stronger than at any time since transition in Europe and Central Asian countries. Based on this strong growth performance, the estimated number of extremely poor people (living on $1 per day) fell by 135 million between 1999 and 2004.

Although still uneven, progress with poverty reduction is evident across all regions. Sub-Saharan Africa reduced the share of people living in extreme poverty by 4.7 percentage points over five years to 41 percent, although high population growth left the same absolute number of poor, at nearly 300 million. South Asia, Latin America, and East Asia all appear to be roughly on track to halve extreme poverty by 2015 from 1990 levels. Europe, Central Asia, and the Middle East and North Africa have largely eliminated extreme poverty. There are also hopeful signs that international development efforts may be gaining momentum, and new innovations in resource mobilization for development are taking shape.

Yet in spite of this optimistic outlook, the international community faces a much more demanding agenda in advancing the MDGs as 2015 draws nearer. Despite progress, nearly 1 billion people remain in extreme poverty. All regions are off track to meet the target for reducing child mortality; nutrition is a major challenge, with one-third of all children in developing countries underweight or stunted; half the people in developing countries lack access to improved sanitation.

Action to scale up development efforts needs to accelerate, but steps forward still appear tentative. Nearly seven years after the Millennium Summit and five years after the Monterrey summit, there has yet to be a country case where aid is being significantly scaled up to support a medium-term program to reach the MDGs. While there has been modest progress in Paris or Brussels or London to address the well-recognized problems in designing and delivering international aid—proliferation of aid channels, weak coordination, lack of resource predictability, misalignment with country strategies, and so on—viewed from the capitals of Ethiopia, Madagascar, or Bolivia, this progress appears to be slow.

This *Global Monitoring Report* (GMR) highlights two areas that require greater international attention if higher global growth trends are to translate into sustainable development outcomes and if the gains are to be shared more evenly:

- *Gender equality*. The first of these arises from gender inequality and lost opportunities for *all* people to help generate and participate in the gains from economic growth. The choice to focus the 2007 report on the third MDG—the promotion of gender equality and empowerment of women—reflects a recognition by the international community that more is needed to support equality for the half of humanity disadvantaged through less access than men to *rights* (equality under the law), to *resources* (equality of opportunity), and to *voice* (political equality).
- *Fragile states*. The second risk arises from the especially difficult development challenges and greater needs facing *fragile states*. Fragile states—countries with particularly weak governance, institutions, and capacity—comprise 9 percent of the developing world's population but over one-fourth of the extreme poor. They represent an enormous challenge: how can the international community provide resources to support efficient service delivery, postconflict recovery, and reform? Without addressing these development challenges the fragile states pose risks that can cross borders—through civil conflicts, risks to public health, and humanitarian crises.

Two additional risks pertain to environmental sustainability and securing the gains from trade liberalization. Natural resource depletion and environmental degradation pose risks to both the quality of growth, and the potential for sustaining future growth. Growth based on the depletion of natural wealth, rather than through increasing wealth for current and future generations, is unsustainable. The "adjusted net savings rate" measures national savings after accounting for resource depletion and damage to the environment, raising broad policy questions about environmental policies that are beyond the scope of this report but may be tackled in future GMRs.

Risks from failure to advance multilateral trade liberalization and expand market access are also highlighted in this year's report. The Doha Round of trade negotiations was effectively suspended in July 2006, but early in 2007 there was an informal agreement to resume talks. Failure to make progress means depriving many countries of vital opportunities for accelerating their growth through trade.

To address these risks and advance the MDG agenda there is a pressing need for better aid coordination to strengthen aid quality and scale-up assistance. This requires efforts by all parties—donors, international financial institutions (IFIs), and developing countries. Agreement needs to be forged at the global level on practical mechanisms and instruments to scale up aid and on measures to reduce the costs of aid fragmentation. Progress with scaling-up will require more and better aid resources (donors); sound, sequenced development strategies (developing partners); better technical support for strong strategies (the IFIs); and a more coherent "aid architecture" to reduce the costs of fragmentation.

Progress toward the MDGs

Growth and Poverty Reduction

The world economy is growing at a pace last seen at the beginning of the 1970s. This is welcome news for developing countries in view of its implications for trade, aid, private financial flows, and remittances. Both low- and middle-income countries have benefited from the trend. Performance varies widely across regions, but there is a favorable trend evident in East Asia, South Asia, Eastern Europe, and Central Asia, and particularly Sub-Saharan Africa, where the sustained and rising growth performance since the late 1990s is in sharp contrast to the weak performance evident over the last three decades. Average per capita income growth in Sub-

---

BOX 1   Global Monitoring Report 2007: Five key messages

Growth is reducing poverty, but not everywhere or always sustainably. Continued strong growth is generating significant progress in poverty reduction globally. But many countries are failing to benefit, especially fragile states, and for some others the sources and quality of growth (unsustainable resource extraction; accumulating pollutants) undermine environmental sustainability and future growth potential.

Investing in gender equality and empowerment of women is smart economics. Greater gender equality helps to create a fair society, raises economic productivity, and helps advance other development goals. Major gains have been achieved, particularly in education, while in other areas progress is lagging. Better monitoring and mainstreaming of women's empowerment and equality into policy formulation and programs of international assistance are therefore vital to the development agenda.

Fragile states are failing to keep up—speed and staffing by development agencies are critical. The largest "MDG deficit" is in states with weak institutions and governance, and often in conflict—the "fragile states." With 9 percent of the developing world's population, they account for over one-fourth of the extreme poor and nearly one-third of child deaths and 12-year olds who do not complete primary school. Efforts to support their transition from fragility must be deepened through improving response time to crises and opportunities, increasing field presence, better interagency collaboration, and building on lessons from successful state-building transitions.

Quality lags quantity—children enroll in school but don't always learn. Advancement in primary school completion has been rapid and encouraging in many countries. Yet cross-country evaluations suggest improvement in cognitive skills has often not kept pace. Quantity and quality in education and health need to proceed in tandem. More effort is needed to monitor outcomes (especially student learning). This provides an essential platform for tracking over time whether policies and incentives are truly producing more effective service delivery.

Scaling up "quality" aid requires greater coherence among donors, developing countries, and international agencies. Donor commitments to scaling up aid have so far been unrealized as real aid flows have faltered and a more complex aid architecture—proliferation of donor channels, fragmentation of aid, ear-marking of funds—undermines aid quality and effectiveness. Scaling-up aid to meet the MDGs requires more and better aid resources (donors); sound, sequenced development strategies (developing partners); better technical support for strong strategies (the IFIs); and a more coherent "aid architecture" to reduce the costs of fragmentation.

Saharan Africa has recently been at about 3 percent and is forecast to continue at this level in 2007. By contrast, growth among low- and middle-income countries in Latin America, and the Middle East and North Africa, continues to be more modest.

Evidence suggests that better growth is translating into declining poverty levels. The most recent data show that all regions except for Sub-Saharan Africa are on track to reach the MDG1 poverty target. In Sub-Saharan Africa the share of people living in extreme poverty has declined little from its 1980 level, but this masks the protracted deterioration during the 1980s and first half of the 1990s,

along with marked improvements since the late 1990s. The share of people in poverty fell by nearly 7 percentage points between 1996 and 2004, although the absolute number of poor has stagnated.

Preliminary estimates suggest that, on average, growth (in GDP) during the late 1990s through 2003/04 resulted in lower poverty incidence: for a sample of 19 low-income countries, 1 percent of GDP growth was associated with a 1.3 percent fall in the rate of extreme poverty and a 0.9 percent fall in the $2-a-day poverty rate. For middle-income countries the impact of GDP per capita growth on poverty was much less, and average poverty has not declined with recent growth. Moreover, changes in income distribution have not, on average, reduced the impact of income growth on poverty reduction in low-income countries, whereas income inequality widened on average in middle-income countries.

One factor behind this favorable performance has been the continuing strength of macroeconomic policies, as evident through continued moderate inflation rates and average fiscal balances that shifted from deficit into balance in low-income countries during 2006. The quality of macroeconomic policies, particularly fiscal policy, in low-income countries shows considerable improvement over recent years.

The stronger growth performance in low-income countries is encouraging, particularly in Sub-Saharan Africa where the higher growth may mark a potential turnaround from the region's protracted stagnation. However, this has to be interpreted with caution. Concerns persist over the potential for a growth slowdown resulting from a disorderly unwinding of global imbalances, protectionism, the future behavior of world oil prices, or a possible global pandemic triggered by avian influenza.

Optimism over the prospects for improved growth and poverty reduction, however, does not apply to the many fragile states. Extreme poverty is increasingly concentrated in these states: by 2015 it is estimated that given projected growth performance, extreme poverty levels in nonfragile states will decline to 17 percent, more than achieving the MDG1 target, while levels of extreme poverty in fragile states will remain at over 50 percent, *higher* than the level in 1990.

Progress with the Human Development MDGs

Broad MDG trends do not change appreciably year to year, and remain much as described last year: all regions are off track on the child mortality goal, and some regions are off track on at least some of the other MDGs. The two regions that lag the most are South Asia and Sub-Saharan Africa. As *regions* they remain off track on all the goals; however, there is considerable variation within regions. MDG trends in fragile states are also examined; while there is variance within the group, fragile states have lower absolute performance and slower improvement than nonfragile ones.

It must also be recognized that there have been some significant successes. Since 2000, over 34 million additional children in developing countries have gained the opportunity to attend and complete primary school—one of the most massive expansions of schooling access in history. Over 550 million children have been vaccinated against measles, reducing death from measles in Sub-Saharan Africa by 75 percent. By mid-2006 the number of AIDS (acquired immunodeficiency syndrome) patients with access to antiretroviral treatment had increased nearly sevenfold to over 1.6 million from 2001 levels. There is little question that the MDG targets have helped stimulate more rapid expansion of basic health and education services.

Nutrition (MDG1). Nearly one-third of all children in developing countries are estimated to be underweight or stunted, and an estimated 30 percent of the total population in the developing world suffers from micronutrient deficiencies. Undernutrition is not only a threat to progress with poverty reduction; it is the underlying cause of over 55 percent of all child deaths, linking nutrition directly to reduction of child mortality (MDG4). In striking contrast to the region's strong growth performance, the highest rates of malnutrition are found in South Asia: underweight prevalence is estimated between 38 and 51 percent in the large countries, none of which appears on track to meet the nutrition goal. Sub-Saharan Africa is estimated to have a 26 percent prevalence of child malnutrition, and in some countries— Burkina Faso, Cameroon, Zambia—trends are worsening. East Asia, Latin America, and Eastern Europe show better performance although all have some countries that are off track.

Universal primary completion (MDG2). Globally the primary school completion rate rose between 2000 and 2005 from 78 to 83 percent and the pace of progress in many countries has accelerated. Gains are especially strong in North Africa, Sub-Saharan Africa, and South Asia. But 38 percent of developing countries are unlikely to reach 100 percent primary completion by 2015 and another 22 percent of countries, which lack adequate data to track progress, are also likely to be off track. The most intractable groups to reach with primary education are those that are "doubly disadvantaged": girls from ethnic, religious, or caste minorities. About 75 percent of the 55 million girls who remain out of school are in this group. But recent data also reveal countries that have made remarkable progress in recent years; six of the seven top countries in expanding primary completion rates (all by over 10 percent per year between 2000 and 2005) were in Sub-Saharan Africa (Benin, Guinea, Madagascar, Mozambique, Niger, and Rwanda). The weakest performers were also primarily in Africa, however, showing the sharp contrasts across countries in the region. And in Asia, Cambodia has made exceptional progress.

Child mortality (MDG4). Progress on child mortality lags other MDGs, despite the availability of simple, low-cost interventions that could prevent millions of deaths each year. Oral rehydration therapy, insecticide-treated bednets, breastfeeding, and common antibiotics for respiratory diseases could prevent an estimated 63 percent of child deaths. Yet in 2005 only 32 of 147 countries were on track to achieve the child mortality MDG. Moreover, 23 countries reveal stagnant or worsening mortality rates. Problems in fragile states are particularly severe: nearly one-third (31 percent) of all child deaths in developing countries are in fragile states, and only two of the 35 states currently considered fragile are on track to meet MDG4. The experience of countries that have achieved rapid gains is also noteworthy, including in Eritrea which, despite per capita income of only $190, cut child mortality in half between 1990 and 2005. This success appears in large measure attributable to implementation of the integrated management of childhood illness and points to the serious need to strengthen policy coherence and improve donor coordination in the health sector.

Maternal health (MDG5). Ninety-nine percent of maternal deaths, about 500,000 annually, occur in developing countries. Lack of direct data on maternal mortality requires the use of "skilled attendance at delivery" as a proxy measure. Survey evidence shows progress in 27 of 32 countries but also suggests that this is highly concentrated among richer households—*equity gaps* in access to skilled attendance are larger than for any other health or education service. Evidence on the main constraints to reducing maternal mortality in three low-income countries reaffirms the importance of early recognition of the need for emergency medical attention, access to adequate medical facilities, and receiving appropriate treatment. But it also underscores the essential need for skilled attendance at birth.

AIDS, malaria, and tuberculosis (MDG6). By end-2006 an estimated 39.5 million people were living with the human immuno-deficiency virus (HIV), up 2.6 million since 2004. An estimated 3 million people died from AIDS in 2006. While the spread of this disease has slowed in Sub-Saharan Africa, it is a rapidly growing epidemic in Eastern Europe and Central Asia. Recent experience in combating the spread of AIDS has demonstrated some important messages: reversing its spread *is possible*, treatment *is effective* in the developing world, but prevention efforts need to be intensified.

Annually there are an estimated 300 to 500 million cases of *malaria*, and 1.2 million deaths, mainly among children and mostly in Sub-Saharan Africa. Several new initiatives hold promise for making inroads against malaria: with support from the Dutch and the "Roll Back Malaria" initiative, the World Bank is leading efforts to implement a global subsidy for artemisinin-based combination therapy, the most promising new treatment available because resistance to traditional drugs has grown. The Malaria Booster Program, which supports country-led efforts to deliver concrete and measurable results, such as delivery of insecticide-treated bed nets and malaria treatment for young children and pregnant women, is currently operating in 10 countries and aims to expand to 20 over the next five years.

Tuberculosis (TB) is estimated to have led to 2 million deaths in 2004, and 9 million new cases. While incidence of TB is falling in five of six regions, global growth of 0.6 percent annually is attributed to rapid increases in infections in Sub-Saharan Africa, linked to the greater likelihood of TB appearing from latent infections in HIV carriers. The Directly Observed Treatment, Short-course (DOTS) is the main strategy to combat TB, and has expanded rapidly, with high-burden countries showing large decreases in TB incidence due to DOTS (for instance, Cambodia and Indonesia). In 2006 a new strain of TB—extensively drug-resistant TB—was discovered in South Africa. International efforts to stop its spread are being led by the World Health Organization (WHO) and the Stop TB Partnership.

Water supply and sanitation (MDG7). There has been significant progress on water supply; globally access has increased from 73 percent in 1990 to 80 percent in 2004, but only Latin America and South Asia are considered on track to meet this part of the goal (although more than one-quarter of developing countries lack data). However, within Africa there are some promising trends: 5 of the 10 countries making fastest progress are in Africa, and 17 of the 36 countries for which data are available are on or almost on track. By contrast, global progress on sanitation has lagged, increasing only from 35 percent in 1990 to 50 percent in 2004 and only three regions (East Asia and the Pacific, Latin America, and the Middle East and Northern Africa) are on track. Only 2 of the 32 African countries for which data are available are on track. Despite its importance for achievement of multiple MDGs, official development assistance (ODA) for water supply and sanitation (WSS) declined significantly from the mid-1990s through 2002. Although

it rebounded somewhat after 2003, it still has not returned to the 2000 level. Recent efforts to ramp up financing for WSS, especially for Africa, through such initiatives as the Africa Infrastructure Consortium and the Rural Water Supply and Sanitation Initiative—even if successful—will take some time to have clear impact on the WSS target, given the long lead time for investments.

A continuing concern for all these aggregate data is whether poor households participate in the progress made. Demographic and Health Survey data allow comparison across income quintiles on relative progress. While gaps in access between rich and poor households remain significant, they are narrowing; the poor have had equal or faster rates of progress in child mortality reduction, immunization coverage, and primary completion in most countries.

Financing Trends and Alignment in Health and Education MDGs

External financing for health and education has nearly doubled in real terms since the MDGs were adopted. Aid for health continued to rise from 2004 to 2005, whereas education ODA commitments showed their first decline, reflecting lower commitments to China and India. Aid commitments for education are expected to have increased again in 2006 and beyond, owing in part to a major initiative announced by the United Kingdom.

Funding for health has grown even more strongly, from private sources such as the Gates Foundation; from global partnerships such as the Global Fund for AIDS, TB, and Malaria; and from bilateral donors: France, Norway, Spain, and the United States have increased health funding between two- and fourfold since 2000. Innovative financing mechanisms targeting the health sector are also getting off the ground: the international finance facility for immunization ($1 billion in 2006), advance market commitments for vaccines ($1.5 billion expected in 2007), and the airline ticket tax implemented by 21 countries ($300 million expected in 2007) are all mobilizing new funds for health interventions. Despite this influx of funds for health, there remains a large shortfall relative to financing needs to reach the health MDGs, conservatively estimated at between $25 billion and $50 billion annually.

While increased external funding is crucial for progress on the health MDGs, there are growing concerns about policy coherence, aid alignment, and transactions costs in the sector, given the number of players and the absence of effective coordination mechanisms—a topic taken up below.

The Role of Quality in MDG Progress

Evidence is emerging that in many countries rapid progress in improving schooling enrollment and completion is not translating into better cognitive skills. New research suggests that this may have a high cost for countries: returns to investment in education appear to accrue to the skills of the population and not to the quantity of schooling attained.

Figure 1 illustrates weak learning outcomes and the gap across countries between education level and cognitive skills. By age nine reading skills in developing countries can significantly lag those in developed countries. While over 96 percent of children in Sweden, Latvia, and the Netherlands can read above the lowest—threshold—level of literacy on OECD-benchmarked tests by age nine, less than half the children in Argentina, Colombia, and Morocco can read at this level. Results from a regionally benchmarked assessment for Southern African countries are similarly distressing: in several countries, less than 50 percent of children are able to read by age 12.

It does not follow from this that there exists an inherent trade-off between quantity and quality in education. In fact, cross-country data show a strong positive correlation between schooling coverage and cognitive skills, at least over the long term. There are also numerous countries that have increased learning outcomes at the same time as they

FIGURE 1 Learning levels of primary school–aged children

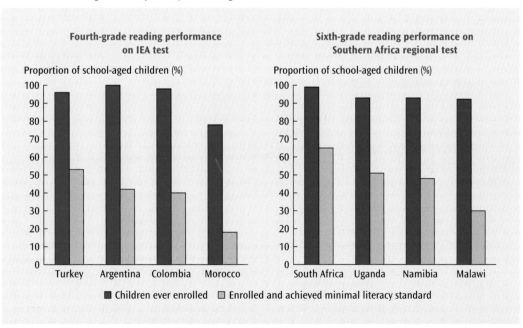

Source: Fourth-grade test: International Association for the Evaluation of Educational Achievement (IEA), Progress in International Reading Literacy (PIRLS) 2001, Sixth-grade test: Southern African Consortium for Monitoring Educational Quality (SACMEQ). Enrollment data: Demographic and Health Surveys.

have expanded access. While this is not easy to do, and there are many cases where quality has been strained as countries rapidly scale up access, it is important to focus on the strategies for managing expansion better. Many poor countries are far from achieving universal primary completion and must accelerate service delivery to reach the MDG by 2015. Slowing expansion would harm the poorest and most marginalized groups most. The challenge must be to expand access while enhancing learning outcomes.

Progress on this challenge requires stronger efforts to monitor student learning in the developing world; most countries today lack national assessment systems and extremely few have engaged in any internationally benchmarked tests. Regular tracking of student learning is essential for accountability in education—for equipping teachers to manage their class time better, for empowering parents to hold schools accountable, and for allowing administrators to evaluate the effectiveness of education spending.

There is a strong case for donor support in developing benchmarked standards of competency linked to critical thinking skills expected by the end of primary school—in other words, basic learning goals for primary education to complement the quantitative goal of universal primary completion. An internationally benchmarked test to measure end-of-primary learning levels could be expensive and technically difficult to produce, but there is a clear public goods argument for such an investment. Precisely at a time when the global community is scaling up aid for the education MDG, a globally benchmarked assessment covering large numbers of developing countries would provide the strongest platform yet for generating knowledge on "what works" to promote learning in different country contexts.

Moving a proposal for basic learning goals for primary education forward will involve costs and face political and technical obstacles. But an internationally supported effort in this area could help countries build national capacity to track learning outcomes

and create incentives to accelerate progress, *alongside efforts to expand school completion rates.*

The same concerns over quality arise in *health care*—and data are even harder to collect. Creative efforts have been made to measure the quality of health care providers across countries and measure the overall quality of care. The extent of misdiagnosed ailments, failure to complete basic checklists for major diseases, and mal-adherence to recommended protocols is alarming. The implication is that there are gaps between what health providers know is right and what they do. It suggests that greater attention to work incentives and institutional settings is needed rather than reliance on input-based approaches, such as raising training requirements or expanding medical schools. Performance contracting is one promising approach for effectively improving health coverage and quality. Greater attention is also needed to bring greater coherence and donor coordination to health sector strategies, as discussed below.

Governance Indicators: An Update

Recently released *aggregated* governance indicators (Kaufman-Kraay) suggest patterns of performance that reinforce key messages from the 2006 GMR. Governance is multidimensional, and there is no unique path from poor to good governance. Actionable indicators to track performance are being developed in several areas, including contributions from independent civil society organizations: Global Integrity released 43 new country reports, the Afrobarometer network released the results for 18 African countries of its third round of surveys, and a new index that monitors transparency in public budgets—the Open Budget Index—was released after four years of development. The World Bank Group also released publicly for the first time its Country Policy and Institutional Assessment (CPIA) scores—an important step in strengthening transparency and disclosure of these scores, which play an important role in allocating concessional financing. By contrast, Public Expenditure and Financial Accountability (PEFA) assessments made less encouraging progress. While the use of PEFA indicators has greatly expanded and many new country assessments are planned, so far only 4 of 33 country reports have been made public, limiting the potential benefits from this valuable tool for analysis.

Promoting and Monitoring Gender Equality and Empowerment of Women

The Importance of Promoting Gender Equality

The 2006 *World Development Report* on equity and development refers to gender inequality as the "archetypal inequality trap," pointing to the sharp differences between men and women in access to assets and opportunities in many countries, and the negative consequences for the well-being of

women, families, and society. The disadvantage of women in *rights* (equality under the law), *resources* (equality of opportunity), and *voice* (political equality) restricts basic freedom to choose and is unfair. This inequality is reflected in the poorer performance by women and girls across many of the MDGs.

"Improving gender equality and empowering women" (MDG3) thus stands on its own merits as a development objective. In addition to this intrinsic importance, gender equality and women's empowerment are also important channels to attain other MDGs. Gender equality and women's empowerment promote universal primary education (MDG2), reduce under-five mortality (MDG4), improve maternal health (MDG5), and reduce the likelihood of contracting HIV/AIDS (MDG6).

Improving gender equality also influences poverty reduction and growth directly through women's greater labor force participation, productivity, and earnings as well as indirectly through the beneficial effects of

FIGURE 2 Pathways from increased gender equality to poverty reduction and growth

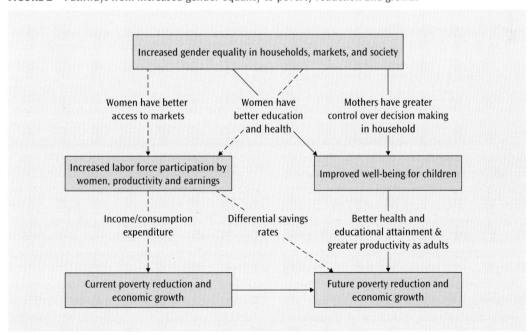

Source: World Bank staff.

women's empowerment on child well-being. Figure 2 identifies the main pathways leading from gender equality to both current and future growth and poverty reduction. One path is through increasing the productive opportunities and higher incomes that women have, raising consumption and savings that help to raise investment rates. Another is through improving women's control over decision making in the household. Several studies have shown that the greater the mothers' control over resources, the more resources households allocate to children's health, nutrition, and education. Better maternal education also benefits children through improved hygiene practices, better nutrition, lower fertility rates, and hence higher per child expenditures. Taken together, these contribute to future growth and poverty reduction.

Progress toward Meeting MDG3

The four official MDG3 indicators—measuring gender equality in enrollments, literacy, and the share of women in nonagricultural employment and national parliaments—provide an important, albeit incomplete, snapshot of progress toward gender equality.

Thanks to efforts to achieve universal primary education (MDG2), girls' enrollments in all levels of schooling have risen significantly (figure 3). Most low-income countries made substantial progress between 1990 and 2005. By 2005, 83 developing countries (of 106 with data) had met the intermediate MDG3 target of parity in primary and secondary enrollment rates. Most of these countries are in regions where enrollment has historically been high—East Asia and the Pacific, Eastern Europe and Central Asia, and Latin America and the Caribbean. In the Middle East and North Africa, most countries met the target by 2005, but some still have a significant female disadvantage in enrollments. In Sub-Saharan Africa performance has been varied; less than one-quarter of countries met the enrollment targets for 2005, but some have attained parity (for example, Botswana,

Rwanda, and South Africa). Of the 14 fragile states for which data are available, 9 are not expected to achieve the primary and secondary enrollment targets.

The female *tertiary* enrollment rate lagged behind the male rate in 63 countries (of 130 countries with data) and *exceeded* the male rate in 65 countries. The female disadvantage was evident mainly in Sub-Saharan Africa, South Asia, and in fragile states.

Progress in basic literacy skills and school enrollments over the years has resulted in higher literacy rates among youth (age 15–24), but gender gaps remain: the United Nations Educational, Scientific and Cultural Organization (UNESCO) estimates that of the nearly 137 million illiterate youths in the world, 63 percent are female. The female-to-male literacy ratio is lowest in Sub-Saharan Africa, Middle East and North Africa, and South Asia—regions that also have female disadvantages in primary and secondary enrollment.

Progress is also evident in women's share of nonagricultural wage employment, which increased modestly in all regions during 1990–2005, and with significant variation across regions and countries (figure 3). In 2005 the share of women in nonagricultural employment was highest in Europe and Central Asia (47 percent), lowest in the Middle East and North Africa (20 percent), and in-between in Latin America and the Caribbean and East Asia and the Pacific (over 40 percent). Trends and patterns in this indicator are difficult to interpret without accounting for country circumstances, such as the share of nonagricultural employment as a percentage of total employment. A favorable score on this indicator might on the surface seem to indicate equitable conditions for women in labor markets, but it may capture conditions for only a very small proportion of the total labor force.

The fourth official MDG3 indicator is the proportion of seats held by women in national parliaments (with no set target). Between 1990 and 2005, all regions except Europe and Central Asia increased women's

FIGURE 3   Progress in official indicators of gender equality and women's empowerment, by region, 1990–2005

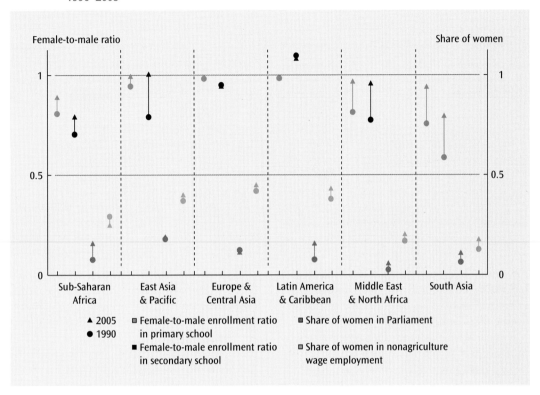

Source: World Bank Indicators. The regional averages are calculated using the earliest value between 1990 and 1995 and the latest value between 2000 and 2005. The averages are weighted by the country population size in 2005.

proportion of the seats in national parliament, but starting from a very low level (figure 3). However, in no region did the average proportion exceed 25 percent, at either the beginning of the period or the end.

Strengthening Official Indicators

The shortcomings of the official indicators for monitoring progress in attaining MDG3 are widely recognized (see, for example, the report of the UN Millennium Project Task Force on Education and Gender Equality, UN Millennium Project 2005). Five supplemental indicators to better measure gender equality are proposed to address this (table 1). These indicators, complementary to the official MDG3 indicators, meet three criteria: data availability (wide country coverage), strong link to poverty reduction and growth,

and amenability to policy intervention. Indicators that met all the three criteria but were highly correlated with other indicators were dropped from the list.

This proposed list draws on the recommendations of the UN Millennium Project Task Force, but is more parsimonious. It takes into account data availability, additionality (does it add new information), and the high costs associated with imposing additional monitoring burdens on already taxed national statistical offices. It also draws on a proposal to refine the existing MDG indicators that was put before the UN Secretary General's office for consideration in March 2007.

Four of the five indicators monitor gender equality in the household; the remaining indicator monitors gender equality in the economy. No additional indicators are recommended to monitor gender equality in

TABLE 1 Recommended additional indicators for MDG3

Household		Economy and markets
Modifications of official MDG indicators	Additional indicators	Additional indicators
Primary completion rate of girls and boys (MDG2)[a]	Percentage of 15- to 19-year-old girls who are mothers or pregnant with their first child[b]	Labor force participation rates among women and men aged 20–24 and 25–49[b]
Under five mortality rate for girls and boys (MDG4)		
Percentage of reproductive-age women, and their sexual partners, using *modern* contraceptives (MDG6)		

Source: World Bank staff.
a. Recommended by the UN Millennium Project Task Force on Education and Gender Equality.
b. Under consideration by the Inter-Agency and Expert Group for MDGs.

the domain of society, because none of the indicators considered for inclusion met the criteria of data availability. Three of the recommended indicators are modifications of official indicators already being monitored as part of the MDGs, while two are indicators not currently part of the official set.

Strengthening International Support for Gender Equality

The success in increasing girls' enrollments in schooling shows that progress in gender equality is possible. This progress, however, requires political will (high-level leadership) and concerted effort from countries and international development agencies. Donors and the multilateral development banks (MDBs) need to significantly improve the support and coordination for gender equality issues to accelerate progress toward MDG3; these issues should become central in their dialogue with partner countries. Since the 1995 Beijing Women's conference, which marked a milestone in international commitment to gender equality issues, donor support improved somewhat, and more resources are devoted to gender equality targets, particularly in the social sectors. Overall, a quarter of bilateral aid by sector—around $5 billion annually—is now focused on gender equality.

However, in spite of strong donor policy commitments to gender equality objectives, implementation has been disappointing. Self-evaluations of nine donor agencies' performance reflect a gap between words and deeds. One of the reasons for this gap is the diffusion of responsibility that resulted from the shared responsibility gender mainstreaming called for: all staff were responsible for promoting it, yet no one group in particular was held accountable for results.

These self-assessments have helped reenergize donors' commitments. Donors are revamping their approaches and setting more realistic targets to both strengthen mainstreaming and introduce specific actions to advance gender equality. There is wide agreement that high-level leadership, technical expertise, and financial resources remain key to implementing donor agencies' gender policies.

The MDBs have made similar progress in advancing their support for gender equality and women's empowerment. Systems to monitor progress with mainstreaming gender equality policies have been introduced, and suggest there has been modest but steady progress. Most MDBs have recently adopted Gender Action Plans to make their gender mainstreaming policies more strategic and operationally effective.

Nonetheless, significant gaps remain. Progress has been greater in the social sectors (especially health and education) than in productive sectors (agriculture, infrastructure, private sector development, and the like). There is also evidence that attention to gender issues is greater in project design than in implementation, and there has been little effort to monitor or evaluate outcomes. Institutions have generally been slow to develop and adopt measurable indicators of progress in gender equality, and the rating systems primarily measure good intentions rather than results. Nor can the resources spent on gender mainstreaming be measured. Clearly much more is needed to strategically realize the comparative advantage that the MDBs have in knowledge generation and analysis, in their convening and coordinating roles, in leading high-level dialogue, and in helping formulate development policy strategies. The MDBs should utilize their comparative advantage and take up a visible leadership role in investing dedicated resources to include gender equality and women's empowerment in the results agenda, in leading international efforts to strengthen MDG3 monitoring, and in better assisting client countries in scaling up MDG3 interventions. The business case for MDBs' investments in MDG3 is strong—it is nothing more than smart economics.

Addressing the Special Challenge of Fragile States

Fragile states are generally characterized by weak institutional capacities and governance, and by political instability. These countries are the least likely to achieve the MDGs and they contribute significantly to the MDG deficit. They account for 9 percent of the population of developing countries, but 27 percent of the extreme poor (living on US$1 per day, see table 2), nearly one-third of all child deaths, and 29 percent of 12-year olds who did not complete primary school in 2005. Of all low-income countries that are unlikely to achieve gender parity in primary and secondary enroll-

TABLE 2 Fragile states face the largest deficit in most MDGs

Indicator	Total in developing countries (millions)	Total in fragile states (in millions and % share)
Total population (2004)	**5,427 million**	**485 million (9%)**
MDG1—Poverty (2004)		
Extreme poverty	985	261 (27%)
Malnourished children	143	22.7 (16%)
MDG2—Universal Education		
Children of relevant age that did not complete primary school in 2005	13.8	4 (29%)
MDG4—Under-Five Mortality		
Children born in 2005 not expected to survive to age five	10.5	3.3 (31%)
MDG5—Maternal Health		
Unattended births	48.7	8.9 (18%)
MDG6—Diseases		
TB deaths	1.7	0.34 (20%)
HIV+	29.8	7.2 (24%)
MDG7—Environmental Sustainability		
Lack of access to improved water	1,083	209 (19%)
Lack of access to improved sanitation	2,626	286 (11%)

Source: World Bank staff estimates; for notes see table 2.9.

ments, half are fragile states. Their performance is clearly linked to chronically weak institutional capacity and governance and to internal conflict, all of which undermine the capacity of the state to deliver basic social and infrastructure services and offer security to citizens.

Conflicts are a major reason why countries slide into fragility; they extract high costs in terms of lives and physical damage, they reduce growth and increase poverty. While there are fewer conflicts in low-income countries than before, conflicts have become shorter and more intense, with an enormous negative impact on GDP growth averaging about 12 percent decline per year of conflict.

Despite the enormous challenges of poverty in fragile states, progress against the MDGs is possible. A number of countries (Mozambique, Uganda) have made a successful transition from weak institutions and/or the legacy of conflict to sustained gains in growth and poverty reduction. In countries that remain fragile, successful progress against the MDGs has been achieved: Timor-Leste, Eritrea, and the Comoros, for example, decreased child mortality by 7.1 percent, 4.2 percent, and 3.5 percent, respectively, between 2000 and 2005.

Aid is particularly important in fragile states because it constitutes the main source of development finance. However, IFIs account for only about 8 percent of total Development Assistance Committee (DAC) ODA flows to fragile states, with the rest coming from bilateral sources. The IFIs, nevertheless, have an important role to play in financing postconflict reconstruction, in aid coordination, and in policy dialogue and technical assistance. The MDBs have recently started to converge around four areas of specialized response to the development challenge in fragile states: (1) strategy, policy, and procedural frameworks; (2) exceptional financial instruments; (3) customized organizational and staffing approaches; and (4) partnership work.

Accelerating progress toward the MDGs in fragile states requires attention to several issues and lessons of recent experience. First, since many fragile states are emerging from conflict, the sequencing and coherence of support for security, electoral efforts, and aid-financing to boost growth and employment are critical for minimizing the risk of reversion to conflict. Donors need to consider whether current instruments provide adequate continuity of support to minimize risks of renewed conflict.

Second, engaging in fragile states requires the IFIs and other donors to review their business practices and procedures, to ensure that these are adapted to low-capacity and sometimes volatile environments. Taking advantage of new peace-building or governance reform opportunities, or adjusting programs in the event of a crisis, requires a rapid response from all international partners engaged in these countries. Supporting reforms in low capacity states also requires increased field presence.

Third, fragile states are especially vulnerable to donor fragmentation and its potential burden on government capacity. This makes implementation of the Principles for Good International Engagement in Fragile States and advancing principles of the Paris Declaration on Aid Effectiveness particularly important. The IFIs need to work both between themselves and with other international partners to develop common approaches and operating principles in fragile states, in particular through efforts to improve coordination and division of labor with organizations leading peace-building efforts, such as the United Nations and regional institutions.

Making Aid, Trade, and Debt Relief Responsive to Country Needs

The expansion in global aid has stalled, and two years after the Gleneagles summit the trends in real aid flows suggest that DAC donors' promises of higher aid to Sub-Saharan Africa appear increasingly unlikely to materialize. Seven years after the Millennium Summit at which the MDGs were adopted, there is yet to be a single country case where aid is being scaled up to support achieving the MDG agenda. Most "low hanging fruit" identified in the Millennium Report of 2005 have yet to be harvested. Progress with multilateral debt relief was rapid after the Gleneagles meetings in 2005, demonstrating how quickly initiatives can advance when there is a strong international commitment. The lack of progress with multilateral trade reforms in the Doha Round similarly demonstrates just how weak international commitment and consensus stymies change. Forging an international consensus beyond rhetoric is needed to accelerate progress.

Aid Volumes Trends: Bringing Actions in Line with Commitments

Although aid was on an upward trend through 2005 as DAC members, non-DAC donors, and nontraditional donors expanded assistance to developing countries, in 2006 the level of real aid from DAC members fell. After reaching a record level in 2005, total DAC member aid fell by about 5 percent to about just below $104 billion in 2006. These trends suggest that real aid delivery is falling well short of donor commitments. Doubling of aid to Africa by 2010 looks increasingly unlikely.

There has also been a continuing concentration of aid in a small number of countries, leaving the majority of countries with little or no real increase. Between 2001 and 2005, real aid volumes grew by more than 50 percent, but nearly 60 percent of International Development Association (IDA) countries saw a decline or little change in aid over this period. Such heavy concentration is not consistent with efforts to broadly accelerate progress toward the MDGs. Even as assistance from DAC donors has declined in 2006, aid from nontraditional donors is on an upward trend: Non-DAC OECD donors are expected to double their assistance to over $2 billion by 2010; Saudi Arabia and other Middle East countries provided nearly $2.5 billion in assistance in 2005; and other emerging donors, China in particular, are also rapidly expanding aid and becoming significant foreign creditors. Much of this aid targets infrastructure and productive sectors

that DAC donors have moved out of.

Progress with scaling up aid to Africa has been disappointing. Five years after the Monterrey Conference and two years since the G-8 pledges at Gleneagles, country examples of programs to scale-up aid to support the MDG agenda are lacking. Beyond debt relief (important to improving future growth opportunities), most countries in Sub-Saharan Africa are seeing stagnant or declining aid inflows. Excluding Nigeria (a recipient of exceptional debt relief) real bilateral ODA from DAC members to the region fell in 2005 and was unchanged in 2006.

There is evidence that aid allocation is becoming increasingly selective on the basis of need (poverty) and the quality of policies (governance). Selectivity varies across different aid instruments. Flexible ODA—aid that can be used toward regular project and program support as opposed to special-purpose grants such as technical or emergency assistance—has been the most responsive to country improvements in governance and greater need. Technical assistance (much of which is for consultants and never leaves donor countries) is the least responsive.

Attention by donors to the needs of fragile states is beginning to translate into increased assistance. Overall aid to fragile states rose by more than two-thirds in 2005 to nearly $20 billion (in 2004 dollars), of which about half was in debt relief and humanitarian assistance. Fragile states are seeing an improving trend in aid received per capita, although they receive somewhat less aid (excluding humanitarian assistance and debt relief) than other low-income countries. Aggregate trends mask the wide variation across different types of fragile states: those emerging from violent conflict typically receive much more aid than other fragile states, and more than other low-income countries.

Progress with Harmonization and Aid Effectiveness

A critical agenda for improving aid effectiveness is progress with harmonization and alignment of aid with country strategies, both by donors and the international aid agencies. There is evidence of some progress in these efforts. Two-thirds of donors place strategic priority on implementation of the Paris Declaration on aid effectiveness, and efforts to monitor its implementation are gaining traction. However, translating this good intent to outcomes on the ground remains extremely challenging: the greatest need for better aid harmonization is often in countries least capable of leading donor coordination themselves.

A baseline survey for monitoring the Paris Declaration was undertaken in mid-2006, yielding benchmarking data on the constraints facing donors and partner countries. On ownership by partnership countries it finds the story is mixed: while comprehensive national strategies are being developed, they lack well-specified prioritization and sequencing of objectives and actions, leaving them operationally weak. Less than one-fifth of countries had developed operational strategies at the time of data collection. The survey also finds that overall public financial management systems are weak in over one-third of countries, and moderately strong or better in less than a third.

Regarding donor actions, it finds that about 40 percent of aid is disbursed using a partner's public financial and procurement systems; about two-thirds of aid is disbursed on time; nearly half of technical cooperation is already coordinated—which is the 2010 target, although different interpretations of "coordination" require caution. The survey finds that donors *are trying* to harmonize. Forty-two percent of aid is provided through program-based approaches such as direct budget support or sectorwide approaches. One-third of missions and one-fifth of country analytic work is joint. However, strategic partnership "satisfaction" surveys in Africa suggest increased dissatisfaction over donor reporting requirements and coordination of donor support.

Pledges of harmonization remain abstract unless tested in the field. A recent review of aid for the health sector in Rwanda illustrates some key problems on the ground. First, the government's ability to achieve *policy coherence* is undermined by donors channeling the majority (86 percent) of total reported aid for health outside the Ministry of Health through direct transfers to local NGOs, local governments, and other providers. Second, most on-budget donor funding is earmarked for HIV/AIDS and malaria (85 percent in 2005), to the relative neglect of capacity building, human resource development, and other sectorwide needs. Only 1 percent was allocated to child health. Third, aid is volatile as much is committed for only 1 to 2 years, constraining ability to scale up health services which require mainly stable recurrent expenditures for salaries and facility maintenance. Finally, there is a sharp disparity between donor funding for health, which has increased sharply, and infrastructure and agriculture, which have been neglected. These factors point to the need for coordination among donors, agencies, global programs, and developing countries, to develop an adequate coordinating mechanism and more coherent approach.

Harmonization in the health sector is particularly difficult: the number of donors is large and includes numerous vertical programs; there is usually no critical mass of health financiers "on the ground" who can meet regularly to coordinate and harmonize. There is also an inherent tension between the goals of harmonized aid through country systems and the explicit mandates of vertical funds—whose successful advocacy for specific global health issues depends critically on their ability to show direct results. A viable harmonization strategy may be to move toward a country-led arrangement whereby (1) all donor support is "on plan" and aligned with government priorities and initiatives; (2) funding is primarily through the government budget, and where this is not possible a share is specified for support to system capacity building; and (3) reporting to donors is less frequent and done through multipurpose reports that meet multiple donor needs.

The Rwanda health sector example points more broadly to challenges posed by the evolving and more complex aid architecture. The proliferation of new aid sources—donors, private foundations, global funds—increases total resources, but also the difficulty of coordination and coherence, and the costs posed by fragmentation and resource earmarking. The average number of official donors has tripled since the 1960s, and since 1990 the number of countries with over 40 active bilateral and multilateral donors increased from zero to over 30. Emerging donors are also expanding their presence rapidly, along with global funds, although these are difficult to track due to insufficient data. The problem of a large number of aid channels is compounded by the trend towards small size of funded activities, which declined on average from $1.5 million to $1 million between 1997 and 2004, while their number surged from 20,000 to 60,000.

This places particular stress on countries with weak capacity. Countries with lower institutional capacity are found to have higher aid fragmentation, with negative implications for aid quality through higher transaction costs and a smaller donor stake in country outcomes. Clearly excessive fragmentation is a serious problem and measures to address it, possibly through donors limiting their focus countries, providing larger funds, or adopting more efficient vehicles (including through multilateral channels), and donors committing to delegate authority to lead donors, could help reduce transactions costs and improve aid effectiveness.

Developments in Debt Relief

The past year saw important progress in deepening debt relief to the poorest countries. The African Development Fund (AfDF), IDA, and the International Monetary Fund (IMF) all implemented the Multilateral Debt Relief Initiative (MDRI), described in the 2006 GMR. This initiative provides 100 percent debt relief on eligible claims to countries that have reached, or will eventually reach, the completion point under the Heavily Indebted Poor Countries (HIPC) Initiative. Twenty-two postcompletion-point HIPCs (and two non-HIPCs) have benefited from the MDRI to date, providing $38 billion, in nominal terms, in debt relief. The ongoing HIPC initiative also saw substantial progress, and 30 HIPCs had reached the decision point and were receiving debt relief as of end-2006.

Developments in Global Trade

World trade in 2006 continued the strong growth trends of recent years. Merchandise exports expanded by 16 percent in value, well above the average of 8 percent experienced during 1995–2004. Developing-country export growth continued to outpace the global average, growing by 22 percent. In addition to cyclical factors, trade performance reflects continuing unilateral trade reforms. Average tariffs in developing countries have fallen from 16 percent in 1997 to around 11 percent in 2006. As the pace of global integration accelerates, harnessing the new opportunities and managing the risks places a premium on a strategy of greater openness, coupled with behind-the-border reforms.

Owing to the steady reduction of tariffs, overall trade restrictiveness has declined in recent years. With the exception of a number of African countries, most economies are now less trade restrictive than they were in 2000. Much of this observed liberalization pertains to manufacturing. Much less has been done in agriculture. For a number of countries (such as India) the agricultural sector is now more restrictive than six years ago; in the European Union there has been no change, while Canada and the United States have registered a small decline since 2000.

Progress with the Doha Round. Despite intensive efforts to conclude the Doha negotiations in 2006, they were effectively suspended in July amid disagreement on the level of ambition in agricultural market access and over reductions in domestic support. However, in early 2007 there was an informal agreement by World Trade Organization members to restart talks, providing a narrow window of opportunity to reach agreement in the first half of 2007 on the key elements of a deal.

Failure to conclude the Doha Round would send a strong negative signal to the world economy about the ability of countries to pursue multilateral solutions. It could weaken the multilateral trading system, which provides developing countries with guaranteed nondiscriminatory market access; the rules-based settlement of disputes; and the transparency of trade regimes. But the biggest risk of failure is to countries' own economic growth, as trade reform is fundamentally about self-interest.

Aid for trade. Progress was made on aid for trade in 2006. Donors indicated that they are prepared to offer large increases in aid for trade to help developing countries address the supply-side constraints to their increased participation in global markets and any transitional adjustment costs from liberalization. How much of this would be additional to existing aid remains unclear. Also, more remains to be done to operationalize this agenda.

Monitoring IFI Performance

Enhancing IFIs' effectiveness in advancing the MDG agenda requires adapting their strategies and developing capacity to be responsive to (1) changing demands, including those related to globalization and global public goods; (2) growing differentiation among clients; (3) the availability of alternative financial resources; and (4) the growing number of actors on the development landscape. Several commissioned reports and events in 2006 reflect on the evolving responsibilities of the IFIs and the need to strengthen performance and collaboration. More coherent efforts may be needed to strengthen the results management capacity of the IFIs, both to support capacity building in partner countries and to reflect on their own performance.

Evolving Roles

A number of commissioned reports or initiatives were completed in the last 12 months with implications for the changing demands on IFI resources and responsibilities. Discussions have highlighted five key challenges: support to the poorest countries; strengthened engagement in middle-income countries; responding on critical global public goods; promoting coherence and collaboration; and strengthening the voice and representation of developing countries. Reports released in September 2006 included the IMF's Medium-Term Strategy and the Report of the International Task Force on Global Public Goods; in the same month the Middle Income Country Strategy Report was reviewed by the World Bank's Board. The Review Committee on IMF–World Bank Collaboration released its report in early 2007. In addition, initial measures were taken to address the need for changing voice and participation in the IMF and the World Bank.

These reports conclude that there is significant progress in assisting poor countries toward achieving the MDGs and in working to promote country-led efforts in partnership with other donors. Connecting results and resources remains a major challenge, however. There is broad recognition of the importance of continuing to engage with middle-income countries, which are home to some 70 percent of the world's poor, but also of the need to improve the responsiveness of the IFIs and tailor support to specific country conditions. Critical public goods include international financial stability, a strong international trading system, preventing the emergence of infectious diseases, generating knowledge, and tackling climate change.

Cooperation among MDBs is underpinned by Memoranda of Understanding between them, and in 2006 the managing director of the IMF and the president of the World Bank commissioned an external review of collaboration between the two institutions. The report noted many examples of good collaboration, but also identified scope for improvement, including clarifying the role of the IMF in low-income countries. Concerning voice and representation, a program of revisiting quotas and governance reforms in the IMF was launched in 2006 to be completed by the 2008. The first step was to revise quotas for a group of the most underrepresented countries: China, the Republic of Korea, Mexico, and Turkey. The changes approved in 2006 increased these countries' total IMF quotas by 1.8 percent, raising their share to 7 percent of total voting shares. Further steps are under way to develop a new formula for a second-round quota adjustment, and preparation of a proposal to increase basic votes in order to enhance the voice of low-income countries. Consultations on voice and representation are also under way in the World Bank.

Assessing Effectiveness: Financial Flows, Results, Harmonization, and Alignment

Assessing the effectiveness of the IFIs poses difficult challenges. Development results often lag policies and programs, and are hard to measure, but the bigger problem is that of attribution of results. Each IFI has an independent evaluation agency that plays an important evaluative role, but it remains difficult to address the results and attribution problems. Three aspects of international financial institutions' performance—financial support, results-based management, and progress toward harmonizing and aligning aid through the Paris Declaration—are highlighted.

Financial flows. Despite the rapid growth in private capital flows to developing countries, the financing role of the IFIs remains an important one. In 2006, the five MDBs disbursed $43 billion, up 20 percent over 2005 levels. It is premature to assess whether this increase is a temporary trend. Nonconcessional gross disbursements increased by 29 percent to $32 billion. After strong growth in concessional gross disbursements since 2000, peaking at just over $11 billion in 2004, flows slightly declined in 2005 and 2006.

These trends suggest that while demand for MDB lending from middle-income countries has increased, the supply of concessional funds to low-income countries is now stagnant. This has implications for the role of MDBs in the future, particularly their ability to respond to demands for scaling up multilateral assistance. Viewed from the perspective of overall ODA flows, the share of MDB financing has fallen significantly since 1998; if disbursements continue to stagnate while donors scale up bilateral ODA, the MDBs will represent only about 6 percent of total ODA flows by 2010. This poses important questions for the international community over the implications of declining multilateralism, or of the shifting multilateralism to other agencies, primarily the UN system and the European Union.

Debt relief under the MDRI has further potential repercussions for IFI financing, in particular for AfDF and IDA, which have provided debt relief extending out to 40 years. The MDRI commits donors to providing additional resources, on a "dollar-for-dollar" basis over four decades, to ensure that the cost of debt forgiveness does not undermine these institutions' overall financial integrity or ability to provide future financing. Firm financing commitments cover 10 percent of the total cost, and qualified commitments another 56 percent, leaving a gap of 34 percent between total costs and commitments for the MDRI. IDA 15 will be an important test of donors' intentions regarding the MDRI and future role of the MDBs.

Results management. The Third Roundtable on Managing for Development, held in Hanoi in February 2007, provided a venue for many country delegations to compare experiences and learn from them. The Roundtable included a meeting of the Asian Community of Practice, and the launching of a similar Community of Practice in the Africa region. Five factors were highlighted as important in building country capacity to manage for development results: leadership and political will, strong links between results and planning practices, evaluation and monitoring tools to generate feedback on programs, mutual accountability between donors and country partners, and statistical capacity (both to supply, and help generate greater demand for, managing for results). The need to scale up both financial and technical support for statistical capacity-building was underscored as an essential element of the agenda—particularly as the financial costs of strengthening systems are relatively modest.

The Common Performance Assessment System (COMPAS) is an interagency effort to develop a common system across the MDBs for monitoring their results orientation, particularly with regard to their internal practices. Its three-pillar structure was described in detail in the 2006 GMR. A report for 2006, prepared under the leadership of the Inter-American Development Bank (COMPAS' chairmanship rotates), examines the seven performance categories that were developed for the 2005 report. In 2006, however, changes were made to improve the indicators, limiting performance comparisons over the two years. A number of findings emerged, including the need to better communicate the results of COMPAS within each MDB.

IFIs and the Paris Declaration. Results of the country-level monitoring of the implementation of the Paris Declaration's mutual commitments, which took place for the first time in 2006, will serve as a baseline to review progress in 2008 and against the 2010 targets. They suggest that substantial actions are being taken by the MDBs in many areas of harmonization and alignment, including the use of joint or collaborative country assistance strategies, but that continued efforts will be needed to achieve the 2010 targets. Over half the country analytic work of the MDBs is joint with other donors and/or partner governments, relative to the target of 66 percent, but only 21 percent of MDB missions are joint with other donors, relative to a target of 40 percent, and there is an urgent need to reduce the large number of parallel implementation units.

Millennium Development Goals—Charting Progress

The following figures and commentary provide an overview of the main trends in country and regional progress toward achieving the Millennium Development Goals. Owing to the limitations of both data and space, the coverage here is selective. An overview of performance can be seen from the figure below showing the shares of all developing countries globally that have achieved or are on track to meet the development goals, are off track and seriously off track to meet them, or countries for which there are insufficient data. It is immediately evident that for these targets many countries simply do not have adequate data to measure their performance, partic-

ularly for poverty (over half), malnutrition, gender, and access to improved water. From the available data, those targets for which the greatest progress has been made include gender equality (as measured by gender parity in primary and secondary school enrollment), access to skilled care at birth (a proxy measure for maternal mortality), and reaching 100 percent primary school completion. Those targets lagging most severely include reducing child mortality, halving extreme poverty, and improving child nutrition. The global challenge of meeting the MDGs remains daunting.

Global Progress toward the MDGs—Select indicators

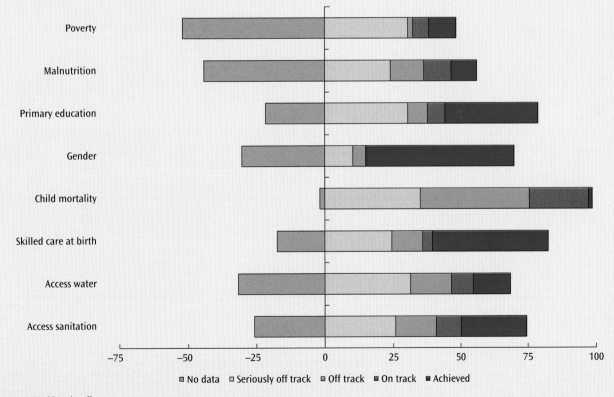

Source: World Bank staff.
Note: Country on track means that the rate of progress is superior to the required growth rate to achieve the goal. Country off track means that the rate of progress is inferior to the required growth to achieve the goal, and superior to the required growth to achieve the half of the target. Country seriously off track means that the rate of progress is inferior to the required growth to achieve the half of the target.

Eradicate Extreme Poverty and Hunger

Extreme poverty—the proportion of the population in developing countries living on less than $1 a day—fell from 29 percent in 1990 to 18 percent in 2004. East Asia and Pacific experienced the most impressive reduction in poverty, and South Asia is now on track, but Sub-Saharan Africa lags behind. Over the same period, the number of people in developing countries grew by 20 percent to more than 5 billion, including 1 billion people in extreme poverty. Global poverty is projected to fall to 12 percent by 2015—a striking success.

Approximately 27 percent of the extreme poor in developing countries live in fragile states. Fragile states have consistently grown more slowly than in other low-income countries. Clearly, this has been, and will likely continue to be, an obstacle to the achievement of MDG1 in those countries. A typical fragile state had made negative progress toward MDG1 by 2005, at which point its poverty rate by the $1 per day measure was about twice that of a typical nonfragile state.

MDG 1 FIGURE 1   Share of people living on less than $1 or $2 a day in 2004, and projections for 2015

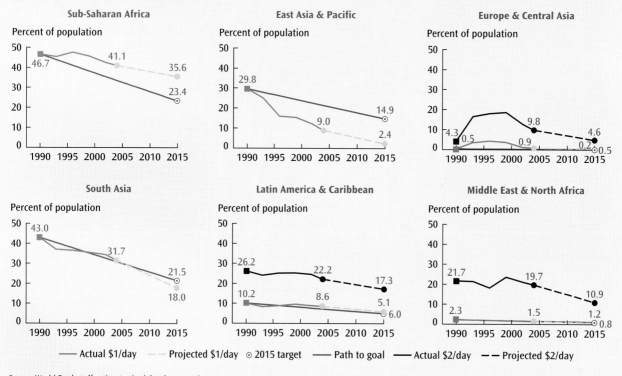

Source: World Bank staff estimates (weighted averages).

While accelerating growth in India has put South Asia on track to meet its goal, Sub-Saharan Africa lags behind.

East Asia has experienced a sustained period of economic growth, led by China, while Latin America and the Caribbean has stagnated, with modest poverty reduction.

The transition economies of Europe and Central Asia saw poverty rates rise in the 1990s and then fall. There and in the Middle East and North Africa, consumption of $2 a day may be more relevant.

TARGET 1: Halve, between 1990 and 2015, the proportion of people who live on less than $1 a day.

TARGET 2: Halve, between 1990 and 2015, the proportion of people who suffer from hunger.

MDG 1 FIGURE 2 Proportion of countries on track to achieve the poverty reduction target

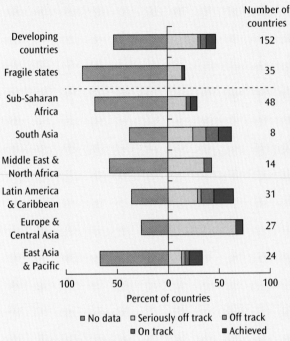

MDG 1 FIGURE 3 Proportion of countries on track to reduce under-5 malnutrition by half

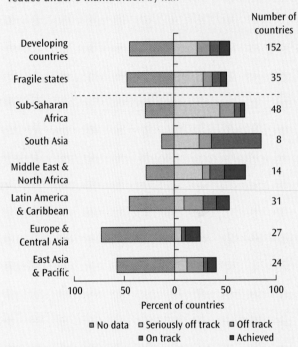

Source: World Bank staff estimates.

Source: World Bank staff estimates.

This chart shows the percentage of countries in each region that are on track to achieve the poverty reduction target of the MDGs. Some have already achieved the target. Those shown as on track could reach the target by 2015, if they maintain current progress. But those shown as off track and seriously off track are reducing poverty too slowly. Eighty percent of fragile states lack the data needed to estimate their progress.

More than half of countries in Sub-Saharan Africa are off track to reach the 2015 target of cutting malnutrition rates by half. Half of the countries in South Asia are on track to reach the target, but they also have the highest rates of malnutrition in the world and will continue to have the largest share of malnourished children, even if the target is achieved. Malnutrition rates in fragile states are similar to those found in other developing countries.

MDG 1 FIGURE 4 Number of people living on less than $1.08 a day (millions), 1981–2004

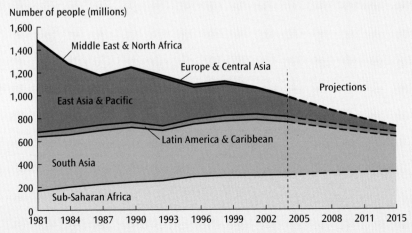

Source: World Bank staff estimates.

Between 1981 and 2004, the number of people in the world who lived in extreme poverty fell from nearly 1.5 billion to just under 1 billion. Both the Middle East and North Africa and Europe and Central Asia regions had essentially eliminated extreme poverty by 1981, but nearly 800 million poor people lived in East Asia—over half of the global total. By 2004 extraordinary progress had been made to lower poverty incidence in East Asia, lifting nearly 630 million people from extreme poverty in under a quarter of a century, which lowered the region's share of total poverty from 58 percent to just 9 percent. At the same time, poverty fell in South Asia from 52 percent of the population in 1981 to 32 percent in 2004, but absolute numbers have been persistent at around 470 million people. In contrast, in Sub-Saharan Africa poverty incidence hovered around 46 percent between the early 1980s and 1999, and declined to 41 percent in 2004. Despite this better trend, the absolute number of poor is still around 300 million.

Achieve Universal Primary Education

Globally, the primary completion rate has increased from 63 percent in 1990 to an estimated 83 percent in 2005, and the pace of annual improvement has accelerated significantly since 2000 in the three regions furthest from the goal—North Africa, South Asia, and Sub-Saharan Africa—a sign of the increasing priority given in these regions to universalizing primary education (see figure 2.1). Latin America and the Caribbean, which started from a higher base, has also sustained an exceptionally strong rate of progress. The number of countries that have achieved universal primary completion increased from 37 in 2000 to 52 in 2005, and this includes some low-income countries: Bolivia,

Indonesia, and Kenya. Notwithstanding these very positive trends, the goal of universal primary completion by 2015 will be difficult to reach: 57 of the 152 developing countries (38 percent) for which data are available are considered off track—meaning that they will not reach the goal on current trends (figure 2). Most of the 33 countries that lack data are also likely off track. Among African countries, 65 percent are considered seriously off track, defined as unlikely to reach the goal before 2040. Among fragile states, only 11 percent have achieved universal primary completion or are on track to doing so, and 50 percent are considered seriously off track.

MDG 2 FIGURE 1   Primary school completion rate

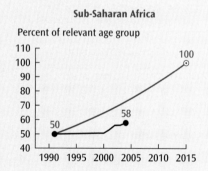

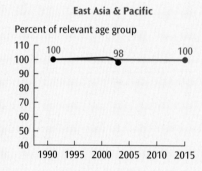

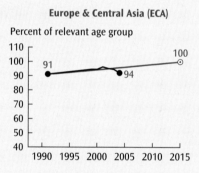

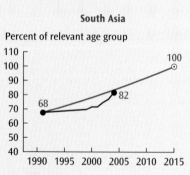

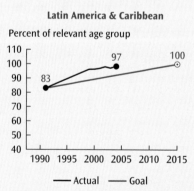

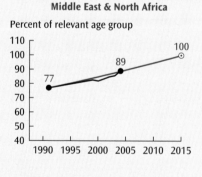

—— Actual   —— Goal

Source: World Bank staff estimates (weighted averages).

Despite faster progress since 2000, Sub-Saharan Africa remains very far from the goal. In South Asia, populous India's strong progress boosts the regional picture, although some countries remain off track.

East Asia, Latin America and the Caribbean, and Europe and Central Asia are all close to the goal.

Strong progress since 2000 in the Middle East and North Africa has put that region on track to achieve universal primary completion, although the regional average hides some variance across countries.

TARGET 3: Ensure that by 2015 children everywhere, boys and girls alike, will be able to complete a full course of primary schooling.

MDG 2 FIGURE 2 Proportion of countries on track to achieve the primary education target

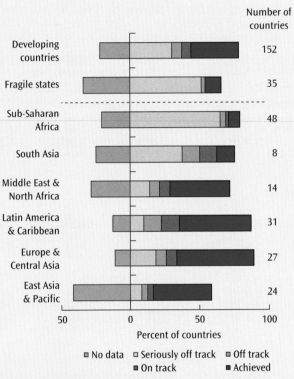

Source: World Bank staff estimates.

In many developing countries children are able to complete a full course of primary education, but in all regions at least a few countries remain off track and unlikely to reach the primary education target. In Sub-Saharan Africa, the poorest-performing region, 65 percent of countries are seriously off track and only 8 percent are on track. We observe a huge lag for fragile states, of which 50 percent are seriously off track.

MDG 2 FIGURE 3 Percent of 15- to 19-year-old cohort that has completed primary education by household wealth quintile and location

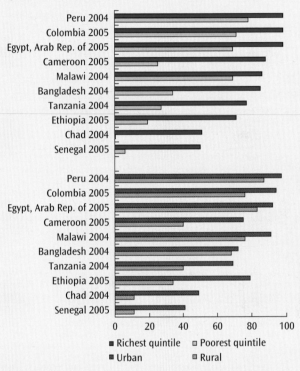

Source: DHS Surveys.

Data from household surveys indicate that the largest gaps in primary completion rates in virtually every developing country are between wealthy and poor populations (figure 3). But gaps between urban and rural populations can also be very large, especially in Africa. Completion rates for girls, which are discussed in the next section, also lag behind those of boys in some countries, but in general—thanks to strong progress on gender equity in education over the past 15 years—these gaps are smaller than those linked to wealth or location. However, while expansion of primary education coverage tends to be pro-poor, pro-rural, and pro-girls in terms of equalizing access and completion, country experience also shows that specific actions to lower direct and opportunity costs or eliminate discrimination are often needed to keep vulnerable children in school, be they orphan, poor, rural, or female.

Promote Gender Equality and Empower Women

When a country educates its girls, its mortality rates usually fall, fertility rates decline, and the health and education prospects of the next generation improve. Unequal treatment of women—by the state, in the market, and by their community and family—puts them at a disadvantage throughout their lives and stifles the development prospects of their societies. Illiterate and poorly educated mothers are less able to care for their children. Low education levels and responsibilities for household work prevent women from finding productive employment or participating in public decision making. To improve girls' enrollments, the social and economic obstacles that keep parents from sending their daughters to school must be overcome. For many poor families, the economic value of girls' work at home exceeds the perceived returns to schooling. Improving the accessibility of schools and their quality and affordability is a first step. Globally, 55 percent of countries achieved the first target by 2005. Latin America and Europe and Central Asia can now focus on the second target. But huge improvement is required in Sub-Saharan Africa and South Asia, where only 20 percent and 35 percent, respectively, of countries reached the 2005 target.

MDG 3 FIGURE 1   Ratio of girls to boys enrolled in primary and secondary education

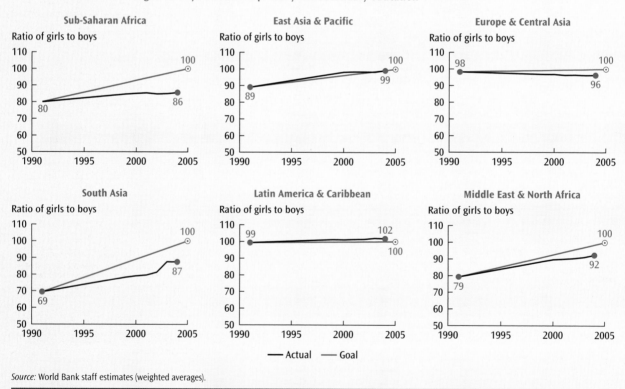

Source: World Bank staff estimates (weighted averages).

The differences between boys' and girls' schooling are greatest in regions with the lowest primary school completion rates and the lowest average incomes.

East Asia and Pacific has almost achieved the 2005 target. In some Latin American countries, girls' enrollments exceed boys'.

In Europe and Central Asia a strong tradition of educating girls needs to be sustained. In Middle East and North Africa more girls are overcoming the strong bias against them.

TARGET 4: Eliminate gender disparity in primary and secondary education, preferably by 2005, and at all levels of education no later than 2015.

MDG 3 FIGURE 2 Proportion of countries on track to achieve gender parity in primary and secondary enrollment

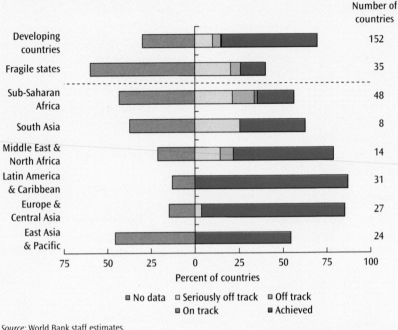

Source: World Bank staff estimates.

Even in regions that have achieved the target on average, such as Eastern Europe and Central Asia, some countries still fall short. And in South Asia and Sub-Saharan Africa, where large numbers of children are out of school, girls are at a severe disadvantage. Fragile states lag behind in achieving gender parity in enrollment, and more than 50 percent of these countries do not have sufficient data to assess their progress.

MDG 3 FIGURE 3 Gender inequality in primary completion rate: The girl/boy gap

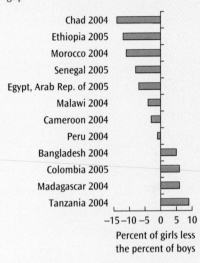

Source: DHS surveys.

Sub-Saharan Africa countries have some of the largest and smallest gender inequality gaps. In Kenya, Madagascar, and Tanzania, girls' completion rates are over 5 percent higher than boys' completion rates, while boys' completion rates are over 10 percent higher in Chad, Ethiopia, Nigeria, and Morocco.

MDG 3 FIGURE 4 Share of men and women participating in the labor force, 1991–2004

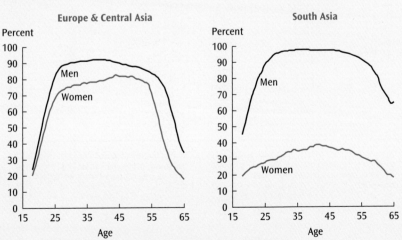

Source: Computed using household surveys (1991–2004, unweighted averages).

Although the gender gap in school enrollments has declined in most regions, the gender gap in labor force participation remains. Age patterns of labor force participation show that compared to young men, fewer young women make the transition from school to work, and this gender gap tends to persist throughout the life cycle. However, the size of this gap varies considerably across regions. The gender gap is the largest in South Asia and the smallest in Europe and Central Asia.

Reduce Child Mortality

Every year over 10 million children in developing countries die before the age of five. Most die from causes that are readily preventable or curable with existing interventions—such as acute respiratory infections, diarrhea, measles, and malaria. Rapid improvements prior to 1990 provided hope that mortality rates for infants and children under five could be cut by two-thirds in the ensuing 25 years, but progress slowed almost everywhere in the 1990s. Progress on the child mortality MDG lags behind all other goals. While the majority of countries have reduced child mortality since 1990, progress has been insufficient to reach the MDG target—which requires an annual decline of 4.3 percent over the entire period. Only two regions, East Asia and Pacific and Latin America and the Caribbean, are close to achieving the MDG target. But even in those two regions, more than half the countries are off track. Progress has been particularly slow in Sub-Saharan Africa, where civil disturbances and the HIV/AIDS epidemic have driven up rates of infant and child mortality. As of 2005, no Sub-Saharan Africa country was on track to achieve the goal, and only 33 out of 147 (22 percent) of developing countries are making enough progress to achieve the goal on current trends.

MDG 4 FIGURE 1   Under-five mortality rate (deaths per 1,000)

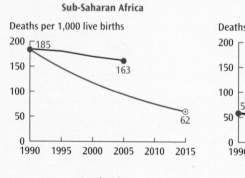

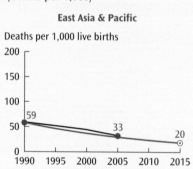

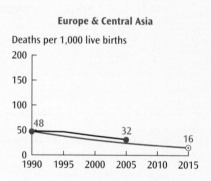

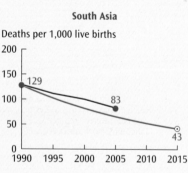

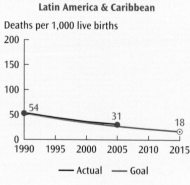

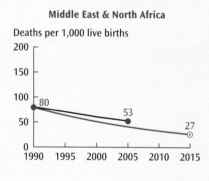

— Actual   — Goal

Source: World Bank staff estimates (weighted averages).

The gap between goal and reality is greatest in Sub-Saharan Africa, but millions of children are also at risk in South Asia.

East Asia and Pacific and Latin America and the Caribbean are nearly on track, but the regional averages disguise wide variations between countries.

More than half the countries in the Middle East and North Africa and Europe and Central Asia regions are off track to reach the target.

TARGET 5: Reduce by two-thirds, between 1990 and 2015, the under-five mortality rate.

MDG 4 FIGURE 2 Proportion of countries on track to achieve the child mortality target

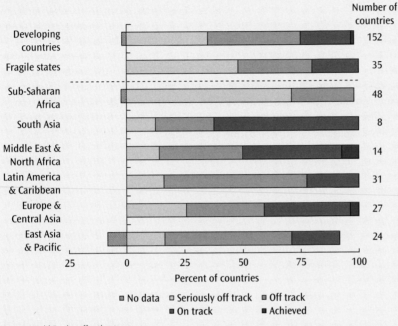

Source: World Bank staff estimates.

A concerted effort to improve the measurement of infant and child mortality has filled many gaps in the international data set and reveals that many countries still fall short of achieving the target, even where regional averages have been improving. Based on estimates through 2005, only 33 countries are on track to achieve a two-thirds reduction in the mortality rate. Every country in Sub-Saharan Africa is off track, and in some countries mortality rates have increased since 1990. Some recent surveys have found rapidly falling mortality rates.

MDG 4 FIGURE 3 Under-five mortality rate by quintile

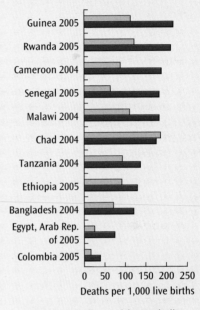

Source: DHS surveys.

Except in Chad, under-five child mortality is over 40 percent higher in the poorest quintile than in the richest quintile. The greatest percentage disparity is in Egypt, where the number of deaths per 1,000 live births is nearly 3 times higher for the poor than for the rich.

MDG 4 FIGURE 4 Composition of under-five mortality in developing regions based on most recent data, 1995–2003

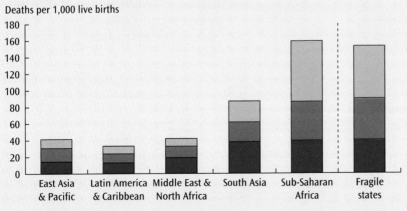

Source: WHO report, 2005 (unweighted averages).

The gap in under-five mortality between Sub-Saharan Africa and other regions is due mostly to higher child mortality (between ages 1–4), yet neonatal and post neonatal mortality are also highest in the Sub-Saharan Africa Region.

Improve Maternal Health

Death in childbirth is a rare event in rich countries, where there are typically fewer than 10 maternal deaths for every 100,000 live births. But in the poorest countries of Africa and Asia the ratio may be 100 times higher. Ninety-nine percent of maternal deaths occur in developing countries—around 500,000 annually. The MDG target—to reduce by 75 percent the maternal mortality ratio between 1990 and 2015—remains difficult to measure for almost all developing countries. No current direct estimates of the maternal mortality ratio or trends exist. Because few countries are able to measure maternal mortal-

ity over time, other indicators are often used instead, such as the skilled health personnel who are needed to deal with the complications of childbirth that can claim mothers' lives. Survey evidence shows progress in 27 of 32 countries, but also suggests that this is highly concentrated among richer households. While survey data also show progress in coverage for the poorest quintiles in many countries, differences in access to skilled delivery care between the poorest and richest quintiles in most countries represent larger equity gaps than for any other health service.

MDG 5 FIGURE 1   Maternal mortality ratios in 2000

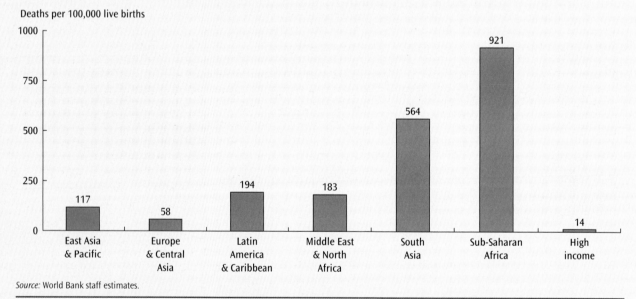

Source: World Bank staff estimates.

Maternal deaths are still unacceptably high in many developing countries of Sub-Saharan Africa and South Asia as a result of high fertility rates and a high risk of dying each time a woman becomes pregnant. Some developing countries in East Asia and Pacific and Latin America and the Caribbean have substantially improved maternal health through better health services, including increased numbers of trained birth attendants and midwives. Still others, in Europe and Central Asia and Middle East and North Africa, have improved maternal health and significantly lowered fertility rates through the use of contraceptives and increased female education.

TARGET 6: Reduce by three-quarters, between 1990 and 2015, the maternal mortality ratio.

MDG 5 FIGURE 2 Proportion of countries on track to provide adequate coverage of births by skilled health personnel

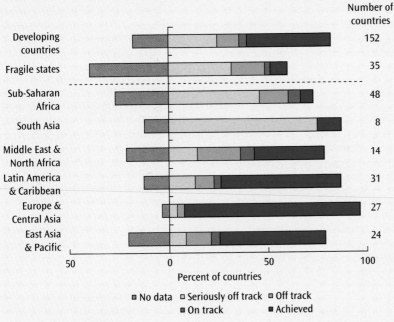

MDG 5 FIGURE 3 Access to delivery by medically trained personnel by household wealth quintile

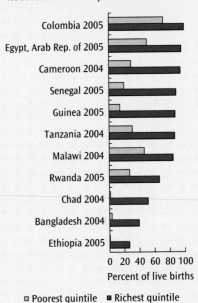

Source: World Bank staff estimates.

This figure shows the proportion of countries in each region that provide skilled health personnel for 90 percent of births or could do so by 2015 based on current trends. Countries that are off track may be able to achieve 75 percent coverage by 2015, while seriously off-track countries will not reach even that level unless they make rapid progress in the next decade. More fragile states are seriously off track compared to other developing countries.

Source: DHS surveys.

In countries with the lowest access to a medically trained personnel for delivery, women in the richest quintile are six times more likely to have access than women in the poorest quintile. In most developing countries, the greater the access, the lower the inequality; however, inequality is still high in Bolivia, Cameroon, and Morocco.

MDG 5 FIGURE 4 Adolescent (15–19) fertility rate by household wealth quintile

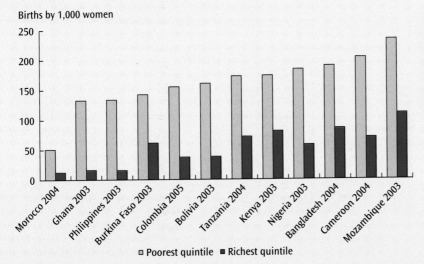

Pregnancy at a young age puts the mother and child at higher risk of serious health consequences. In developing countries, maternal mortality in girls under 18 years of age is estimated to be two to five times higher than in women between 18 and 25. Adolescent fertility rates are higher among poorer people, often substantially so. Poor young women typically have less access to reproductive health services, but the choice to have children very early also reflects low-income girls' lack of access to schooling and limited economic prospects.

Source: DHS surveys.

Combat HIV/AIDS, Malaria, and Other Diseases

Epidemic diseases exact a huge toll in human suffering and lost opportunities for development. Poverty, armed conflict, and natural disasters contribute to the spread of disease—and recovery, in turn, is often endangered by disease. In Africa, AIDS has reversed decades of improvements in life expectancy and left millions of children orphaned. By end-2006 an estimated 39.5 million people globally were living with HIV, up 2.4 million since 2004, and an estimated three million people had died from AIDS. While the spread of AIDS has slowed in parts of Sub-Saharan Africa, it remains the center of the epidemic; home to just over 10 percent of the world's people, 64 percent of all HIV-positive people, and 90 percent of all HIV-positive children. About 60 percent of HIV-positive adults in Africa are women.

The largest recent increases in the number of people with HIV have been in Eastern Europe, and Central and East Asia (21 percent higher in 2006 than in 2004). Recent experience in combating the spread of AIDS has demonstrated three important messages: reversing its spread is possible, treatment is effective in the developing world, and prevention remains a crucial challenge. More effective, evidence-based approaches to prevention are required—drawn from careful evaluation of what works in different contexts and the continued tailoring of responses to the changing epidemic.

Increasing the awareness of the impact of malaria and tuberculosis on human development has been matched with a commitment to fight these diseases, and fight them more effectively. There are an estimated 300–500 million new cases of malaria each year, leading to more than 1 million deaths. Nearly all the cases and more than 95 percent of the deaths occur in Sub-Saharan Africa. Tuberculosis (TB) strikes 9 million people each year and kills 2 million. But there has been clear progress in reducing TB prevalence and deaths in recent years. The only region where TB incidence is still growing is Africa, because of the emergence of drug-resistant strains and the greatly reduced resistance to TB among people with HIV.

MDG 6 FIGURE 1 HIV prevalence and deaths in the developing world, 1990–2006

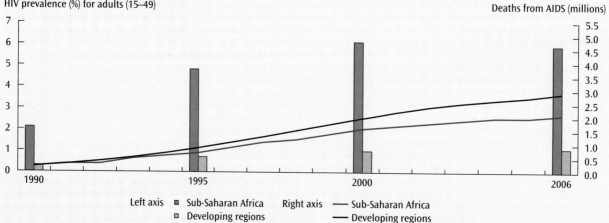

Source: UNAIDS/WHO, November 2006.

TARGET 7: Have halted by 2015 and begun to reverse the spread of HIV/AIDS.

TARGET 8: Have halted by 2015 and begun to reverse the incidence of malaria and other major diseases.

MDG 6 FIGURE 2 Number of people receiving antiretroviral therapy by region

People receiving antiretroviral therapy (thousands)

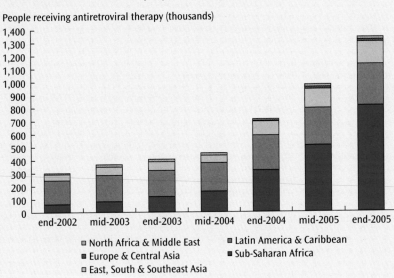

□ North Africa & Middle East   ■ Latin America & Caribbean
■ Europe & Central Asia   ■ Sub-Saharan Africa
□ East, South & Southeast Asia

Source: WHO and UNAIDS report, 2006.

Impressive progress has been made in extending antiretroviral coverage in Sub-Saharan Africa, where the number of people receiving treatment has more than doubled since 2004. While the number of people receiving antiretroviral therapy (ART) in East, South, and Southeast Asia has increased rapidly, progress in Europe and Central Asia and in North Africa and the Middle East has been less dramatic. Nonetheless, antiretroviral treatment in the developing world still reaches just 24 percent of those who need it.

MDG 6 FIGURE 3 Tuberculosis prevalence and number of TB deaths, 1990–2005

TB prevalence (%)   Deaths due to TB (millions)

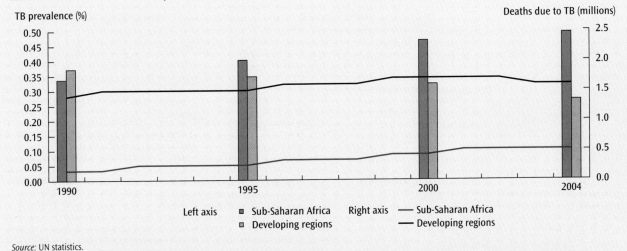

Left axis   ■ Sub-Saharan Africa   Right axis   — Sub-Saharan Africa
            □ Developing regions   — Developing regions

Source: UN statistics.

Many developing countries have successfully reduced TB's prevalence since 1990. Sub-Saharan Africa is the only region where TB prevalence continues to increase; TB-related deaths reached 600,000 in 2004.

Ensure Environmental Sustainability

Sustainable development can be ensured only by protecting the environment and using resources wisely. Less than 20 percent of developing countries are on track or have achieved the 2015 target to increase access to water, and less than 35 percent have increased access to sanitation, but Sub-Saharan African countries are lagging behind other regions. And in the fragile states, the proportion of countries on track to achieve the target for increased access to water and sanitation is 6 percent and 15 percent, respectively.

Around the world, land is being degraded and carbon dioxide (CO_2) emissions are driving changes in global climate. Climate change is a grave threat to the developing world and a major obstacle to continued poverty reduction across many dimensions. First, developing regions are at a geographic disadvantage: they are already warmer, on average, than developed regions, and they suffer from high rainfall variability. Second, developing countries—in particular the poorest—are heavily dependent on agriculture, the most climate-sensitive of all economic sectors, and they suffer from inadequate health provision and low quality public services. Third, low incomes and vulnerabilities make adaptation to climate change particularly difficult. Global emissions of CO_2 rose by 4 billion metric tons between 1990 and 2003.

MDG 7 FIGURE 1   Population without access to an improved water source or sanitation facilities

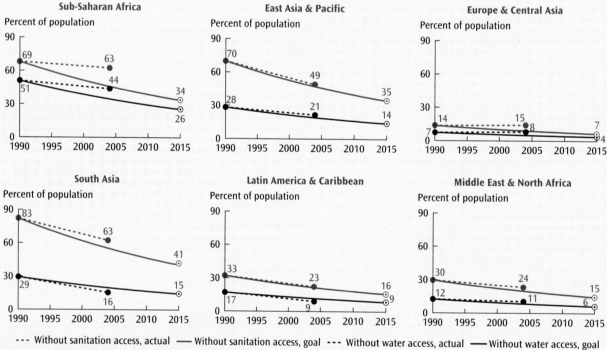

--- Without sanitation access, actual —— Without sanitation access, goal --- Without water access, actual —— Without water access, goal

Source: World Bank staff estimates (weighted averages).

In Sub-Saharan Africa, 300 million people lack access to improved water sources, and 450 million lack adequate sanitation services. South Asia has made excellent progress in providing water, but progress has been slower in providing sanitation.

In East Asia, rapid urbanization is posing a challenge for the provision of water and other public utilities. Latin America and the Caribbean, the most urban developing region, has made slow progress in providing sanitation.

Many countries in Europe and Central Asia lacked reliable benchmarks for measuring improved access to water and sanitation in the early 1990s. In the Middle East and North Africa, Egypt, Morocco, and Tunisia have made the fastest progress.

TARGET 9: Integrate the principles of sustainable development into country policies and programs and reverse the loss of environmental resources.

TARGET 10: Halve by 2015 the proportion of people without sustainable access to safe drinking water and basic sanitation.

TARGET 11: Have achieved a significant improvement by 2020 in the lives of at least 100 million slum dwellers.

MDG 7 FIGURE 2 Proportion of countries on track to achieve the target for access to improved water

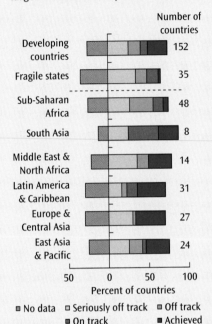

Number of countries

Developing countries	152
Fragile states	35
Sub-Saharan Africa	48
South Asia	8
Middle East & North Africa	14
Latin America & Caribbean	31
Europe & Central Asia	27
East Asia & Pacific	24

Percent of countries

■ No data □ Seriously off track ■ Off track
■ On track ■ Achieved

Source: World Bank staff estimates.

MDG 7 FIGURE 3 Adjusted net saving

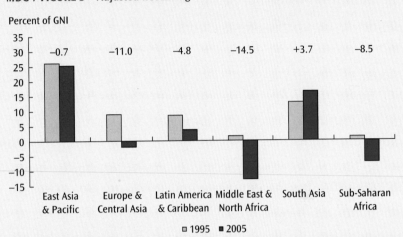

Percent of GNI

□ 1995 ■ 2005

Source: World Development Indicators.
Note: Numbers above bars show percent change from 1995 to 2005.

Are countries saving enough for future growth? Adjusted net saving measures the rate of saving in an economy after taking into account investments in human capital, depreciation of produced capital, depletion of natural resources, and damage caused by pollution. A negative saving rate implies that current levels of welfare and growth may be threatened by resource depletion. The Middle East and North Africa, Sub-Saharan Africa, and Eastern Europe and Central Asia had negative saving rates in 2005 when depletion of natural resources was taken into account. The largest decline in saving between 1995 and 2005 occurred in these three regions, while the largest gain, 3.7 percent of GNI, was in South Asia.

Lack of clean water is the main reason that diseases transmitted by feces are so common in developing countries. Water is a daily need that must be met, but in some places people spend many hours to obtain water from sources that are not protected from contamination. Even the modest target of halving the number of people without access to an improved water source will not be met in many countries at the current rate of progress. Only 35 percent of countries are on track to achieve or have achieved the target.

MDG 7 FIGURE 4 CO_2 emissions, 1990–2003

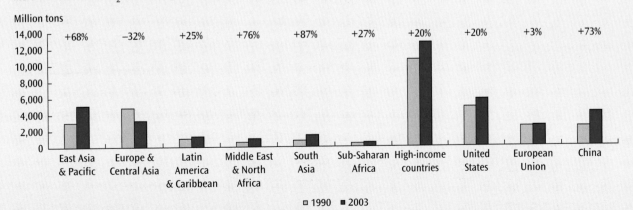

Million tons

□ 1990 ■ 2003

Source: World Development Indicators.
Note: Numbers above bars show percent change from 1990 to 2003.

Carbon dioxide (CO_2) is a greenhouse gas that contributes to global climate change. Global emissions of CO_2 from burning fossil fuels and manufacturing cement rose by 4 billion metric tons between 1990 and 2003. Most of the increase in these emissions came from high-income countries (2.09 billion metric tons) and East Asia and the Pacific (2.07 billion metric tons). South Asia and the Middle East and North Africa have regions with the largest percentage increase in emissions, followed by East Asia and the Pacific. Conversely, owing to the economic recession and restructuring of the 1990s, the transition economies of Europe and Central Asia emitted less CO_2 in 2003 than in 1990.

Fostering Global Partnerships

Important steps toward global partnership were taken at the international meetings in 2001 in Doha, which launched a new "development round" of trade negotiations, and in 2002 at the International Conference on Financing for Development in Monterrey, Mexico, where high-income and developing countries reached consensus on mutual responsibilities for achieving the Millennium Development Goals. The consensus calls for developing countries to improve governance and policies aimed at increasing economic growth and reducing poverty and for high-income countries to provide more and better aid and greater access to their markets.

Total aid rose in recent years through 2005, and declined 5 percent in 2006. But much of the recent increase was due to debt relief, and this may provide less than full additionality as measured by the current flow of new resources for development.

Owing to the steady reduction of tariffs, overall trade restrictiveness has largely declined in recent years. However, the poorest developing countries faced the highest barriers, notably from developed countries. South-South trade faces a high level of protection. Most of this protection is in agriculture.

MDG 8 FIGURE 1   Overall Trade Restrictiveness faced by countries in 2006

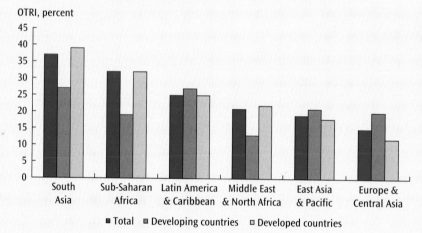

OTRI, percent

The effect of policies on exporters' access to markets differs by region. South Asian, Sub-Saharan African, and Latin American and Caribbean countries faced the highest barriers to their exports, since they export mainly agricultural products. For South Asia and Sub-Saharan Africa, restrictions by developed countries are especially high. East Asia and Pacific countries face less restrictions; the same is true for Europe and Central Asia and Middle East and North Africa.

■ Total   ▨ Developing countries   ▫ Developed countries

Source: OTRI (World Bank).

MDG 8 FIGURE 2   Share of total aid toward fragile states

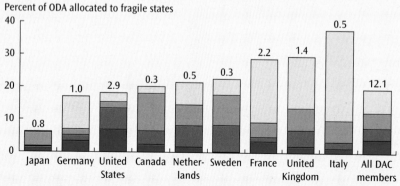

Percent of ODA allocated to fragile states

Donor focus on fragile states is translating into substantial assistance to some of those countries and the group as a whole. On average, DAC countries allocated 20 percent of bilateral aid to fragile states in 2003–05. However, more than half of fragile states received less ODA in 2005 than in 2001. Aid flows were dominated by debt relief; several donors provided over 50 percent of their aid in debt relief. Humanitarian aid also accounted for a substantial share of assistance to fragile states. By contrast, "other ODA," which traditionally finances development projects and programs, was less than a quarter of aid.

■ Technical cooperation   ▪ Food & humanitarian aid   ▨ Other ODA   ▫ Debt relief

Source: OECD DAC Development Committee Report and DAC database.
Note: Numbers above bars reflect average ODA volumes given to fragile states, 2003–05 (2004 US$ billions).

TARGET 12: Develop further an open, rule-based, predictable, nondiscriminatory trading and financial system.

TARGET 13: Address the special needs of the least developed countries.

TARGET 14: Address the special needs of landlocked developing countries and small island developing states.

TARGET 15: Deal comprehensively with the debt problems of developing countries through national and international measures in order to make debt sustainable in the long term.

TARGET 16: In cooperation with developing countries, develop and implement strategies for decent and productive work for youth.

TARGET 17: In cooperation with pharmaceutical companies, provide access to affordable essential drugs in developing countries.

TARGET 18: In cooperation with the private sector, make available the benefits of new technologies, especially information and communications.

MDG 8 FIGURE 3 Sectoral allocation of DAC members' bilateral aid

Percent of allocable aid

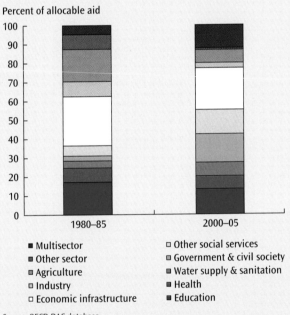

- Multisector
- Other sector
- Agriculture
- Industry
- Economic infrastructure
- Other social services
- Government & civil society
- Water supply & sanitation
- Health
- Education

Source: OECD DAC database.

The chart shows the breakdown of bilateral, sector-allocable aid, by social services, economic infrastructure (roads . . .), sector production, and multisector (environment . . .). The share of aid devoted to government and civil society has increased. Also, the shares of aid for agriculture, industry, and economic infrastructure have declined.

MDG 8 FIGURE 4 Selected indicators on aid harmonization and alignment in 2006

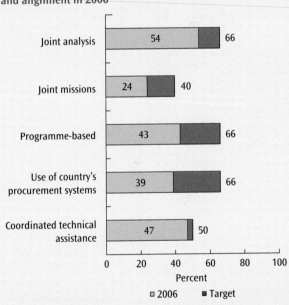

Source: OECD DAC database.

In several areas, donors are coming quite close to reaching the 2010 goals for harmonization and alignment. The largest gap involved the use of country procurement systems, an area slowed by concerns over the quality of financial management.

1

Growth, Poverty Reduction, and Environmental Sustainability

Under the first Millennium Development Goal (MDG1), the international community aims to halve the global rate of extreme income poverty—as measured by the share of the population living on less than $1 per day—between 1990 and 2015. Current trends and growth forecasts indicate that this goal will be achieved, although not in Sub-Saharan Africa. High growth in China and India explains much of the reduction in the global poverty rate, although progress toward MDG1 has also quickened in many other developing countries. High growth has continued in most of the developing world in the past year as a result of better policies in developing countries and a favorable global environment. The outlook for growth and poverty reduction remains favorable, although some risks remain. In particular, low-income country per capita growth is expected to remain above 5 percent in 2007.[1]

Addressing the problems of fragile states (box 1.1) is central to the development agenda and to furthering progress toward the MDGs.[2] Nine percent of the population, and about 27 percent of the extreme poor in developing countries live in fragile states. This situation will not improve unless fragile states become less vulnerable to adverse shocks, and they increase their capacity to absorb external funds and to mobilize internal resources for sustained poverty reduction and improved economic security. This chapter focuses on the growth and macroeconomic policies of fragile states, while later chapters deal with other aspects.

The chapter also reports on recent progress in further areas covered in last year's *Global Monitoring Report* (GMR) that are central to achieving higher sustained growth, promotion of a better investment climate, and improvements in governance. A better investment climate is key to attaining higher growth and employment creation, while, as noted in last year's GMR, governance is an ongoing part of MDG monitoring, because it is an important factor underpinning a country's development effectiveness and progress toward the MDGs.

While higher economic growth is generally desirable, one should also be aware of its environmental costs. Although the recent boom in commodity prices has helped to underpin strong growth in many of the most natural resource–dependent economies, high resource dependence can lead to high rates of resource depletion. Countries are liquidating assets when they extract minerals and energy, harvest forests and fish unsustainably, or deplete their agricultural soils, and this can have consequences for future growth.

BOX 1.1   Definition of fragile states

Fragile states is the term generally used to refer to countries that are facing particularly severe development challenges such as weak governance, limited administrative capacity, violence, or the legacy of conflict. In defining policies and approaches toward fragile states, different organizations have used different criteria and terms. Despite methodological variations, however, development partners have been converging around an approach developed at the OECD, which recognizes common characteristics of weak governance and vulnerability to conflict, together with differentiated constraints and opportunities in fragile situations of (1) prolonged crisis or impasse, (2) postconflict or political transition, (3) gradual improvement, and (4) deteriorating governance.[a]

While important for the development of shared strategic and operational approaches, the OECD-DAC typology does not generate a country time series that can be used for research purposes. This year's GMR uses the World Bank definition of fragile states, which is based on a measure of the countries' Country Policy and Institutional Assessment (CPIA) and governance scores.[b] The CPIA-based definition also has the advantages of (1) being a multidimensional concept; (2) being development-oriented, (3) stemming from a robust, review-based process; (4) giving weight to governance, a crucial variable that reflects the capacity of states; and (5) strongly correlating with conflict-related variables.

a. "Fragile States: Policy Commitment and Principles for Good International Engagement in Fragile States and Situations," DAC Senior Level Meeting, December 5–6, 2006.
b. The World Bank definition covers countries scoring 3.2 and below on the CPIA. This is similar to the bottom two quintiles of the CPIA, which the OECD-DAC has used for research purposes on fragile states, but has the advantage of being an absolute rather than a relative threshold, allowing the total number of countries covered to vary from year to year depending on changes in performance. This classification—previously referred to as "Low Income Countries Under Stress" (LICUS)—has been in use in the Bank since 2003; CPIA scores over the years 1998 to 2005 are used to determine what states were fragile over this time period. For years before 1998, cutoff values were determined by comparing the distribution of the CPIA in each year with that for 1998–2001. Since it is determined for each year, fragility is a status, not a permanent classification. Countries may thus be intermittently fragile, although the data used throughout this report are smoothed to avoid excessive volatility in the classification of borderline cases.

Gender equality—in the sense of equality of opportunities, not outcomes—plays an important role in development. Cross-country data show an inverse relationship between the incidence of poverty and the level of gender equality as measured by the rate of female labor market participation. Greater gender equality in access to education, land, technology, and credit markets is also associated with lower poverty. While the direction of causality of these relationships is unclear, it is evident that higher gender equality is associated with better MDG outcomes, including higher nutritional status and lower poverty. These themes are explored in chapter 3.

Poverty Reduction and Growth

Progress on Poverty Reduction

The prospects for achieving MDG1—halving poverty by 2015—are largely unchanged from last year's *Global Monitoring Report*. Overall, the world as a whole is on track to meet the goal with the population share of the extreme poor in developing countries projected to fall from 29 percent in 1990 to 12 percent in 2015. By 2004, over halfway through the goal period, this share had already dropped to 18 percent. Preliminary estimates suggest that the number of extremely poor people in developing countries fell by 135 million between 1999 and 2004.

FIGURE 1.1 Progress toward the poverty MDG target 1990–2004, and a forecast for 2015

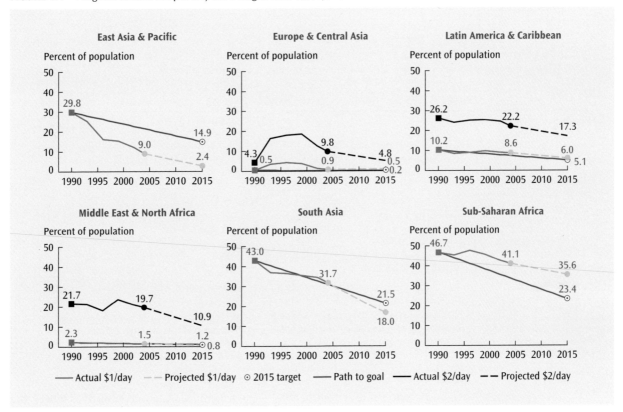

Source: World Bank staff.
Note: The graphs show preliminary data with growth forecasts under review.

This positive assessment overshadows significant regional differences (see figure 1.1). Sub-Saharan Africa remains a long way off the path that would take it to MDG1, even assuming projected growth rates higher than the historic averages since 1990. Between 1999 and 2004, the share of people in extreme poverty in the region fell to 41 percent, a decline of 4.7 percentage points, but higher population growth left the same absolute number of poor at nearly 300 million. The region now accounts for 30 percent of the world's extreme poor, compared with 19 percent in 1990 and only 11 percent in 1981. The Europe and Central Asia region has lost ground since 1990, and may not meet the development goal. The Middle East and North Africa region is expected to achieve MDG1, albeit narrowly, while the Latin America and Caribbean region is likely to come close. However, the main drivers of poverty reduction globally continue to be countries in the East Asia and Pacific and South Asia regions, which—thanks to spectacular rates of growth in the last decade—are both set to overshoot the poverty target. By 2015, extreme poverty rates are projected to be below 3 percent for EAP countries, and 18 percent for SA countries, as compared to MDG1 targets of 15 and 22 percent respectively.

For a number of countries,[3] it is possible to go beyond the regional estimates presented in figure 1.1, and use poverty estimates from household surveys to examine whether, for a typical country, the upturn in growth since the late 1990s led to poverty reduction (table 1.1). The countries included

TABLE 1.1 Impact of growth of GDP per capita on poverty[a]
Averages (percent)

Region or Income Grouping	Number of Countries	Annual Percent Growth in GDP per capita	Initial Poverty Rate ($1/day)	Annual Percent Change in Poverty Rate ($1/day)	Elasticity[b]	Initial Poverty Level ($2/day)	Annual Percent Change in Poverty Rate ($2/day)	Elasticity[b]	Initial Gini Index	Annual Diff. in Gini
Low-income countries	**19**	**3.7**	**23.5**	**−4.85**	**−1.32**	**54.0**	**−3.12**	**−0.85**	**40.5**	**−0.12**
Sub-Saharan Africa	5	1.7	48.8	−2.50	−1.46	78.5	−1.05	−0.61	47.1	−0.14
East Asia and Pacific	4	3.2	16.9	−9.36	−2.91	60.8	−4.04	−1.26	34.5	−0.02
Europe and Central Asia	7	6.0	8.6	−26.05	−4.31	33.7	−9.81	−1.62	36.3	−0.41
Middle-income countries	**26**	**2.1**	**5.7**	**−1.51**	**−0.72**	**19.7**	**−1.06**	**−0.51**	**44.7**	**0.20**
Europe and Central Asia	8	5.2	0.8	−2.32	−0.45	9.9	−1.27	−0.25	33.7	0.45
Latin American and the Caribbean[c]	14	−0.1	7.7	0.02	−0.21	21.5	0.20	−2.78	50.5	0.07
Memorandum items										
India (1994–2005)		4.55	42.1	−1.47	−0.32	85.5	−0.48	−0.11	32.8	0.36
China (1999–2004)		8.11	17.8	−11.73	−1.45	81.1	−7.23	−0.89	41.6	0.44

Source: World Bank and IMF staff.
a. Two surveys for each country were undertaken at intervals of three to eleven years. The last survey for each country was undertaken between 2002 and 2005. Estimates of GDP per capita growth and changes in poverty rates are annualized proportional changes in cross-country averages. All averages are unweighted.
b. Percentage change in poverty rate divided by percentage growth in GDP per capita.
c. Includes data for Argentina and Uruguay based on urban household surveys.

are those with household surveys conducted during both the middle/late 1990s and after 2001. The results must be interpreted with caution in view of possible survey measurement and sampling errors, and, in view of the limited number of countries for which there are appropriate data, may not be representative of entire regions or country groups. Furthermore, the relationship between growth and poverty may be obscured by changes in relative prices, taxes and transfers, including worker remittances, and, as noted below, changes in income distribution.

In low-income countries the preliminary estimates suggest that, on average, growth has clearly resulted in lower poverty incidence: for a sample of 19 low-income countries, 1 percent of GDP growth was associated with a 1.3 percent fall in the rate of extreme poverty and a 0.9 percent fall in the $2-a-day poverty rate. Clear poverty impacts are also evident in the three regions for which sufficient country-level data are available. The picture is somewhat differ-

ent for middle-income countries where the impact of GDP percapita growth on poverty was less. While a high negative elasticity was obtained for the Latin America and the Caribbean sample by the $2-a-day poverty defintion, this reflects increased poverty in a context of near-zero negative growth. One hypothesis is that the poor in the middle-income countries examined were drawn relatively heavily from economically productive groups, who did not enjoy the benefits of growth given its sectoral and geographic composition, and from groups such as retirees and the unemployed, who may depend substantially on public transfers.

There was also a somewhat different impact of growth on poverty incidence in China and India. In China, high growth led to very substantial decreases in poverty rates, while in India, the gains in poverty reduction were more modest. In both countries, poverty reduction took place despite a worsening of the income distribution. Between 1981 and 2004, there was an estimated decline in the absolute number of extreme poor in China of over 500 million people, while in India, the number of extreme poor remained roughly constant (see annex table 1A.3).

Changes in income distribution have not, on average, reduced the impact of income growth on poverty reduction in low-income countries. Inequality in income as measured by the Gini index declined on average for the overall sample of low-income countries. In contrast, income inequality widened on average in middle-income countries, thus hindering poverty reduction.

Improvements in Long-Term Growth

It is reassuring that the pick-up in low-income-country per capita growth rates that started in the 1990s continued in 2006 with an estimated overall per capita GDP growth of 5.9 percent, up from an average of 4.0 percent in 2001–05 (table 1.2). As in previous years, most regions show strong growth performance, with a particularly impressive rate of growth in the low-income countries of Europe and Central Asia, which are still experiencing a rebound after the transition recession of the mid-1990s. The region continues to benefit from strong com-

TABLE 1.2 Per capita GDP growth for high-, middle- and low-income countries

	1986–90	1991–95	1996–2000	2001–05	2004	2005e	2006f	2007f
Real per-capita GDP growth[a]								
World	1.8	0.8	2.0	1.5	2.9	2.3	2.9	2.2
Memo item: World (PPP weights)[b]	..	..	3.9	4.0	5.2	4.7	5.3	4.5
High income	2.9	1.4	2.4	1.4	2.6	2.0	2.6	1.9
Low-income countries	2.9	1.8	2.2	4.0	5.0	5.6	5.9	5.4
East Asia and Pacific	4.7	5.4	0.4	3.8	4.1	4.9	4.7	5.1
Europe and Central Asia	6.6	−11.3	3.8	6.8	7.1	10.2	11.5	9.3
Latin America and Caribbean	−1.1	−0.3	1.4	0.7	1.8	1.7	1.8	1.8
Middle East and N. Africa	6.8	0.9	2.1	0.4	−0.7	0.6	0.8	−0.6
South Asia	3.6	3.0	3.5	4.7	6.1	6.5	6.8	5.9
Excluding India	2.0	2.3	1.9	2.9	4.2	4.8	4.4	4.5
India	4.1	3.2	4.0	5.2	6.7	7.0	7.5	6.4
Sub-Saharan Africa	0.1	−1.6	1.0	2.4	3.1	4.0	4.0	4.4
Middle-income countries	1.0	1.8	3.3	4.3	6.4	5.6	6.2	5.4
East Asia and Pacific	6.1	9.6	6.2	7.9	8.7	8.5	9.1	8.1
Excluding China	5.4	4.9	1.0	3.2	5.0	3.3	4.0	3.7
China	6.3	11.1	7.7	8.8	9.4	9.5	10.0	8.9
Europe and Central Asia	0.6	−4.5	2.9	5.2	7.3	6.0	6.4	5.6
Latin America and Caribbean	−0.2	1.8	1.6	0.9	4.5	3.1	4.0	2.9
Middle East and N. Africa	−0.6	1.7	2.3	3.0	3.2	2.7	3.3	3.2
South Asia	..	..	..	..	..	..	..	..
Sub-Saharan Africa	−0.2	−1.3	1.4	3.0	3.8	4.4	4.2	3.3
Fragile States	3.4	−2.6	0.9	2.5	3.4	4.7	4.6	4.7
Memorandum items								
Developing countries	1.1	1.5	2.8	3.9	5.8	5.3	5.9	5.2
excluding transition countries	1.6	3.4	2.9	3.8	5.8	5.3	5.9	5.1
excluding China and India	0.2	−0.4	1.5	2.2	4.5	3.6	4.2	3.5

Source: World Bank.
Note: PP = purchasing parity; e = estimate; f = forecast.
a. GDP in 2000 constant dollars; 2000 prices and market and exchange rates.
b. GDP measured at 2000 PPP weights.

modity prices and export earnings. In South Asia, growth in India continues at a formidable pace, but other countries in the region are also doing well with the exception of Nepal, which has been suffering from political unrest. Most importantly, in view of the high poverty in the region, Sub-Saharan African countries are also experiencing sustained and rising growth rates. Oil-exporting countries have contributed significantly to this strong performance. Increased oil production and the large terms-of-trade gains from the oil price hike have boosted domestic incomes and spending. Non-fuel-exporting African countries seem to have weathered the adverse shock of high oil prices well, thanks to a mixture of improved policies and strong non-fuel commodity prices. In contrast with the high rates of per capita growth in other regions, growth among low-income countries in the Middle East and North Africa and Latin America and the Caribbean regions continues to be much lower.

Growth in middle-income countries also continues to be strong. China remains the star performer with an estimated per capita growth of 10 percent in 2006. But other middle-income countries in the region and elsewhere are also growing at sustained rates, thus improving prospects for the gradual reduction of the pockets of poverty that still exist in these countries. Recent outcomes suggest that per capita growth rates in middle-income countries have increased, with average rates in the last few years significantly and consistently higher than pre-2000 values.

Weak Growth and Less Poverty Reduction in Fragile States

Fragile states have consistently grown more slowly than other low-income countries (table 1.3). Although the average per capita growth of such states has picked up in recent years, this is partly due to accelerated expansion in a few fuel-producing countries and a fall in the number of conflicts. Among non-fuel-producing fragile states, while growth has increased since 2000, the outlook is for per capita growth to remain a full percentage

TABLE 1.3 Real per capita growth and investment and savings rates of fragile and nonfragile states (percent)

Real per capita growth, investment and savings rates	1986–90	1991–95	1996–2000	2001–05	2004	2005	2006e
Per capita GDP growth							
Fragile states	0.1	−2.5	0.3	2.1	3.2	3.3	2.6
Fuel producers	1.7	−5.5	2.4	2.9	2.2	5.9	4.0
Non–fuel producers	−0.1	−2.0	−0.1	2.0	3.4	2.8	2.3
Nonfragile states	1.3	−0.1	2.9	3.0	3.5	4.1	4.5
Gross fixed capital formation/GDP							
Fragile states	16.1	17.7	17.7	18.3	18.3	19.2	20.4
Fuel producers	16.9	21.5	25.7	20.4	18.4	21.4	31.1
Non–fuel producers	16.0	17.0	16.4	18.0	18.3	18.8	18.6
Nonfragile states	21.4	24.6	22.6	24.1	25.5	25.2	25.6
Gross national savings/GDP							
Fragile states	11.3	11.1	9.8	12.6	15.7	15.8	18.8
Fuel producers	14.3	15.5	14.7	23.6	28.7	38.9	47.7
Non–fuel producers	10.9	10.3	8.9	10.7	13.6	11.0	12.8
Nonfragile states	14.6	15.9	14.4	16.6	18.0	17.2	18.6

Source: IMF staff.
Note: Unweighted country averages; e = estimate.

point lower than that experienced by low-income countries as a whole. Lower investment relative to GDP in fragile states linked in part to lower national savings rates (domestic savings and net transfers from abroad, including official transfers and worker remittances) has been one cause of their slower growth.

Clearly the inferior growth performance of fragile states has been, and is likely to continue to be, an obstacle to the achievement of MDG1. Fragile states by the LICUS definition are home to 9 percent of the population of developing countries, and have nearly twice the incidence of extreme poverty of other low-income countries. About 27 percent of the extreme poor in developing countries live in fragile states. Moreover, fragile states can have adverse spillovers on neighboring countries through conflict, refugee flows, organized crime, spread of epidemic diseases, and barriers to trade and investment.[4]

The rate of extreme poverty in the current set of fragile states is estimated to have risen somewhat in 1990–2004 from 49 percent to over 54 percent (figure 1.2). The projected poverty rate for this group of countries in 2015 is slightly higher than in 1990 under current assumptions about future growth and income distribution, suggesting that no overall progress will be made toward MDG1 over the goal period as a whole. In contrast, nonfragile states made significant progress in reducing poverty by 2004, and are projected to overachieve MDG1 by 2015.

Conflicts have undermined growth performance at various times in most fragile states. Conflicts are a major reason why countries slide into fragility; they extract high costs in terms of lives and physical damage, but also reduce growth and increase poverty. There is consensus in the relevant literature[5] that civil conflict reduces gross domestic product (GDP) growth, although estimates of the size of this impact vary. The impact of conflict on growth and poverty incidence seems to have worsened since the beginning of the 1990s (see Staines 2005). Conflicts have become shorter and more intense than before; their average impact on GDP growth is now about

FIGURE 1.2 Rates of extreme poverty (percent)

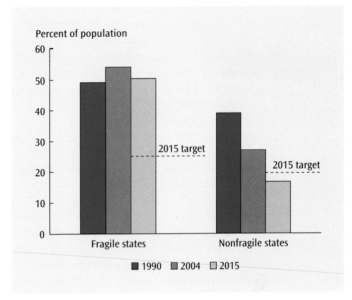

Source: World Bank staff calculations.

−12 percent per year of conflict. While in the past, the fall in growth was more gradual, and was followed by a gradual and prolonged recovery within the conflict period, since 1990 the period of the growth collapse has largely coincided with that of the conflict, leading to this higher annual GDP loss. It has also taken longer for countries to regain their preconflict per capita income levels than would have been the case before 1990.

Because conflict is both a major cause and consequence of poverty in fragile states, the coherence and sequencing of international diplomatic, security, and development engagement is more important in these environments than elsewhere. Recent research (for example, Chauvet and Collier 2004) demonstrates that the risk of reversion to conflict is significantly higher in the period following postconflict elections than in the period preceding elections. This increased risk does not diminish for the first postconflict decade. In discussions of these results at the United Nations (UN) Peace-Building Commission, participants noted that this risk may have important implications for the sequencing of electoral, peacekeeping, and development assistance, underlining the importance of efforts to ensure that electoral assistance in fragile transitions is properly sequenced with decisions to maintain or draw down peace-keeping troops, and with aid-financed efforts to support measures to generate growth and employment and other initiatives that may mitigate the risks of reversion to conflict.

Conflict aside, all fragile states have weak institutions and governance, hindering growth.[6] Some states may be willing to promote growth and reduce poverty, but are unable to do so for a variety of reasons such as a lack of territorial control, political cohesion, and administrative capacity. In other states, governments may be unwilling to take necessary actions because they are not substantively committed to overall poverty reduction, or they may promote poverty reduction while excluding certain social or geographical groups.

State fragility has proven to be a persistent condition. Of the 34 states judged as fragile in 1980, 21 were still viewed as such in 2005, although of these, 6 had left and later resumed fragile status during the period. The average duration of fragility among the 2005 group of fragile states was 16.6 years. For the 20 countries that entered and permanently left the fragile states list since 1980, the average duration of fragility was 7.8 years. Of these, Mozambique experienced the shortest duration of fragility (3 years), and Niger the longest (15 years).

Nevertheless there are some success stories. Specifically, Vietnam, Mozambique, and Uganda have graduated from fragile state status. All three experienced severe violent conflict but managed to achieve a durable cessation of hostilities. Conflict ended either because there was a change in geopolitical conditions that provided incentives for warring parties to lay down their arms, or because there was a military victory by one party involved in the conflict that eliminated opposition groups or gave them a stake in the postconflict politi-

cal order. Subsequently in all three countries, growth was enabled by the introduction of at least modest programs of market-oriented economic reform that were managed so as to keep interested elites on board.

Limited capacity and willingness to undertake needed reforms in fragile states undermine the mainstream poverty reduction approach based on partnership as exemplified by the Poverty Reduction Strategy Paper (PRSP). Difficulties donors experience when working in these countries, particularly the ones with limited geopolitical relevance, can lead to excessively low or volatile aid flows even after taking into account the countries' low level of governance (see OECD/DAC 2005). The international community is increasingly aware of issues particular to fragile states, and has been considering alternative approaches tailored to the characteristics of specific countries, for example, emphasizing humanitarian assistance and relying where possible on help from nonstate actors such as nongovernmental organizations (NGOs). In this context, the OECD/DAC has recently issued a set of "Principles for good international engagement in fragile states."

Macroeconomic Performance

Continued good macroeconomic policies—as shown by continued low inflation and budget deficits—have helped underpin improved growth performance in low-income countries (table 1.4). At about 6.2 percent, median inflation in 2006 is estimated to have decreased from a 2005 peak of 7.2 percent associated with the sharp rise in oil prices, and is forecast to slow further in 2007. Since 2000, inflation has been substantially lower than 10 years earlier. The external indebtedness of low-income countries relative to GDP has also been declining, in part reflecting the impact of the Heavily Indebted Poor Countries (HIPC) Initiative and the Multilateral Debt Relief Initiative (MDRI). In 2006, the average debt-to-GDP ratio was 61 percent, compared to over 90

TABLE 1.4 Macroeconomic indicators for low-income countries
Annual averages, except where indicated[a]

	1986-90	1991-95	1996-2000	2001-05	2006 est.	2007 proj.
Inflation (median annual %)[b]						
Low-income countries	7.1	14.3	6.8	5.4	6.2	5.3
Fragile states	10.2	19.8	9.1	7.7	6.8	5.5
Nonfragile states	6.3	11.4	6.2	4.9	5.9	5.2
Middle-income countries	9.9	18.0	6.8	4.4	4.6	4.6
External debt (% of GDP)						
Low-income countries	84.9	97.5	92.2	89.5	61.0	51.1
Fragile states	129.9	115.9	116.1	110.1	81.7	63.2
Nonfragile states	57.0	85.2	75.2	76.0	47.7	43.3
Middle-income countries	44.3	46.7	44.5	46.9	41.9	40.2
Fiscal balance (% of GDP)						
Low-income countries	−6.5	−6.9	−4.9	−3.5	0.4	2.2
Fuel producers	−8.7	−11.2	−5.6	6.7	23.9	58.7
Non–fuel producers	−6.4	−6.6	−4.9	−4.3	−1.6	−2.7
Fragile states	−10.0	−7.8	−4.9	−2.6	3.8	10.4
Of which: Fuel producers	−11.5	−12.1	−7.2	8.2	29.3	71.4
Non–fuel producers	−9.9	−7.1	−4.7	−4.5	−1.4	−1.8
Nonfragile states	−4.2	−6.3	−4.9	−4.1	−1.8	−3.2
Middle-income countries	−3.5	−2.7	−3.2	−2.6	−0.7	−1.2

Source: IMF staff.
a. Averages are calculated as unweighted means of country values.
b. Median inflation is calculated from the annual medians and then averaged over five-year periods.

percent throughout the 1990s. This decline is particularly apparent for HIPCs that have passed the HIPC Initiative completion point, for which the external debt-to-GDP ratio in 2006 was half its average for 2001–05. The dramatic swing in average fiscal balances from a deficit to a small surplus in low-income countries in 2006 is mainly explained by sharp increases in oil revenues in a few fuel producers. However, in non-fuel-producing countries there has been a reduction in the size of fiscal deficits relative to GDP since the late 1990s.

Fragile states' macroeconomic indicators have tended to be inferior to those of other low-income countries. Until recently, inflation rates were on average at least 2.9 percentage points higher than in nonfragile states, possibly because of recourse in some countries to monetary financing of the budget. External

debt indicators are also higher, reflecting in some cases excessive past external borrowing. In addition, fragile states have found it difficult to satisfy the conditions for reaching the HIPC Initiative completion point and hence debt relief under the MDRI. Of the states classified as fragile in 2005, only three, Mauritania, São Tomé and Principe, and Sierra Leone, had reached the completion point as of end-March 2007. Although fuel-producing fragile states have recently attained large fiscal surpluses through high oil export revenues or oil-related fees and transfers, prior to the early 2000s, fiscal deficits relative to GDP among fuel-producing fragile states were consistently higher than in non-fragile states, reflecting limited fiscal discipline. Deficit ratios have, however, been similar in non-fuel producing fragile states to those of nonfragile states.

Quality of Macroeconomic Policies

For the fourth consecutive year, International Monetary Fund (IMF) staff have carried out assessments of the quality of macroeconomic policies in each low-income country (table 1.5). In addition to providing a snapshot of the quality of the main dimensions of macroeconomic policies for each year, these assessments can be used to evaluate developments since 2003, the first year of the exercise.

The assessment of fiscal policy continues to be mixed: almost 50 percent of countries have earned a good rating, but 21 percent are regarded unsatisfactory. A significant proportion of countries have moved out of the unsatisfactory category—a marked improvement compared to 2003. However, the composition of expenditures continues to be rated unsatisfactory in almost half of low-income countries. In contrast, access to foreign exchange, the quality of monetary policies, and the governance and transparency of monetary and financial institutions have consistently rated relatively well, with a majority of countries rated good and a relatively small percentage rated unsatisfactory. In addition, more than half the countries surveyed in 2006 received favorable ratings regarding the consistency of their policy mix.

Consistent with the evidence on macroeconomic indicators, assessments of macroeconomic policies in fragile states are markedly more negative in some areas than those for low-income countries as a whole. The composition of public spending receives a much worse assessment in fragile states, reflecting the inappropriateness of expenditure composition for poverty reduction in these countries. The picture for monetary policy and the financial sector is more mixed. The quality of monetary policy is considered good for a similarly large proportion of fragile and nonfragile states, underlining the relative insulation of monetary authorities from weaknesses in administrative capacity. However, the governance and transparency of monetary and financial institutions is seen as worse in fragile states. That said, there is significant variance across the group: countries such as Timor-Leste, and more recently, Haiti and Liberia have made significant progress in this regard.

Although the assessments are not strictly comparable,[7] the World Bank 2005 CPIA ratings of low-income-country macroeconomic

TABLE 1.5   Quality of macroeconomic policies in low-income countries, 2006
Share of countries falling into each category (percent)

Rating	Fiscal policy	Composition of public spending	Monetary policy	Consistency of macro policies	Governance in monetary and financial institutions	Access to foreign exchange
2006 survey						
Unsatisfactory	20.5	48.7	10.3	15.4	15.4	3.8
Adequate	33.3	38.5	19.2	32.1	28.2	12.8
Good	46.2	12.8	70.5	52.6	56.4	83.3
2003 survey						
Unsatisfactory	33.8	49.4	11.7	22.4	17.1	9.2
Adequate	19.5	32.8	11.7	28.9	22.4	13.2
Good	46.8	18.2	76.6	48.7	60.5	77.6
Fragile states (2006)						
Unsatisfactory	*46.7*	*70.0*	*20.0*	*30.0*	*30.0*	*10.0*
Adequate	*26.7*	*20.0*	*10.0*	*30.0*	*33.3*	*20.0*
Good	*26.7*	*10.0*	*70.0*	*40.0*	*36.7*	*70.0*

Source: IMF staff assessments.

policies are broadly similar to those of IMF staff. In particular, the CPIA ratings indicate less satisfaction with fiscal policies than with macroeconomic policies as a whole: 36 percent of countries were given a score of 3.0 or less for fiscal policy, compared with 21 percent for macroeconomic management. Roughly consistent with the relatively low assessments given by IMF staff for the composition of public spending, the CPIA also shows that 37 percent of all low-income countries and 78 percent of fragile states score 3.0 or less regarding the equity of public resource use.

Prospects for the Global Economy

The world economy is growing at a pace last seen at the beginning of the 1970s. This is welcome news for developing countries in view of its implications for trade, aid, private financial flows, and remittances. In 2006, the United States continued to expand at a strong pace, but global activity was more balanced owing to an acceleration of growth in European countries. The exceptional growth performances of China and India also continued. In the coming years, growth is expected to slow down slightly in most advanced countries, on the back of a gradual resolution of the large global current account imbalances that have been accumulating in the last decade.

However, the risks of growth slowdown remain, although the likelihood of these materializing has diminished recently. If the pace of economic activity were to translate into higher inflationary pressure in developed countries, this might trigger more dramatic rises in interest rates than experienced so far, with the attendant danger of a sharp slowdown in these countries' growth. The unwinding of global imbalances, and in particular of the exceptionally large U.S. trade deficit, could also take place at a much faster pace than expected, if the U.S. economy were to slow down significantly, following, for example, an acceleration in the fall of housing prices. The future behavior of world oil prices is another area of uncertainty. While further sharp increases are not anticipated,

they cannot be ruled out in view of possible stronger-than-expected demand and the ongoing instability in the Middle East. There is also a danger that protectionism could rise in the years ahead, reversing some of the gains from an increasingly integrated global economy. Lastly, the chances of a global pandemic derived from avian influenza remain.

There are also some risks that could impinge more directly on the growth prospects of developing countries. As noted above, the negative impact of high oil prices on many non-fuel-commodity-exporting developing countries has been limited by the improvement in their terms of trade arising from strong demand growth. In the future, however, while a fall in oil prices is unlikely, a relative decline in non-fuel-commodity price could occur. In addition, a rise in real interest rates in developed countries could create turbulence in emerging-market financial sectors, with possible adverse macroeconomic consequences.

Need to Make Progress in Other Areas

To sustain and accelerate growth and poverty reduction, developing countries will not only need to maintain and, in many cases, improve their macroeconomic frameworks, but also make efforts in other areas. This chapter monitors progress in two such areas, the private investment climate and governance.

Monitoring the Investment Climate

The World Bank monitors the investment climate through two main vehicles: the Investment Climate Surveys (ICS) and the Doing Business (DB) surveys. The former draws data from firms, while the latter relies on the views of experts.

In 2006, new firm-level ICS data became available for 27 countries, bringing the total to 73,000 firms in 104 countries. The year marked the beginning of a shift to regional rollouts of the surveys, with 8 Latin American countries and 17 Sub-Saharan countries covered in the latest round. Several fragile states

(Burundi, Democratic Republic of Congo, Côte d'Ivoire, Guinea, Guinea-Bissau, and Mauritania) were included. Key areas of interest in Latin America include innovation and technology. The Africa report focuses on issues of competitiveness, gender, and the extent to which the investment climate can compensate for geographic challenges such as being landlocked or natural resource intensive.

Several countries are now collecting follow-on surveys, making it possible to evaluate changes in the investment climate and policy reforms. For example, a survey was fielded in Egypt in 2004 prior to a series of reforms of the tax system, licensing, permits, and customs. The 2006 survey picked up clear indications of the impact of these reforms. Whereas taxes had ranked as the top constraint in 2004, it became only the fifth-highest constraint in 2006. Significantly, there were fewer inspections by tax authorities and fewer petty bribes associated with taxes. In addition, streamlining of licensing permits led to a decline in the time to get an operating license from 3.3 months to 2.0 months.

Moreover, petty bribery associated with permits and with customs clearance declined. While corruption remains an issue, there is evidence of significant progress.

In Bangladesh, a set of firms were surveyed every six months for three years. The impact policy change can be seen in international trade reforms, licensing reforms, and tax reforms. With the end of the Multi-Fiber Agreement, international competition in garments and textiles intensified as reflected in falling garment export and textile input prices. The demand for skilled workers also rose, with skilled workers receiving higher wage increases, and firms reporting greater delays in hiring new skilled workers. In addition, the automation of municipal licensing through a new interface provided by the Dhaka Chamber of Commerce and Industry resulted in dramatic declines in the time taken to renew business licensing permits through Bangladesh's Municipal Corporations. There was also a decline in the incidence and value of bribes (figure 1.3).

The 2007 *doing business* indicators measure the status of *de jure* business environ-

FIGURE 1.3   Regulatory reforms can increase efficiency and reduce corruption

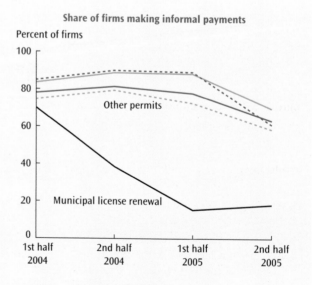

Source: Hallward-Driemeier (2006): Bangladesh Panel Survey.

ment in which private firms operate, with commonly defined indicators across 175 countries. The goal is to benchmark and monitor efforts to improve the business climate and provide policy makers with a set of indicators as to how they compare with other country practices. Donors and foreign investors can make use of the indicators to measure progress in them. The transparency and simplicity of the indicators also facilitate efforts to identify areas of inefficiency and shortcomings in country regulatory frameworks. While there are many other factors affecting investors' decisions, improvement of the regulatory environment can have spillover benefits on other areas of public policy, further improving the attractiveness of good reformers in the eyes of investors.

The 2007 Doing Business report recognized the accomplishments of countries that were able to improve their regulatory environments. Georgia was 2006's most impressive reformer, making reforms in 6 of 10 areas studied by *Doing Business* and improving its world ranking on the ease of doing business from 112 to 37 in the span of one year, pointing to the capacity of countries to quickly and significantly progress. Mexico and Romania also improved their rankings through major reforms. The African region, which had been the slowest-reforming region in the previous two reports, picked up pace in 2006, and, with the exception of Europe and Central Asia made more progress than other developing-country regions. Tanzania and Ghana were Africa's top reformers, but others also made significant progress. Many of the reforms in Africa were easy, stroke-of-the-pen reforms—one simple reform in Côte d'Ivoire cut the time it takes to register property from 397 days in 2005 to 32—although more difficult reforms will soon be necessary. Other countries, including two fragile states, Zimbabwe and Timor-Leste, were identified as having deteriorating business environments. Eritrea, another fragile state, was noted as having the single worst reform of the year, which suspended all construction licenses and prohibited private businesses from entering the construction sector.

Monitoring Governance Trends

The 2006 GMR highlighted governance monitoring as a core ongoing part of the broader task of monitoring progress in reaching the MDGs. The 2006 analysis underscored the following:

■ Governance is multidimensional, with no unique path from weaker to stronger governance. The quality of bureaucracy and of checks-and-balances institutions comprise two broad dimensions along which governance might change, with the pattern of change varying from country to country.
■ Governance monitoring is an imperfect science. All measures have margins of error. It would be a mistake to read significance into small differences across countries or modest changes over time.
■ Monitoring at aggregate levels, using broad measures, can provide an overview of trends in governance change and cross-country patterns. But efforts at reform invariably focus on specific governance subsystems, and (unless they can be disaggregated) broad measures are too imprecise to be useful for monitoring whether specific interventions create progress.
■ There is strong potential for monitoring at a disaggregated level, "using specific measures of the quality of key governance subsystems, and using the results as 'actionable indicators' to identify specific strengths and weaknesses in individual countries." The 2006 GMR advocated strongly for greater investment in developing such measures.

Broad Governance Trends in Low- and Middle-Income Countries, 1996–2005

The 2006 GMR identified schematically three distinct trajectories of governance improvement: disproportionate gains in bureaucratic capability, disproportionate gains in checks-and-balances institutions, and balanced gains. The 2006 GMR also suggested ways to measure both bureaucratic capability[8] and

FIGURE 1.4   Trajectories of Governance Improvements

TRAJECTORY I: Balanced—Significant Improvements in both Government Effectiveness and Quality of Checks and Balances Institutions

TRAJECTORY II: More Improvement in Government Effectiveness

TRAJECTORY III: More Improvement in Quality of Checks and Balances Institutions

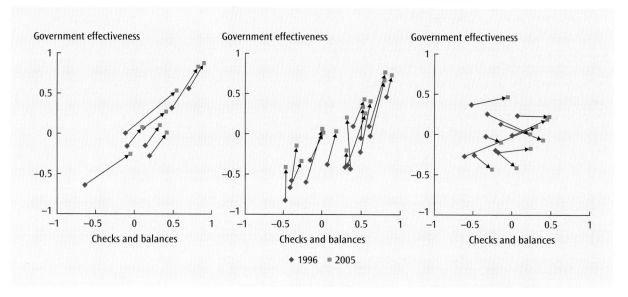

Countries: Nigeria, Mozambique, Mexico, Mali, Croatia, Slovenia, Slovak Republic, and Estonia.

Countries: No significant improvement in Quality of Checks and Balances Institutions: Turkey, Ukraine, Hungary, Belarus, Bulgaria, Azerbaijan, Paraguay, Panama, and Madagascar. Quality of Checks and Balances Institutions saw significant improvement, but the improvement in the Government Effectiveness dimension is double or more the size of improvement in the Checks and Balances dimension: Russia, Tajikistan, Romania, Tanzania, Lithuania, and Latvia.

Countries: No significant improvement in Government Effectiveness dimension: Ghana, Kenya, Bhutan, The Gambia. Government Effectiveness dimension saw significant improvement, but the improvement in the Quality of Checks and Balances dimension was double or more the size of improvement in the Government Effectiveness dimension: Serbia, Senegal. Significant decline in Government Effectiveness dimension: Peru, Indonesia, Syria, Sierra Leone.

Sources: Kaufmann, Kraay, and Mastruzzi 2006; Polity IV Database 2005.

the quality of checks and balances.[9] Figure 1.4 uses aggregate governance indicators to depict empirically these three trajectories of improvement for 1996–2005. Forty-four of the 111 countries experienced governance changes that were both relatively large and at least moderately significant.[10]

The measures are sufficiently loosely defined,[11] and the margins of error of the estimates sufficiently large, that the results are best viewed as heuristic. Even so, the systematically divergent patterns across the three sub-figures[12] seems to underscore that there is no unique path from poor to good governance:

- Eight countries—including three in Africa and three in Eastern Europe—improved governance in a balanced manner over the course of the decade.

- Fifteen countries—including 10 from Eastern Europe or the former Soviet Union—improved mostly in bureaucratic capability/government effectiveness.

- Ten countries saw disproportionate improvement in the quality of their checks-and-balances institutions. In four of these (Indonesia, Peru, Sierra Leone, and Syria) the gains in accountability were offset by declines in bureaucratic capability/government effectiveness. Four of the six countries that improved checks and balances over the decade without a corresponding decline were in Sub-Saharan Africa (The Gambia, Ghana, Kenya, and Senegal).

■ Eleven countries, of which six are currently classified as fragile states, experienced governance declines in at least one dimension without improvement in the other. For five of these (Central African Republic, Côte d'Ivoire, Eritrea, Nepal, and Zimbabwe) the declines were both relatively large and moderately significant across both dimensions; for three (Argentina, Guinea-Bissau, and the Lao People's Democratic Republic) the declines were mostly in bureaucratic capability; and for the remaining three (Ecuador, Guyana, and República Bolivariana de Venezuela—all in Latin America) mostly in the quality of checks-and-balances institutions.

The data suggest broadly divergent patterns among African countries relative to countries in Eastern Europe and the former Soviet Union in the trajectories of governance reform. The most common improvements were, in the former group, a further consolidation of the political openings of the early 1990s, and in the latter group, gains mostly in government effectiveness. Country-specific starting points thus surely matter in shaping the agenda for governance change, although understanding of these dynamics is still in its infancy. Tracking the impact of specific governance reforms requires more disaggregated "actionable" indicators.

Growing Momentum for Actionable Governance Indicators

Over the past year, initiatives by independent civil society organizations, work within the World Bank Group, and multidonor initiatives all have contributed to progress in the development of specific governance indicators that, given repeated measurement over time, can be used to monitor operationally, in a disaggregated way, the effectiveness of efforts to strengthen governance subsystems.

Independent civil society organizations made a variety of noteworthy contributions to the monitoring of the quality of checks-and-balances institutions, three of which are illustrated here. First, in May 2006 the Afrobarometer network released the results for 18 African countries of its third round of surveys. Afrobarometer provides scientifically reliable data, comparable across countries and over time, on citizen perceptions vis-à-vis a variety of governance issues including popular understanding of, support for, and satisfaction with democracy; the demand for, and satisfaction with effective, accountable, and clean government; satisfaction with education, health, and local government services; and citizen participation in both democratic processes and development efforts. Second, in January 2007, Global Integrity (whose GII index was introduced in the 2006 GMR) released 43 additional country reports. These included follow-up reports for 17 of the 25 countries surveyed in the initial, 2004 round.

The third contribution by civil society was the release in October 2006 (after four years of work) by the International Budget Project of a new index to monitor the transparency of public budgets. As with the GII, the Open Budget Index is based on a combination of expert assessments and peer review at both country and global levels. Key findings include the following:

■ Only 6 of 59 countries surveyed—France, New Zealand, Slovenia, South Africa, the United Kingdom, and the United States— were reported as consistently providing "extensive" budget information to citizens in their budget documents. An additional 30 countries provide "significant" or "some" budget information.

■ Twenty-three countries were reported as providing "minimal" or "scant or no" information—with 10 countries (Angola, Bolivia, Burkina Faso, Chad, the Arab Republic of Egypt, Mongolia, Morocco, Nicaragua, Nigeria, and Vietnam) in the latter, weaker category.

■ In 32 of the countries surveyed, the government does not make available to the public information it is already producing for its own internal use or for donors. Thus, many countries could sharply improve their transparency and accountability simply by providing information they already produce to the public.

The World Bank Group has made three sets of contributions. First was the publication, for the first time (but only for low-income countries), of disaggregated CPIA scores. The 2006 GMR detailed the potential for using some of the CPIA results—especially those on public financial management, on the quality of public administration, and on property rights and the rule of law—as governance measures. As these data have long been used in the allocation of International Development Association (IDA) resources, their release is an important contribution not only to the endeavor of governance monitoring, but also to the transparency of the international financial institutions (IFIs). The second contribution was the release of the 2005 updates for both the Doing Business (DB) indicators and the Kaufmann-Kraay/World Bank Institute (aggregate) governance indicators; for the first time, the detailed indicators used to construct the KK measures have also been made available on the KK/WBI Web site. The third contribution was in systematizing and scaling up further its efforts on enterprise surveys. Prior to 2006, only in Europe and Central Asia were surveys systematically done across all countries within a region, rather than on a demand-driven country-by-country basis. Regional rollouts currently are under way worldwide, including for 30 countries in Africa and 15 in Latin America. As of February 2007, enterprise survey results were available on a new streamlined Web interface for 100 countries—up from only 37 a year earlier. Research is under way that links the DB and Enterprise Survey (ES) results.

Multidonor initiatives have resulted in significant progress on two sets of indicators: the Public Expenditure and Financial Account-ability (PEFA) public financial management indicators, and the OECD/DAC work on procurement. Use of the PEFA indicators (which were described in depth in the 2006 GMR) has expanded rapidly. As of October 2006, public financial management assessments had been completed (to the point of final draft reports) in 33 countries and were under way in an additional 15, and 34 more assessments had been planned (but not yet begun). In July 2006, following a long gestation period, the OECD/DAC Joint Venture for Procurement published a revised tool—*Methodology for Assessment of National Procurement Systems (version 4)*—and an accompanying guidance note for scoring each of its 54 indicators on a four-point scale. The tool has successfully been piloted in five countries (Albania, Bangladesh, Ghana, the Philippines, and Turkey) and is currently being used in 15–20 more. So far, however, these multidonor initiatives have been characterized by a notable disconnect between scaled-up in-country efforts (that have made an important contribution to harmonized monitoring at country-level of trends in the quality of public expenditure management), and transparent availability of the fruits of that effort.

For PEFA (table 1.6), only 8 of 45 "substantially completed" assessments have so far found their way into the public domain, and even those have been made available only as individual reports, with no effort to consolidate and contrast the results. The remaining reports, although their drafting apparently has been finalized, currently are in a consultation (or postconsultation) limbo; the problem is seemingly especially acute for assessments led by the World Bank or the European Commission. The OECD/DAC-sponsored work on procurement assessments is less advanced than PEFAs. But here too, there are no plans to make available in a consolidated way the results of the ongoing country-level work.

Underlying this caution is a concern among donors as to how the findings will be used. In particular, there is a fear that cross-country comparisons will be used to construct new "red-lines"—absolute thresholds as to which

TABLE 1.6 Status of "finalized" PEFA assessments (as of February 23, 2007)

Number of assessments	WB leading	EC leading	WB and EC jointly leading	Other agency leading	Total assessments
Substantially completed draft/final report	20	16	1	8	45
Of which final report completed	4	11	0	4	19
Of which final report in the public domain	4	2	0	2	8

Source: PEFA Secretariat.

countries should receive aid, and the form in which that aid should be provided. This fear is misplaced. Certainly, it is not relevant for the World Bank Group—where the performance-based allocation system (using the CPIA) is the basis for allocation of IDA resources. More broadly, as highlighted in the 2006 GMR, there is a growing consensus that scaling up aid, and moving to country systems, principally should be based not on absolute thresholds but on *country-specific trends* in the quality of these systems, as evidenced by improvement in actionable indicators.

Growth, Poverty, and the Environment

The Environment as a Source of Growth and Poverty Reduction

Higher economic growth is clearly desirable, but rather than a goal in and of itself, it should be a process of increasing the wealth of present and future generations. Defining wealth as including not only physical and human capital, but also natural assets, leads to concerns that current rates of depletion and degradation of natural resources may be undermining the sustainability of higher growth, particularly in developing countries. Such concerns have motivated four recent major reports on environmental issues (box 1.2).

A distinguishing characteristic of developing countries is their high dependence on natural resources. When agricultural land, minerals, energy resources, and forests are taken into account, the share of natural resources in total wealth is substantially higher than produced capital in the poorest regions—Sub-Saharan Africa and South Asia—and in the oil-producing countries of the Middle East and North Africa. In lower-middle-income countries the shares of produced and natural capital in total wealth are roughly equal. Only in upper-middle-income countries is there a consistently higher share of produced capital compared to natural capital in total wealth. For a broad spectrum of developing countries, the effectiveness of natural resource management can therefore have a significant impact on development prospects and performance.

As noted in the introduction to this chapter, countries are liquidating assets when they extract minerals and energy, harvest forests and fish unsustainably, or deplete their agricultural soils. This liquidation of natural assets is obscured in traditional national accounts measures, such as gross national income (GNI), which treat depletion and depreciation as part of income. Careful analysis of the net rate of wealth creation presents a very different picture of economic performance. In Sub-Saharan Africa, for example, the net creation of wealth has been effectively zero over the last three decades, a period in which total population more than doubled. In countries such as Cameroon, Benin, Burkina Faso, Mozambique, and Rwanda, low saving effort, resource depletion, and high population growth combined to yield net reductions in wealth per capita of more than 10 percent of GNI in 2000.

BOX 1.2 Current issues in the environment debate

Four recent reports have highlighted the urgency of many environmental and natural resource problems globally, and helped to link environmental factors to development outcomes.

The Millennium Ecosystem Assessment: Ecosystems and Human Well-Being (MA)
One of the central messages of the MA, a multiyear nongovernmental process involving nearly 1,400 experts, is that the unprecedented exploitation of ecosystems is rapidly destroying those ecosystems' abilities to continue providing services that are essential to our well-being. For example, in recent years, human activity has enhanced the ability of the ecosystem to provide crops but decreased the ability of marine fisheries to provide fish, a consequence of overfishing. The MA concludes that such unsustainable activity will prevent future generations from enjoying the benefits of certain ecosystem services. It also highlights the importance of valuing ecosystem services appropriately compared to the more common practice of valuing them primarily for the services that can be exploited for more private and immediate gains, including from revenues from harvested timber and food. The content and lessons of the MA are directly relevant to the pursuit of sustainable poverty relief.

The Stern Review on the Economics of Climate Change
This review provides a thorough analysis of how climate change may impact the world economy and what can be done to minimize its costs. The review estimates that irreversible damages to the world from unabated climate change could entail a cost equivalent to a permanent drop of 5–20 percent of global per capita consumption depending on the climate scenario, with that cost being disproportionately borne by the poorest people. This drop in GDP could cause as many as 220 million people in Africa and South Asia alone to remain below the $2-a-day poverty line at the century's end, with equally severe impacts on human development indicators. Changing precipitation patterns, extreme temperatures, increasingly violent storms, and rising sea levels could also lead to massive migration and increased conflict, compounding the misery of already suffering populations.

The review argues that significant and immediate action can greatly reduce the likelihood of the direst scenarios. The cost of action to stabilize the climate at moderate levels of warming would be a permanent 1 percent drop in global per capita consumption. The review also advocates that the international community needs to invest more in adapting to climate change because the global temperature has already risen by 0.7° C, and will increase more because of the presence of past and projected emissions. Adaptation will be particularly difficult for people in low-income countries, and "should be an extension of good development practice," including promotion of growth and economic diversification, and investing in education, health, water management, and disaster preparedness.

While there has been an active debate over the assumptions and conclusions of the review, the importance of the issue calls for greater attention, possibly in future GMRs.

Where Is the Wealth of Nations?
This World Bank study aims to increase understanding of the role of natural resources and the environment in the development process. It provides a comprehensive analysis of the different sources of wealth in developed and developing countries, and reveals some strong tendencies in wealth composition: (1) in low-income countries natural resources are a much larger share of total wealth than produced capital—29 percent compared with 16 percent; (2) agricultural land makes up two-thirds of the natural capital of low-income countries; and (3) the largest share of wealth across all income classes consists of less tangible items such as human and institutional capital.

The study shows that the majority of low-income countries are actually dissaving in per capita terms when resource depletion and population growth are taken into account. Policy responses for donors and developing countries include placing greater emphasis on improving natural resource

continued

BOX 1.2   Current issues in the environment debate *(continued)*

management, such as efforts to preserve soil quality in agriculture; reducing incentives to over-exploit natural resources, particularly living resources; and balancing investment in the overall portfolio of natural, produced, human, and institutional capital.

At Loggerheads? Agricultural Expansion, Poverty Reduction, and Environment in the Tropical Forests
This World Bank Policy Research Report discusses the dual goals of preserving rapidly shrinking tropical forests and relieving the poverty of the hundreds of millions of people who live in and near them. The report emphasizes that the causes of deforestation are varied. Some forests are cleared to expand commodity production in order to meet the demands of wealthy urbanites. Other forests are cleared by poor people who rely on expanding low-productivity agriculture. Timber prices have a more ambiguous effect as they often encourage sustainable management of timber rather than clear-cutting.

The consequences of continued high rates of deforestation include the annual emission of 3 billion tons of CO_2, the disappearance of entire ecosystems and the species that inhabit them, and widespread changes in water flows, scenery, microclimates, pests, and pollinators. To reduce deforestation the report discusses the pros and cons of different land management strategies—protected areas, regulated logging concessions, community forest management—and their appropriateness in different contexts.

The policy recommendations in the report include building local institutions and social capital in forested areas, particularly among indigenous groups and communities that will collectively manage forests. The report stresses the need to mobilize international resources, especially conservation and carbon finance. Two cross-cutting recommendations include equitably assigning property and land use rights where they are weak or absent and, as recommended in the Millennium Ecosystem Assessment, actively encouraging markets for environmental services at local, national, and international levels.

Natural wealth is a potential contributor to growth and poverty reduction, but policies, institutions, and political economy can all influence the strength of the contribution. Exports of commercial natural resources (minerals, energy, forest products, and fish) are a source of development finance, but many countries do not use this finance effectively, and are consuming resource rents rather than investing them. Nature tourism is a growing source of exports in many countries, but government policies often hamper the expansion of the sector. The productivity of agricultural land—55 to 65 percent of the value of natural resources in developing countries—has a profound impact on growth and poverty, particularly in low-income countries. For poor households, the environment and natural resources contribute directly to health, livelihoods, and vulnerability. For women in par-

ticular, the management of natural resources has significant impacts on welfare (box 1.3).

While natural resources can potentially make large contributions to growth and poverty reduction, they present specific risks as well. Commodity boom and bust cycles can stress fiscal systems and increase the volatility of exchange rates. "Easy money" in the form of resource rents can reduce the impetus for economic reforms. The evidence suggests that a combination of sound macroeconomic policies and strong sectoral policies and institutions is required in order to parlay natural resource wealth into successful development.

Update of Key Indicators

MDG7 calls for integrating the principles of sustainable development into country policies and reversing the loss of environmental

---

BOX 1.3   Gender and the environment

In most regions women are more commonly burdened with handling domestic work. Children, especially girls, also spend much of their time helping with these tasks. A major component of domestic work is retrieving water and firewood for the home. The amount of time and effort needed to complete these tasks is highly dependent on environmental conditions. For homes with access to piped water and modern fuels, the time burden can be minimal. However, in places where water and fuel are more difficult to access these tasks can take hours every day, reducing the amount of time women and girls can spend on other activities, including out-of-home employment or school. Deforestation and pollution of water resources exacerbate the problem, requiring people to continually travel longer distances to fetch firewood or potable water (Barwell 1996).

Malawi is a country where access to water and firewood is particularly critical and also precarious. More than 90 percent of people use fuel wood as their main source of cooking energy. During the 1990s, Malawi's deforestation rate was 3 times that of the rest of Sub-Saharan Africa's and 10 times that of the world as a whole, making this vital resource more difficult to access. Malawi is also expected to experience a water crisis by 2025 that will make this resource scarcer. As noted above, these developments are likely to decrease female school attendance and performance compared to those of boys. This result suggests that the gender disparity in schooling may not be the result of conscious discrimination but instead of traditional gender inequalities in the division of labor (Nankhuni 2004).

Additionally, some environmental health hazards fall disproportionately on women. Exposure to indoor air pollution, especially particulates, is a major factor causing lower-respiratory infections, the leading cause of death from infectious diseases. Women are at greater risk than men because they are more commonly responsible for household tasks that expose them to indoor air pollution, such as cooking with biomass fuels. A Kenya study shows that young and adult women are exposed to, respectively, 2.5 and 4.8 times the particulate matter that men are exposed to in their age groups (Ezzati and others 2000). Correspondingly, the acute respiratory infection rate for women was twice that of men (Ezzati and Kammen 2001).

Projects that reduce indoor air pollution, promote reforestation, and improve water quality are often thought of as environmental projects that help serve the health and economic interests of local populations. However, these projects, if well targeted, can have disproportionate benefits for women, because they can ease burdens that have traditionally reduced women's ability to participate in more empowering activities.

resources. Given the high resource dependence of many developing countries, there is a strong link between this goal and that of reducing poverty. Table 1.7 provides an update on key indicators in the context of trends of the past 15 years. The indicators chosen—adjusted net saving, rates of deforestation, CO_2 emissions, and reliance on biomass fuels—aim to represent both a general view of sustainability and the progress in specific areas relevant to development. "Adjusted net saving" measures countries' net saving effort after accounting for depletion and damage to the environment, thus providing an indicator of the sustainability of development.[13] For-

est loss is crucial because of the environmental goods and services provided by forests, including CO_2 sequestration. CO_2 emissions contribute to global climate change, a long-run threat to development. Household reliance on traditional biomass energy affects both pressures on forest resources and damages to human health from indoor exposure to smoke.

Each of these indicators entails specific policy goals: (1) for adjusted net saving the aim is to achieve positive saving rates that are consistent with growth targets; (2) goals for CO_2 emissions are driven by the individual targets for the industrialized

TABLE 1.7 Key indicators of environmental sustainability

| Group | Adjusted net saving | | | Carbon dioxide emissions | | Annual deforestation | | Use of traditional fuels | |
| | Percent of GNI | | | Metric tons per capita | | Forest cover lost 1990–2005 | | Combustible renewables and waste (% of total energy) | |
	2005	of which, global damages caused by CO_2 emissions	Annual change (percentage points, 1990–2005)	2003	Percent increase 1990–2003	Annual area lost (sq km)	Annual percent lost	2004	Annual change (percentage points, 1990–2004)
World	7.4	0.4	−0.19	4.0	−0.2	83484	0.14	10.3	−0.03
Low income	6.2	1.0	0.24	0.9	1.6	71694	0.59	44.9	−0.53
Fragile states	−25.1	0.8	−0.57	0.5	−2.0	31799	0.56	78.1	0.07
Non-fragile states	11.0	1.0	0.31	1.0	2.5	39891	0.62	39.1	−0.76
Middle income	9.5	0.9	−0.12	3.9	−0.4	18288	0.03	9.0	−0.08
Low & middle income	8.0	1.0	−0.01	2.4	−0.6	90621	0.21	17.5	−0.07
East Asia & Pacific	25.3	1.2	0.45	2.7	1.3	4939	−0.22	16.1	−0.61
Europe & Central Asia	−2.0	1.2	−0.89[a]	6.9	−3.1	−1789	−0.02	2.4	0.04[c]
Latin America & Caribbean	3.7	0.4	−0.11	2.4	0.4	45753	0.44	14.8	−0.25
Middle East & North Africa	−13.0	1.2	−0.92[b]	3.4	2.4	−747	−0.49	1.2	−0.04
South Asia	16.4	1.1	0.64	1.0	3.0	−831	−0.18	38.0	−0.79
Sub-Saharan Africa	−7.3	0.7	−0.20	0.8	−0.8	43296	0.58	55.7	−0.01
High income	7.7	0.3	−0.21	12.8	0.7	−7137	−0.09	3.1	0.01
High income: OECD	8.2	0.3	−0.19	12.8	0.6	−7041	−0.09	3.3	0.01

Source: World Development Indicators.
Note: Carbon dioxide figures refer to emissions from combustion of fossil fuels and cement manufacture.
a. Annual change refers to the period 1995–2005.
b. Annual change refers to the period 1993–2005.
c. Annual change refers to the period 1992–2004.

country signatories to the Kyoto Protocol of the UN Framework Convention on Climate Change, which aims to reduce global emissions by 5.2 percent from 1990 levels by 2012; (3) bringing deforestation down to zero is the appropriate policy goal for many countries, preserving the environmental services provided by forests and protecting the sustainable flow of timber and nontimber products derived from natural forests; and (4) reducing and ultimately eliminating household use of traditional biomass fuels through provision of affordable substitutes.

Saving Rates across the World

Saving is a core aspect of development. Without the creation of a surplus for investment,

countries cannot escape a state of low-level subsistence. In an effort to comprehensively assess a country's rate of saving, "adjusted net saving" modifies traditional saving measures to take into account depreciation of produced capital, the depletion of natural resources, pollution damages, and investment in human capital (box 1.4). Negative saving rates are a clear indication that an economy is not on a sustainable path. Figure 1.5 shows trends in gross and adjusted net saving over time.

In East Asia and the Pacific and in South Asia, adjusted net saving has been steady at about 20 percent and 10 percent, respectively, owing to strong saving efforts. In Sub-Saharan Africa, it has been hovering around zero. Latin America and the Caribbean and Europe and Central Asia have had modestly positive

BOX 1.4 Adjusting saving rates to reflect a wider range of assets

The following figure presents the calculation of adjusted net saving in Bolivia in 2005.

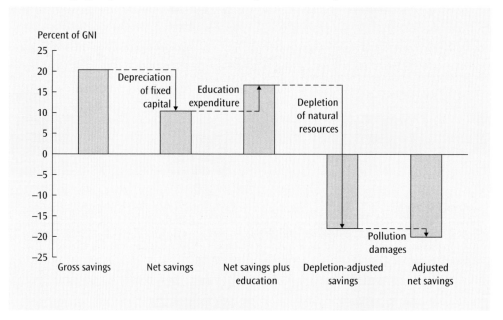

Source: World Development Indicators.

Gross saving in Bolivia in 2005 was roughly 20 percent of GNI. This falls to 10 percent when depreciation of fixed capital is deducted, but the drop is partially offset by investment in human capital (as measured by education expenditure). Deducting the depletion of natural resources (mostly natural gas in Bolivia's case) and damages from emissions of PM10 (particulate matter less than 10 microns) and CO_2 leads to the bottom-line value of –20 percent of GNI as the adjusted net saving rate of Bolivia. In net terms the country is consuming wealth, with negative consequences for potential growth.

As just noted, while adjusted net saving focuses primarily on the net accumulation of wealth within a country's borders, it also accounts for damages inflicted on all countries when a unit of CO_2 is emitted. This overall approach to accounting is based on two assumptions about property rights: (1) that countries own the natural assets lying within their borders, and (2) that countries have the right not to be polluted by their neighbors. The latter assumption is what underpins the Kyoto Protocol. If countries have the right not to be polluted by their neighbors, then the economic accounts of pollution emitters should show a charge for the damage inflicted—these figures are broken out in table 1.7. With the conservative carbon price used in the saving calculation ($24 per metric ton of carbon), these damages vary from 0.3 percent of GNI in high-income countries to 1.0–1.2 percent in most developing regions. This largely reflects the efficiency of energy use in the different regions.

saving rates over time. However, in Europe and Central Asia there has been a downward trend in saving owing to an increasing extraction of oil, which has not been offset by an equivalent increase in gross saving. Resource rents are clearly being consumed in many of these countries. While not shown in figure 1.5, adjusted net saving rates in high-income

FIGURE 1.5 Adjusted net saving rates by region

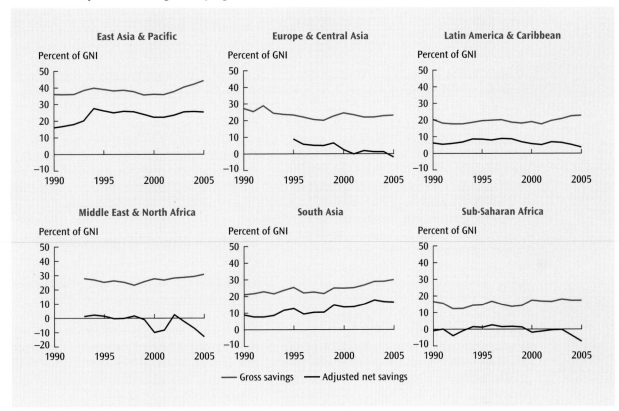

Source: World Development Indicators.

countries have fallen steadily from nearly 20 percent in the early 1970s to less than 10 percent in 2005—this is largely a reflection of falling gross saving rates.

For countries with growing populations, there is an additional factor not included in table 1.7—the reduction in wealth *per capita* associated with each new population cohort. For a population growth rate of 2 percent per year this "wealth dilution" effect would imply a deduction from wealth per capita on the order of 10–12 percent of GNI in a typical developing country. The change in wealth per capita is negative in the majority of low-income countries, often by significant proportions of GNI.

Low or negative adjusted net saving places growth at risk. The policy responses to insufficient saving include (1) reducing government dissaving, a common source of low gross saving rates; (2) investing more in human capital; (3) reducing incentives to overexploit natural resources, particularly forests and fish; and (4) reducing excess pollution emissions through market-oriented policies.

Energy: From Global to Local Issues

Carbon dioxide emissions from fossil fuel combustion and cement manufacture worldwide topped 27 billion metric tons in 2003, an increase of 19 percent compared to 1990 levels. In the absence of policy interventions, this trend will likely continue as economic activity grows. China, which is already the second-largest emitter, has increased its emissions per capita by 52 percent between 1990 and 2003, while India's emissions per capita have grown 50 percent in the same period—note, however, that the 2003 level of emissions per person in each country is still a fraction of high-income-country levels.

The major part of CO_2 emissions from fossil fuel combustion and cement manufacture stems from rich countries, however, with the United States contributing 22 percent of total emissions, the European Union 9 percent, and Japan 5 percent in 2003. But the share of developing-country contributions is rapidly increasing. From 2000 to 2003, global CO_2 emissions increased by 2.9 percent annually, and about 83 percent of this increase came from low- and middle-income countries. If CO_2 emissions from deforestation and CO_2-equivalent emissions from agriculture are included, the annual contribution of developing countries to greenhouse gas concentrations exceeds that of high-income countries.

The lowest level of CO_2 emissions per capita is in Sub-Saharan Africa. This is mainly driven by the lack of access to modern sources of energy, which leads people in poor countries to depend on traditional biomass fuels for their energy needs. Solid biomass is associated with respiratory problems caused by indoor smoke. Most of the victims are infants, children, and women from poor rural families.

Globally, 2 billion people rely on biomass fuels for energy. The regions with the highest level of biomass fuel use are Sub-Saharan Africa and South Asia. The data show very little progress between 1990 and 2004 for Africa and more generally for low-income countries, where the use of biomass products and waste as a percentage of total energy use has gone from 55 percent in 1990 to 48 percent in 2004.

Deforestation

Forests provide important ecosystem services (CO_2 sequestration and regulation of water flows, for example) and host most of the world's biodiversity. The causes of deforestation and ecosystem loss include conversion to agriculture and unsustainable commercial timber extraction, particularly in the presence of ill-defined property rights and corruption. Forests can be used wastefully if they are cleared for low-productivity ranches that are ultimately abandoned The net change in forest area during 1990–2005 is estimated to be a loss of 8.3 million hectares a year (an area about the size of Panama or Sierra Leone). Deforestation is highest in Sub-Saharan Africa (0.6 percent per year between 1990 and 2005) and in Latin America and the Caribbean (0.4 percent per year). While fragile states contained 8.2 percent of the world's forest area in 2005, they also accounted for 28.6 percent of world deforestation.

Update on Country Programs and Policies

Sustainable development requires that actions by the current generation not damage the development prospects of future generations. This can be achieved by ensuring that wealth, broadly conceived to include human-made and natural assets, does not decline from one generation to the next. Sustainability presents a significant challenge, especially in the presence of public goods and externalities, because markets by themselves are not able to ensure efficient outcomes. In addition to market failures, policy failure is also a distinct possibility. The "resource curse" literature (see, for example, Auty and Gelb 2001) argues that natural resource wealth may dampen economic growth owing to the political economy of rent-seeking that occurs in many resource-rich countries, while the volatility of natural resource prices presents risks to macroeconomic stability.

Whether the problem is a market failure or a policy failure, sustainable development requires strong institutions that are able to pursue a coherent economic policy and the objective of raising social welfare. Population-weighted environment CPIA scores for regions and income groups for 2005 (figure 1.6) show that Sub-Saharan Africa scores lowest (3.2), while East Asia and Latin America have the highest regional average (3.8). The regional average scores mask good performance in

FIGURE 1.6 Environment and overall CPIA score by region and income group

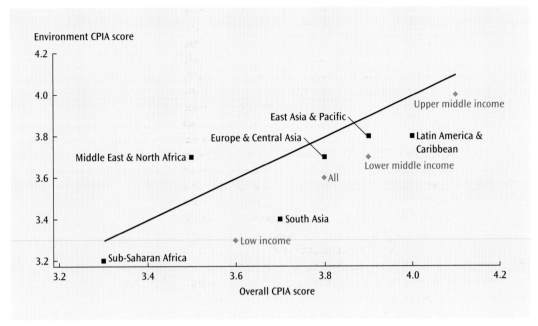

Source: CPIA database.
Note: Scores are population weighted.

many countries—Mauritius and South Africa are strong performers in Sub-Saharan Africa, for example, while the Republic of Korea, Malaysia, Thailand, Costa Rica, and Mexico top the lists in East Asia and Latin America. As might be expected, there is a wide difference between the environment scores of low-income countries (3.3) and upper-middle-income countries (4.0). Figure 1.6 shows that environment CPIA scores are generally lower than overall CPIA scores, indicating that the quality of environmental institutions in developing countries is lagging in relative terms.

Looking Ahead

This brief update on MDG7 has necessarily neglected many issues that could be taken up in future GMRs. Potential issues for consideration include (1) climate change and development; (2) poverty-environment links, including evidence on the environmental contribution to the health and livelihoods of poor households; and (3) natural resources as assets for devel-

opment, emphasizing the key roles played by agricultural land, forest and fisheries in generating income, and natural areas as a resource for nature tourism.

Notes

1. In this report, low-income countries are those eligible for IDA assistance. Other developing countries are classified as middle income.

2. As box 1.1 indicates, fragility is defined according to cutoff values of the World Bank's country policy and institutional assessment (CPIA). In 2005 the list of countries and territories for which the CPIA rating (see World Development Indicators 2007) was at 3.0 and below includes Afghanistan, Angola, Burundi, Central African Republic, Chad, Comoros, Democratic Republic of Congo, Republic of Congo, Côte d'Ivoire, Eritrea, Guinea, Guinea-Bissau, Haiti, Kosovo, Lao PDR, Liberia, Myanmar, Solomon Islands, Somalia, Sudan, Timor-Leste, Togo, Tonga, Uzbekistan, West Bank and Gaza, and Zimbabwe. Marginal fragile states, for which the CPIA rating is at 3.1 or 3.2 include Cambodia, Djibouti, The Gambia, Mauritania, Nigeria, Papua

New Guinea, São Tomé and Principe, Sierra Leone, and Vanuatu. As CPIA ratings change, countries move in and out of the list.

3. The low-income countries are Albania, Armenia, Bolivia, Burkina Faso, Côte d'Ivoire, Georgia, Honduras, India, Indonesia, Kyrgyz Republic, Lao PDR, Moldova, Mongolia, Mozambique, Nigeria, Tajikistan, Uzbekistan, Vietnam, Zambia. The middle-income countries are Argentina (urban), Brazil, Chile, China, Colombia, Costa Rica, Dominican Republic, El Salvador, Estonia, Guatemala, Jamaica, Jordan, Kazakhstan, Latvia, Lithuania, Macedonia, Mexico, Paraguay, Peru, Philippines, Poland, Romania, Russia, Thailand, Uruguay (urban), República Bolivariana deVenezuela.

4. Chauvet and Collier (2004) estimate that when a fragile state is a neighbor, the result is a loss of 1.6 percent of GDP per year.

5. Those who performed studies of the negative impact of conflict on GDP include Knight and others (1996); Collier (1999); and Caplan (2001). Collier (1999) also found that a negative impact persisted long after conflict.

6. Chauvet and Collier (2004) estimate that state fragility as measured by LICUS status typically reduces the annual growth rate of peacetime economies by 2.3 percent relative to other developing economies.

7. Not only are the questions underlying the macroeconomic assessments different in the CPIA, but the 2005 survey also omits four fragile states in the IMF staff assessments.

8. The 2006 GMR suggested that bureaucratic capability was best measured using the World Bank's CPIA measures of budget and financial management, and administrative quality. However, these measures are only available publicly for one year and for IDA recipients. The Kaufmann-Kraay (KK) government effectiveness indicator is closely correlated with these measures (the correlation coefficients for 2005 data with the CPIA Budget and Financial Management, and Administrative Quality measures are 0.71 and 0.81, respectively) and is used as an alternative.

9. The suggested checks-and-balances measure is a composite of three indicators: KK Voice and Accountability, KK Rule of Law, and Polity IV Executive Constraints. The Executive Constraints

variable for 2004 is used in the construction of the 2005 Quality of Checks and Balance Institutions dimension.

10. A two-step filtering process was used to identify significant governance improvements between 1996 and 2005. Under this process a country should experience (1) improvement in at least one of its Government Effectiveness, Voice and Accountability, and Rule of Law indicators at the 75 percent confidence level; and (2) an increase in its score on either the Government Effectiveness or Quality of Checks and Balance Institutions dimension by at least 0.15 points.

11. Each of the KK measures is a composite that combines distinct but related concepts. Thus KK Government Effectiveness measures "the quality of public services, the quality of the civil service and the degree of its independence from political pressures, the quality of policy formulation and implementation, and the credibility of the government's commitment to such policies" (Kaufmann, Kraay, and Mastruzzi 2006).

12. A country is placed in Trajectory II if there is significant improvement along both dimensions according to the two filters, but the improvement in the Government Effectiveness dimension is two times or greater than the improvement in Checks and Balances. Similarly, if the improvement in the Checks and Balances dimension is two times or greater than the improvement in the Government Effectiveness dimension, the country is placed in Trajectory III.

13. "Adjusted net saving" modifies traditional gross savings measures to account for depreciation of produced capital, the depletion of natural resources, pollution damages, and investment in human capital. The lack of comparable international data on many natural resources such as fishery depletion, diamond resources, and extraction of subsoil water means that the adjusted savings figures published here and in the World Development Indicators will be incomplete for some countries. In addition, a portion of health expenditures should be viewed as investment in human capital and captured in the adjusted savings measure, but data are again a problem. The divergence between local and international prices may distort both gross and adjusted net savings figures, because some investments (in education, or nontradables such as buildings) are valued at local prices, while natural resources and machinery and equipment are valued at world prices.

ANNEX TABLE 1A.1   Share of people living on less than $1.08 a day (%)

Region	1981	1990	1993	1996	1999	2002	2004	Forecast 2015
EAP	57.7	29.8	25.2	16.1	15.5	12.3	9.1	2.4
China	*63.8*	*33.0*	*28.4*	*17.4*	*17.8*	*13.8*	*9.9*	*2.6*
ECA	0.7	0.5	3.6	4.4	3.8	1.3	0.9	0.5
LAC	10.8	10.2	8.4	8.9	9.7	9.1	8.6	6.0
MNA	5.1	2.3	1.9	1.7	2.1	1.7	1.5	0.8
SAR	51.6	43.0	37.1	36.6	35.8	34.7	31.9	18.0
India	*54.3*	*44.3*	*42.1*	*40.6*	*38.8*	*37.5*	*35.8*	*22.1*
SSA	42.3	46.7	45.5	47.7	45.8	42.6	41.1	35.4
Total	**40.6**	**28.7**	**25.6**	**22.8**	**22.3**	**20.4**	**18.4**	**11.8**
Fragile states		*49.0*					*54.2*	*50.4*

ANNEX TABLE 1A.2   Share of people living on less than $2.15 a day (%)

Region	1981	1990	1993	1996	1999	2002	2004	2015
EAP	84.8	69.7	65.0	52.5	49.3	41.7	36.6	15.3
China	*88.1*	*72.2*	*68.1*	*53.3*	*50.1*	*40.9*	*34.9*	*14.1*
ECA	4.6	4.3	16.5	18.0	18.6	12.9	9.8	4.7
LAC	28.4	26.2	24.1	25.2	25.3	24.8	22.2	17.3
MNA	29.2	21.7	21.4	21.4	23.6	21.1	19.7	10.9
SAR	89.1	85.7	82.4	82.4	80.8	80.3	77.7	60.1
India	*89.6*	*86.4*	*85.5*	*84.5*	*83.2*	*82.1*	*81.1*	*66.8*
SSA	74.5	77.1	76.1	76.4	75.8	73.8	72.0	64.7
Total	**67.1**	**60.8**	**59.4**	**55.5**	**54.4**	**50.8**	**47.7**	**34.2**
Fragile states		*73.4*					*75.8*	*72.7*

ANNEX TABLE 1A.3   Number of people living on less than $1.08 a day (millions)

Region	1981	1990	1993	1996	1999	2002	2004	2015
EAP	796	476	420	279	277	227	169	48
China	*634*	*374*	*334*	*211*	*223*	*177*	*128*	*37*
ECA	3	2	17	21	18	6	4	2
LAC	39	45	39	43	49	48	47	38
MNA	9	5	5	4	6	5	4	3
SAR	473	479	440	459	475	485	462	304
India	*382*	*376*	*379*	*385*	*387*	*393*	*386*	*283*
SSA	168	240	252	286	296	296	298	326
Total	**1489**	**1247**	**1172**	**1093**	**1120**	**1067**	**986**	**721**
Fragile states		*172*					*261*	*306*

ANNEX TABLE 1A.4   Number of people living on less than $2.15 a day (millions)

Region	1981	1990	1993	1996	1999	2002	2004	2015
EAP	1170	1113	1083	908	883	766	684	312
China	*876*	*819*	*803*	*650*	*628*	*524*	*452*	*196*
ECA	20	20	78	85	88	61	46	23
LAC	104	115	111	122	128	131	121	109
MNA	51	49	52	55	65	61	59	40
SAR	818	954	976	1035	1073	1124	1124	1015
India	*630*	*734*	*769*	*801*	*832*	*861*	*876*	*853*
SSA	296	396	422	458	491	513	522	597
Total	**2457**	**2647**	**2722**	**2664**	**2727**	**2655**	**2556**	**2095**
Fragile states		*257*					*365*	*441*

Source: World Bank staff estimates.

2

The Role of Quality in MDG Progress

Since 2000, over 34 million additional children in the developing world have gained the chance to attend, and complete, primary school—one of the most massive expansions of schooling access in history. Over 550 million children have been vaccinated against measles—doubling the coverage rates in some countries, and driving down measles deaths in Sub-Saharan Africa by 75 percent. The number of developing-country AIDS (acquired immunodeficiency syndrome) patients with access to antiretroviral treatment increased from 240,000 in 2001 to over 1.6 million at mid-2006. Despite migration and resource constraints, health workers and clinic visits across the developing world are increasing significantly, as are the share of pregnant women with access to health care when they deliver, and the share of young children with regular health and nutrition screening. There is now little question that the "stretch" goals adopted by the global community in 2000 to promote human development have helped stimulate and support more rapid expansion of basic health and education services across the developing world.

The progress in service delivery is not even, of course—and it is not enough. Across every region there are lagging countries, and within every country there are poor people, rural areas, women, girls, and vulnerable groups who lack fair access to schooling,

basic health care, and water and sanitation. In reviewing overall progress toward the human development Millennium Development Goals (MDGs), this chapter examines where the worst gaps persist and what policies can work to redress them.

The chapter also explores whether this strong push to expand coverage is eroding service quality. Measuring quality in education and health poses very different challenges, but in both cases limited data have inhibited comparisons across developing countries. In education, while student learning outcomes offer a straightforward and meaningful way to measure system quality, few developing countries have tracked these systematically. But new education research in 2006 has built directly comparable measures of what children are learning in the developing world, and the results have clear implications for MDG progress. In health, the latest research exploits creative ways to measure the quality of services that health workers actually deliver to patients, rather than what they are capable of delivering; the implications for health policy are equally important.

The first half of this chapter provides a brief overview of progress on each of the human development MDGs, except the gender goal (MDG3), which is the subject of chapter 3. The chapter also reviews global trends in financing for human development sectors and the performance of major global programs. The second half of the chapter focuses on the role of quality in promoting progress on the human development MDGs.

Human Development MDG Status 2007

Broad regional trends of MDG progress have not changed since last year. All regions are off track on the child mortality goal, and at least some of the others. The two regions lagging most seriously behind—South Asia and Sub-Saharan Africa—are off track on all of the goals. This section highlights some of the countries making exceptionally fast progress toward different MDGs, countries where outcomes are worsening, the performance of major global programs, and new evidence from research on what drives country progress. The chapter gives special attention to the performance of fragile states—which lag far behind other developing countries on most MDGs—and the special challenges they face in reaching the goals.

MDG1—Nutrition Target

Access to adequate food is one of the most basic conditions of survival and escape from poverty. Accordingly the first MDG links two measures of poverty: *income poverty*, which is discussed in chapter 1, and *hunger*. The target is to halve between 1990 and 2015 the proportion of people who suffer from hunger, as measured by the percentage of children under five who are underweight. Undernutrition is not only a threat to poverty reduction progress, it is also the underlying cause of over 55 percent of all child deaths. In 2007 nearly a third of all children in the developing world remain underweight or stunted, and an estimated 30 percent of the overall population of the developing world suffers from micronutrient deficiencies. But the picture differs across regions:

- *South Asia* has the highest rates and largest numbers of malnourished children. Under-

weight prevalence rates are 38–51 percent in the most populous countries—India, Bangladesh, Afghanistan, and Pakistan. Progress is being made in these countries, but none is on track to reach the MDG.

- *Sub-Saharan Africa* has an estimated 26 percent of all children suffering undernutrition. Of concern are worsening trends in countries such as Cameroon, Burkina Faso, and Zambia.

- *East Asia, Latin America, and Eastern Europe* all have some countries off track to reach the MDG. The highest levels of malnutrition and micronutrient deficiencies are in Cambodia, Indonesia, Lao People's Democratic Republic, the Philippines, Guatemala, Haiti, Honduras, and Uzbekistan. Vietnam, on the other hand, has made impressive progress in improving child nutrition.

MDG2—Universal Primary Completion

Globally the primary completion rate has increased from 78 percent in 2000 to an estimated 83 percent in 2005, and the pace of annual improvement has accelerated since 2000 in all regions except Latin America, where completion rates were already high. Progress has been especially strong in North Africa, South Asia, and Sub-Saharan Africa. Although some 38 percent of all developing countries are considered off track, and another 22 percent have inadequate data, the number of countries that have achieved universal primary completion increased from 37 in 2000 to 52 in 2005. Nine of the 10 countries making fastest progress globally are low-income countries in Africa, but given the low base they started from in 1990, most are still off track to reach the MDG (table 2.1). Of 38 African countries for which there are data, 33 are off track, with a few countries showing actual declines in primary completion.

The two largest challenges for all countries are ensuring that primary completion means completion with adequate learning—discussed later in this chapter—and extending schooling access to the last 10 percent of children. While survey data indicate that the largest gaps in schooling access in virtually every developing country are between high- and low-income populations, an overlay of issues can make particular groups of poor students especially hard to reach. A recent study (Lewis and Lockheed 2006), for example, showed that nearly 75 percent of the 55 million girls who remained out of school in the developing world in 2000 were "doubly disadvantaged"—female *and* from excluded ethnic, religious, or caste groups (figure 2.1). Achieving universal primary completion in these cases will require more than just building schools. It will also require actions to eliminate discriminatory policies, change teachers' attitudes, provide compensatory preschool and in-school programs to help disadvantaged girls catch up, and tools such as targeted stipends to overcome parents' reluctance to send girls to school and the direct and opportunity costs of doing so. The encouraging fact is that many policies and efforts to reach the "doubly disadvantaged" in fact will benefit all disadvantaged students, and bring countries closer to the goals of education for all.

TABLE 2.1 Several low-income countries are making strong progress on universal primary completion

Country	Primary completion rate 2000	Primary completion rate 2005	Annual percentage increase 2000–2005
Strong performers			
Mozambique	16.2	42.0	20.9%
Cambodia	46.6	92.3	14.7%
Benin	34.9	65.0	13.2%
Rwanda	22.4	39.0	11.7%
Niger	16.8	28.1	10.9%
Guinea	33.3	54.5	10.4%
Madagascar	35.6	57.7	10.1%
Ethiopia	36.7	55.0	8.4%
Senegal	36.0	52.2	7.7%
Burundi	25.1	35.7	7.3%
Poor performers			
Mauritania	51.6	44.5	−2.9%
Namibia	85.4	75.3	−2.5%
Malawi	67.2	60.7	−2.0%

Source: UNESCO Institute of Statistics., 2007.

FIGURE 2.1 Most out-of-school girls are "doubly disadvantaged": Female and from minority groups

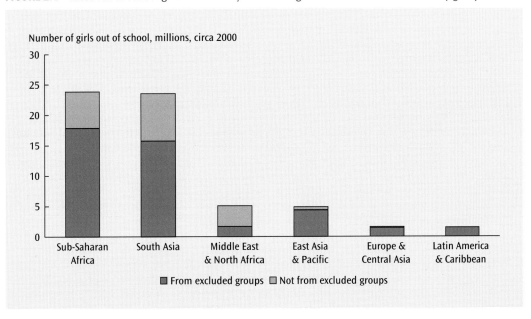

Source: Lewis and Lockheed 2006.

Donor aid for education fell in 2005, for the first time since 2000. Reasons for the decline appear to be short term in nature and are discussed later in this chapter. With its announcement in April 2006 of a $15 billion commitment over the next 10 years, the United Kingdom is now the leading bilateral source of support for education. Other European Union and Group of Eight (G-8) donor countries have also pledged to increase support for education within their rising overall levels of official development assistance. The Education for All-Fast Track Initiative (EFA-

FTI) (see box 2.1) appears to provide a useful framework to ensure that increased finance is used effectively to accelerate countries' progress toward MDG2 and harmonize donor assistance.

MDG4—Child Mortality

Over 10 million children under five in the developing world die each year of diseases that are preventable and curable with a handful of simple, low-cost interventions. An estimated 63 percent of child deaths could

---

BOX 2.1 Early evidence that the EFA Fast Track Initiative is making a difference

The EFA Fast Track Initiative. The EFA Fast Track Initiative, launched in 2002, is the major global program promoting attainment of the education MDG, and Education for All Goals more broadly. The FTI is a "results-focused" partnership of all major donors for education and all low-income developing countries willing to commit to ongoing benchmarking of their education system performance, to ensure that spending produces results. The FTI is managed by a small secretariat staffed and supported by partner agencies and housed in the World Bank. Starting with 8 developing countries in 2002, the FTI had expanded to 28 countries by end-2006. At end-2008, it expects to involve 60 low-income countries, covering approximately 70 percent of the out-of-school children in the world. The FTI also has a special focus on supporting progress in fragile states.

Donor financing for FTI countries is channeled both through expansion of existing donor programs and the multidonor FTI Catalytic Fund, administered by the Secretariat. Although the Catalytic Fund was originally conceived as a small and short-term source of bridge financing for countries entering the initiative without many active bilateral donors, the Fund has continued to attract donor pledges. At end-2006, the Fund totaled $1.1 billion in donor contributions and was disbursing approximately $150 million per year in grants to FTI countries. In FY 2008, Catalytic Fund disbursements are expected to be about 10–15 percent of total aid for basic education in low-income countries. In 2008, the Fund's initial limit on support of up to three years will also be relaxed.

The FTI has sought to tighten the "compact" for results by monitoring the performance of both countries and donors. Among countries, the FTI's performance benchmarks promote sound policies and results focus; among donors, the FTI encourages more harmonized and efficient aid.

A review of the program in 2006 concluded that the FTI is making progress on these goals (World Bank 2006). The FTI's performance benchmarks have acquired growing international consensus and, while there is less progress in some areas than others, FTI has helped some of the world's lowest enrollment countries substantially increase primary school coverage and girls' enrollments; reduce repetition; increase domestic spending on primary education; and boost spending on books, supplies, and maintenance. The FTI also seems to have had a large effect on donor harmonization and sector planning. Joint sector reviews, pooled funds, single reporting arrangements, and joint missions are becoming the norm in FTI countries, reducing transactions costs and increasing aid efficiency. By simultaneously promoting a scale-up of spending on primary education and policy reforms among both recipient countries and donors to improve the effectiveness of that spending, the Initiative appears to have created a useful framework for education MDG progress.

be averted with oral rehydration therapy to combat diarrhea, insecticide-treated bednets to prevent malaria, breastfeeding to improve nutritional status, and antibiotics to treat acute respiratory infections, if these were implemented universally (Jones and others 2003). But progress on the child mortality MDG lags other goals. In 2005, only 32 out of 147 developing countries (22 percent) were making enough progress to achieve a two-thirds reduction in child mortality between 1990 and 2015.

Moreover, 23 low- and middle-income countries show worsening or stagnant child survival trends. Many of these countries are either in conflict, emerging from conflict, or are heavily affected by HIV (Human Immu-nodeficiency Virus)/AIDS. Among the worst are Iraq (150 percent increase) and four countries in Southern Africa (Botswana, Zimbabwe, Swaziland, and Lesotho) in which child mortality increased because of HIV/AIDS.

The majority of countries have reduced child mortality since 1990, but not at the pace required to reach the MDG—an annual decline of 4.3 percent over the entire period. Progress is possible, though, as shown by sharp declines even in some low-income countries: between 1990 and 2005, under-five mortality per 1,000 live births declined from 177 to 61 in Timor-Leste, from 53 to 19 in Vietnam, from 147 to 78 in Eritrea, and from 166 to 75 in Bhutan (table 2.2). However, of the best performing Sub-Saharan

TABLE 2.2 Progress on child mortality in a few countries

	Under-five mortality rate per 1,000 births				Annual percent change 1990–2005
	1990	1995	2000	2005	
Strong performers					
Low-income countries					
Timor-Leste	177	154	107	61	−7.1
Vietnam	53	44	30	19	−6.8
Bhutan	166	133	100	75	−5.3
Mongolia	108	87	65	49	−5.3
Lao PDR	163	131	101	79	−4.8
Sub-Saharan Africa					
Eritrea	147	122	97	78	−4.2
Malawi	221	193	155	125	−3.8
Cape Verde	60	50	42	35	−3.6
Comoros	120	101	84	71	−3.5
Mozambique	235	212	178	145	−3.2
Middle-income countries					
Czech Republic	13	10	5	4	−7.9
Egypt, Arab Rep. of	104	71	49	33	−7.7
Peru	78	63	41	27	−7
Turkey	82	63	44	29	−6.9
Syrian Arab Rep.	39	28	20	15	−6.6
Poor performers					
Iraq	50	122	125	125	6.1
Botswana	58	66	101	120	4.8
Zimbabwe	80	90	117	132	3.3
Swaziland	110	110	142	160	2.5
Lesotho	101	91	108	132	1.8

Source: World Bank

BOX 2.2 Fast progress on child mortality in Eritrea

What made it possible for Eritrea, a fragile, postconflict country with annual per capita income of just $190 and a primary completion rate for girls of only 33 percent to reduce under-five mortality by nearly 50 percent between 1990 and 2005? Based on assessments of child health services, the decline in mortality has been attributed in part to the implementation of the IMCI (integrated management of childhood illness) approach, including the training of over 500 health workers at different levels of the health care system in IMCI case management. Following the IMCI implementation, it was found that availability of drugs and equipment in health centers had improved, and that providers were doing a better job of following protocol for diagnosis and prevention of disease. Immunization coverage for fully vaccinated children increased from 41 percent in 1995 to 76 percent in 2002 in two Demographic and Health Survey (DHS) rounds. Encouraging and plausible as these factors are, programs such as Eritrea's should undergo well-designed evaluations before conclusions can be confidently drawn. The evidence used to explain changes in mortality often consists of after-the-fact rationalizations that link the implementation of specific activities with observed trends in mortality, an unscientific approach that does not take into account what might have happened without the intervention.

Source: http://www.usaid.gov/stories/eritrea/cs_eritrea_mortality.html, retrieved in 2006.

African countries, only Eritrea, described in box 2.2, is close to the MDG pace.

MDG5—Maternal Health

Each year an estimated 500,000 women in the developing world die in childbirth. While this number is far lower than annual child deaths, reducing maternal mortality is a global preoccupation because deaths during delivery are highly preventable. Maternal mortality has been called a "tracer condition" for health systems (World Bank 1999), because if countries can ensure the three basic conditions of adequate access to antenatal care, medical attendance at delivery, and a health referral system that ensures prompt treatment of emergencies at adequately equipped clinics, deaths during childbirth can be virtually eliminated. Ninety-nine percent of maternal deaths occur in the developing world.

The MDG target—to reduce the maternal mortality ratio by three-fourths between 1990 and 2015—remains difficult to measure; for almost all developing countries, no current direct estimates of the maternal mortality ratio or trends exist. A new joint effort by the World Health Organization (WHO), the United Nations Children's Fund (UNICEF), the United Nations Population Fund (UNFPA), and the World Bank in 2007 will update the data with 2005 estimates. In the absence of direct estimates, monitoring of progress toward the goal has focused on one of the key determinants of maternal mortality: the presence of a medically skilled attendant at the time of delivery.

The latest survey data show that in 27 out of 32 developing countries (84 percent) the proportion of deliveries with a skilled attendant has increased in recent years (table 2.3). Morocco, Nicaragua, Indonesia, and Egypt registered especially impressive progress. Survey data also show that differences in access to skilled delivery care between the poorest and richest quintiles in most countries present larger equity gaps than for any other health or education service. Even in some of the poorest low-income countries, such as Benin, Cameroon, Mali, Mozambique, Zambia, or Zimbabwe, skilled attendance at delivery for the upper income groups reaches levels near or above 90 percent, several times the coverage for the poorest quintile. Finally, the surveys show that what constitutes "skilled attendance at delivery" varies across countries. In Jordan, for example, where over 95 percent of women deliver with skilled

TABLE 2.3 Progress in assisted births

Country	Births attended by a medically trained person (percent of all births)				Absolute change between surveys
	Percent	Year	Percent	Year	
Strong performers					
Morocco	30.8	1992	62.6	2004	31.8
Nicaragua	64.6	1997	89.7	2001	25.1
Indonesia	49.1	1997	66.2	2003	17.1
Egypt, Arab Rep. of	46.2	1995	60.9	2000	14.7
Benin	63.9	1996	72.9	2001	9
India	34.3	1993	42.4	1999	8.1
Vietnam	77	1997	85.1	2002	8.1
Namibia	68.2	1992	75.5	2000	7.3
Burkina Faso	30.9	1998	37.8	2003	6.9
Guatemala	34.8	1995	40.6	1998	5.8
Poor performers					
Haiti	46.3	1995	24.2	2000	−22.1
Peru	56.4	1996	46.9	2000	−9.5
Zambia	46.5	1996	43.4	2001	−3.1
Kenya	44.4	1998	41.6	2003	−2.8

Source: Demographic and Health Surveys.

care, 63 percent of deliveries take place with the assistance of a doctor, and 37 percent with a midwife or nurse, but virtually all occur in hospitals. But in Benin, while a relatively high 73 percent of deliveries are assisted, only 5 percent of these are with a doctor, and 23 percent of births occur at home.

Maternal deaths most commonly result from three critical sources of delay in accessing appropriate emergency care during pregnancy and delivery: (1) inadequate recognition of the need for care; (2) difficulty in getting to facilities (due to lack of transportation, poor roads or high costs); and/or (3) lack of adequate treatment once a facility has been reached (Thaddeus and Maine 1994). Box 2.3 summarizes new research from Ghana, Kenya, and India which sheds light on the relative contributions of these "three delays" to poor maternal outcomes, and how their underlying causes can differ in different country contexts.

One country whose progress in reducing maternal mortality has been researched is Honduras. In the 1990s Honduras adopted a four-pronged strategy to reduce its high maternal mortality rate: (1) training traditional birth attendants in how to recognize high-risk pregnancies and deal with obstetric emergencies; (2) increasing health personnel and birthing centers in remote areas; (3) strengthening emergency obstetric care in rural health centers and district hospitals; and (4) improving emergency transportation and communication systems. At the same time, the country introduced improved surveillance to establish the cause of maternal deaths in all recorded cases. The successful implementation of this strategy is credited with reducing maternal mortality across Honduras by more than 50 percent over the past decade, including in the most remote and poorest areas (Danel 1999; Ransom and Yinger 2002).

MDG6—AIDS, Tuberculosis, and Malaria

HIV/AIDS. No single MDG has galvanized as much global attention and financial support since 2000 as the goal of "halting and reversing the spread of HIV/AIDS." What

BOX 2.3 Preventing maternal mortality: Findings from three countries

To examine the relative contribution of the "three delays" to poor maternal care, the World Bank collaborated with research institutions in Ghana, India, and Kenya to carry out in-depth studies in very different settings: in northern Ghana (Kassena-Nankana District, a predominantly rural area, with population scattered and mainly dependent on subsistence farming); in Kenya, the Nairobi slums of Korogocho and Viwandani; and in Uttar Pradesh, India's most populous state, with a predominantly rural population and low status of women. Household survey data, verbal autopsies, facility surveys, and in-depth interviews were used to analyze the three delays.

In Ghana, although almost all women saw a midwife or nurse for antenatal care, the majority (59 percent) eventually delivered at home with a traditional birth attendant. Of the women who developed complications, about half recognized the problem as serious within a day, but 36 percent took three days or more. Sixty percent of these women reported the distance and travel time to a health facility as the major constraint to seeking service there. Three percent of women delivered while en route to a health facility, indicating the difficulty of getting to facilities in time. But women who did deliver in health facilities gave strongly positive opinions of the quality of obstetric care they received, notwithstanding reports from health workers at these facilities that they lacked adequate staff, supplies, and equipment.

In the Nairobi slums, 70 percent of women delivered with the assistance of a health professional—a substantially higher rate than in other parts of Kenya. Of the 62 percent who experienced obstetric complications, four-fifths made the decision to seek care within 24 hours, and distance and transportation were not major obstacles. In focus groups, women reported that the overriding factor against seeking care is cost. About 62 percent of women paid more than 1,000 KSh ($14) for delivery care in health facilities, and the requirement for a cash deposit prior to admission was an important obstacle. In Nairobi, women with obstetric complications frequently did not receive care promptly—owing to long queues, unavailability of health professionals, the demand for a deposit, or lack of equipment—and at times were sent to another health facility as a result. In contrast to Ghana, a large majority of Kenyan women reported poor treatment by health personnel, especially nurses and midwives at facilities.

In Uttar Pradesh, India, antenatal care is nominally free of charge at government health facilities, but just 40 percent of women utilize it. Only 21 percent of women deliver at a health facility, and a higher share of these are at private facilities than government ones. The survey showed that the majority of women thought antenatal care or delivery with the assistance of skilled medical attendants was unnecessary; birth was viewed as something that should normally take place unassisted at home. Unlike rural Ghana, access factors such as long distance to health facilities and difficulty in obtaining transport were less frequently cited reasons for not delivering at the health facilities. However, 40 percent of the facilities indicated that they were not equipped to deliver basic emergency obstetric care, given limited staffing and equipment. While the study pointed to the need to improve the quality of government health facilities, it also suggests the need for outreach to women about the importance of professional assistance at births, since obstetric complications are unpredictable.

Source: Mills and others 2007.

---

has been achieved over the past six years—especially the expansion of treatment across the developing world—stands as a tribute to the power of concerted global action. But what remains to be done is also substantial—partly because of the unique nature of AIDS, a disease that mutates faster than any known virus and radiates along myriad societal transmission fault lines, but also because of the inherent challenges of rapidly scaling-up global action and funding in any area.

From just a few localized spots of infection just 25 years ago, AIDS has spread to nearly every country in the world, and by end-2006 an estimated 39.5 million people were living with HIV, an increase of 2.6 million compared with 2004 (figure 2.2). Behind these numbers is an increasingly heterogeneous epidemic ranging from Sub-Saharan Africa, where a mature, largely heterosexually transmitted epidemic has slowed its spread, to rapidly growing epidemics in Eastern Europe and Central Asia, linked to high-risk behaviors in segments of the population.

Globally, financial resources available for implementing the AIDS response have increased from $1.6 billion (about 20 percent of total development assistance for health) in 2000 to nearly $8 billion (60 percent of total health support) in 2006. In numerous low-income countries, external support earmarked for AIDS is half or more of the entire public health budget. However, external funding is concentrated in relatively few developing countries, and large unmet needs remain. What has been achieved, and what have we learned to guide future action? From the vantage point of 2007, five cautious conclusions can be drawn:

■ **Reversing the spread of HIV/AIDS is possible.** The first signs of declining HIV

prevalence at the national level have been recorded in eight countries at the national level (Kenya, Uganda, Thailand, Zimbabwe, Barbados, Bahamas, Cambodia, and Thailand) and in urban areas in six other countries (Burkina Faso, Côte d'Ivoire, Ethiopia, Ghana, Malawi, and Rwanda). In India, declines have been recorded in four southern states. In Latin America and the Caribbean new infections in 2006 remained at about the same level as in 2004.

The underlying drivers of the declines are not fully understood, but it is likely that they reflect a different mix of factors in each context. It also seems likely that this progress is easily reversible, so there is no cause for complacency. Recent surveillance data from Uganda—one of the first of the above countries to show signs of declining prevalence—suggest that condom use has started to decline, numbers of sexual partners have increased, and seroprevalence may again be increasing in some sites.

In most of the countries, the natural course of the epidemic may be playing the most important role in reducing the number of new infections; once epidemics reach

FIGURE 2.2   Global HIV/AIDS epidemic, 1990–2006

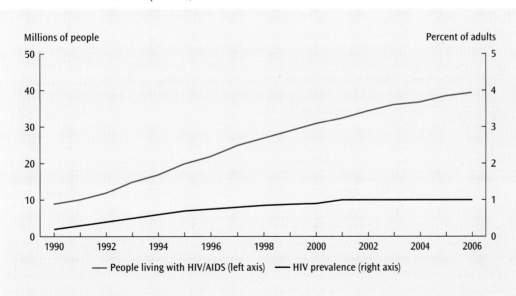

Source: UNAIDS, AIDS epidemic update, 2006.

a critical scale, "burnout" occurs since there are fewer uninfected individuals left to infect. But in the countries where prevalence declined, there is also evidence of behavioral changes, including reductions in the number of partners, increased use of condoms, and delays in the age of first sexual intercourse (UNAIDS 2006).

■ **Treatment is effective in the developing world.** When the MDGs were adopted, there was glaring global inequity in the chances an AIDS patient had of accessing treatment depending on "which world" he or she lived in: in 2001, only 240,000 people were on antiretroviral treatment (ART) of an estimated 5 million people in the developing world with advanced HIV disease who needed treatment. By mid-2006 there were 1.6 million people on treatment.[1] Botswana, Kenya, South Africa, Uganda, Rwanda, and Zambia have made strongest progress, and were among the 14 countries providing treatment to at least 50 percent of those in clinical need by June 2005 (UNAIDS and WHO 2005).

It is now confirmed that the same gains in life expectancy achieved in high-income countries are attainable in resource-scarce environments. Adherence to antiretroviral regimens in developing-country settings is also as high as in high-income countries (Mills and others 2006). Large cohort studies have examined survival in over 27,000 patients from developing and industrialized countries and found similar levels of viral suppression and declines in mortality (Stringer and others 2006). UNAIDS estimates that expanded provision of antiretroviral treatment resulted in a gain of 2 million life-years in low- and middle-income countries in 2005 (UNAIDS 2006).

Globally, the WHO goal of putting 3 million people with AIDS on ART by end-2005 was not reached, but numbers are increasing rapidly. More important, access to treatment has not only improved health and saved the lives of numerous adults but also helped restore the well-being of other household members, especially children.

A recent analysis found that, on average, within six months of starting treatment, patients were able to increase their working hours substantially (Thirumurthy, Graff-Zivin and Goldstein 2005). Owing to increased work, even for low-income day laborers, the study estimated that the incremental costs of treatment were fully covered by the higher income generated, and there were other social benefits accruing to the household.

■ **Prevention efforts are inadequate.** Prevention will make the difference in the global trajectory of the AIDS epidemic. While 3 million people died of AIDS in 2006, there were 4 million new cases of infection—over 70,000 per week. Until progress is made in reducing this number substantially, the battle against AIDS will continue uphill. Coverage of prevention efforts is too low almost everywhere, especially among populations most at risk. A recent survey of more than 10,000 people living with HIV in 69 countries found that less than 1 percent of adults aged 15–29 had utilized voluntary counseling and testing and only about 11 percent of pregnant women had access to services for preventing mother-to-child transmission (Stover and Fahnenstock 2006). Prevention efforts aimed at high-risk populations only reached an estimated 33 percent of commercial sex workers, 34 percent of prisoners, 9 percent of homosexuals, and 8 percent of injecting drug users, far short of the coverage of over 60 percent that is needed for effective impact. Finally, although some 5 billion condoms were distributed in 2005, survey data suggest that this covered only an estimated 20 percent of risky sex acts.

■ **More evaluation of "what works" in different contexts to prevent HIV is needed.** While many approaches to prevention have been tried, few approaches have been rigorously evaluated, and some evaluations have revealed unimpressive or mixed results for programs previously believed to be effective. While a WHO review found that 13 of 23 evaluations of school-based

HIV education showed some beneficial impact, some of the most rigorous evaluations—randomized controlled trials in Western Kenya (Duflo and others 2006) and Mexico (Walker and others 2006)—found no evidence that HIV education courses in secondary schools affected key outcomes such as condom use. However, these and other studies have helped to identify other interventions that could be cost-effectively scaled up. Dupas (2005) found that informing young Kenyan girls about the higher risk of infection they face when engaging in sexual relationships with older men had a positive impact; one year after the intervention, girls were 65 percent less likely to have gotten pregnant by adult partners. A randomized experiment conducted in rural Malawi found that knowing one's serological status led to only small behavioral changes—suggesting that universal HIV testing might not be the most cost-effective way of **preventing** infections (Thornton 2005). However, offering an incentive equal to about one-tenth of a rural laborer's daily wage increased the demand for testing, overcoming stigma and offsetting opportunity costs of time. There may also be scope for incentives for other positive health behaviors, such as avoiding risky behaviors or adhering to ART.

■ **The world has much more to do in fighting HIV.** Treatment access has expanded, but it still reaches only one-quarter of all people with AIDS in the developing world. Prophylactic care for opportunistic infections also only reaches about one patient in four. Effective HIV prevention strategies need to be scaled up aggressively in all parts of the world—and these investments would yield high returns. A 2006 study calculated that large-scale and effective prevention strategies implemented today in 125 low- and middle-income countries could avert more than half of the 28 million new infections projected to occur between 2005 and 2015—and by 2015 could save $24 billion per year in associated treatment costs

(Stover and others 2006). The experience of Brazil and Thailand is instructive; early and determined government action focused both on preventing HIV in high risk groups and making ART affordable has kept both countries on a trajectory of very low prevalence.

To meet the needs of all target populations and truly reverse the epidemic, UNAIDS estimates that $22 billion per year in external funding is required, almost a tripling of the current level. Yet even the current levels of external financing for AIDS have had major effects on the allocation of health resources in developing countries and placed strain on scarce factors of supply and costs.

In this environment, several areas stand as urgent priorities for action. The first is better harmonization and alignment of donor efforts. The "three ones" platform—ensuring that in every country there is only one national AIDS leadership body, one national plan, and one system for monitoring progress—has made some headway. Key agencies are working on an explicit division of labor and better coordination in providing technical support; there has been an increase in joint donor reviews and supervision visits and agreement on a harmonized set of HIV indicators. But there is still much more to be done. The second priority is strengthening health systems in developing countries to enable them to absorb additional funding and deliver expanded services efficiently. Third is the imperative of scaling up effective, evidence-based prevention strategies.

Malaria. Malaria is both preventable and curable, but each year an estimated 300 to 500 million cases of malaria result in an estimated 1.2 million deaths. The majority of malaria deaths are among children, and an estimated 80 percent occur in Sub-Saharan Africa. Malaria also causes severe anemia and maternal illness, and contributes to low birth weight, a leading risk factor for child morbidity and mortality. In most countries in Africa south of the Sahara, malaria cases are diagnosed and reported based on clinical grounds, such as fever, without laboratory testing. Since fever is common to many infectious diseases, misdiagnoses are common and the actual number of cases is unknown. As a result, malaria incidence and mortality data by country generally do not accurately reflect the true scope of the disease, and are not reliable for monitoring trends. Instead, use of insecticide-treated bednets is tracked to monitor whether countries are addressing the disease through an effective preventive strategy. Table 2.4 shows that coverage rates are still low in many countries.

Drug resistance and a global subsidy for antimalarial drugs. One reason for the resurgence and increased burden of malaria is the development of resistance to traditional first-line antimalarial treatments, such as chloroquine (CQ) and sulfadoxine pyrimethamine (SP or Fansidar) by the parasite that causes a severe form of malaria. In some areas of Southeast Asia an artemisinin-based combination therapy (ACT) has been successful in treating and reversing the spread of drug-resistant malaria, and WHO recommends use of ACT when new drugs are required. But ACTs are 10–20 times as expensive as first-line treatments, and there is a risk that malaria's toll could rise even higher if resistance to artemisinin were to spread. The challenge is thus to facilitate the use of artemisinins where appropriate while preserving their effectiveness for as long as possible. Arrow and colleagues (2004) and a separate study by the World Bank and the Roll Back Malaria (RBM) Partnership concluded that actions to delay the development of resistance to ACTs create a benefit for all—"a global public good." This would justify a sustained global subsidy for ACTs, to ensure that artemisinins are used with other antimalarials, and used judiciously.

With support from the Netherlands and the RBM Partnership, the World Bank is leading an effort to translate this proposal for a high-level global subsidy into reality. The Bank is facilitating the analysis, consultations, and the design of possible management arrangements for the subsidy, which could be hosted in an existing agency as appropriate.

The Malaria Booster Program. In 2005 the World Bank renewed its commitment to the Roll Back Malaria Partnership, and the Africa Region launched the Malaria Booster Program to support country-level efforts to deliver concrete and measurable results. Over the next five years, the Bank expects to commit up to $500 million of International Development Association (IDA) resources to support the program in approximately 20 countries. As of mid-December 2006, 11 projects totaling $357 million had been approved—funding malaria-control projects in 10 countries and a subregional multisector project in the Senegal River Basin. The 11 projects are expected to deliver at least 19 million long-lasting insecticide-treated bednets, primarily to young children and pregnant women, and about 29 million doses of ACT, primarily to children.

TABLE 2.4 Use of insecticide-treated bednets by children under five

	Poorest quintile	Richest quintile	Population average
Colombia 2005	85.2	73.4	79.2
Cambodia 2000	57.3	80.7	67.5
Chad 2004	67	71.2	55.8
Mali 2001	34.4	48	38.3
Tanzania 2004	17.8	71.3	33.9
Benin 2001	24.7	57	33.8
Burkina Faso 2003	25	30.1	23.3
Zambia 2001	6.4	29.8	17.7
Kenya 2003	8.1	36.3	16.7
Ghana 2003	19.6	10.8	16.2
Cameroon 2004	5	21.5	13.7
Mozambique 2003	4.7	20.9	10.1
Uganda 2000	6.3	23.3	9.4
Nigeria 2003	11	3.3	7.1
Namibia 2000	11.3	5.5	6.6
Rwanda 2000	1.8	24.7	5.8
Zimbabwe 1999	0.2	7.3	2.9

Source: Demographic and Health Surveys.

Tuberculosis. There were 9 million new TB cases and approximately 2 million TB deaths in 2004, making this the second deadliest communicable disease, after AIDS. As table 2.5 shows, while TB incidence was stable or falling in five out of six World Bank regions, it is growing at 0.6 percent per year globally, owing to rising incidence in Sub-Saharan Africa. People latently infected with TB are at a much greater risk of developing active TB if they are concurrently infected with HIV, and this has contributed to dramatically worsening TB incidence in southern African countries and Kenya (table 2.6). In the Europe and Central Asia Region, incidence per capita increased during the 1990s, but peaked about 2001, and has since fallen. The main strategy to combat TB is careful treatment with a protocol called Directly Observed Treatment, Short-course (DOTS). In 2004, DOTS was being used in 183 countries, with 100 percent population coverage in 9 of 22 high-burden countries, and almost complete in 5 others. By the end of 2004, 83 percent of the world's population lived in countries, or parts of countries, covered by DOTS. High-burden countries with high levels of DOTS coverage, such as Indonesia and Peru, have shown large decreases in TB incidence in recent years (table 2.6).

Tuberculosis can usually be treated with a course of four standard, or first-line, anti-TB drugs, which cost $14–18 per patient (Stop TB Partnership 2006). If these drugs are misused or mismanaged, however, multidrug-resistant TB (MDR-TB) can develop, which must be treated with more expensive second-line drugs, which have more side-effects and take longer to work. In September 2006, WHO detected a deadly new strain of the bacteria—called extensively drug-resistant (XDR) TB—in Kwazulu Natal Province, the epicenter of South Africa's HIV/AIDS epidemic. XDR-TB is resistant to a number of first- and second-line anti-TB drugs, and treatment options are very limited. Because of constraints on equipment and skills for diagnosis in poor countries, the global distribution of XDR-TB is not known with accuracy at the moment. However, WHO estimates that there were almost

TABLE 2.5 TB incidence trends by region

Region or classification	Incidence of tuberculosis (per 100,000 people)	
	1990	2004
East Asia & Pacific	161	138
Europe & Central Asia	51	83
Latin America & Caribbean	103	64
Middle East & North Africa	66	54
South Asia	180	177
Sub-Saharan Africa	162	363
High income	28	17
Low income	177	224
Lower middle income	134	115
Upper middle income	69	114
World	124	140

Source: WHO.

TABLE 2.6 Changes in TB incidence, 1990–2004

Country	Incidence of tuberculosis (per 100,000 people)		Absolute difference 1990 and 2004
	1990	2004	
Increasing incidence			
Swaziland	263	1,226	963
Zimbabwe	135	674	539
Lesotho	179	696	517
Kenya	108	619	511
Namibia	260	717	456
South Africa	268	718	450
Declining incidence			
Peru	394	178	−215
Haiti	484	306	−178
Maldives	148	49	−99
Indonesia	343	245	−98

Source: WHO.

half a million cases of MDR-TB worldwide in 2004, and MDR-TB can presage XDR-TB. WHO is leading international efforts to address the XDR-TB problem in collaboration with countries and the Stop TB Partnership.

MDG7—Water and Sanitation

MDG7 "Ensure Environmental Sustainability," includes a target that is interlinked

> **BOX 2.4   Measuring health progress**
>
> The health MDGs, and especially maternal mortality and AIDS, malaria, and tuberculosis (TB) goals, are difficult to monitor, owing to the absence of vital registration and disease surveillance systems in many countries. The Health Metrics Network (HMN) is a global network launched in 2005 to help developing countries improve the availability and quality of their health statistics. Partners include developing countries, multilateral agencies (including the World Bank), bilateral donors, the Gates Foundation, and the major global partnerships.
>
> While many donors have supported monitoring and evaluation units (M&E) to report on specific project activities, or have supported the DHS and other household surveys, they have never before worked together to strengthen health information systems in the developing world. Improving countries' capacity to establish vital registration, disease and risk factor surveillance, national health accounts, and regular household surveys promises over time to reduce the costs of generating the information that both policy makers and donors need and avoiding uncoordinated M&E activities.
>
> The HMN has developed a common framework setting out the standards, policies, capacities, and processes needed at the country level. The framework also serves as a diagnostic tool to establish a baseline of currently available health statistics, and provides a roadmap for development and implementation of health statistics strengthening. During 2006, some 40 countries received grants from the HMN to carry out baseline assessments using the common framework. The network is currently developing time-bound plans for strengthening health information systems in an initial batch of countries.
>
> *Source:* Health Metrics Network.

to progress on most of the human development MDGs—the target of halving by 2015 the proportion of people without sustainable access to safe drinking water and basic sanitation. Hygiene, sanitation, and water supply have important influences on child health, schooling attendance, gender equity, and other human development outcomes. Hand-washing initiatives have been shown to reduce the probability of contracting diarrheal diseases—an important cause of child morbidity and mortality—by 44 percent, sanitation improvements produced a 32 percent decrease, and improved water supply resulted in a 25 percent reduction (Fewtrell and others 2005). A recent international poll by the *British Medical Journal* chose sanitation as the greatest medical breakthrough since the 1840s.

Globally, there has been significant progress on water supply; access to improved water sources has increased from 73 percent in 1990 to 80 percent in 2004 but only Latin America and South Asia are considered on track to reach the target (and about 26 percent of developing countries lack adequate data to judge).[2] Sub-Saharan Africa is the region most seriously off track, but there are also some promising trends: Malawi and Namibia have reached the MDG target; 17 of 36 African countries for which data are available are on or almost on track; and 6 of the 10 countries making fastest progress globally are low-income African countries (table 2.7).

There has been progress on sanitation too, but not enough. Globally, access to improved sanitation has increased from 37 percent in 1990 to 52 percent in 2004—which is not on pace to the goal of 69 percent coverage by 2015. Only two regions (East Asia and the Pacific and Latin America) are on track for basic sanitation. While the South Asia region is not on track given its very low starting base, large gains in access have been made, especially in India, where sanitation coverage more than doubled between 1990 and 2004. About 46 percent of all developing countries are considered off-track to the sanitation target, while another 34 percent have inadequate data. Progress in Africa has been slow. Only one of the 32 African countries for which data are available is on track. This makes the performance of that country—Senegal—all the more noteworthy (table 2.8).

The three largest challenges in achieving the water supply and sanitation MDG targets are: (1) ensuring that sanitation gets sufficient attention in national investment programs; (2) reducing rural-urban disparities in the access of water supply and sanitation services; and (3) ensuring the sustainability of investments already made.

Access to sanitation tends to lag behind water supply, which has historically been accorded a higher priority both by governments and households. The lag is due to a number of factors, including limited demand from households, institutional fragmentation, poor coordination, and limited capacity to address the problem at scale. While the poorest quintiles in every region have the least access to water and sanitation, the biggest gaps in access fall along the rural-urban divide. In developing countries, 92 percent of the urban population has access to improved water sources and more than 73 percent to sanitation, while coverage in rural areas is 70 percent for access to water and only 33 percent for basic sanitation. The rural-urban disparities are especially sharp in Africa and South and East Asia.

A major lesson of the past decade is that water supply and sanitation investments are not sustainable unless adequate attention is paid to the institutional context and performance of service providers. Principles for a sound operating environment include the use of demand-responsive approaches in service provision, managing services at the lowest appropriate level, adherence to cost recovery policies where necessary in combination with transparent subsidies targeted to the poorest users, appropriate technologies and standards to ensure cost effectiveness of investments,

TABLE 2.7 Access to improved water is growing

Countries	Percent of population with access to improved water sources		Average annual percentage point increase, 1990–2004
	1990	2004	
Strong performers			
Malawi	40%	73%	2.4%
Namibia	57%	87%	2.1%
Paraguay	62%	86%	1.7%
Burkina Faso	38%	61%	1.6%
Central African Republic	52%	75%	1.6%
Ecuador	73%	94%	1.5%
Vietnam	65%	85%	1.4%
Ghana	55%	75%	1.4%
Eritrea	43%	60%	1.2%
El Salvador	67%	84%	1.2%
Poor performers			
Maldives	96%	83%	−0.9%
Uzbekistan	94%	82%	−0.9%
Algeria	94%	85%	−0.6%
Comoros	93%	86%	−0.5%

Source: WHO-UNICEF Joint Monitoring Program, Meeting the Drinking Water and Sanitation Target: The Urban and Rural Challenge of the Decade, 2006.

TABLE 2.8 Access to improved sanitation is growing

Countries	Percent of population with access to improved sanitation		Average annual percentage point increase, 1990–2004
	1990	2004	
Strong performers			
Guatemala	58%	86%	2.0%
Ecuador	63%	89%	1.9%
Dominican Republic	52%	78%	1.9%
Vietnam	36%	61%	1.8%
Senegal	33%	57%	1.7%
Nepal	11%	35%	1.7%
Sri Lanka	69%	91%	1.6%
Paraguay	58%	80%	1.6%
Pakistan	37%	59%	1.6%
Benin	12%	33%	1.5%
China	23%	44%	1.5%
Mexico	58%	79%	1.5%
Poor performers			
Liberia	39%	27%	−0.9%
Burundi	44%	36%	—0.6%
South Africa	69%	65%	−0.3%

Source: WHO-UNICEF Joint Monitoring Program, Meeting the Drinking Water and Sanitation Target: The Urban and Rural Challenge of the Decade, 2006.

and a shift from sewerage systems to on-site sanitation and hygiene promotion programs. Different management models are appropriate for different country contexts and increasingly diverse management models are being successfully used in both the public and private sectors. Increasing use of public-private partnerships is another promising trend.

Despite its importance for directly supporting achievement of the WSS MDG and indirectly contributing to progress on health, education, and gender MDGs, ODA for water and sanitation declined significantly from the mid-1990s through 2002. Since 2003, assistance for WSS has begun to swing upwards again, but even in 2005 had not recovered to the 2000 level. In the past two years, efforts have been made to ramp up financing for WSS, especially for Africa. This has resulted in the recent establishment of the Africa Infrastructure Consortium, and the Rural Water Supply and Sanitation Initiative led by the African Development Bank. Although this is a positive development, given the long lead time for investments, it will be several years before new

funding through these initiatives translates into improved access to water sources and sanitation, and faster progress on the WSS targets.

Financing MDG progress

External financing. External financing for health and education has nearly doubled in real terms since the MDGs were adopted. While aid for health continued to rise from 2004 to 2005, education-related official development assistance commitments showed their first decline (figure 2.3). The decline reflects a drop in commitments for China and India, both of which received large commitments linked to new multiyear programs in 2004. On a sectoral basis, basic plus general education funding rose to 53 percent of the total volume, and the share for postsecondary education fell to 38 percent. Commitments for Sub-Saharan Africa increased, to 29 percent of the total volume. Education commitments are expected to increase again in 2007.

In health, much attention has been given to the expansion of private funding sources

FIGURE 2.3 Development assistance for education and health, 2000–05

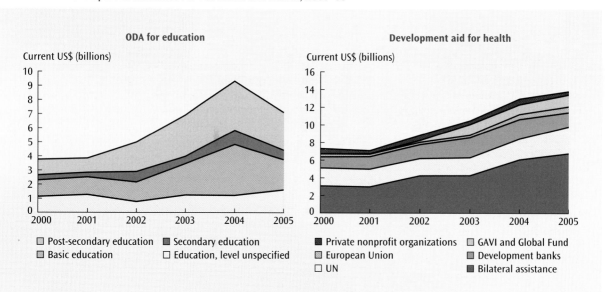

Source: OECD/DAC data.

over the past five years, with the Gates Foundation in particular increasing from about $0.6 million to $1.2 billion per year in assistance, two-thirds of which is channeled to countries through global programs such as the Global Fund for AIDS, TB and Malaria (GFATM); and the Global Alliance for Vaccines and Immunizations (GAVI). But as can be seen from figure 2.3, a number of bilateral donors have increased their core assistance levels at least as strongly—the United States has more than doubled its health funding, reaching close to $4 billion in 2005; Spain has also doubled its assistance; and France and Norway have quadrupled their official development assistance for health. A number of new financing modalities have also been established with support from bilaterals. In contrast, support for health from multilateral development banks has been flat in real terms since 2000, most likely reflecting recipient countries' preference for grant funding over even highly concessional lending.

As large as the expansion of bilateral and private assistance has been, current support levels are still far short of the estimated financing needs to reach the health MDGs, the most conservative of which calls for $25–50 billion per year in external support. There is also a growing imbalance between the volumes of funding mobilized for specific diseases and the core funding needs of health systems for scaling up basic service delivery. Multilateral development banks (MDBs) could potentially play a key role in the provision of "complementary"

BOX 2.5 Innovative new financing mechanisms for health are getting off the ground

Along with mobilizing more funding, donors for health have worked since 2000 to improve aid quality and address market failures in the supply of global public goods for health through the development of innovative financing methods:

The International Finance Facility for Immunization (IFFIm) was designed to increase the stream and predictability of funding for health and immunization programs. A pilot for the larger International Finance Facility, the IFFIm mechanism converts donor pledges of off-budget commitments of future resources into funds available for near-term disbursement through bond markets. In 2006, $1 billion was raised in an initial bond offering and channeled to GAVI, which is now committing these resources to country programs for the introduction of new vaccines and health system strengthening.

Advance Market Commitments (AMCs) for vaccines are financial commitments from donors to subsidize future purchases of yet-to-be-developed vaccines. AMCs were designed to increase the incentives for global drug companies to invest in research, development, and production of vaccines that would serve developing-country markets. The first AMC pilot is targeting pneumococcal vaccines, which could avert 1.6 million developing-country deaths a year. Donors will launch the AMC Pilot in February 2007, committing $1.5 billion to support the purchase of pneumococcal vaccines through roughly 2019.

UNITAID, financed through a tax on airline tickets and other sources, was designed to provide a long-term, predictable funding stream for drugs and diagnostic kits to fight HIV/AIDS, TB, and malaria. In 2007, UNITAID is expected to receive $300 million from ticket levies implemented in France, Chile, and 19 other countries including Brazil. UNITAID will work with global funds and agencies such as the Clinton Foundation on the supply side of the international pharmaceutical market—pooling orders, stimulating competition, and negotiating lower prices for drugs—as well as providing support for programs on the ground, mostly through the Global Fund. In 2007, UNITAID expects to supply drugs for 100,000 people in 16 countries, and to reach 130,000 children with an "HIV pediatric package" of drugs, diagnostic kits, and nutrition.

un-earmarked financing and technical support aimed at overall strengthening of health systems. However, the trend in MDB financing for health over the past several years has been flat.

Developing-country spending. Government spending on health and education has grown as a share of the gross domestic product (GDP) in all regions (figure 2.4). The largest increase has been for education in South Asia—from 3 to 3.8 percent, driven by India—but the share of GDP devoted to education in that region still remains the lowest in the world. In both the Middle East and North Africa and Sub-Saharan Africa, education shares were already a relatively high share of GDP and they have increased further. At 5.5 percent and 5 percent of GDP, respectively, these two regions now trail only East Asia and the Pacific in the national fiscal priority given to education.

In health, spending shares increased in all regions except Latin America and the Caribbean. The largest increase was in Sub-Saharan Africa, where government health spending as a

percentage of GDP rose by 26 percent between 2000 and 2004.[3] However, the region still trails all other regions except South Asia in its spending share for health.

Donor harmonization. Efforts to improve the "quality" of donor assistance are on very different trajectories in education and health. In education, an increasing number of developing countries are joining the EFA-FTI, which the OECD/DAC Forum recently ranked as one of the most effective among global programs in promoting donor harmonization and aid alignment with country-led priorities. Core principles of the FTI are to unify donors in reviewing and endorsing a credible education sector strategy for each FTI country and committing development partners to align aid with that framework. Off-plan and off-budget support are not permitted. FTI donors have also been making progress on the ground in implementing the Paris Harmonization accords: they have reduced the number of separate donor missions, increased their use of country systems, and pooled their financing. The review paper

FIGURE 2.4 Developing countries are devoting more national resources to education and health

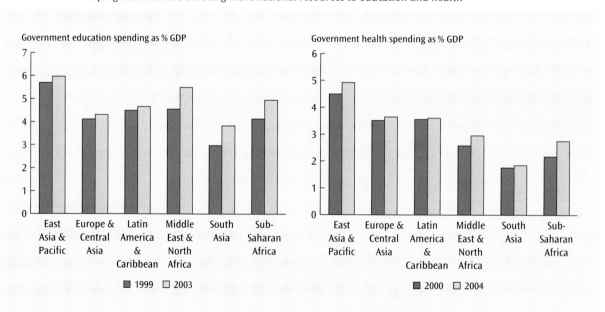

Sources: UNESCO Institute of Statistics; WHO.

cited earlier concluded that harmonization progress under the FTI was real, significant, and a major achievement of the initiative to date (World Bank 2006).

In health, progress has been largely based on country-specific efforts, and there is no comparable organizing entity for unifying donors around coherent national strategies. Previous GMRs have documented the "verticalization" of global support for health over the past seven years and growing concerns about transactions costs, coordination failures, and poor alignment with recipient countries' national health priorities. A 2006 case study of Rwanda, whose strong national commitment to achieving the health MDGs and innovative policies have attracted large increases in donor funding, provided some graphic examples of the difficulties recipient countries face in achieving policy coherence, aligning aid to sectorwide financing needs, and mapping volatile annual or biannual aid commitments onto long-term recurrent fund-

ing needs (see box 2.6.) A recent analysis of Ethiopia confirmed similar patterns.

The global health community has acknowledged these issues at successive international fora. In 2004–05 WHO and the World Bank convened a *High-Level Forum on the Health MDGs* (HLF) to examine aid effectiveness in health. Major issues highlighted by the HLF included poor alignment of aid with government priorities; the volatility and short-term nature of many commitments; harmonization and alignment issues created by the large number of different donors in health, particularly Global Health Partnerships; and the need for closer monitoring of the impact of increased general budget support on funding available for health. Perhaps the most important outcome of the HLF is the development of a set of Best Practice Principles for Engagement of Global Health Partnerships at the Country Level—based on the Paris Declaration—which are now being implemented by major health partnerships. Other contributions include

---

BOX 2.6 Managing aid for health in Rwanda

Rwanda has made impressive progress in health over the past several years, with innovative reforms, sustained implementation and increased domestic spending supported by burgeoning donor support: the health sector share of total government spending grew from 2.5 percent in 1998 to 10 percent in 2005. By 2004, donor grants represented about half of total government spending in Rwanda, but this figure actually underestimates the importance of foreign aid, because of large off-budget funding, especially in the health sector. There is no question that the current partnership between the government and donors is supporting the country's progress. But a recent review of Rwanda's development assistance for health documented some of the issues in aid delivery that the government must navigate in translating aid resources into results (Republic of Rwanda 2006).

The first is the challenge of achieving policy coherence—and even basic fiscal monitoring—given that only 14 percent of total donor support for health is channeled through the budget of the Rwandan Ministry of Health or through local governments and health districts (12 percent). The remaining 74 percent of aid is channeled by donors directly to NGOs or their own-managed projects. This aid may be effectively used: even the government has recognized the efficiency of contracting services to NGOs. The issue is that it is difficult for the Ministry of Health—which remains responsible for health outcomes in the country—to account for, or track, the total volume of health spending.

A second issue is alignment: while Rwanda is trying to implement a major reform of its overall health delivery system, out of total on-budget official development assistance to the health sector

continued

BOX 2.6 Managing aid for health in Rwanda *(continued)*

in 2005 of $75 million, $46 million was earmarked for HIV/AIDS, $18 million for malaria, and only $1 million for child health. Although external funding for HIV/AIDS is still short of estimated needs, it far exceeds support available for other health priorities—although some HIV/AIDS funding supports facilities upgrading that has broader benefits.

A third issue is volatility: much of the assistance for Rwanda, like other countries, reflects commitments from bilateral donors that are for 1–2 years at most—although the United Kingdom is a notable exception. This leads to substantial variations in funding levels from year to year, and inhibits long-term planning. In two areas in particular—national decisions to scale-up health service provision by training and hiring more doctors and nurses, and the expansion of AIDS patients on antiretroviral treatment—Rwanda and other governments currently incur major risks of sustainability.

Finally, the Rwanda case illustrates, from a country's viewpoint, the disparity between funding available for vertical health programs and other development priorities. The report notes that "spending on health has increased markedly in recent years…(but) infrastructure and agriculture have been relatively neglected. Major investments in the road network are needed to support economic growth and poverty reduction. Major investments are needed in energy and in water and sanitation." While such multisectoral investments can have important effects on human development outcomes, the current aid architecture makes it difficult for countries to allocate resources efficiently across sectors to capture these complementarities.

On-budget donor assistance to the health sector in Rwanda, 2005

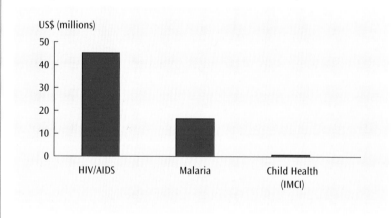

Source: Republic of Rwanda, 2006.

analyses of the challenges of scaling up service delivery, including human resource constraints, and the "fiscal space" for sustainable health financing.

Tanzania and Uganda are good examples of country leadership in pulling health donors into coordinated sectorwide approaches (SWAps). The Rwandan government has also recently developed an "Aid Policy and a Joint Agreement"—a compact to be signed with development partners—as part of the new Economic Development and Poverty Reduction Strategy in 2007. Elements of the compact include donors' agreement that all aid will be included in the government budget, and a stipulation that aid projects not meeting this requirement will only be accepted if they are sustainable. Donors have also been asked to assess how well their practices align with the draft policy, and to discuss all planned activities with the government. Resource flows to the sector will be through a SWAp. Donors providing budget support will be guided by a new Partnership Framework for Harmonization and Alignment of Budget Support.

Fragile States

Fragile states or low-income countries under stress (LICUS) account for 9 percent of the population in developing countries but 27 percent of those living on less than US$1 per day. These countries are least likely to achieve

the MDGs: almost one-third (31 percent) of all child deaths and 29 percent of all 12-year-olds who fail to complete primary school in developing countries are in fragile states. As table 2.9 shows, on virtually every MDG, fragile states acccount for a disproportionate share of the world's people who suffer from poor outcomes and poor services. Only two of the 35 states considered fragile in 2005 are on track to reach the child mortality MDG: Timor-Leste and Lao PDR. And 25 percent of the countries where child mortality rates are actually worsening are fragile states.

Even when compared with other low-income countries, the performance of fragile states is considerably weaker; as figure 2.5 shows, child mortality in fragile states over the past 15 years has remained higher and progressed more slowly than in other low-income countries.

Primary completion rates in fragile states also trail those of other low-income coun-

TABLE 2.9 Fragile states lag most on MDGs

MDG indicator	Millions of people		
	Total developing countries	Total fragile states	Percent of total fragile states
Total population	**5,427**	**485**	**9%**
MDG1—Poverty and hunger			
Underweight children	143	22.7	16%
MDG2—Universal education			
Children of relevant age that did not complete primary school in 2005	13.8	4	29%
MDG4—Under-five mortality			
Children born in 2005 not expected to survive to age five	10.5	3.3	31%
MDG5—Maternal health			
Unattended births	48.7	8.9	18%
MDG6—Diseases			
HIV+	29.8	7.2	24%
TB deaths	1.7	0.34	20%
MDG7—Environmental sustainability			
Lacking access to improved water	1,083	209	19%
Lacking access to improved sanitation	2,626	286	11%

Source: World Bank staff estimates.

FIGURE 2.5   Child mortality is higher and showing less progress in
fragile states

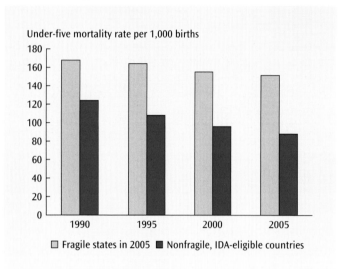

Source: World Bank.

FIGURE 2.6   Primary completion rates are lower in fragile states, but
improving

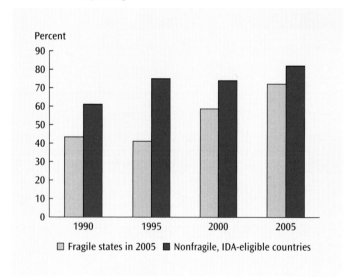

Source: UNESCO.

sively quickly. In 7 out of 12 cases studied in a 2005 review, primary school enrollments were higher in the year after conflicts than in the year before they began—including in countries where 50 percent or more of schools were damaged or destroyed by hostilities. (Buckland 2005). The "surprising resilience" of primary education systems is attributed to a number of factors: the strong priority given to schooling by communities, which often strive on their own to keep schools open during conflicts; the high and immediate priority education typically receives from donors and countries once conflicts end; and the opportunities for education reform that postconflict settings can present. Since 1995, buoyed by the exceptional progress in Cambodia, the fragile states as a group have increased primary completion faster than nonfragile low-income countries.

But primary education may be an exception. The effects of conflict on child health can be more severe and harder to reverse. More than 2 million children have died over the past decade as a direct result of armed conflict, and at least 6 million children have been seriously injured or permanently disabled (Bustreo and others 2005). A 2003 study found that during a typical five-year war, infant mortality increases by 13 percent and the effect is persistent: in the first 5 years of postconflict peace the infant mortality rate remains 11 percent higher than the preconflict baseline (Hoeffler and others 2003). In general, weak institutions—whether or not they are marked by conflict—constrain progress in expanding basic services in fragile states. As figures 2.7 and 2.8 show, while average access to improved water supply and measles immunizations have expanded in fragile states, they have not kept pace with the rates of improvement in nonfragile low-income countries.

Although the gap in average aid flows between fragile states and other low-income countries has narrowed over the past five years, aid to fragile states is particularly volatile. When donors do engage, they often establish parallel systems because government

tries (figure 2.6), but the gap is not as great. Indeed, the data suggest that at least under some circumstances, such as restoration of primary school functioning after conflicts, it is possible for fragile states to rebound impres-

systems are weak. This approach can further undermine fragile states, and can make future capacity building difficult. A particular issue in the human development sectors is the potential for gaps in service delivery in the "transition phase" between the end of a humanitarian crisis and the beginning of longer-term recovery and reconstruction projects.

Aware of these issues, donors assisting in the postconflict reconstruction of Afghanistan and Timor-Leste have worked carefully to implement strategies to smooth the transition (box 2.7). The positive results of these experiences may hold lessons for donors working in other fragile states, and possibly in other sectors.

Is MDG Progress Reaching the Poor?

Equitable country progress toward the MDGs comes from reaching the poorest citizens—bringing up average national indicators by extending services and achieving outcomes for the lowest quintiles of the population. Few sources of data allow national indicators to be "unpacked" to see which groups within countries have benefited most, but the international DHS does. As of end-2006, 21 developing countries had survey results that enable us to analyze MDG progress since the goals were adopted in 2000. While these countries are not a representative sample, they span all regions and different levels of per capita income.

In every country, both access to services and outcomes for the poorest quintiles are lower than for other income groups, and the gaps are often disturbingly large. While child mortality rates across these 21 countries are 79 per 1,000 live births for the top quintile and 125 per 1,000 births for the population as a whole, they average 148 per 1,000 live births for the lowest quintile. While primary completion rates average 81 percent for the highest income quintile and 55 percent for the population as a whole, they average 36 for children from the poorest quintile. Similarly for the delivery of services such as immunizations, 82 percent of children in the top quintile and 69 percent of all children

FIGURE 2.7 Measles immunization in fragile states remains lower

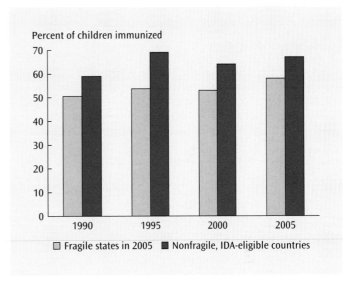

Source: WHO.

FIGURE 2.8 A growing gap in access to improved water

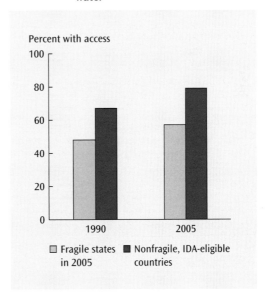

Source: UN Joint Monitoring Project.

were immunized for measles in these countries, but only 59 percent of children in the bottom income quintile.

It is sobering to keep these gaps in mind. But the data also show some encouraging

---

> ## BOX 2.7 Rebuilding health services after conflict: Strategies from Timor-Leste and Afghanistan
>
> After the violent withdrawal of Indonesian troops in 1999, more than 70 percent of Timor-Leste's health facilities were destroyed or badly damaged and approximately 80 percent of the country's health managers had left the country. The government faced the immediate challenge of restoring health services and a longer-term challenge of rebuilding a sustainable health system. With support from IDA and other donors, the government implemented a two-tier strategy that addressed both. Under the first Health Sector Rehabilitation and Development Project (HSRDP I), the government addressed the short-term need to get services going again by contracting with local and international relief NGOs; for a time, NGOs became the main health service providers.
>
> At the same time, the government implemented strategic longer-term investments in a sustainable national health system—by reconstructing facilities, developing national health policies and regulations, redeveloping the organizational structure of the health system, and training new human resources.
>
> Afghanistan faced a similar challenge after the collapse of Taliban rule. The country had some of the worst health indicators in the world, with estimated under-five mortality of 256 per 1,000 births, compared to 92 for South Asia. To address urgent needs, the World Bank and the Ministry of Public Health initiated the Health Sector Emergency Reconstruction and Development Project, and similarly contracted with 10 local and international NGOs to deliver a priority basket of health services in 12 provinces.
>
> The results in both countries were impressive. In Timor-Leste, the use of health services increased from one visit per person per year on average to at least 2.5. Measles immunizations rose from 26 percent to 73 percent of cildren; skilled attendance at birth increased from 26 percent to 41 percent; and child mortality declined dramatically. In Afghanistan, even in provinces such as Helmand, where continuing violence cost the lives of several health workers, patient visits more than doubled, from 157,000 in 2004 to 338,000 in 2006. Across all 12 provinces, there was a fourfold increase in the number of people visiting rural health centers, a 60 percent increase in the number of functional health centers, and an increase from 5 percent to 63 percent of pregnant women receiving prenatal care.
>
> Afghanistan and Timor-Leste illustrate the potential of approaches that integrate the best features of the public and private sectors. In each case, the government led the strategy and oversaw implementation, but delegated the role of principal service provider to NGOs. In Timor-Leste, subsequent projects have supported a progressive transition of service delivery from international NGOs to government district management teams. In Afghanistan, owing to the perceived success of the current contracting arrangements, the possibility of a longer-term partnership is being considered.
>
> *Prepared by:* Fadia Saadah, EAHD and Benjamin Loevinsohn, SASHD.

trends. In the countries where service delivery is expanding—for primary education, immunizations, and other health services—there are many countries where the gains in service access for the poorest children are larger than for the population as a whole. Child mortality outcomes—which generally take longer to produce and reflect many factors beyond direct service delivery in health—also show some progress for the poor, although not as strongly. Specifically, the data show the following:

- In 15 of the 17 countries making progress in reducing child mortality, there is either little gap between the rates of improvement for the lowest quintile and the population average or faster progress for the poor.
- In 14 of the 15 countries that have increased measles immunization rates, coverage increased faster for the poorest children than for the population as a whole.
- In 11 of the 13 countries which show increased primary completion rates, the poorest quintile improved more than the

population as a whole.

Child mortality. The 21 countries with recent data include 14 Sub-Saharan African countries, 2 in East Asia, 2 in North Africa, and 2 in Latin America (figure 2.9). The continued progress in Egypt, which trend data since 1990 show to be on

FIGURE 2.9 Child mortality progress

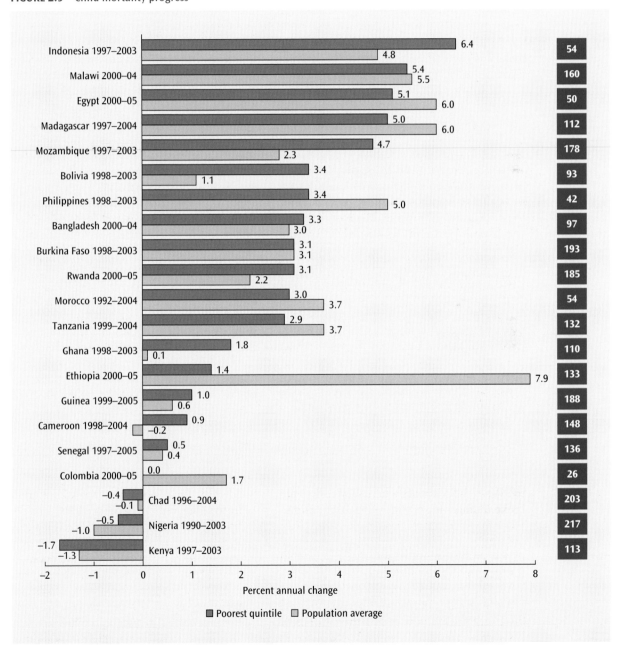

Source: Demographic and Health Surveys.
Note: The boxed numbers show the numbers of child deaths per 1,000 live births in the most recent surveys.

track to reach the child mortality MDG, is clear. But these data suggest that several other countries—Indonesia, the Philippines, Malawi, Madagascar, Mozambique, and Ethiopia—have accelerated their progress on under-five mortality since the MDGs were adopted. While Egypt has maintained a decline in under-five mortality of over 4.3 percent per year for the full period since 1990, the four African countries and Indonesia and the Philippines have all begun registering the necessary rate of progress over the past several years. This is encouraging.

These data also show that in virtually all the countries where there is progress, it is reaching the poor. In nine countries—Indonesia, Mozambique, Bolivia, Bangladesh, Rwanda, Ghana, Guinea, Cameroon, and Senegal—children in the poorest quintiles are showing faster improvement in health than for the population as a whole. In six other countries (Malawi, Egypt, Madagascar, Burkina Faso, Morocco, and Tanzania) there is little gap. Only in two countries (Ethiopia and Colombia) is the rate of improvement in child health for the poorest groups seriously lagging behind the average. And in Chad and Kenya, overall deterioration is hurting the poor worst. In Nigeria, there is a long gap in time between the surveys, which could affect the comparability of the results. But the general picture of very slow MDG progress in these countries is corroborated by other data and is troubling.

Immunization against measles. Given the aggressive global campaign since 1999 to increase measles immunizations, the DHS data offer a measure of the success of this effort. The data for 21 countries indicate that especially in Sub-Saharan Africa, measles vaccination rates have increased and children in the poorest income quintile have benefited substantially (figure 2.10). There is only one case, Bangladesh, where measles coverage has grown without benefiting the lowest quintile relatively more. It should be recalled, however, that Bangladesh has invested heavily in vaccination programs

for several decades and has a high level of overall coverage, including for the lowest quintile. Kenya, Malawi, Chad, and Nigeria again appear as troubling cases of decline for all segments of the population, but with the poorest harmed most.

Primary completion. In the 18 countries with comparable education data, the picture that emerges is that primary completion progress is strongly pro-poor. In all but two of the countries that registered increases in the share of youths who completed primary education, the poorest quintile improved more than the average, and in most of those countries the differential was large. Burkina Faso, Madagascar, Ethiopia, Bangladesh, and Morocco stand out as making exceptional progress in extending basic education to all segments of the population (figure 2.11).

As with the other indicators, Kenya and Chad show no evidence of progress. More surprising, perhaps, are the declines for Tanzania and Mozambique—both of which have been strongly committed to education for some time and are considered high performers by donors. The explanation may be that the share of the cohort aged 15–19 that has completed primary education reflects changes in the education system and participation rates from roughly a decade earlier; in a sense, these data "look in the rearview mirror." Policy changes of the last few years—such as Kenya's 2002 adoption of free primary education—will not be reflected in these results. But the impact of Mozambique's civil war of a decade ago on schooling participation at that time would be. Neither of these explanations is fully satisfying in the case of Tanzania, however, which has sustained educational progress for many years. While rates of improvement will necessarily slow in countries with high levels of primary school coverage, which applies to Tanzania as well as several others of these countries, the poor should not necessarily show worsening trends.

FIGURE 2.10 Measles vaccines are reaching the poor in many countries

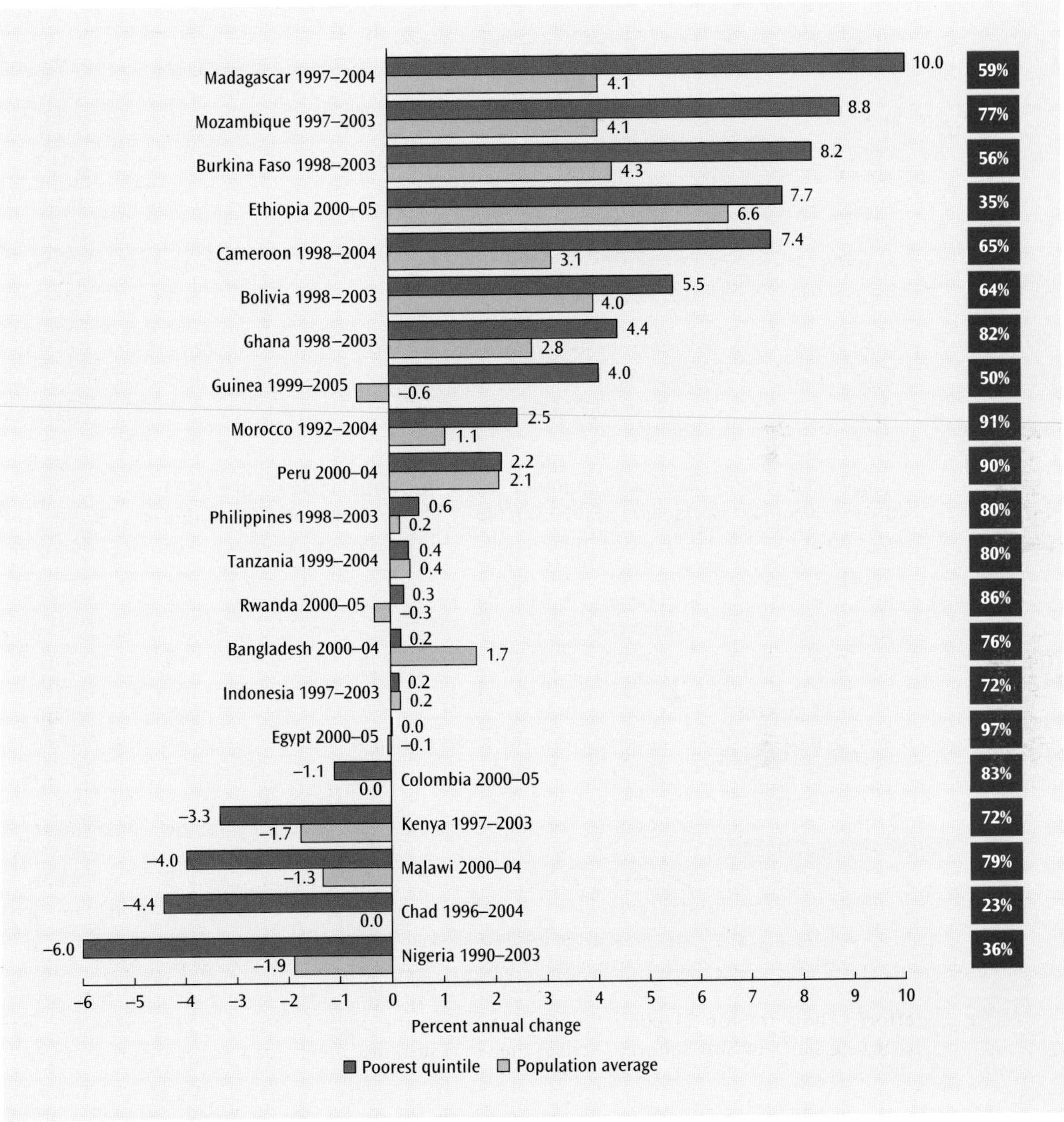

Source: Demographic and Health Surveys.
Note: The boxed numbers show the immunization coverage (for children 12–24 months) in the most recent survey.

FIGURE 2.11   Primary completion progress is benefiting the poor in many countries, but not all

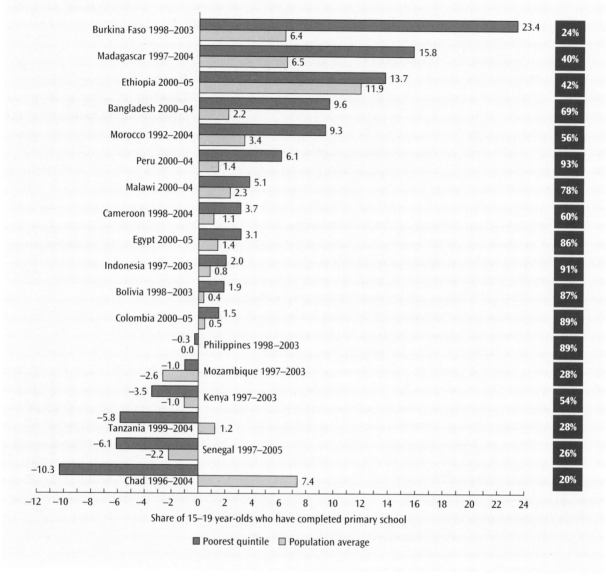

Source: Demographic and Health Surveys.
Note: The boxed numbers show the share of 15- to 19-year-olds who have completed primary school in the most recent surveys.

The Role of Quality in MDG Progress

Education: Are Developing-Country Students Learning?

In 2005, a respected NGO in India shocked the nation by publishing the results of a test administered to 300,000 primary school–aged children across the country. Using a network of NGO volunteers, the simple test of reading and math skills was given to children at home, whether enrolled in school or not. The good news was that over 90 percent of all Indian children reported being enrolled. The sobering result: 68 percent of primary school students could not read a simple (second grade-level) paragraph and 54 percent of children could not solve a simple two-digit math problem (Pratham 2005). The results varied across states, but the mean performance was troubling. What was India's tremendous progress in expanding primary access over the past decade really producing?

Other developing countries are confronting the same question. An NGO-administered test in a small set of low-income schools across Peru in 2005 found that 50 percent of children at the end of second grade could not read a single word of a simple first-grade text (Cotlear 2006). A similar reading test in rural Cameroon showed that 80 percent of the *third* grade children tested could not read a single word of a first-grade text (Walter 2007).

New research shows that such learning failures have high costs for countries, as well as the children involved. In a comprehensive review this year, two leading education researchers show that most of the economic returns to education are a return to the cognitive skills of the population, and not to the average levels—or quantity—of education attained (Hanushek and Woessman 2007). If two countries have the same average years of schooling but in one country average learning levels are higher, individual earnings, the distribution of income, and the long-term rate of economic growth will all be higher in that country.

While it has long seemed intuitively obvious that a year of schooling in Mali is not equal to a year of schooling in the Republic of Korea or Finland, it has never before been possible to "unpack" the differential quality element. Using a new data set that combines the results of all major international tests over the past 40 years, Hanushek and Woessman draw several important conclusions for education policy. First, they demonstrate that a large part of the higher incomes that more highly educated individuals earn, in both developed and developing countries, is a function of cognitive skill levels (as measured on international tests), rather than years of schooling completed. Second, they document a tight correlation across countries between the degree of earnings inequality in the labor force and the degree of dispersion in adult literacy scores across the population (Nickell 2004). While learning disparities do not *cause* income inequality, the research does suggest that policies to lessen gaps in average learning levels across different segments of the population may have direct and positive impacts on income distribution.

Finally, they find a connection between education quality and growth that "dwarfs the association between quantity of education and growth." A one standard-deviation increase in a country's average performance on international tests is associated with a 1–2 percentage point higher annual per capita GDP growth—a huge effect. Although small subsamples make these effects more tentative, Hanushek and Woessman also find that effects for developing countries (an increase of 2.29 percentage points per year) are higher than for OECD countries (1.7 percentage points per year), and that countries' trade openness and institutional quality significantly enhance the impacts.

Does it matter whether countries' average scores reflect broad-based education systems of reasonable quality or systems with a pinnacle of very high-scoring students? Both seem to be important. Countries' mean scores are highly correlated with the share of students who reach a threshold level of skills on international tests. In other words, countries' achievement of "education for all" by bringing all students to basic levels of literacy and numeracy is key for capturing the economic benefits of education. But the share of top performers is also important, and "seems to exert separately identifiable effects on economic growth." Hanushek and Woessman postulate that top performers afford an economy the capacity to innovate, and a large population with basic skills provides the ability to diffuse and apply new knowledge broadly.

What does this mean for the education MDG? First, it provides powerful economic arguments to support the goals of Education for All as universal primary completion with adequate levels of learning, and not simply completion of a target cycle of schooling. The 2000 Dakar Education for All goals were framed in these terms—universal coverage *and* learning—and many observers have urged that targets for the primary education MDG should explicitly include learning goals as well.

Second, it points to the value of measuring learning outcomes in relation to internationally benchmarked standards. The economic benefits identified were associated with learning levels that met an international threshold.

How many developing-country students meet this threshold today? Very few can be directly compared, as only 7 developing countries—and no low-income countries—participated in the latest OECD cross-country assessment, and only about 20 developing countries have participated in any major international assessment. However, figure 2.12 provides a graphic image of the large gap in performance between OECD and developing-country participants on recent exams to measure math, literacy, and thinking skills among 15-year-old students.

Poor as these country results are, they represent the upper bound of student learning in

FIGURE 2.12 Reading and math performance on the OECD PISA Exams, 2000 and 2003

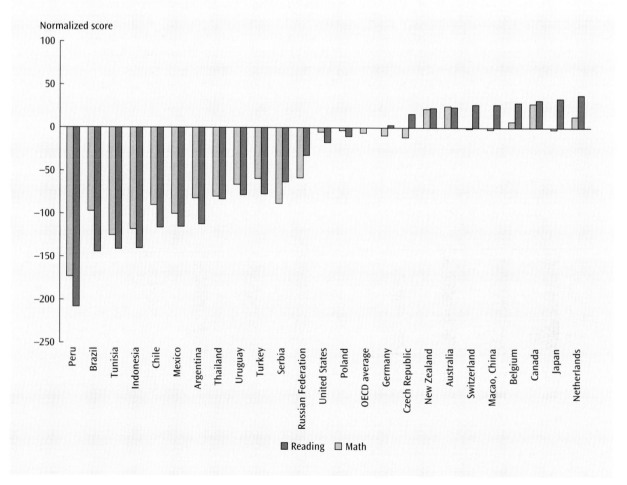

Source: PISA 2003 and PISA 2000.
Note: PISA = Program for International Student Assessment.

the developing world, because only relatively high-income developing countries have participated in any international tests to date, and in these countries, the pool of students tested represents only the relatively privileged 15-year-olds still in school at that age. In the regions where achievement of the education MDG is at greatest risk—Sub-Saharan Africa and South Asia—very few countries have participated in any OECD-benchmarked assessment. But figure 2.13 shows how even by age nine reading ability in developing countries can lag that in OECD countries by a significant margin. By the fourth grade in Argentina, Colombia, and Morocco, less than 50 percent of all children can read at the lowest-threshold-level of literacy, on an international test normed for OECD countries. In contrast, 96 percent or more of fourth graders in Sweden, Latvia, and the Netherlands read at this level (Greaney and Prouty 2007).

Although the level of "minimum literacy" in the regionally benchmarked assessment for Southern African countries cannot be directly compared with that of the IEA test, the results are similarly distressing. In several countries in the region, 50 percent or less of children are able to read by age 12. In Malawi, high dropout rates in primary school combined with low learning results in only an estimated 30 percent of children being able to read at that age.

Is there a quality-quantity trade-off in education? The fact that rapid enrollment expansion in developing countries is often associated with strains on quality leads to speculation that there is an inherent trade-off between schooling coverage and learning levels. But UNESCO's 2005 report on education quality, which looked carefully at the available evidence on learning outcomes, and other recent cross-country studies do not support this (UNESCO 2005, Crouch and Fasih 2005). In fact, cross-country data show a positive correlation between education coverage and average learning levels, at

FIGURE 2.13   Many children do not attain minimum learning levels

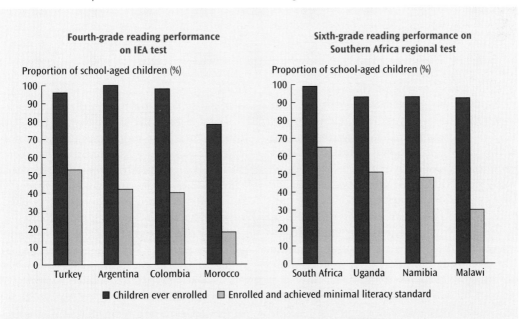

Source: Fourth-grade test: International Association for the Evaluation of Educational Achievement (IEA), Progress in International Reading Literacy (PIRLS) 2001; Sixth-grade test: Southern African Consortium for Monitoring Educational Quality (SACMEQ). Enrollment data: Demographic and Health Surveys.

least over the long term. There is no case of an education system with high average learning levels that has not also achieved universal primary completion and virtually universal secondary school completion. There are also cases of countries that have simultaneously increased schooling access and raised learning levels. There is no *inherent* tradeoff.

That does not mean it is easy to maintain school quality as enrollments swell, especially when enrollments increase dramatically, as in response to policy changes such as the elimination of school fees. But the essential fact that there is no inherent trade-off is important, because a large number of countries are still far from universal primary completion and many will need to find ways of scaling-up service delivery even faster from now to 2015 to reach the MDG. Slowing expansion would harm the poorest and most marginalized groups most. The evidence suggests that most developing countries are striving to universalize primary education as quickly as they can. The strategy must be to support their efforts to give adequate attention to quality and ensure that children learn. And even many countries which have reached or are on track to the MDG in terms of coverage must do more to improve learning, to equip youth with the literacy, numeracy, and critical thinking skills needed for full participation in civic life and economic productivity.

Support for measuring learning outcomes. The policies that can help countries achieve improvements in quality and learning at the same time as they expand access and completion have been analyzed comprehensively by UNESCO (GMR 2005), and other studies. A relevant question from the standpoint of MDG progress is whether donors are currently giving adequate support to developing countries' efforts to monitor student learning. Today, a developing country that wishes to benchmark its students' learning performance against that of other countries lacks good instruments for doing so. All of the currently available international tests have been developed for advanced countries. They do not provide useful information for developing countries because they tend to be too difficult. It is important that developing countries have access to evaluation and testing methodologies that allow them to link to performance in the developed world, but also provide good measures of the range of performance in their own populations.

One approach that has been proposed is the development of a set of global learning goals—a core set of literacy, numeracy, and critical thinking skills that children should master by the end of primary school (Filmer, Hasen, and Pritchett 2006). While in a world of global economic competition, the most relevant benchmark for learning is arguably a global one, there are many alternative ways to support a stronger focus on learning outcomes. An internationally normed subset of questions, for example, could be built into national or regionally benchmarked assessments. The important thing is to generate a valid measure of student learning levels that can be tracked over time and directly compared with results for other countries.

An important issue for cross-country comparisons in an MDG context is that the average learning levels achieved by children in school must be adjusted for the share of students not in the school system to generate a true picture of the average literacy and numeracy skills of the population. To do otherwise creates adverse incentives for expansion, particularly for marginalized students.

Regular tracking of student learning is also essential for establishing accountability systems in education that focus teachers, parents, and administrators on the right outcomes. When results are fed back to teachers, they become a tool for classroom improvement. When results are fed back to communities, they can strengthen local voice in school governance. And when results are tracked by system administrators, they help evaluate the effectiveness of education spending. Abundant research from developed countries and increasing evidence from developing countries shows a consistently weak correlation between higher spending and improved student learning (Hanushek and Kimko 2000;

Woessman 2003; Pritchett 2004; Hanushek and Luque 2003; Mizala and Romaguera 2002). This does not mean that learning can be improved *without* more resources, and there is some evidence that a minimum set of inputs (basic facilities, teacher presence, and the availability of books) is a threshold condition for education to occur (Duflo 2001). But it is evidence that many common and costly "input based" strategies for strengthening education systems—such as upgrading teacher qualifications or lowering class size—do not work. Only by tracking student results over time can school systems gauge whether teacher quality is truly improving, and which policies and investments aimed at making teachers perform better really produce results.

There are political and technical challenges to standardized learning measurement. Political challenges in part stem from the power that exposing student learning results can have in holding education stakeholders accountable. But there are also legitimate concerns in developing countries that OECD benchmarked tests do not measure their reality or their curriculum.

Designing valid and reliable tests is costly, takes time, and requires sophisticated skills. If a test is internationally benchmarked, sustained and intensive international cooperation is also required. For this reason, the approach being piloted in some developing countries—to use simple tests of reading fluency at the end of second grade—is a welcome development. Such tests are low cost, relatively easy to administer, and provide early feedback on literacy development that school systems can act on.

But such nationally oriented tests are not a substitute for more systematic tracking of learning *across* developing countries. Existing research points to the need for countries and donors to shift from spending and aid based on inputs to spending based on education results—and specifically, measurable improvement in student learning. There is a genuine global public goods dimension in cross-country assessment, and donor support is justified to underwrite its costs. The key is to develop new assessment instruments that are suitable for developing countries, but linked to existing international tests. However costly it might be to develop, pilot, and sustain such assessments, the sums would be small in relation to the billions of dollars in new aid being mobilized to support universal primary completion. Globally benchmarked assessments covering large numbers of developing countries would provide the strongest platform yet for research on "what works" to promote learning results in different country contexts.

Measuring learning outcomes per se does not improve education systems; it does not eliminate the political obstacles to key reforms or ensure that better policies are well implemented. Some OECD countries that regularly participate in internationally benchmarked assessments, such as the United States, have been notably unsuccessful in improving their results. But other countries have done so: the United Kingdom, Australia, and Finland are good examples. Clearly, testing is not a panacea. But it is an essential tool for countries that want their policy and program choices to be guided by evidence that they work. Such evidence holds crucial potential for more effective developing-country policies, more productive aid, and faster and more meaningful progress toward the education MDG.

Promoting Quality in Health

Quality in health can be measured in terms of the structure of supply, process, or outcomes. As in education, the most meaningful measures of a system's quality are the outcomes it produces. But in health, data on key outcomes such as child or maternal mortality are difficult to collect, slow to change, and heavily influenced by factors beyond health. Process data also present collection challenges. As a result, as in education, the most commonly used quality measure is inputs—such as the distribution of health clinics, drug supplies, and the quantity and qualifications of health providers—and is the basis for most health sector planning (Collier, Dercon, and Mackinnon 2003; Lavy and Germain 1994).

Much of the attention in relation to the health MDGs has focused on the challenge of scaling up one key input: health providers. The Joint Learning Initiative of the WHO and other health donors has estimated that large increases in doctors and nurses in the developing world will be needed to attain the health MDGs. In Africa alone, an estimated 1 million new health workers are required by 2015, to increase the current ratio of 1 provider per 1,000 people to a target of 2.5. While cross-country studies provide some evidence that provider density is correlated with services such as immunization rates and assisted births, it is equally clear from research that weak incentives for performance can drive a large wedge between the theoretical availability of providers and the quantity of care they actually deliver. Chaudhury and others (2006), for example, found an average provider absence rate of 35 percent in surprise visits to health facilities in six developing countries, with an absence rate for doctors in some rural areas reaching as much as 75 percent.

Measuring the quality of clinical practice. Some of the most recent research in health is going a step further, analyzing the extent to which even when providers are present, they may deliver suboptimal care. Drawing on creative strategies—doctor and patient interviews, direct observation of doctor-patient interactions, and vignettes (or the use of actors to simulate sample patient cases)—researchers are gathering direct estimates of provider quality through key process measures. The implications for attainment of the health MDGs are substantial. If health provider *availability* does not guarantee adequate care, strategies to achieve better health outcomes by training and recruiting more workers will fail. But if effective strategies exist for getting more performance out of existing providers, availability could greatly accelerate progress.

Recent studies have explored these issues in five countries with very different levels of economic development and very different health systems—India, Indonesia, Tanzania, Mexico, and Paraguay. There was substantial variation across and within countries, but the overall quality of care was low. In a disturbing number of cases, clinicians routinely misdiagnosed and mistreated common illnesses, not because of lack of training or medicines, but because they did not exert the effort necessary to find the correct diagnosis (Leonard, Masatu, and Vialou 2005).

In Tanzania, 33 percent of clinicians misdiagnosed a woman with pelvic inflammatory disease and 60 percent mistreated the condition. This disease—which is caused by untreated sexually transmitted diseases—makes a woman more susceptible to HIV/AIDS and more likely to spread the illness to partners if untreated. While 86 percent of clinicians correctly diagnosed a patient suffering from classic symptoms of TB, 67 percent mistreated the disease. Less than 20 percent of clinicians informed TB patients of the importance of taking medicine consistently, even though they knew that effective treatment of TB requires careful ongoing management (Leonard, Masatu, and Vialou 2005).

In India, doctors completed only 26 percent of the tasks medically required for a patient presenting with TB—the number one killer among infectious diseases in India—and only 18 percent of recommended tasks for a child with diarrhea (Das and Gertler 2007). Doctors in Tanzania completed less than 24 percent of the essential checklist for a patient with malaria (Leonard, Masatu, and Vialou 2005). In the face of major global efforts to curb HIV/AIDS, TB, and malaria, these data are troubling: the impact of substantially increased funding will clearly be blunted if clinicians in the target countries cannot diagnose patients who suffer from these illnesses or effectively treat them.

The important finding for policy makers is that large gaps can exist between what providers know and what they do. On questionnaires about their standard practice, many doctors knew the correct diagnostic protocols to follow for different patient conditions. But in actual practice—particularly for patients seen later in the day—adherence to protocols was low. In India and Tanzania, the biggest gaps were found in the public sector. While competency levels were often higher among public sector doctors (all doctors in this sector are medical board qualified), their "effort" was sharply lower than in the private or NGO sector (Das and Hammer 2004). As figure 2.14 shows, in India the increased value of competence in the public sector was completely offset by decreased effort. Although private doctors lacking the Indian medical board certification are significantly less well-trained than doctors in the public sector, the quality of care they delivered to patients was significantly better.

These findings offer two potentially important policy implications. First, they suggest that trying to improve health care delivery by raising training requirements, expanding medical schools, or other input-based policies countries often rely on may be an inefficient route to better health care performance. Second, it suggests that countries concerned about a "brain drain" of their trained physicians to OECD markets might be able to reduce those risks by setting national training requirements slightly lower than the rich countries' standards. These data suggest that there might be very little trade-off in terms of delivered health quality.

Institutional setting—along with incentives—makes a large difference for the quality of service delivered. In Tanzania, clinicians working in facilities with "high-powered incentives"—measured by factors such as the ability of facility managers to hire or fire personnel, set salaries, determine the number and types of staff who work for them, and the degree of financial independence at the facility level—were much more likely to perform up to their ability than equivalently trained and paid doctors in less autonomous facilities (Leonard, Masatu, and Vialou 2005).

Contracting for results. An increasing number of developing countries are experimenting with ways to inject "high-powered

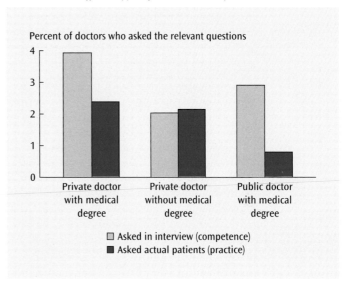

FIGURE 2.14 The quality of health care is not just a function of doctors' training
(percent of recommended diagnostic protocol followed by different types of doctors in India)

Percent of doctors who asked the relevant questions

☐ Asked in interview (competence)
■ Asked actual patients (practice)

Source: Das and Hammer 2004.

incentives" for performance into public health systems. One approach is to contract private providers for the delivery of public health services. While the first and most rigorously evaluated such experience is Cambodia (see box 2.8), contracting has also been tried on a fairly large scale in nine other countries. In a recent review of the experience, Loevinsohn and Harding (2005) conclude that contracting for primary health care services has been effective and can produce rapid improvements. Positive results have been achieved in a wide range of country settings and for a range of different services, from nutrition in Africa to primary health care in Guatemala. In most places where it has been tried, governments have subsequently decided to scale-up contracting more broadly. The biggest impacts generally have been for services that are relatively easy to deliver such as immunizations, vitamin A supplementation, and prenatal care. Services such as family planning and assisted deliveries have shown smaller changes, likely

---

BOX 2.8   Contracting for health services in Cambodia

As part of a major effort to expand and improve health service delivery, Cambodia since 1999 has contracted out to private bidders the management of government health services in five rural districts. In each district, contractors were required to provide a "Minimum Package" of preventive care, health promotion, and simple curative services. Contractors were also responsible for services at district hospitals, subdistrict health centers, and rural health posts. Performance was measured against eight service delivery indicators. Contracts were for a fixed period and inadequate performance could lead to sanctions and nonrenewal. The five districts covered 1.2 million people, 11 percent of Cambodia's population. All of the contractors were international NGOs.

Since the districts were randomly selected for the program, it has been possible to evaluate its impacts rigorously—in other words, to determine with confidence that the health delivery improvements seen in these districts were actually caused by the program.[a] Some of the effects have been large: immunization coverage increased by 21 percentage points, vitamin supplementation to children under age five increased by 42 percentage points, and antenatal care delivered to pregnant women increased by 36 percentage points. Contracting improved the management of government health centers, as measured by availability of 24-hour service, reduced staff absenteeism, increased supervisory visits, and continuous availability of supplies and equipment. It also led to lower out-of-pocket spending by patients, who shifted back to using public health facilities instead of private sector drug sellers and traditional healers. As the districts eligible for the experiment were in poor regions, this is an important equity effect. While measuring the impact on final health outcomes such as child mortality would require a larger-sized experiment, the researchers could conclude that health status in the five districts improved as a result of the program: both the average number of reported illnesses in a typical month and the incidence of diarrhea in children under five were reduced.

A cautionary note from Cambodia's experience is that even though some of the program's impacts were genuinely large, they were less than would have been estimated through a simple "before and after" comparison of health service delivery in the districts implementing the reform. This is because over the period of the contracting experiment, there was a strong general improvement in health system performance. The careful manner in which the government rolled out this program allowed for accurate estimate of its causal impacts, and more confidence about what can be expected now that it is being scaled-up further.

a. Bloom and others 2007.

---

because these imply more behavioral change on the part of patients.

In all cases where contractor performance was directly compared with government provision of the same services, contractors were more effective in expanding coverage and delivering quality care. In Hyderabad, India, for example, an NGO achieved a TB treatment completion rate that was 14 percentage points higher than the public clinic in a nearby area, and at a lower cost (Murthy and others 2001).

The cases to date provide suggestive evidence that the most successful approaches base the contracts on specified outputs and outcomes, rather than inputs, and give contractors autonomy over how they use resources to produce the contracted outcomes—including the ability to offer differential pay to the public sector health workers they supervise and to hire and fire with greater flexibility.

Contracting out services to private providers is not the only formula for strengthening performance incentives in health systems.

Rwanda is experimenting with performance-based contracting for both public and NG0 providers, using some of the same principles. The system pays facilities (which in turn pay individual providers) bonus payments for incremental improvements in basic health services and HIV/AIDS testing and treatment. Facilities have autonomy over how funds are used, including topping up staff salaries and freedom to raise outside sources of income, such as from user fees. Strong monitoring and auditing arrangements (including periodic surveys to track patient satisfaction) allow for verifying the quality of care and making payments conditional on quality. Argentina's innovative *Plan Nacer* program is similarly using bonus payments to create incentives for better quality maternal and child health services no matter where they are provided—in public, semi-public, or private facilities.

It is encouraging that countries such as Cambodia, Rwanda, and Argentina are not only developing new strategies to improve quality in health, but also rolling out reforms in a careful manner that permits rigorous evaluation of their impact. The creative new research exposing the large wedge between doctors' ability and their practice makes it clear that attaining the health MDGs in most developing countries will depend at least as much on getting better performance from providers as on scaling up their numbers.

Conclusions

From the vantage point of 2007, the stretch goals to promote human development progress set by the international community in 2000 have made an appreciable difference. They have put a significant number of developing countries on a faster trajectory to universal provision of basic health and education services. They have demonstrated the commitment of the rich world to mobilizing increased aid for specific human development goals. And they have given rise to a large number of new global institutions and programs to support these processes. Not all of these developments are unalloyed goods; there is

growing concern about the quality of rapidly expanding services, the "earmarking" of development dollars to specific diseases and goals, and the transactions and coordination costs associated with proliferating funding channels. But actions in each area could mitigate some of the problems and enhance the positive trends. Some of the most important are summarized below:

- *Intensified Focus on Learning.* The international community could strengthen the incentives for developing countries to keep focused on student learning and school quality as they pursue universal primary completion. There is a public goods argument for donors to support developing countries in defining a relevant set of basic literacy, numeracy, and critical thinking skills that should be attained by the end of primary school. International support could also help build appropriate national and regional assessment systems to track student learning in developing countries and permit them to benchmark their progress.

- *Health system strengthening.* There is an urgent need for scaled-up and stronger health systems in developing countries, to stretch absorptive capacity and avoid the risks that large amounts of needed aid are lost to mal-coordination and corruption. There is also need for appropriate incentives to improve outcomes, and actions to ensure that levels of support are sustainable and not distortionary at the macro level. The new World Bank Health, Nutrition, and Population (HNP) sector strategy commits the Bank to a central focus on health system strengthening, but it will require internal staffing changes and other actions to develop this potential fully.

- *Donor harmonization in health.* Action is needed to curb the transactions costs and coordination failures increasingly associated with verticalized and proliferating health programs. The way forward should be country-led processes that set clear national priorities in health and insist on more rapid progress toward the Paris Harmonization targets: donor alignment with national plans, joint supervision missions, use of national systems, and other goals.

■ *Monitoring results.* For too many MDG targets and in too many countries, lack of data makes it impossible to track progress. There are several sources of support for statistical strengthening in developing countries, including new initiatives since the MDGs were adopted, such as the Health Metrics Network, but collectively these efforts are not enough. Expanded donor support is needed for building countries' ability to monitor trends in key areas.

■ *Evaluating impact.* The key to faster MDG progress is basing policies, programs, and donor support on evidence of what works. Too few innovative programs in the developing world are rigorously evaluated today, and those that are often show that program impacts in reality are lower than advocates predicted. This is not bad news; it is the reality that explains why, in aggregate, "aid effectiveness" is not higher. Only rigorous evaluations—which establish that the program *caused* the observed results—can build a solid base for policy and program design. Because such evaluations are expensive and have a public good

element in that they benefit all countries, there is a strong case for increased donor support.

Notes

1. There is no official estimate for the end of 2006, but Peter Piot of UNAIDS expected the number would "probably approach 2 million" by year end (remarks on November 27, 2006, Washington DC).

2. Because the World Bank uses an exponential, rather than linear, method to model progress to MDG targets, these estimates of the number of countries and regions on track to the goal differ slightly from those of the UN Joint Monitoring Program.

3. In previous years, this report cited IMF public expenditure data for health and education in developing countries. In 2005, the Fund stopped collecting sector-level expenditure data, so GMR 2007 relies on data from UNESCO for education, and on WHO for health spending. Both series show numerous inconsistencies with IMF data (which we have reported previously), with particularly large inconsistencies for education. Country coverage of UNESCO's spending data is also much weaker than WHO's. For 2004, UNESCO's developing country coverage was extremely low, so the terminal years presented above for education and health are different.

Promoting Gender Equality and Women's Empowerment

The 2006 *World Development Report* acknowledges the importance of ensuring equal opportunities across population groups as an intrinsic aspect of development and as an instrument for achieving poverty reduction and growth (World Bank 2005). Noting that men and women have starkly different access to assets and opportunities in many countries around the world, the report refers to gender inequality as the archetypal "inequality trap," reproducing further inequalities with negative consequences for women's well-being, their families, and their communities. MDG3 reflects the strong belief by the development community that redressing gender disparities and empowering women is an important development objective on grounds of both fairness and efficiency.[1]

This chapter reviews the evidence on the relationship between gender equality, poverty reduction (MDG1), and growth. There is also compelling evidence that gender equality and women's empowerment are channels to attaining other MDGs—universal primary education (MDG2), lower under-five mortality (MDG4), improved maternal health (MDG5), and lower likelihood of contracting HIV/AIDS (MDG6).[2]

The chapter also tracks progress of countries toward meeting MDG3 since 1990, using the official MDG3 indicators. Because these indicators only partially capture the elements of gender equality, the chapter introduces five complementary indicators that provide a more complete and nuanced description of gender equality and women's empowerment. The indicators are measurable, actionable, and parsimonious; three of the five build on existing measures of other MDGs, so the data requirements for monitoring them are not onerous. Further, some of these complementary indicators (or similar measures) are being considered for inclusion in the MDGs as part of new targets for decent and productive work and for reproductive health services. Finally, the chapter extracts preliminary lessons from countries that have achieved high levels of—or fast progress toward—gender equality, but does not undertake a systematic analysis of policies. Countries that perform well on MDG3 illustrate that investments in equality in rights, resources, and voice can make a difference.

Thanks to the push to achieve universal primary education with gender-informed education policies, girls' enrollments at all levels of schooling have increased, and several countries have achieved gender parity in primary enrollments. Their success story suggests that concerted action can foster progress in gender equality not only in education but also in the economy and the society, where advances have been more modest.

Success in boosting girls' enrollment may offer important lessons for the unfinished agenda in education and the largely unaddressed agenda in the other domains of gender equality:

- Closing the gaps in well-being (health and education) and opportunities for girls and women in disadvantaged subgroups within nations who face multiple exclusions on the basis of their sex and their race, residence, ethnicity, caste, and disability. It is also essential to monitor progress in gender equality and women's empowerment for these subgroups.
- Giving priority to improving and monitoring gender equality and women's empowerment in Sub-Saharan Africa, which consistently lags behind in most areas measured by MDG3.
- Paying special attention to gender equality and women's empowerment issues in fragile states where progress on MDG3 is hampered both by slow economic advancement and gender-specific consequences of conflict.
- Scaling up significantly the collection and analysis of sex-disaggregated data to measure more accurately and fully the progress in achieving MDG3. Data on all six official indicators of MDG3 are available for only 59 out of 154 developing countries (for 2000–05), and even fewer countries have time series data that would allow tracking over time. For both the official and expanded list of indicators recommended in this chapter, only 41 countries have current (2000–05) information. This lack of data limits considerably the ability to monitor progress, learn from success, and, ultimately, to make informed decisions regarding scaling up investments.

Gender Equality and Economic Performance: A Framework

Gender equality does not necessarily mean equality of *outcomes* for males and females. Using the definition in the *World Develop-ment Report 2006*, gender equality means equal access to the "*opportunities* that allow people to pursue a life of their own choosing and to avoid extreme deprivations in outcomes"—that is, gender equality in rights, resources, and voice (World Bank 2001; World Bank 2005). Equality of rights refers to equality under the law, whether customary or statutory. Equality of resources refers to equality of opportunity, including equality of access to human capital investments and other productive resources and to markets. Equality of voice captures the ability to influence and contribute to the political discourse and the development process.

Figure 3.1 presents a framework that ties together key elements of gender equality. Gender inequality in rights, resources, and voice can surface in three domains: in the *household*, in the *economy and markets*, and in *society*. In the household, evidence suggests that increased gender equality between men and women changes the allocation of household expenditures, resulting in a larger share of resources devoted to children's education and health. Gender inequalities influence the distribution of household tasks, often limiting women's ability to work outside the home, as well as women's control over fertility decisions. In the market, gender inequality is reflected in unequal access to land, credit, and labor markets, and in significantly less access to new production technologies. In society, gender inequality is expressed as restrictions to women's participation in civic and political life. Finally, as figure 3.1 shows, in addition to improving individuals' lives, increased gender equality can contribute to better aggregate economic performance.

These long-term benefits, of course, come with costs in the short run. Policies to achieve gender equality (for example, introducing quotas in representation in parliament or labor legislation prohibiting discriminatory practices) could have political costs for their proponents when some groups win and some lose. Some policies may also have economic costs that come from unintentionally under-

FIGURE 3.1 Gender equality, domains of choice, and economic performance: A framework

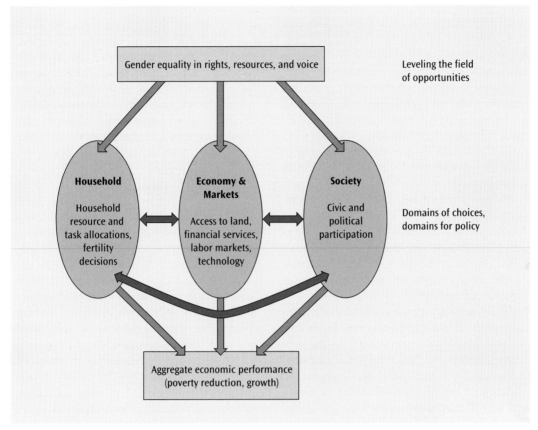

Source: World Bank staff.

cutting individual incentives in the name of gender equality. These costs are additional to the budgetary expenditures associated with implementing the policies. It is important to keep these short-term trade-offs well in mind in assessing specific policies.

Gender Equality, Poverty, and Economic Growth

Poverty incidence tends to be lower in countries with more gender equality. This relationship is quite robust to various measures of poverty and of gender equality—in terms of the latter, the female-to-male ratio of sex-specific Human Development Indices, the ratio of the gender-related development index to the human development index (GDI-HDI ratio), and the gender empowerment measure

(GEM).[3] Economic growth also appears to be positively correlated with gender equality. This correlation is robust to changes in the length of the period over which per capita GDP growth rates are averaged and to two alternative measures of gender equality (the female-to-male ratio of sex-specific HDI indices and the GDI-HDI ratio).[4] When gender equality is measured by the GEM, however, the relationship is not statistically significant.

Simple correlations across countries—while suggestive—do not imply a causal relationship between gender equality and poverty reduction or economic growth: gender equality could "cause" faster growth and accelerated poverty reduction, but faster development could also spur improvements in gender equality. Alternatively, the causal arrows may point in both directions, or a third factor may be responsible for both faster development and greater improvements in gender equality—perhaps better governance.

Regression analyses that control for other (possibly confounding) factors have also been employed, although the estimated coefficients by themselves do not imply causality. Cross-country growth regressions, building on widely accepted macroeconomic growth models, have examined the link between greater equality in educational opportunities and growth rates or levels of per capita income.[5]

Recent studies using cross-country regressions typically find that female education has a larger impact on growth than male education (Abu-Ghaida and Klasen 2004).[6] Klasen (2002), for example, finds that the direct and indirect effects of gender inequality in educational attainment account for 38 percent of the 2.5 percentage point gap in growth rates between South Asia and East Asia, 17 percent of the 3.3 percentage point gap between Sub-Saharan Africa and East Asia, and 45 percent of the 1.9 percentage point gap between the Middle East and North Africa and East Asia.[7]

Growth regressions have serious limitations, however, and those that use gender-disaggregated data are no exception. One serious limitation is the ad hoc nature of extensions to the augmented Solow model, which underlies growth regressions. Variables have been added to capture economic openness, government spending, political instability, ethnic diversity, and a host of other potential determinants of growth—frequently with little or no justification in economic theory. A second weakness is a simultaneity problem that results in biased results: gender equality affects growth, but growth presumably also affects gender equality, because the economic pressure in rapidly growing markets makes gender discrimination much more costly. Finding appropriate identification factors to address this bias is extremely difficult, which leads to a search for other evidence.

Cross-country correlations and growth regressions can be suggestive, but they do not explain *how* gender equality might be associated with poverty reduction or faster growth. There are several *pathways* through which gender equality in rights, resources, and voice stimulate productivity, earnings, and better child development outcomes, thus generating better development outcomes in an economy. Figure 3.2 depicts the pathways of women's labor force participation and earnings (identified by dashed arrows) and children's well-being (identified by solid arrows).

Women's Labor Force Participation, Productivity, and Earnings

Whether engaged in self-employment or wage employment, working women contribute to household income and expenditure. In poor households, such contributions can be crucial for keeping the household out of poverty; this is a reason to increase access to education, markets (labor, land, credit), and technology. This increased access can contribute to current poverty reduction and economic growth through higher consumption and to future poverty reduction through the impact on children's accumulation of human capital and the potential impact on aggregate saving (the dashed arrows in figure 3.2).[8]

Women face many constraints at home and in the marketplace when they decide to seek paid employment. Numerous studies point to women's reproductive role as affecting female labor force participation, in general, and work for pay, in particular. In the Kyrgyz Republic, for example but not atypically, 24.8 percent of women reported that "housekeeping, taking care of children, sick persons, or the elderly" kept them from working outside the home, but only 1.5 percent of men reported these reasons (Morrison and Lamana 2006). Besides child care, women also face the time burden of domestic tasks, especially collecting water and firewood. In rural areas of Burkina Faso, Uganda, and Zambia the potential time savings from locating a potable water source within 400 meters of all households range from 125 hours per household per year to 664 (Barwell 1996)—time that could be used to work for pay.

FIGURE 3.2   Women's earnings, children's well-being, and aggregate poverty reduction and economic growth—The pathways

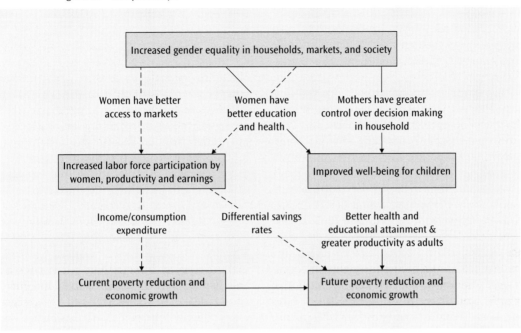

Source: World Bank staff.

Wage gaps and discrimination against women in labor markets may lower labor force participation, both contemporaneously and for future generations. The contemporaneous effect occurs as the wage loss due to discrimination persuades some women to stay at home rather than engage in paid work. The wage loss due to discrimination will also cause parents to systematically underinvest in the education of girls relative to boys (see Anderson and others 2003 for evidence on Malaysia). The segregation of women into low-paying occupations may be another important driver of underinvestment in girls' education. But empirical documentation of the impact of these two disincentives to female labor for participation has been limited, and further research is needed.

For self-employment, imperfections and discrimination in other markets constitute barriers for women. If access to inputs such as land, credit, capital, and technology is limited for noneconomic reasons, women's productivity and earnings in self-employment will

be lower than those of self-employed men. These lower potential earnings may discourage women from entering self-employment.

For households dependent on agriculture, land is the most important productive asset. The limited evidence available, however, indicates that the distribution of land ownership is heavily skewed toward men. For example, in a set of Latin American countries, roughly 70–90 percent of formal owners of farmland are men (Deere and Leon 2003). When women do own farmland, their holdings are typically smaller than men's.[9] Similar evidence is found for Sub-Saharan Africa (Doss 2005; Udry 1996; Quisumbing and others 2004). The evidence also clearly points to the importance of access to land and land size for increasing income.[10]

When they do have access to land, women frequently have less secure tenure rights. For example, under customary law in much of Sub-Saharan Africa, permanent land rights are held by men, typically male household heads. In contrast, women traditionally held (strong) usufruct rights to individual plots offered by men (Lastarria-Cornheil 1997). Land redistribution reforms and land titling and registration programs have, in many cases, either maintained the rights status quo or weakened women's rights (Jacobs 2002; Agarwal 1994; Agarwal 1993; Lastarria-Cornheil 1997).[11]

Most studies find that women are not more likely to be rejected for loans or be subject to higher interest rates by lenders, but they are often less likely to apply for loans than men, partly because they do not have land, property, or other assets to offer as collateral (Baydas and others 1994; Storey 2004; Ratusi and Swamy 1999; Buvinic and Berger 1990). As a result, in both Malawi and Bangladesh, women are more likely than men to face constraints to credit, as measured by credit limits (the maximum amount individuals report they can borrow from various sources) and unused credit lines (the difference between the credit limit and amounts borrowed) (Diagne and others 2000). But when women are the direct beneficiaries of credit rather than men, the impact of credit on various measures of household welfare is greater.

Technological innovation and adoption have undoubtedly been key drivers of increases in productivity and household incomes. Most empirical studies of the determinants of technology adoption and diffusion in developing countries examine the adoption decision at the level of the household. They have not examined how female farmers fare relative to male farmers in terms of schooling and literacy (considered to be critical for processing relevant new information); access to information (through social networks and agricultural extension services); access to credit, labor, and commodity markets; risk exposure and risk aversion; and land size and land rights.[12] Most of the evidence suggests that many of the barriers to adoption are not related to the characteristics of the technology, but originate in other markets relevant for the adoption decision, such as land, labor, credit, and information. For example, Croppenstedt and others (2003) find that female-headed households in Ethiopia have

significantly lower endowments of land, and that land size is a significant positive determinant of fertilizer use.

Children's Well-Being

Women's education, health, and greater control over household resource allocation improve children's well-being (figure 3.2, solid arrows). Studies from developing and developed countries consistently show that when mothers have greater control over resources, more resources are allocated to food and to children's health (including nutrition) and education. In Ghana, an increase in the share of women's assets raises household spending on food and children's schooling (Doss 1996). Similarly, in Côte d'Ivoire, the higher women's share of cash income, the higher is the household budget share allocated to food (Hoddinott and Haddad 1995). In Ghana, in years when the production of women's crops is higher, the household spends a large share of its budget on food and on private goods for women; in years when the production of men's crops is higher, however, the household spends more on goods consumed by men (Duflo and Udry 2004).

Better nutritional status of mothers is associated with better child health. In Brazil maternal height has a large impact on infants' height (length) while paternal height has no impact (Thomas and Strauss 1992). One way this happens is that mothers who are underweight or who suffer from micronutrient deficiency before pregnancy are more likely to give birth to low-birth-weight infants (Galloway and Anderson 1994).

The benefits of mother's education for children are well known; they flow through several pathways:

- Safer health and hygiene practices, which improve children's health (Cebu Study Team 1991).
- More time and resources for children's health and education (Brown 2006).
- More exposure to information from a wider range of sources, and higher ability to process and act on the information received

(Webb and Block 2004; Thomas, Strauss, and Henriques 1991; Caldwell 1979).

- Better nutritional outcomes, in part because of higher ability to process and act on information (Glewwe, Jacoby, and King 2001; Alderman, Hoddinott, and Kinsey 2006; Behrman and Rosenzweig 2004).

- Fewer children, reducing household dependency ratios and increasing per-capita consumption expenditure (Schultz 1997, 2002).

- Higher labor force participation and earnings, which in turn increase household consumption expenditures (see review in Schultz 2002).

- Greater bargaining power within the household and therefore a higher ability to act on preferences for investing in children (World Bank 2001).

Several studies have estimated the welfare effects of participation in programs where women are the main direct beneficiaries. In their study of microcredit programs in Bangladesh, and after controlling for self-selection in program participation, Pitt and Khandker (1998) find that female borrowing has a larger impact on children's school enrollment than male borrowing. Exploiting a natural experiment in which black families became eligible for large old-age pension payments in South Africa, Duflo (2003) finds that girls who live with a grandmother who is eligible to receive pension benefits are healthier (measured by anthropometric measures) than those who live with a grandmother who is not eligible to receive pension benefits; in contrast, the effects were not statistically significant for households in which the pension was received by a man. Comparing the marginal effect on household expenditure patterns of transfers received by mothers through *Oportunidades*—a conditional cash transfer program in Mexico initially implemented as a randomized social experiment—with the marginal effect of other sources of household income, Rubalcava and others (2004) find that cash transfers from the program increased the household budget shares allocated to children's schooling, clothing, and protein-rich foods.[13]

Given the evidence linking increases in women's productivity and earnings to lower household poverty and better outcomes for children, it is clear that barriers to women's labor force participation, productivity, and earnings also constrain poverty reduction. Given the weaker evidence linking increased women's productivity and incomes to faster growth, it is less certain that removing those barriers will generate a growth dividend. Nevertheless, it is difficult to imagine that higher female labor force participation and earnings would not lead to higher levels of total output and per capita output. Similarly, increases in productivity and earnings in health and education, and in control over resources, lead both to better child development outcomes in the present and to an intergenerational transmission of earnings capability that improves the prospects for future poverty reduction and growth.

Monitoring Progress Toward MDG3 Using the Official Indicators

Progress toward attaining MDG3 is measured by the target and four indicators defined in the Millennium Declaration (table 3.1). The target is "the elimination of gender disparities in primary and secondary education, preferably by 2005, and at all levels of education no later than 2015." The target and the first two indicators measure progress in gender equality in the household, the third measures progress in the economy generally, and the fourth measures progress in society. They provide important, albeit incomplete, measures of achievements (since 1990) in gender equality for the three domains identified in the framework in figure 3.1.

Progress in the Household Domain: School Enrollment and Literacy

Through concerted efforts by government, civil society, and the development community, girls' enrollments in all levels of schooling rose significantly in the last decade. Indeed, thanks to these efforts, most low-income countries made substantial progress during the 1990s in reaching gender parity in primary school enrollments and literacy (Lewis and Lockheed 2006; EFA Global Monitoring Report 2007). Between 1990 and 2005, girls' enrollment in primary education increased in virtually all regions; the sole exception was East Asia and the Pacific, where girls' gross enrollment rate already exceeded 100 percent in the early 1990s (figure 3.3). Girls' enrollment in secondary school increased as well.

Gains in girls' secondary school enrollment were notable in East Asia and the Pacific, Latin America and the Caribbean, and Middle East and North Africa. This progress is quite remarkable and shows the responsiveness of girls' school enrollments to gender-informed policy interventions such as stipends, conditional cash transfers, and vouchers.

These improvements in girls' enrollment helped increase gender parity ratios. Figure 3.4 shows that between 1990 and 2005, there were notable improvements in gender parity ratios in enrollments at all levels of schooling,

TABLE 3.1 Official indicators for MDG3

Household	Economy and market	Society
Ratio of girls' to boys' enrollment in primary, secondary, and tertiary education[a]	Share of women in wage employment in the nonagricultural sector	Proportion of seats held by women in national parliaments
Ratio of literate females to males among 15–24-year-olds		

Source: United Nations 2003.
a. Measured using gross enrollment rates.

FIGURE 3.3 Progress in girls' enrollment rates between 1990 and 2005

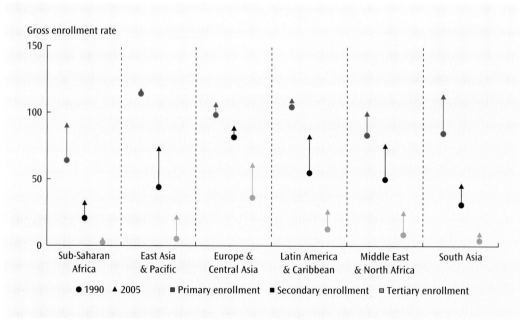

Source: World Development Indicators 2006.

FIGURE 3.4   Trends in gender parity in enrollment and literacy rates, 1990 and 2005

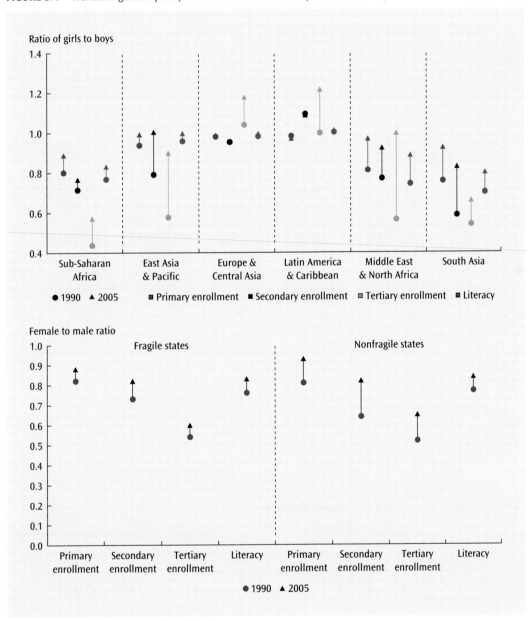

Source: World Bank Indicators (top); World Development Indicators 2006 (bottom).
Note: The regional averages are calculated using the earliest value between 1990 and 1995 and the latest value between 2000 and 2005 for each country. The averages are weighted by the country population size in 2005. In the second figure, trend is shown for countries that were fragile states in the 2000–05 period. For fragile states, data are available for 25 countries for primary enrollment, 22 for secondary enrollment, 8 for tertiary enrollment, and 13 for literacy. For nonfragile comparator countries, corresponding sample sizes are 36, 31, 21, and 25.

particularly in regions that had large disparities at the beginning of the period.

Combining performance in primary and
secondary enrollments, by 2005, 83 developing countries (out of 106 with data) had
met the intermediate MDG3 target of parity
in primary and secondary enrollment rates
(table 3.2).[14] Most of these countries are in
regions where enrollment has historically
been high—East Asia and the Pacific, Europe
and Central Asia, and Latin America and the
Caribbean. In the Middle East and North
Africa, most countries met the target by 2005,
but this region also included 3 countries (out
of 11 with data) with significant female disadvantages in enrollment. In Sub-Saharan
Africa, less than one-quarter of all countries
met the target by 2005.

Among 14 fragile states with data, five
countries met the target by 2005. Poor data
availability for this group of countries makes
it difficult to accurately compare their progress with that of nonfragile states. However,
an analysis of averages for countries that have
data for the two periods shows that, as compared to nonfragile states, fragile states made
only modest progress in moving toward gender parity in enrollments (figure 3.4).

Despite significant improvements in girls'
primary school enrollment, half of all countries
in South Asia failed to meet the target because
of low gender parity in secondary school enrollment. In South Asia, Bangladesh and Sri Lanka
are notable for achieving parity.

In 2005 the female tertiary enrollment rate
lagged behind the male rate in 63 countries (of
130 countries with data) and exceeded the male
rate in 65 countries. Female disadvantage was
evident mainly in Sub-Saharan Africa, South
Asia, and in fragile states. Male disadvantage
was notable in Middle East and North Africa
(Algeria, Iran, Jordan, and Libya), East Asia
and the Pacific (the Philippines and Thailand),
Latin America and the Caribbean (Honduras,
Nicaragua, Panama), and Europe and Central Asia. Reflecting the legacy of the Soviet
Union and historically high enrollment rates
in Europe and Central Asia, countries there
had high female tertiary enrollment rates that
exceeded male enrollment rates.

The education system's ability to deliver
basic literacy skills and progress in school
enrollments over the years has resulted in
higher literacy rates and greater gender parity
among youth (ages 15–24). But gender gaps
remain: UNESCO estimates that of the nearly
137 million illiterate youths in the world, 63
percent were female (UNESCO, EFA Global
Monitoring Report, 2005). The female-to-
male literacy ratio was lowest in Sub-Saharan

TABLE 3.2 Regional performance in attaining the primary and secondary enrollment target by 2005

	Achieved target by 2005	On track to achieve target by 2015	Off track or unlikely to achieve target by 2015	No data	Total
Sub-Saharan Africa	10	1	16	21	48
East Asia and the Pacific	13	0	0	11	24
Europe and Central Asia	22	0	1	4	27
Latin America and the Caribbean	27	0	0	4	31
Middle East and North Africa	8	0	3	3	14
South Asia	3	0	2	3	8
Total	83	1	22	46	152
of which: Fragile states	5	0	9	21	35

Source: World Bank estimates using data on enrollments between early 1990s and 2004/2005.
Note: The column showing countries with no data indicates the number of countries with missing data either at the start of the period or at the
end of the period or both. Of the 49 non-fragile low-income countries, 25 had met the target by 2005, 1 was on track to meet the target by 2015, 9
were unlikely to meet the target, and 14 had no data.

Africa, Middle East and North Africa, and South Asia—regions that also had female disadvantages in primary and secondary enrollment (figure 3.4). In 25 countries in these regions, there were fewer than 80 literate young women for every 100 literate young men. The ratio was lowest in Yemen and Afghanistan, where only 36 young women were literate for every 100 literate young men.

The Unfinished Education Agenda

Despite the considerable success in increasing girls' enrollment and improving gender parity ratios at all levels of schooling, several challenges remain.

Fragile states and countries unlikely to attain the enrollment target. For the 23 countries that did not meet the enrollment target by 2005, the World Bank estimates, based on the rate of change in the ratios over the 1990s, that 22 countries are unlikely to achieve the target by 2015; 16 of these countries are in Sub-Saharan Africa (table 3.2). This list includes 9 low-income countries such as Benin and Burkina Faso, where improvements in gender parity ratios in the 1990s might not compensate for large pre-existing gender disparities. The list also includes 9 fragile states (all in Sub-Saharan Africa).

Disadvantaged and excluded groups. A second challenge is uncovered when average national gender parity ratios are disaggregated by income, location, race, ethnicity, disability, or other features that identify disadvantaged or socially excluded populations within a country. Large gender gaps in education and literacy in rural areas, among minority groups or lower-income quintiles may explain why some countries have not reached the gender parity target (Bolivia, Cambodia, Ecuador, Guatemala, Lao PDR, Morocco, and Pakistan). For education and literacy, the female disadvantage is always larger in rural areas and among lower-income households (figure 3.5). This is further accentuated in countries that have not reached overall gender parity in school enrollments (largely in Sub-Saharan Africa and Middle East and North Africa).

It has been estimated that of the 60 million girls not in primary school in 2002, 70 percent were from excluded groups (UNESCO Institute for Statistics 2005). In Bolivia, household survey data show gender gaps in school attainment among indigenous children but not among non-indigenous children (figure 3.6). Although boys and girls have similar profiles at ages 7–13, attainment rates for indigenous girls already start to decline at age 9, with a faster decline after age 13 (Duryea, Galiani, Nopo, and Piras 2006). Even in countries that have attained the gender parity target in education, girls' enrollment in some subgroups continues to lag behind that of boys' (for example, in Chile, Mexico, and Panama). Gender parity ratios in school enrollments and literacy thus need to be disaggregated by characteristics related to disadvantage and exclusion, and targeted policies are needed to increase the school enrollments of girls from disadvantaged groups.

Levels not just ratios. A third challenge is that the ratio of girls to boys in enrollment is silent on levels of enrollment. Although all regions increased their secondary school enrollments since 1990, no region showed universal enrollment in secondary education in 2005 (figure 3.3). Only four regions had two-thirds or more of their eligible population in secondary school in 2005: Europe and Central Asia with 86 percent, Latin America and the Caribbean with 70 percent, Middle East and North Africa with 66 percent, and East Asia and Pacific with 64 percent.[15] In both South Asia and Sub-Saharan Africa, fewer than half of secondary-age students were enrolled (48 percent and 32 percent, respectively). Efforts to increase school enrollments, especially in secondary education, need to be informed by gender equality concerns and scaled up in regions with lagging enrollment rates (see box 3.1).

Transitions from one level to the next and from school to work. Promoting equality in education opportunities involves entering the education system at primary level, progressing through to higher levels, and making the transition to the labor market. But the offi-

FIGURE 3.5 Average youth literacy rates in Africa conceal rural-urban disparities

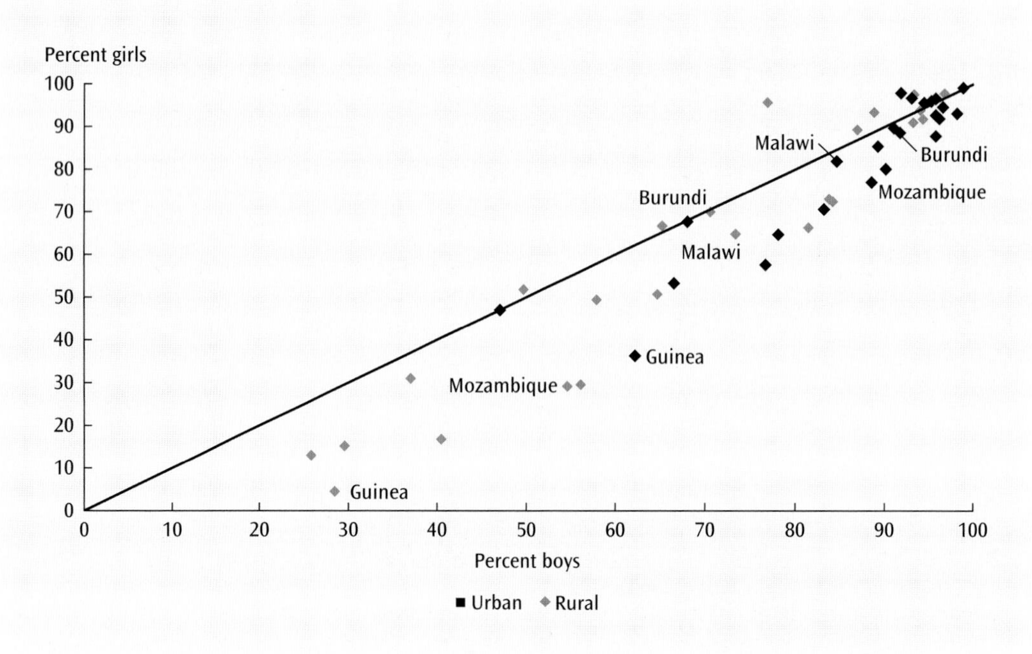

Percent girls

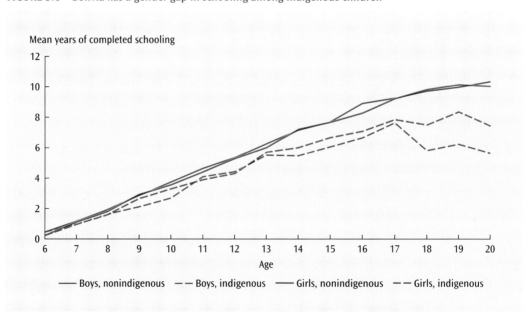

Source: World Bank staff estimates using household survey data from 24 Sub-Saharan African countries. Four countries labeled for illustrative purposes.

FIGURE 3.6 Bolivia has a gender gap in schooling among indigenous children

Source: Duryea, Galiani, Nopo, and Piras 2006.

cial MDG3 indicators measure only parity in school participation at each level. They do not capture potential gender disparities in transition from one level of schooling to the next, in the quality of what is learned in school, and in the transition from school to work.

Progress in the Economy and in Society: Nonagricultural Wage Employment and Political Participation

The MDG3 indicator in the economy and market is the share of women in nonagricultural wage employment (with no set tar-

get). Women's share of nonagricultural wage employment increased in all regions in 1990–2005; this increase was modest, however, with significant variation across regions and countries (figure 3.7). In 2005 the share of women in nonagricultural employment was highest in Europe and Central Asia (47 percent) and lowest in Middle East and North Africa (20 percent). In Latin America and the Caribbean and East Asia and Pacific, it exceeded 40 percent. Women's share of nonagricultural wage employment was highest in the highly urbanized upper-middle-income countries (43 percent) and lowest in the still predominantly

---

BOX 3.1 "Good" parity levels may hide huge enrollment challenges

Gender parity ratios say nothing about absolute levels of enrollment. A ratio of one (perfect equality) may indicate "equality of deprivation" rather than equality of opportunity. In Haiti the parity ratio in secondary enrollment rates was 1.03 in 2003, but only 20 percent of both girls and boys in Haiti were enrolled in secondary school (box figure). In such an environment, the challenge is to boost enrollments while maintaining gender parity.

Parity ratios can be at high and low secondary enrollments

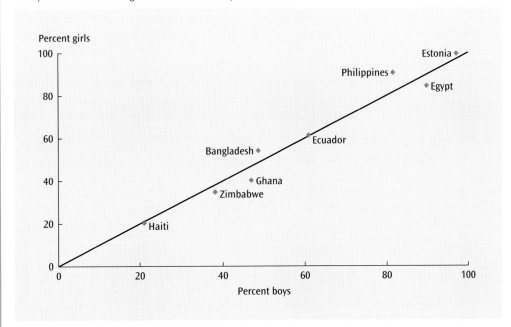

Source: World Development Indicators 2006.

FIGURE 3.7 Progress in share of women in nonagricultural wage employment and proportion of seats in parliament held by women, by region

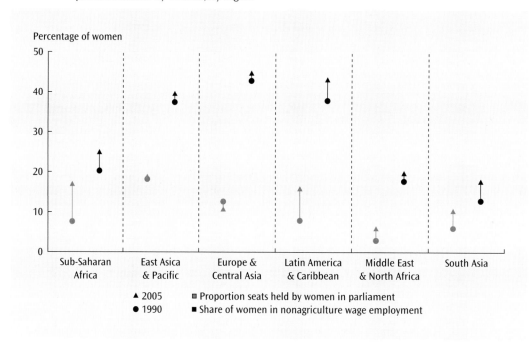

Source: World Development Indicators 2006. The regional averages are calculated using the earliest value between 1990 and 1995 and the latest value between 2000 and 2005 for each country. The averages are weighted by the country population size in 2005.

rural low-income countries (30 percent). In 15 countries, mostly in Europe and Central Asia, women dominated nonagricultural wage work. Women also dominated this work in Cambodia, Honduras, and Vietnam—countries where recent growth in export-oriented manufacturing industries increased the demand for female workers. For 20 countries in Sub-Saharan Africa, South Asia, and Middle East and North Africa, women's share was below 20 percent.

Trends and patterns in this indicator are difficult to interpret without taking into account the circumstances in each country—such as the share of nonagricultural employment as a percentage of total employment. A favorable score on this indicator might, on the surface, seem to indicate equitable conditions for women in labor markets, but it may capture conditions for only a very small proportion of the total labor force (see the following section for a discussion of the limitations of this indicator).[16]

Like the education indicators, the average share in nonagricultural wage employment also conceals inequalities within countries. In several countries of Latin America, indigenous and Afro-descendent women, who have significantly fewer years of education than other women, are also less likely to be employed in nonagricultural paid employment (figure 3.8). For example, nearly 60 percent of all women engaged in nonagricultural paid work in Bolivia in 2002 were nonindigenous, a percentage that far exceeds the population share of nonindigenous women. Duryea and Genoni (2004) find that in Bolivia, Brazil, Guatemala, and Peru, indigenous and Afro-descendant women are overrepresented in low-paying and informal jobs.

The fourth official MDG3 indicator is the proportion of seats held by women in national parliaments (with no set target). Between 1990 and 2005 all regions except Europe and Central Asia saw an increase in the proportion of women's seats in national parliament, but starting from low levels (figure 3.7). However, in no region did the average proportion exceed 25 percent, at either the beginning of the period or the end.

Quotas to increase women's presence in parliament (candidate quotas and reserved seats) were adopted by a large number of countries during the 1990s. By 2005, more than 40 countries had introduced electoral quotas. Because of quotas, countries like Argentina, Costa Rica, Mozambique, Rwanda, and South Africa have reached levels of women's parliamentary representation comparable to those in Nordic countries (Ballington and Karam 2005). However, quota rules are not sufficient by themselves to ensure increased participation by women; implementation and enforcement are key. In addition to quotas at the national level, increasing women's opportunities to participate in local politics can increase the number of women who are able to participate at the national level.

Strengthening the Monitoring of Gender Equality and Women's Empowerment

While the official indicators for MDG3 cover the three domains of society, economy/markets, and the household, they suffer from four serious shortcomings. First, the official MDG3 indicators only partially capture gender equality and empowerment in the areas they are designed to measure: education, employment, and political participation. Education enrollment rates say nothing about equality in learning or educational outcomes. The share of women in nonagricultural wage employment is of limited relevance for low-income countries where wage employment is not a main source of jobs. It does not capture many dimensions of job quality (Grown and others 2005), nor does it quantify the serious barriers that may inhibit women from participating in labor markets: time burdens of domestic tasks; limited availability of child care; lower educational attainment (in some

FIGURE 3.8 Share of women in nonagricultural wage work by ethnicity

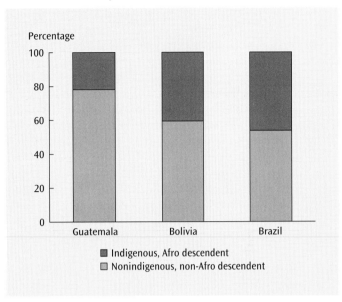

Source: World Bank staff calculations using household survey data from Guatemala (2002), Bolivia (2002), and Brazil (2001).

regions); wage gaps (relative to men); limited access to complementary inputs such as credit, capital, and technology; and the impact of law and custom on women's ability to work outside the home (Morrison, Raju, and Sinha 2007). And political participation is captured only at the national level, not at provincial or local levels where access to women's decision making is also important.

Second, the official indicators do not monitor key elements of gender equality such as health outcomes and disparities in access to productive resources such as land, credit, and technology. Health outcomes are a particularly important determinant of well-being and productivity. Although indicators for other MDGs measure performance on health (MDGs 4, 5, and 6), they are not designed to monitor progress on gender equity in health status.

Third, while MDG3 refers to the promotion of *both* gender equality and women's empowerment, the official indicators are far better at measuring gender equality than empowerment. Gender equality is a measure of the rights, resources, and voice enjoyed by women *relative* to those enjoyed by men. Three of the official four indicators (ratio of girls' to boys' enrollment rates, ratio of literate females to males among 24-year-olds, and share of women in wage employment in the nonagricultural sector) measure the status of women relative to men, rather than whether women are empowered in an absolute sense—that is, whether they have the ability to exercise options, choice, control, and power.[17] Knowing, for example, that girls are equally likely to be enrolled in secondary schools as boys indicates gender equality but not necessarily empowerment if only a small percentage of girls are enrolled (box 3.1).[18] Important elements of empowerment not captured by the official MDG3 indicators include the ability of women to work for pay (economic empowerment) and the ability to control their own fertility.[19]

In addition to being poor measures of empowerment, changes in the indicators based on parity ratios are difficult to interpret (Grown 2006). Increases in female-to-male ratios can result from a fall in male rates with female rates remaining constant, or from a decline in both female and male rates with male rates declining faster, or from female rates increasing faster than male rates. While rising female rates of school enrollment or lit-

eracy are undoubtedly welcome, falling rates of male enrollment or literacy are not.

Finally, national-level indicators—whether parity ratios or absolute levels—can mask inequalities between groups.[20] Improvements in aggregate enrollment ratios, for example, may hide the fact that girls (or in some cases, boys) belonging to socially excluded groups in the population fare much less well. Thus it is critical to disaggregate indicators by characteristics related to disadvantage and exclusion to monitor countries' performance—and to develop targeted interventions not just at the national level, but also for particular subgroups.

A Proposal for Strengthening the Official Indicators

The shortcomings of the official indicators for monitoring progress in attaining MDG3 are widely recognized (see, for example, the report of the UN Millennium Project Task Force on Education and Gender Equality). In response, this chapter recommends that countries consider monitoring five additional indicators complementary to the official MDG indicators, to better measure gender equality (table 3.3). These indicators meet three criteria: data availability (wide country coverage), strong link to poverty reduction and growth,

TABLE 3.3 Recommended additional indicators for MDG3

Household		Economy and markets
Modifications of official MDG indicators	**Additional indicators**	**Additional indicators**
Primary completion rate of girls and boys (MDG 2)[a]	Percentage of 15- to 19-year-old girls who are mothers or pregnant with their first child[b]	Labor force participation rates among women and men aged 20–24 and 25–49[b]
Under-five mortality rate for girls and boys (MDG4)		
Percentage of reproductive-age women, and their sexual partners, using *modern* contraceptives (MDG6)		

Source: World Bank staff.
a. Recommended by UN Millennium Project Task Force on Education and Gender Equality.
b. Under consideration by Inter-Agency and Expert Group for MDGs.

and amenability to policy intervention. Indicators that met all three criteria but were highly correlated with other indicators were dropped from the list.[21]

This proposed list draws on the recommendations of the UN Millennium Project Task Force, but is more parsimonious in its recommendations—both because it explicitly takes into account data availability and collinearity issues, and because of the high costs associated with imposing additional monitoring burdens on already taxed national statistical offices.[22]

Four of the five indicators monitor gender equality in the household; the remaining indicator monitors gender equality in the economy. No additional indicators are recommended to monitor gender equality in society, because none of the indicators considered for inclusion meet the criteria of data availability. Three of the recommended indicators are modifications of official indicators already being monitored as part of the MDGs.

Additional Indicators for the Household Domain

EDUCATION

Primary school completion rates. As mentioned above, the official MDG3 indicator of school enrollment ratios is a far better measure of gender equality than of women's empowerment; it does not indicate whether enrolled students go on to complete primary school—the outcome that brings immense benefits for development. Thus this chapter recommends supplementing the official MDG3 indicators with primary school completion rates for girls and boys.[23] This indicator (without sex disaggregation) is currently monitored as part of MDG2 on attainment of universal primary education, and sex-disaggregated data are reported annually by the World Bank and UNESCO.

Primary school completion is measured as the number of students in the last primary grade minus repeaters in this grade as a proportion of the number of children at the expected graduation age.[24] Girls are less likely than boys to complete the first schooling cycle, particularly in South Asia, where the primary completion rate is estimated at 90 percent for boys and 83 percent for girls; and in Sub-Saharan Africa, the primary school completion rate is 67 percent for boys and 57 percent for girls (table 3.4). Almost all regions made significant progress in raising girls' primary school completion rates between 1991 and 2004. Sub-Saharan Africa, South Asia, and Middle East and North Africa had the largest percentage increases (about 21 percent), followed by Latin America and the Caribbean (14.4 percent). Gaps between girls' and boys' completion rates, however, remain significant in Sub-Saharan Africa and South Asia.

MORTALITY AND MORBIDITY

Under-five mortality. As mentioned above, health is one of the elements of gender equality that is not adequately covered by the official MDG3 indicators. A low-cost step toward remedying this is for countries to disaggregate the MDG4 indicator of under-five mortality by sex. Rates of under-five mortality are typically higher for boys than for girls (because of biological differences between the sexes) in countries where there is no significant discrimination against girls. For example, in four countries considered to be characterized by high levels of gender equality (Denmark, Finland, Norway, and Sweden) the girl-to-boy ratio is

TABLE 3.4 Girls lag behind boys in primary school completion rates in most regions

	Girls		Boys	
	1991	2004	1991	2004
Sub-Saharan Africa	47.1	56.9	62.3	67.3
East Asia and Pacific	92.3	96.3	92.3	95.8
Europe and Central Asia	92.9	92.6	94.3	96.5
Latin America and the Caribbean	88.4	101.1	83.0	99.4
Middle East and North Africa	73.3	89.0	87.8	92.9
South Asia	68.3	83.0	90.4	90.2
Total	78.6	84.0	93.4	89.4

Source: World Development Indicators 2006.
Note: Population weighted regional averages.

between 0.81 and 0.88. Where there is general discrimination against girls, this is manifested in higher under-5 mortality for girls than for boys. This comes about due to inequality in nutrition and health care during childhood.

The data sources for sex-disaggregation of under-five mortality are the same as those for the MDG4 indicator. The data issues are the same as well—although the best source of data is a complete vital statistics registration system, such systems are uncommon in developing countries, so estimates are also obtained from sample surveys or derived by applying direct and indirect estimation techniques to other data sources. One source of internationally comparable data on global and regional trends in under-five mortality by sex is the estimates published by the United Nations using available national data. Using this data, overall levels of under-five mortality indicate where efforts must focus on improving child health outcomes—Sub-Saharan Africa and South Asia (figure 3.9). When sex-disaggregated data are analyzed, East Asia and Pacific,

in addition to Sub-Saharan Africa and South Asia, stand out as regions where efforts must be focused on reducing the health disadvantages faced by girls (figure 3.9).

Prenatal sex selection is one dimension of discrimination against girls that is not captured in under-five mortality. It affects the sex ratio at birth, and is especially prevalent in the East Asia and Pacific region, and to much less extent in South Asia (box 3.2). Because it is not a concern in other regions of the developing world, sex ratio at birth is not recommended as an additional indicator.

Mortality and morbidity beyond childhood. The use of sex-disaggregated data for monitoring under-five mortality is a first step toward measuring gender equity in health. In the area of health, the term "gender equity" is used instead of "gender equality" in order to emphasize that differences between men and women in some health outcomes are due primarily to biological differences between the sexes. Gender differences in average life expectancy at birth are heavily influenced by

FIGURE 3.9   Female under-five mortality rate and female-to-male ratio, 2004

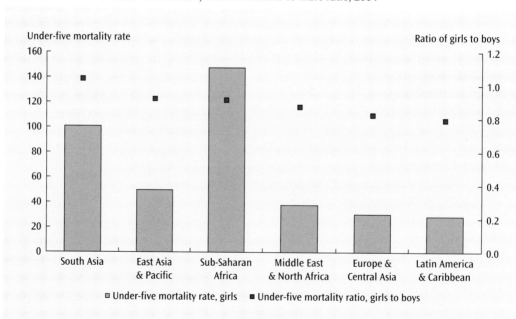

Source: World Population Prospects 2004.

gender disparities in child mortality rates and so they do not reflect sufficiently the health conditions of adolescents and adults. Over the life cycle, males and females face different risks and causes of morbidity and mortality, and monitoring these differences should help inform health policy and programs. While MDG5 monitors maternal health, this indicator misses sources of illness and death among women that are unrelated to maternal causes and are not relevant for women and girls not in the reproductive age group. Monitoring the incidence of specific diseases, as done by MDG6 (HIV/AIDS, malaria, and tuberculosis), while important, also does not offer a full view of sex and gender differences for the design of health policy priorities.

An international attempt to measure adult morbidity and mortality was made by the Global Burden of Disease project, a worldwide collaboration of over 100 researchers, sponsored by the World Health Organization and the World Bank. The study used information from a number of countries to estimate the costs of individual causes of morbidity and mortality to healthy life. This measure, the disability-adjusted life years (DALYs), estimates potential years of life lost due to premature death, poor health, or disability for all age groups. Table 3.5, which summarizes the results of this study for the 15–29 age group, shows that there are important differences in the distribution of the burden of disability and death between males and females; it shows that young women are more likely to suffer from mental health–related issues and HIV/AIDS, while young men are more likely to suffer from the fallout of violence as well as injuries and road traffic accidents.

The first DALY estimates were published in *World Development Report* 1993. Two years of estimates are now available, one for 1990 and another for 2000. The 2000 estimates were subsequently revised, and the most recent estimates are available for 2002. Due to changes in methodology and classification of mortality causes, the 1990 and 2002 estimates are not comparable; hence it is not possible to assess trends in DALYs.

TABLE 3.5 Sources of death and disability with largest gender differentials in disease burden for 15- to 29-year-olds, low- and middle-income countries

Disease/condition	Burden of disease (% of total) Females	Burden of disease (% of total) Males	Gender ratio (female/male)
Females			
Fires	2.13	0.9	2.34
Migraine	1.46	0.68	2.12
Panic disorders	2.49	1.24	2.0
HIV/AIDS	12.76	9.03	1.4
Unipolar depressive disorders	8.05	5.82	1.37
Males			
Other unintentional injuries	4.29	8.09	0.53
Road traffic accidents	2.24	7.73	0.29
Violence	1.24	7.58	0.16
Alcohol use disorders	0.68	4.12	0.16
War	0.13	2.68	0.05

Source: WHO 2002.
Note: The burden of disease has been calculated as the percent of DALYs lost due to a specific cause over the total DALYs lost (for men and women separately). For identifying priority diseases for gender equity, all diseases that primarily affect males (such as prostrate cancer) or females (such as maternal conditions) were removed from the list. The burden of disease for males and females were multiplied by the gender ratio. The diseases with the greatest gender differential are those that have a weighted differential above the statistical threshold of its distribution—mean plus one standard deviation.

> **BOX 3.2 Sex ratios at birth and removing unwanted daughters in East Asia and South Asia**
>
> Sex ratios at birth have been excessively masculine in much of East Asia for decades, compared with the "normal" ratio of 104–106 males per 100 females in most populations. In China and the Republic of Korea, the sex ratio at birth was around 107 in 1982, rising sharply thereafter with the spread of sex-selective abortion in the mid-1980s. In China it increased to nearly 120 in 2005.[a] In the Republic of Korea, it peaked at around 116 in the early 1990s and has since declined to below 108 in 2005.
>
> Skewed sex ratios at birth reflect sex-selective abortion, but may also include some amount of female infanticide, where the child is not reported as a live birth and is therefore indistinguishable in the statistics from an abortion. Another route for removing unwanted daughters is selective neglect during early childhood, typically by giving girls less aggressive health care for illnesses than boys. As sex-selective abortion becomes more accessible, it becomes easier to remove daughters—as a result, sex ratios at birth rise, and selective neglect after birth declines.
>
> The net effect of sex selection before birth, at birth, and after birth is reflected in the sex ratios of children aged 0–4 (box figure). The data show that discrimination against girls is also increasing in India—by 2001 the 0–4 year sex ratio was high in the country as a whole.[b] It is concentrated in the northwestern states of Punjab and Haryana, where the 0–4 year sex ratios have been historically high, rising sharply with the spread of sex-selective abortion in the 1980s and 1990s.
>
> Cultural factors help explain why these parts of Asia exhibit child sex ratios so much higher than anywhere else in the world. These societies have similar lineage-based kinship systems, which effectively ensure that only boys can continue the household and lineage and care for their parents in their old age. In most other societies, daughters are not so sharply excluded from participating

continued

This chapter stops short of recommending that countries use DALYs as a monitoring indicator for adult morbidity and mortality to complement the indicator of child health, since its ultimate practicality and usefulness as an indicator will depend on how frequently estimates will be available. (Given the availability of recent DALY estimates for 2002, however, some of the analysis below incorporates DALYs in exploratory fashion.) One significant shortcoming of DALYs is that the methodology is costly for individual countries to apply. Countries that wish to use the DALYs for results-based monitoring can rely on the WHO's production of country-level estimates.

Reproductive Health

Modern contraceptive use. This proposed indicator responds to the need to better measure women's ability to regulate fertility and choose desired family size. Since ability to regulate fertility is strongly linked to labor force participation and earnings, it also is an indirect measure of the potential for women's economic empowerment. The official indicator for MDG 6—contraceptive prevalence rate—considers all methods of contraception, computed as the percentage of women who are practicing, or whose sexual partners are practicing, any form of contraception, traditional or modern (United Nations 2003). But compared to traditional methods, modern methods offer women and their partners a more reliable way to control their fertility and to prevent the spread of sexually transmitted disease. This indicator also reveals the availability of family planning services to women and their sexual partners. This chapter therefore recommends that countries also monitor the percentage of women of reproductive age (and their sexual partners) who use modern contraceptives. Data on contraceptive use are typically available with a gap of three to four

BOX 3.2 Sex ratios at birth and removing unwanted daughters in East Asia and South Asia *(continued)*

in the well-being of their parental households. Decades of urbanization and industrialization in the Republic of Korea have eased the grip of these traditional social structures, reflected in the trend toward normalizing child sex ratios.

Child (0-4 year) sex ratios in China, India (Punjab and Haryana), and Korea (1950–2000)

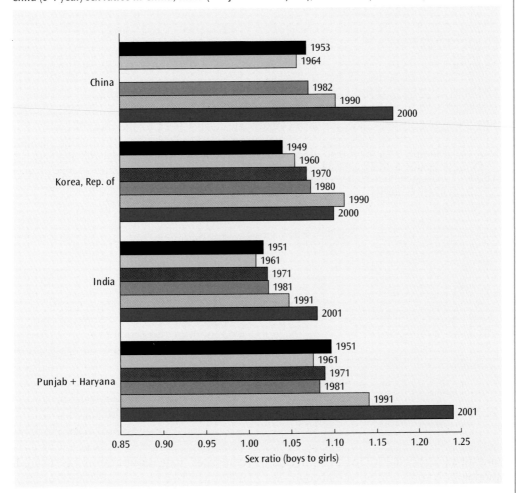

Note: The data for India are for the age group 0–6.

Sources: Korea National Statistical Office 2006; Goodkind 1996; Chung and Das Gupta 2007; and Das Gupta and others 2003.
a. Derived from Chinese census and intercensal survey data: the 1982 estimate is from Zeng and others 1993; the 2000 estimate from Yuan and Tu 2005, and the 2005 estimate is reported by Xinhua (2005.08.24) and Shanghai's Business Weekly citing the Chinese Academy of Social Sciences (http://news.bbc.co.uk/2/hi/asia-pacific/250557.stm).
b. India does not officially estimate the sex ratio at birth, partly because of the absence of good vital registration data.

years from Demographic and Health Surveys (DHS), Multiple Indicator Cluster Surveys, and contraceptive prevalence surveys.

A related indicator, percentage of women with unmet need for contraception, is being considered for inclusion in MDG5.[25] It is defined as the percentage of sexually active women who are not using any method of contraception and who either do not want to have any more children or want to postpone their next birth for at least two more years (Westoff 1978; Westoff and Pebley 1981). Since computation of unmet need requires survey data on intentions for future births, this indicator is available for a smaller set of countries (mainly those with DHS surveys) than is the indicator for use of modern con-

traception. Where available, unmet need can be used as an indicator of availability of family planning services.

The percentage of women reporting use of modern contraceptives has increased over the last two decades, from 47 percent in 1990 to 56 percent in 2000 (United Nations, Department of Economic and Social Affairs, Population Division 2002). Table 3.6 reports data from countries that have had two or more DHS between 1985 and 2005. The percentage of women aged 15–49 reporting use of modern contraceptives has increased over the 1990s in every country in this table.

Adolescent motherhood. Childbearing among teenagers can bring disproportionate health risks to the mother and the baby (maternal mortality, delivery complications, premature delivery, and low birth weight). In parts of Sub-Saharan Africa where female genital mutilation is practiced, pregnancy can also heighten the health risks to teen mothers (Zabin and Kiragu 1997). Beyond health outcomes for mother and baby, adolescent motherhood is associated with early departure from school, lower human capital accumulation, lower earnings, and a higher probability of living in poverty (World Bank 2006). Thus this chapter suggests that countries monitor the percentage of women aged 15–19 who are mothers or are pregnant as an additional indicator of gender equality and women's economic empowerment.[26] Data for this indicator are available from DHS and other reproductive health surveys.

Births to teenage girls are common in many developing countries. Most recent data show that more than 10 percent of 15- to 19-year-olds are mothers in Sub-Saharan Africa, South Asia, and Latin America (figure 3.10). In Bangladesh and Mozambique more than 30 percent of 15- to 19-year-olds are mothers or are pregnant. In most developing countries, unlike in developed countries, teenage childbearing frequently takes place within marriage (World Bank 2006).[27] The percentage of girls marrying before age 18 is high in a number of countries and ranges from less than 20 percent in Central Asia to more than 60 percent in Ban-

TABLE 3.6 Trends in modern contraceptive use, selected countries

	Year	% Using modern contraceptive
Cameroon	1991	4.3
	2004	12.5
Ghana	1988	4.2
	2003	18.7
Kenya	1989	17.9
	2003	31.5
Mali	1987	1.3
	2001	5.7
Uganda	1988	2.5
	2001	18.2
Egypt, Arab Rep. of	1988	35.5
	2000	53.9
Morocco	1987	28.9
	2004	54.8
Kazakhstan	1995	46.1
	1999	52.7
Bangladesh	1994	36.6
	2004	47.6
Indonesia	1987	43.9
	2003	56.7
Philippines	1993	24.9
	2003	33.4
Brazil	1986	56.5
	1996	70.3
Colombia	1986	52.4
	2005	68.2

Source: Demographic and Health Surveys.

FIGURE 3.10   Trend in adolescent motherhood

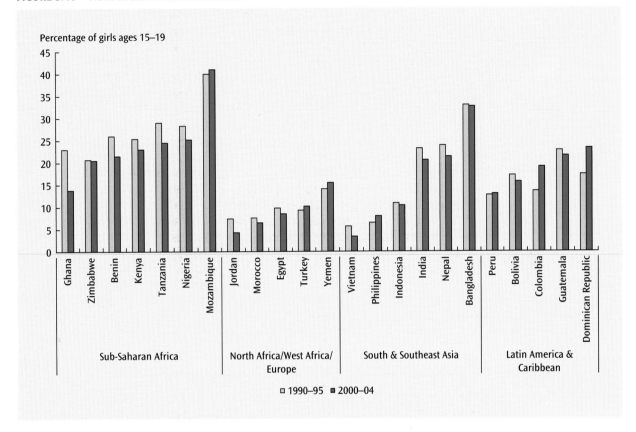

Source: Demographic and Health Surveys.
Note: Percentage of girls who are mothers or are pregnant.

gladesh, Guinea, Mali, and Nicaragua.[28] In Mali nearly 36 percent of young women were married by age 15.

Between the early 1990s and 2000, the percentage of adolescent mothers declined in a number of countries (figure 3.10). This is, however, far from a universal trend: adolescent motherhood increased over this period in Colombia, the Dominican Republic, Mozambique, Peru, the Philippines, Turkey, and the Republic of Yemen.

Additional Indicators in the Economy and Markets Domain

Labor force participation. To strengthen the official MDG3 labor force indicator (share of women in wage employment in the nonagricultural sector), this chapter recommends monitoring the labor force participation rates of men and women aged 20–24 and 25–49.[29] The labor force participation rate is interpreted as indicating women's potential economic empowerment.

Evidence from a number of developing countries shows that girls are less likely than boys to make the transition from school to the labor market (National Academy of Sciences 2005). Monitoring labor force participation among girls aged 20–24 thus indicates the extent to which education and skills acquired in school are used in the labor market. Age patterns of labor force participation show that in almost all regions of the world the greatest gender gap in participation occurs between the ages of 25 and 49. This is not surprising since the gender division of tasks typically results in women in this age group contributing more of their time to child and home care while men increase in work outside the home. Monitoring employment indicators for this age group thus offers potential for policy interventions (such as child care services) to influence labor market behavior of men and women.

Analysis of women's labor force participation in developing countries is sensitive to the data source. The UN Handbook on Indicators for Monitoring Millennium Development Goals (United Nations 2003) recommends using data from population censuses, labor force surveys, enterprise censuses and surveys, administrative records of social insurance schemes, and official estimates. These sources typically undercount women's participation, especially where women workers participate mainly in unpaid agricultural work. Household surveys asking respondents a detailed set of questions about their participation in work activities offer a more accurate estimate of women's labor force activities. Thus, this chapter uses household surveys to calculate the indicators on labor force participation and employment by type.[30]

When data on women's and men's labor force participation rates are examined, three patterns emerge. First, there are regions where women's participation in the labor force itself is low. In these regions, there has been little change in women's participation between 1990 and 2005 (figure 3.11). These are also regions where the greatest gender difference in participation. In a sample of 96 developing countries, female participation rates are the lowest in countries of Middle East and North Africa, South Asia, and Latin America and the Caribbean.[31] For the 20–24 age group in these regions, the average female labor force

FIGURE 3.11 Female and male labor force participation rates by region, 1990–2005

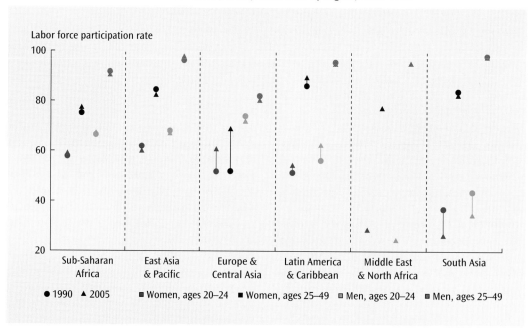

Source: Household and Labor Force surveys. The regional averages are calculated using the earliest value between 1990 and 1995 and the latest value between 2000 and 2005. The averages are weighted by the country population.
Note: Computed from household surveys (1995–2005). Labor force participation rates for males and females aged 20–24 and 25–49. Population weighted regional averages for South Asia (5 countries), Latin America and the Caribbean (20 countries), Sub-Saharan Africa (10 countries), East Asia and Pacific (8 countries), and Europe and Central Asia (13 countries). For 5 countries in Middle East and North Africa, data are only available for 2000–05.

participation rate ranges from 37 percent to 49 percent—below the average of 55 percent or higher for the remaining regions. Similarly, for the 25–49 age group in these regions, the average female participation rate is between 37 and 60 percent, again much lower than that in other regions.

Middle East and North Africa, South Asia, and Latin America and the Caribbean are also the regions with the greatest gender gaps in participation rates (figure 3.11). In these regions, for both age groups, male labor force participation rates are between 1.5 and 2 times the female labor force participation rates. For 20- to 24-year-olds in Latin America and Caribbean, this gender gap is paradoxical, given the region's success in educating girls and eliminating the gender gap in schooling. This gap suggests that, unlike their male counterparts, young women there face barriers to reaping the labor market returns to increased schooling.

Second, there are countries where female participation rates for both age groups are high, the gender gap in participation is low, but women are concentrated in low-paying agricultural employment. These are mainly the countries of Sub-Saharan Africa. Countries in this region have among the highest female participation rates. Of the 29 countries with data, female labor force participation rates exceed 60 percent in 12 countries for the 20–24 age group and in 21 countries for the 25–49 age group. In Benin, Burkina Faso, Burundi, Guinea, Mozambique, Rwanda, Tanzania, and Uganda, female participation rates are close to 80 percent for both age groups.

In these countries, female participation appears to be concentrated in agricultural employment or self-employment in the non-agricultural sector. Of the 28 countries where the female share of agricultural employment exceeds 40 percent (out of 71 countries for which we have data on employment by type), 17 are in Sub-Saharan Africa. For example, in Burundi, Rwanda, and Uganda, close to 60 percent of agricultural workers are female. In Ghana, where women workers dominate nonagricultural employment, most tend to be self-employed.

Third, there are countries where female participation rates are high for both age groups, gender gaps in participation rates are low, and women's share in nonagricultural paid work is high. These countries are mainly in Europe and Central Asia and in East Asia and Pacific where female participation rates are 60 percent or higher (except in Turkey, where the participation rate is 38 percent). Despite this high participation, as well as high educational attainment, women receive lower wages than men (see World Bank 2001; World Bank 2002; Pham and Reilly 2006).[32] An analysis of gender wage gaps in Russia and Poland during the mid-1990s found that only about 20 percent of the gender gap in wages could be explained by male-female differences in observed worker or job characteristics. The remaining gap was "unexplained," which is frequently interpreted as an indicator of labor market discrimination against women.

Of course labor force participation rates do not tell the whole story of women's economic empowerment in labor markets. Additional information on quality of employment—in addition to the official MDG3 indicator on share of women in nonagricultural wage employment—is needed to give a context to participation rates (box 3.3).

Value-Added of the Proposed Indicators

The proposed complementary indicators deal with some of the shortcomings identified in the official MDG3 indicators. They capture additional elements of gender equality in two of the three areas the official MDG3 indicators measure: education (by examining sex-disaggregated completion rates) and employment (by adding sex-disaggregated labor force participation rates); they do not improve, however, the measurement of political participation. The indicators also incorporate an important new area of gender equity in health; due to data limitations, however, it was not possible to incorporate measures of access to remunerated employment and disparities in access to productive assets. These indicators, in conjunction with the official

> ### BOX 3.3 Beyond participation: Self-employment, informality, and household work
>
> When women are employed, it is often claimed that, relative to men, they are more likely to: (1) be self-employed rather than work for wages; (2) work in the informal rather than the formal sector; and (3) work as own-account workers, domestic workers, and contributing family workers, while men are more likely to work as employers and wage and salaried workers (UNIFEM 2005).
>
> The evidence to support these contentions is mixed:
>
> ■ Among 91 countries with recent data, male workers on average appear to be more likely to be self-employed than female workers (KILM, 4th edition).
>
> ■ Whether women are overrepresented or underrepresented in the informal employment sector relative to total nonagricultural employment sector differs across developing countries. In Sub-Saharan Africa, Latin America, and India, the share of women in informal employment is larger than the share of men so engaged. In the Middle East and North Africa, the reverse seems to be the case (Grown and others 2005).
>
> ■ Among 80 developing countries with data, male workers appear to be more likely than female workers to be own-account workers (KILM 4th edition). Female workers are indeed more likely to be domestic workers and unpaid workers in family enterprises than male workers.
>
> A key question is whether women prefer to work at home or in family-owned businesses because of the location or the flexibility of work hours, which allows them to more easily combine work, domestic chores, and care. Or, do prevailing gender norms condition women to assume this triple workload or restrict their mobility? Or, is this pattern a result not of supply considerations, but rather of the gendered demand for labor, which presumably reflects existing societal gender norms?
>
> *Sources:* Grown and others 2005; KILM, 4th edition; Carr and Chen 2004.

MDG3 indicators, do a better job of measuring empowerment of women and of including sex-disaggregated levels of key indicators, thus overcoming some of the interpretation difficulties associated with parity ratios.

The value added of the additional indicators is in part an empirical question and in part a policy question. On the empirical side, the additional indicators are only valuable if they provide a ranking of countries on gender equality that is substantially different than that produced by the official MDG3 indicators—that is, they add information.[33] For each country, we calculate the rank according to the official MDG3 indicators and the proposed indicators.[34] Figure 3.12 plots the scores of 54 countries on the official MDG3 indicators against two of the additional indicators (the female-to-male ratio of primary completion and the under-

five mortality rate).[35] The figure shows that the additional indicators provide significant information beyond that supplied by the official indicators. Thirty-two of 54 countries change rankings. Some countries that score relatively high on the official indicators score relatively low on the additional indicators (for example, the Baltic countries and some other countries in Europe and Central Asia, as well as Cuba, Namibia, and Maldives). On the other hand, some countries with relatively low scores on the official indicators have substantially higher relative scores on the additional ones (for example, Brazil, Indonesia, Mauritius, Morocco, and Swaziland). For both sets of countries, the additional indicators are capturing elements of gender equality not captured by the official MDG3 indicators. For countries close to the diagonal in figure 3.12, the ranking on

FIGURE 3.12 Comparison of country scores on official and expanded MDG3 indicators

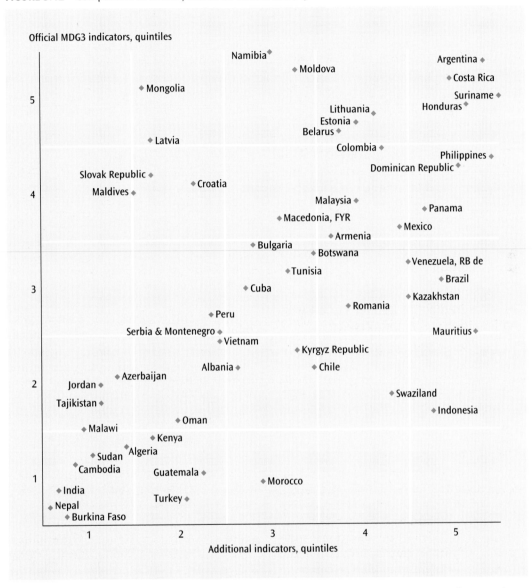

Source: Calculations using data from household surveys, World Development Indicators, and World Population Prospects 2004 for 54 countries 2000–05.
Note: To calculate the aggregate rank of countries for each set of indicators, we rank all countries that have data on the official MDG3 and proposed indicators for the period 2000–05. For purposes of comparability, countries for which the most recent data are older than this period are not considered. Each country is ranked by the value of each component indicator, from lowest to highest, and assigned a consecutive number (starting with 1) in accordance with its rank. Countries with exactly the same value are given the same rank. The sum of these values for each country yields a composite measure for that country, which then becomes the basis for a final ranking of the countries. This composite measure or index takes a minimum value of 6 and a maximum value of 6 times 54. For each set of indicators—official and proposed—we group the countries into quintiles according to this ranking. Because the official MDG3 indicators consist of four education indicators, a country's rank on the official indicators depends heavily on its performance in education. A country's ranking on the official indicators was not adjusted for this overrepresentation of education indicators, because it reflects the priority placed on education in the MDGs.

the official and additional indicators is quite similar; for these countries (for example, Albania, Argentina, Malaysia, Nepal, and Tunisia) the latter indicators provide little extra information on overall levels of gender equality.

On the policy side, the value added of the additional indicators hinges on their policy relevance. One aspect of policy relevance is the ability to identify countries that have scored particularly high or particularly low on specific elements of gender equality and draw conclusions about how public policy has influenced these outcomes. Another related aspect of policy relevance is whether scores on these additional indicators are useful in identifying other areas for public policy intervention. These themes are explored in more detail in the section that follows.

The Measurement of Gender Equality and Empowerment: Data Needs

The proposed complementary indicators discussed above do not remedy all the shortcomings of the official MDG3 indicators. Table 3.7 lists other prospective indicators that meet the criteria of being modifiable by policy and

having a strong link to poverty reduction and growth, but for which data are not currently widely available. Data collection for these indicators should be strongly considered.

Information is most needed for indicators that measure gender equality in society. Data on the share of women in positions in the executive branch of government and in local government are available only for some regions and some countries. Increasing coverage to a larger number of countries and regions should not be too onerous, especially because these data are straightforward and easy to collect. Similarly, voting behavior by sex should be easily obtained from voting records or from international opinion surveys, such as the regional barometer surveys (Latin, African, and Asian barometers) and the World Values Surveys, which now include more questions about voting behavior.

A potentially revealing indicator with direct implications for using services and enjoying citizen rights, is the number and share of women and men with basic citizenship documents, starting with birth registrations (and ending with death registries).[36] Recent research by the Inter-American Development Bank showed

TABLE 3.7 Prospective indicators for which data are not currently available

Household	Economy and markets	Society
Test scores, male and female	Gender gap in wages[a,b]	Percentage voting by male, female, and ratio
Proportion of women who have ever been victims of physical violence by an intimate male partner	Share of women in informal wage and self-employment in nonagricultural employment	Proportion of seats held by women in local government
	Percent of employed women who have access to child care	Proportion of women in the executive branch
	Businesses, by average size and sex of owner[b]	Percentage of individuals who possess basic citizenship documents, female, and ratio
	Access to credit for women and men	
	Land ownership by female, male, and jointly held[a,b]	

Source: World Bank staff.
a. Recommended by UN Millennium Project Task Force on Education and Gender Equality.
b. Included in World Bank's Country Policy and Institutional Assessments (CPIA).

underregistration of births in six Latin American countries, varying from 8.4 percent in Peru to 25.8 percent in the Dominican Republic. Characteristics associated with the risk of a child being undocumented from birth to age five included poverty, rural residence, and teen motherhood (Duryea and others 2006).

In the economy and market, comparable and timely data with good country coverage are urgently needed on the share of women in informal and self-employment (as part of a more comprehensive package of information on women's and men's employment, covering agricultural and nonagricultural activities formal and informal, wage, and self-employment). Data are also needed on wages and earnings by sex and type of employment. This recommendation, made first by the subgroup on gender indicators of the Inter-Agency and Expert Group on the MDG indicators, needs to be implemented, with efforts to improve and expand the collection and analysis of such data by national statistical offices.[37]

There also needs to be a significant international effort to obtain even basic data on both productive and consumer assets—land, livestock, house ownership, other property, credit, business ownership—disaggregated by sex, at the level of individuals, households, and firms. Some countries have information on land tenure by the sex of the owner in agricultural censuses or surveys. But information on access to credit (formal and informal) and business ownership by sex is almost nonexistent, except for micro studies. The international development agencies that produce and run large-scale specialized surveys—such as FAO's and IFAD's agricultural and rural surveys and the World Bank Group's household and business surveys—need to make a special effort to collect and analyze sex-disaggregated information on asset ownership and control.

The most complete existing coverage of reliable and actionable data is for indicators of gender equality in the household (where there has been the greatest advance in gender equality). Additional data-gathering efforts are needed to obtain measures of educational achievement (test scores) by gender and to mea-sure the results of gender-informed educational interventions. On the former, new international tests, such as the TIMSS, PIRL, PISA, and SACMEQ, measure achievement, but coverage of developing countries is still too limited.

Reliable and comparable data with good coverage are also needed on the prevalence of violence against girls and women in the family. Comparable victimization surveys conducted by the World Health Organization in 10 countries and a recently published major study by WHO (2005) are a promising start, as is the initiative by Macro International to include questions about intimate partner violence in Demographic and Health Surveys in nine countries (Kishor and Johnson 2004). These efforts need to be scaled up. WHO should lead an international effort to collect data on an appropriate, measurable, and actionable indicator of violence against women: tentatively, the proportion of women who in the past 12-month period have been victims of physical violence by an intimate male partner.[38]

In describing data that are needed for an expanded set of indicators, one must not lose sight of the fact that data on all six official indicators of MDG3 are available for only 59 out of 154 countries (for 2000–05). Many others have produced data but do not update the information regularly. This limits the number of countries that can be used for making valid cross-country comparisons; of the 154 countries in the database for this report, only 41 have information for both the official and the expanded lists of MDG3 indicators for 2000–05. Collecting and publishing updated information for these indicators is a clear—and doable—priority.

The UN Statistics Division, in collaboration with the World Bank and UNFPA, recently set up an Interagency and Expert Group for Gender Statistics, with broad representation of international organizations, national statistical offices, and nongovernmental institutions. At its inaugural meeting, in December 2006, the group launched a global gender statistics program to strengthen and complement national, regional, and other international gender statistics programs. This and similar efforts need to be fully supported by the international development community—since without good data, little progress will be made in national and international efforts to achieve MDG3.

Learning from Country Experiences

This section identifies outliers—countries that have especially high or low performance with respect to the official and expanded set of MDG3 indicators in the most recent year for which data are available (in the 2000–05 period).[39] This exercise is undertaken in order to extract lessons learned about policies to promote gender equality from both high and low performers, rather than to obtain a global ranking of countries for MDG3.[40] For those countries identified as outliers (*only* with respect to the relatively small subset of countries for which data are available), the section then examines the evolution of these indicators over the 1990–2005 period, both to understand how these countries ended up where they did and to determine whether there has been convergence among countries that started at very different levels of gender equality. Lastly, the section discusses changes in laws, institutions, and policies in outlier countries that may have contributed to the improvement (or worsening) of indicators and the policy framework for gender equality and women's empowerment.

Outlier Countries According to the Official MDG3 Indicators

To identify outlier countries according to the official MDG3 indicators, we use the ranking method described above. We group the countries into quintiles according to this ranking. Of the 12 countries in the top 20 percent or quintile, 10 are in Europe and Central Asia and Latin America and the Caribbean, indicating a clear regional pattern (table 3.8). Mongolia and Namibia deserve a closer look because they differ significantly from the other countries in their regions. Of the 12 countries in the bottom quintile, four are in Sub-Saharan Africa, three are in South Asia, and two are in North Africa. Note that four out of the eight countries in Sub-Saharan Africa and three of the four in South Asia are in this bottom quintile. Guatemala and Cambodia stand out because most other countries in their regions are in the top two quintiles.

To understand better the levels of gender equality achieved in about 2005, the performance of countries in the two quintiles on the official MDG3 indicators is examined over a 10- to 15-year period. Three basic patterns can be observed:

■ For primary enrollment, secondary enrollment, and literacy rates, there has been significant convergence: countries that were in the bottom quintile in 1990 reg-

TABLE 3.8 Countries in the top and bottom quintiles, according to scores on official MDG3 indicators

World region (number of countries with comparable data)	Bottom quintile	Top quintile
Sub-Saharan Africa (8)	Burkina Faso, Malawi, Kenya, Sudan	Namibia
East Asia & Pacific (8)	Cambodia	Mongolia
Europe & Central Asia (20)	Turkey	Belarus, Lithuania, Estonia, Moldova, Latvia
Latin America & the Caribbean (14)	Guatemala	Argentina, Honduras, Colombia, Suriname, Costa Rica
Middle East & North Africa (5)	Morocco, Algeria	
South Asia (4)	India, Pakistan, Nepal	

Source: World Bank staff.
Note: There are 59 countries with data for 2000–05. The number of countries with comparable data for these indicators in each region is given in parentheses.

istered significantly more rapid progress than those in the top quintile. The case of primary enrollment (figure 3.13 shows the size of the change in the levels of one indicator, depicted by the length of the arrows) is especially striking.[41] By 2005, several of the countries that were in the bottom quintile in 1990 had caught up with the top quintile. This reflects the progress of most countries in basic education, a point made in the preceding section and illustrated by the remarkable leaps for

FIGURE 3.13 Changes in official MDG3 indicators for countries in the bottom and top quintiles, 1990–2005

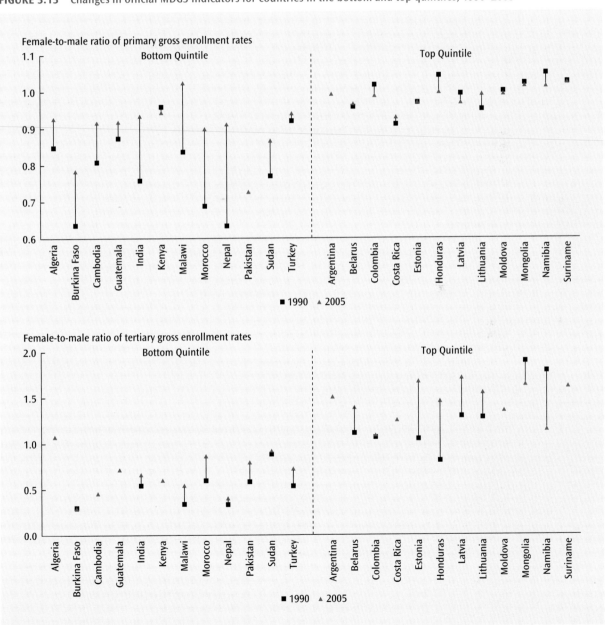

continued

FIGURE 3.13 Changes in official MDG3 indicators for countries in the bottom and top quintiles, 1990–2005 *(continued)*

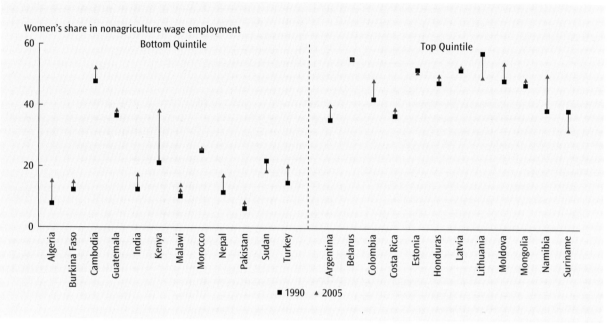

Source: World Development Indicators 2006.
Note: A few countries do not have data around 1990, defined here as 1998–95. The countries for which initial data are missing appear with just one point.

several bottom-quintile countries—especially in comparison with the countries in the top quintile. Note the progress by Burkina Faso, Malawi, Morocco, and Nepal. Countries in the top quintile show little change in this ratio because they were already close to gender equality in 1990.

- In the case of tertiary enrollment (also pictured in figure 3.13), there has been a widening of the gaps between bottom and top quintile countries. By and large, top quintile countries had female-to-male enrollment ratios in excess of one in 1990, and these rates rose substantially over the 1990–2005 period. This is indicative of severe male disadvantage. At the same time, bottom quintile countries, characterized by severe female disadvantage, made significant progress in boosting the female-to-male enrollment ratio; the only two exceptions to this pattern are Burkina Faso and Nepal.
- A third pattern emerges with respect to women's share in nonagricultural wage

employment and political participation. For these two indicators, there is little difference in performance between top and bottom quintile countries.[42] For nonagricultural wage employment (see figure 3.13), Kenya stands out because its rapid progress on this indicator puts its 2005 score at about the initial level for several top-quintile countries. Cambodia also stands out because it begins the period on par with the countries in the top quintile; in contrast, it is in the bottom quintile of performers because of its record on the other MDG3 indicators. In several countries in the top quintile, notably Argentina and Namibia, women's share in nonagricultural employment continues to rise.

Outlier Countries Using the Expanded Gender-Equality Indicators

Now consider the proposed additional gender-equality indicators and how countries perform. Because comparable data across countries on these additional indicators are even more scarce than for the official MDG3 indicators, we focus on two subsets of indicators: (1) the primary completion rates and the under-five mortality rate, for which comparable data are available for 54 countries, and (2) labor force participation rates and DALYs for which comparable data are available for 41 countries. Countries are re-ranked for each subset, and the most gender-equal and the least gender-equal countries are listed in tables 3.9 and 3.10.

As with the official MDG3 indicators, the top quintile features several countries in Latin America, but even more with this new set of indicators. Countries in blue are common to both rankings, four in the top quintile (Argentina, Costa Rica, Honduras, and República Bolivariana de Venezuela) and seven in the bottom (Algeria, Burkina Faso, Cambodia, India, Malawi, Nepal, and Sudan).

How have these countries performed since 1990? Except for Honduras and República Bolivariana de Venezuela, there has been very little change in the gender ratio in primary completion rates in the top-quintile countries; essentially, all these are roughly at parity (figure 3.14). In the bottom quintile, however, five countries achieved notable progress, and with

the exception of Burkina Faso, appear likely to achieve gender equality in this indicator.

The gender ratio for under-five mortality rates is a different story. There has been very little change in or among countries in both quintiles. Remember that in four industrial countries considered to be the most gender equal (Denmark, Finland, Norway, and Sweden), the female-to-male ratio is between 0.81 and 0.88. The developing and transition countries in the top quintile were near this level in about 1990. But for a few of these countries (Indonesia, Kazakhstan, Panama, the Philippines, and Suriname), the indicator suggests worsening mortality rates for boys relative to girls. In contrast, the countries in the bottom quintile are all above this range, with the three South Asian countries having data showing the greatest disadvantage for girls.

On the second subset of proposed indicators (using data on 41 countries) the similarities and differences are striking. In the bottom quintile, five countries are in the bottom quintile on the official MDG3 indicators (table 3.8) and the first subset of proposed indicators (table 3.9). The top quintile consists only of the countries in Europe and Central Asia (table 3.10), who achieve their high ranking due to desirable outcomes for females in labor force participa-

TABLE 3.9 Countries in the top and bottom quintiles, according to primary completion rates and under-5 mortality

World region (number of countries with comparable data)	Bottom quintile	Top quintile
Sub-Saharan Africa (8) East Asia & Pacific (6) Europe & Central Asia (18)	Burkina Faso, Cambodia, Malawi, Sudan	Mauritius, Indonesia, Philippines
Latin America & the Caribbean (14)	Azerbaijan, Tajikistan	Argentina, Brazil, Costa Rica, Dominican Republic, Honduras, Kazakhstan, Panama, República Bolivariana de Venezuela
Middle East & North Africa (5) South Asia (3)	Algeria, India, Jordan, Maldives, Nepal	

Source: World Bank staff.
Note: The total number of countries with data during the period 2000–05 is 54. The number of countries with comparable data for these indicators in each region is given in parentheses. The countries in blue (Algeria, Argentina, Burkina Faso, Cambodia, Costa Rica, Honduras, India, Malawi, Nepal, and Sudan) also appear in the lists in table 3.8.

TABLE 3.10 Countries in the top and bottom quintiles, according to labor force participation rates and disability-adjusted life years

World region (number of countries with comparable data)	Bottom quintile	Top quintile
Sub-Saharan Africa (3)	Burkina Faso, Malawi, Swaziland	
East Asia & Pacific (5)	Indonesia	
Europe & Central Asia (18)	Turkey	Belarus, Estonia, **Kazakhstan,** Latvia, Lithuania, Moldova, **Romania,** Russian Federation, Ukraine
Latin America & the Caribbean (12)	Honduras	
Middle East & North Africa (1)	**Jordan**	
South Asia (2)	India, Pakistan	

Source: World Bank staff.
Note: The total number of countries with data during the period 2000–2005 is 41. The number of countries with comparable data for these indicators in each region is given in parentheses. The countries in blue (Burkina Faso, Malawi, Turkey, Pakistan, India, Latvia, Moldova, Estonia, Lithuania, and Belarus) appear also in the lists in tables 3.8 and 3.9; the countries in bold (Kazakhstan and Jordan) appear also in table 3.9.

tion and an undesirable male disadvantage in DALYs. Five of them are in the top quintile in the previous lists. Due to a lack of comparable data for the beginning of the period, it is not possible to track the progress of countries on this set of indicators.

Changes in Rights, Resources, and Voice in Outlier Countries

Sweeping changes in a country's institutional environment can affect gender equality. Large social and economic transformations tend to change gender structures and relations, with effects on gender indicators. For example, the fall of the Taliban in Afghanistan ushered in the highest increase in school enrollment rates in its history for both boys and girls, but with the previous restrictions harsher for girls, the rise in their enrollment was especially impressive. This change was brought about by a near-doubling in the number of schools in the country after 2003 and cessation of physical threats on girls who attend school. Even so, long-standing institutional obstacles and investment shortfalls will keep Afghanistan's indicators of gender equality below those of other countries in the region for some time.

Equal rights. Both high and low performers have enacted constitutional or legal reforms to "level the playing field" between men and

women by prohibiting discrimination on the basis of sex and by adopting special measures for women's advancement. The difference between high- and low-performing countries is not so much the laws themselves, however, as in the mechanisms to implement them. High-performing countries tend to have more developed policy frameworks to enforce the laws. Without institutions for enforcement, including the information needed for it and the associated budget allocations, good laws can become mere statements of noble intention.

A good illustration of a coherent package of legal reforms that includes provisions for their enforcement is Moldova's Gender Equality Law, passed in February 2006.[43] The law specifies the mandates and responsibilities of public institutions with a role in enforcement, authorizes public budget funding for these agencies, and establishes both penalties and reparations for violations of the law. In Lithuania the office of Equal Opportunity Ombudsman gave "teeth" to a series of antidiscrimination laws passed between 2000 and 2004 by investigating and penalizing offenders for violating the Law of the Republic of Lithuania on Equal Opportunities for Men and Women.

High-performing countries do not have discriminatory laws condoning differential treatment between men and women, while many low-performing countries do. Women

FIGURE 3.14   Changes in two proposed indicators for countries in the bottom and top quintiles, 1990–2005

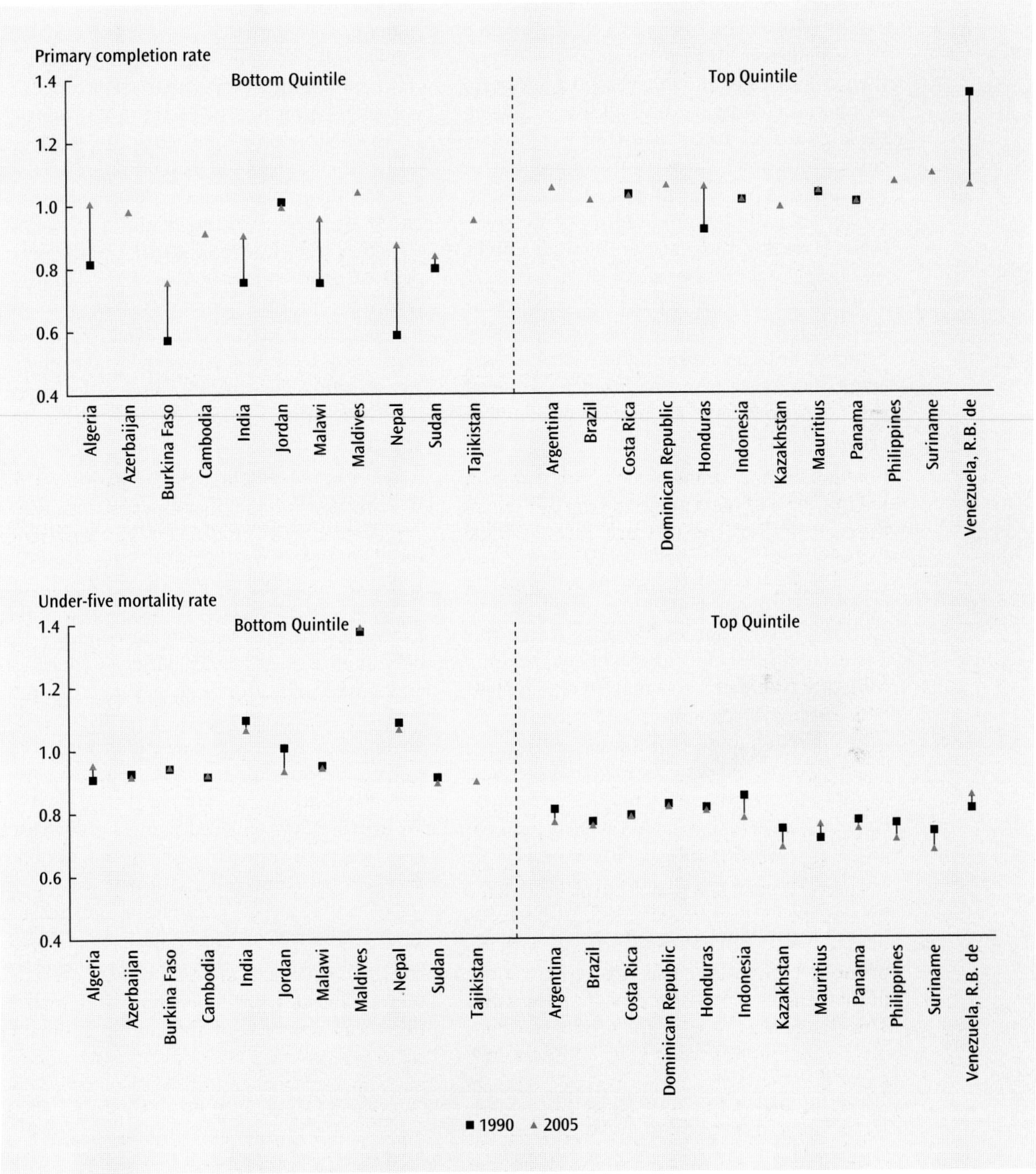

Sources: World Development Indicators (2006) for primary completion rates and World Population Prospects (2004) for under-five mortality rates.

in low performing countries are often treated as minors in family law—for instance, they cannot pass on citizenship to a child, and they need their husband's permission to include their children's names in a passport or obtain a national identity card. In addition, laws in these countries often directly or indirectly constrain women's options for employment and their ownership of productive assets. Examples include supposedly "protective" labor laws, such as bans on women's night work in the agricultural sector (India's Plantations Labor Act of 1951) and the requirement that employers bear all costs of maternity benefits (Burkina Faso, India), that increase employers' costs of hiring women. Some of these countries have no gender-specific provisions in labor laws that ban dismissal during pregnancy (Burkina Faso, Kenya). Land registration laws strengthen the land rights of male heads of household and weaken women's customary land rights (Kenya).

Many legal changes ensuring equal rights for men and women are quite recent, underscoring the fact that legal changes often follow and reflect social changes. Legal reforms have often followed and may have benefited from improvements in gender equality in both high- and low-performing countries.

Pakistan, a low performer, suggests the close connection between social and legal changes. Pakistan's national assembly passed the Protection of Women Bill in November 2006, after much debate and controversy. Removing rape from the jurisdiction of Islamic laws, the bill makes rape a crime punishable under Pakistan's penal code. Despite Pakistan's overall low scores on gender equality in the 1990–2003 period, it improved gender parity ratios considerably in secondary and tertiary schooling, and it increased women's representation in parliament from 10 to 22 percent. These gains in gender equality and women's empowerment quite likely set the stage for or facilitated the bill's passage into law.

Most countries now have separate government offices or agencies to promote gender equality and women's empowerment and to enforce equal opportunity legisla-

tion. And as a result of the commitments at the UN Beijing Women's Conference (1995), many governments elevated these offices to ministerial status. Despite this high profile, a frequent commentary is that these offices or ministries continue to be marginal or fragile in their institutional capacity, budgets, and influence (INSTRAW 2005; UNDAW 2004). Their performance seems to be influenced by their location in the government structure (the closer to the office of the president or prime minister, the better), by their resources, and by their links with women's movements in civil society. Relatively well-resourced women's ministries have played significant roles in promoting gender equality. Cambodia's Ministry of Women's and Veteran's Affairs (established in 1998), for example, was singled out as one of the key ministries to execute the medium- term expenditure framework (2005–08) and to implement Cambodia's National Strategic Development Plan (2006–10) (box 3.4).

Equal resources. A notable feature that differentiates the high-performing countries (by definition) is their gender parity in education and health indicators—suggesting that gender-informed investments in human capital are key to promoting gender equality, and that low-performing countries with aggressive education policies are on a good track. Malawi, for instance, has achieved significant increases in gender parity ratios at all levels of schooling, thanks both to universal free primary education (1994) and to a specific emphasis in increasing girls' attainment in basic education. Gender-informed policy reforms included reducing the direct costs of girls' schooling, increasing access and retention of girls in school, and removing gender bias in teaching (Semu 2003).

Various factors are associated with women's greater opportunities in the labor force in the high-performing countries. For the countries of Europe and Central Asia, gender equality is the legacy of explicit state policies that emphasized employment as both a right and a duty for both men and women. There is little evidence that the treatment of women in the labor market has systematically deterio-

---

BOX 3.4   How Cambodia's Ministry of Women's Affairs addresses the MDG3 challenges

Since peace was restored in 1997, Cambodia has made huge strides to recover from nearly 30 years of conflict. But the legacy of war still constrains growth and gender equality. Cambodia remains one of the poorest countries in East Asia, with 35 percent of households living below the national poverty line, and low levels of health and education in the population. A very unbalanced adult sex ratio during the war—the result of more men dying than women—is evening out, but has left a high percentage of poor households headed by women; it may have worsened gender relations and contributed to rising levels of domestic violence. In response, with backing from the prime minister, the Ministry of Women's Affairs (MWA) has had a major role in integrating gender equality concerns in government plans, including the poverty reduction strategy and the national development plan (2006–10).

At the *macro* level, MWA is institutionally well positioned to influence laws and policies, and it benefits from having gender equality enshrined in the constitution. It has invested in statistics and has expanded the official MDG3 indicators to sharpen the government's focus on gender inequalities. It added the indicators of gender equality in: (1) literacy rates for 25- to 44-year-olds, to cover women in prime childbearing and working ages; (2) wage employment in agriculture, industry, and services, to monitor sex segregation within sectors (women are underrepresented in the service sector); and (3) all elected bodies (National Assembly, Senate, and commune councils) and government positions. In addition, it added a new target focused on reducing all forms of violence against women and children.

At the *meso* level, MWA provides technical assistance and training on mainstream gender issues in line ministries, including agriculture (the most important source of economic livelihood for women and men), education (to increase the number of females in secondary education), and labor (to draft bilateral agreements that will ensure safe international migration for women workers). At the *micro* level, MWA takes the lead in developing services that are not yet a priority for line ministries and in piloting projects—for instance, assistance and business training to women garment workers in order to reduce their vulnerability to garment industry retrenchment.

The MWA active engagement in mainstream policy formulation, collaboration with line ministries, and ability to monitor progress have all contributed to its success. Constraints affecting its performance include insufficient technical and research capacity, limited allocation of resources, and poor understanding of gender equality and gender mainstreaming—on the latter, there is still a tendency to undertake isolated, women-specific activities, with little overall impact.

Source: Phavi and Urashima 2006.

---

rated with the transition to the market economy, though there is concern that women are not taking full advantage of the process of economic liberalization and privatization. These countries thus need to strengthen equal rights to access to resources, such as land, capital, and credit and other financial services (World Bank 2002).

For the Latin American countries that record high rates of women's participation in the official nonagricultural wage employment indicator, the rise in women's participation in the workforce in the 1990s seemed to be the result of neither specific government policy nor economic growth, since women's participation rose despite widespread economic stagnation in the 1990s. Instead, the rise is related to secular changes in the role of women in households and in the labor market, associated with their higher education, lower fertility, and higher wages. While the gender gap in wages is still wide in some countries in the region, it has narrowed significantly in others, and in high-performing Colombia it has already closed (Duryea and others 2004).

Cultural barriers often constrain the employment options of women in low-performing countries, especially in some countries in the

Middle East and North Africa with comparatively high levels of female schooling. In addition, structural changes in the economy—such as losses in the agricultural sector and increased rural to urban migration—can result in a decline in female labor force participation. This was the case in Turkey, where men compensated for the steady fall in agricultural employment by taking up nonagricultural work while women had to leave the market "voluntarily" (World Bank 2003).

Equal voice. Women's representation in parliament is the only indicator currently available to identify high- and low-performing countries on the issue of equal voice, and it is the one area in which changes can be more directly attributed to affirmative government action. The two countries with the highest representation of women in parliament and the largest increases are Argentina and Costa Rica, which adopted quota laws for women's representation in parliament in the early 1990s. In Argentina the current female membership in the National Congress is the highest ever attained—42 percent in the Senate and 33 percent in the House. Namibia, the only high-performing country in Sub-Saharan Africa, adopted quota laws for parliamentary and municipal elections in the mid-1990s. As result, women's representation in parliament rose from single digits to 28 percent during 1990–2003. Quota laws appear to help solidify women's gains in parliamentary representation. Without them, women's gains in representation can be quite volatile. Mongolia is a high-performing country with high gender parity in education and health, growing women's participation in employment and self-employment, and a new constitution that guarantees equal rights and includes many provisions prohibiting gender discrimination (1996). Even so, women's representation in parliament declined sharply in 1990-2003, from the mid–1920s to the single digits.

The Policy Framework for Gender Equality and Women's Empowerment

These examples underscore three main instruments available to governments to advance women's rights, resources, and voice: laws, institutions, and policies. There has been perhaps most progress in reforming constitutional and legal frameworks to ensure equal rights for women under the law. CEDAW and other international and regional conventions have provided a general framework for national legislation that bans discrimination on the basis of sex and protects women's rights. A first challenge is enforcement of these laws. Second, and despite the advancements made, laws in many countries still condone differential treatment between the sexes or, more blatantly, treat women as minors or second-class citizens. Laws without enforcement may not guarantee equal rights but differential treatment under the law seems to be a good predictor of gender inequality in society. Legal reforms, both to change the letter of the law and to strengthen the vehicles for enforcement, need to be paired with efforts to improve the collection and analysis of sex-disaggregated statistics—the basic building blocks for enforcing rights, designing policy, insuring government accountability, and monitoring progress in MDG3.

Institutions, even without the presence of overtly discriminatory rules, can reflect and reinforce gender inequality by restricting women's access to resources and services, or they can enforce equal rights and unlock opportunities for women. Governments have most often promoted an enabling institutional environment for gender equality both by setting aside resources to "mainstream" promotion and enforcement functions in line ministries and other government agencies, and by establishing a separate office or ministry with promotion, oversight, and/or enforcement functions. Mainstreaming should increase the positive impacts of government interventions and prevent unintended negative impacts of government action on gender equality. Because mainstreaming makes it difficult to track the amount of resources allocated to promote gender equality, public scrutiny of budgets is an important tool for holding the government accountable (box 3.5).

Over time, effective mainstreaming should obviate the need for having a separate agency or function for promotion. However, more than two decades of experience with "national women's machineries" (and with the integration of gender concerns in donor and international agencies—see chapters 4 and 5) has shown that mainstreaming is a long-term process, and that technical soundness, instrumental rationales, and financial incentives all help with the mainstreaming task. The experience also suggests that gender mainstreaming does not reduce the continuing need for a separate function or agency with vigilance functions. The challenge is to ensure that separate and mainstreaming functions complement and reinforce each other, rather than duplicate efforts and/or compete for scarce resources.

Advocacy organizations in civil society, including NGOs and grassroots groups, have been central in promoting gender equality and women's rights. Effective action, especially in terms of protecting women's rights, has often been the result of alliances between them and government counterparts.

In terms of policies, there is considerable knowledge on cost-effective ways to promote gender equality in the domain of the household, especially in terms of increasing girls' and women's access to education and maternal and reproductive health services. Demand-side interventions that condition transfers and subsidies to gender equality objectives are increasingly popular and proving to be cost effective. Delivery of health and education services can be designed to promote gender equality by putting in place measures that prevent discrimination by providers and encourage providers to be responsive to gender differences in client needs. Such measures include the provision of single-sex facilities and female providers which have been effective in increasing women's service utilization in a variety of contexts (World Bank 2001).

The promotion of gender equality in the economy is less easily influenced, because it depends not only on gender-targeted policy and project interventions, but also on mac-roeconomic factors, demographic trends, and the functioning of different markets. In Bangladesh, for example, the opening of the economy to trade significantly increased economic opportunities for women in the garment export sector (Kabeer and Mahmud 2004). Globalization and the opening of markets in many other countries, however, have benefited skilled over unskilled workers, which may have widened the differences in economic opportunities between more educated and less educated women, and between women and men. A growing economy and well-functioning markets expand opportunities for all. If women's economic empowerment contributes to poverty reduction and growth, stable growth that generates quality employment and provides an enabling environment for entrepreneurship is necessary, if not sufficient, to expand women's economic opportunities.

Universal programs can work—and have worked—to reduce gender inequalities (as in the case of the push for universal primary education); nevertheless, reducing gender inequalities most often requires targeted action and (sometimes) specialized agencies. There is comparatively good knowledge, for example, on expanding labor market opportunities for women through gender-informed training and job intermediation programs. And there is substantial knowledge on the design of microfinance institutions to increase women's access to credit and other financial services. More knowledge is needed in terms of what works to expand women's access to productive resources and productive infrastructure.

Targeted action is especially needed in the case for those left behind because of the interaction of gender and other forms of exclusion (such as ethnicity, race, location, or disability). Cumulative disadvantages present both institutional and legal challenges on how best to promote opportunities and protect the rights of girls and women who belong to excluded groups in the population.

Much more can be done to promote gender equality in the societal domain, a cornerstone for the promotion of overall gender equal-

BOX 3.5 Gender-informed public finance management

Public scrutiny of the budget from a gender equality perspective is important for both mainstreaming gender in government policies and empowering citizens to influence policy making and hold governments accountable for public finance management. In the last decade, more than 60 countries have undertaken analyses of public budgets to assess differential incidence and effect on men and women, as well as to measure men's and women's economic contributions.

Different approaches to gender-informed budget analysis. Approaches have differed in terms of focus, coverage, and methodology:

■ The Women's Budget Initiative (WBI) in **South Africa** expanded its initial broad focus on the national budget to analyses of specific budgets for domestic violence prevention, treatment, housing, and child support grant programs, among others. The **Uganda** Gender Budget Project analysis covered the national budget by sector. In **Mexico,** the analysis focused on antipoverty programs and public expenditure on health in several states. **Korea** and the **Philippines** analyzed women-targeted policies and activities at the local level. In **Morocco,** gender budgeting is being introduced also at the local level. In general, the more specific or focused the gender-informed budget exercise, the easier its implementation.

■ Most efforts have covered public expenditures, classified into: (1) women-specific expenditures; (2) gender equality expenditures in sectors or line ministries; (3) mainstreamed government expenditures that provide goods or services to the whole community; and (4) expenditures to achieve equity in public sector staff rosters. Some also extended coverage to revenues: the South African WBI looked at taxation to reduce bias against women, and a review of the value-added tax (VAT) in Uganda recommended tax relief on items used by women in the care economy.

■ The most commonly used method takes the government's policy framework and examines it sector by sector, both in terms of utilization of budget expenditures and longer-term impacts on men and women. The **Uganda** analysis compared administration expenditures with public services that citizens received and proposed reallocations within and between sectors. The **Mexico** analysis focused on how "gender-neutral" programs recognized and addressed the limitations women face and whether they covered women's needs and build their capacities. Ideally, these analyses should cover the four dimensions of government budgets and their interaction: expenditure, revenue, the macroeconomics of the budget, and participation in budget decision-making processes.

■ Tools have included gender disaggregated beneficiary assessments, public-expenditure benefit incidence analysis, and tax incidence analysis, among others. **Chile** has included gender as a cross-cutting theme in a performance-based national budget, and is using incentives (salary bonuses) for public sector staff as a tool to achieve measurable results.

■ The World Bank has undertaken gender-disaggregated public expenditure reviews in a number of countries, including Cambodia, Ghana, Morocco, Paraguay, St. Vincent and the Grenadines, Vietnam, and Uganda. Most have combined the use of gender-disaggregated benefit incidence analysis with gender institutional analyses or gender impact assessments of public programs. The reviews have shown that undertaking gender analysis can contribute to better targeted, more efficient, and more equitable public expenditure.

Lesson and challenge. The main lesson from the experience with gender-informed budget analysis is that changing public policy priorities is a more complex process than pointing out gender differences and disparities in budgets. The implementation of budget initiatives requires upgrading the technical skills of budget officials and gender experts; raising public awareness of gender issues to ensure the sustainability of the initiatives; and supporting well-informed coalitions of NGOs for advocacy. Most importantly, effective government agencies are central to their implementation. The key challenge for gender-informed budget analysis and policy making is moving beyond gender-targeted interventions to full and sustained gender mainstreaming in the budget process.

Sources: Asesorias para el Desarrollo (2007); BRIDGE (2003); Budlender and Hewitt (2002, 2003); Elson (2006); UNIFEM (2002); World Bank (2007).

ity. Women's voices in society—expressed through leadership positions in politics and grassroots and other women's organizations in civil society—should continue to be a main driver for gender equality and women's empowerment.

This chapter has highlighted the intrinsic importance of MDG3. It has also documented that progress toward attaining MDG3 should have multiplier effects and spur progress in other MDGs. To monitor this advancement, the chapter has recommended complementing the official indicators with selected additional ones; it has highlighted the need to strengthen the collection and analysis of sex-disaggregated data in all domains of gender equality. The additional investments needed to monitor MDG3 should go hand-in-hand with the scaling up of successful interventions to expand opportunities for girls and women.

Policy lessons from the review of the evidence in this chapter include, first and most importantly, that there can be significant advancement in gender equality when there is the will—as shown by the remarkable leaps that countries, even low-performing ones, have made in improving girls' access to schooling. Second is that laws, institutions, and policies matter. Laws provide an appropriate framework for leveling the playing field between men and women, but have no impact if they are not enforced; enforcement requires institutions with budgets and with reliable information to back enforcement. The promotion of gender equality requires distinct institutional arrangements (for vigilance and accountability), as well as actions to mainstream gender issues across public sector agencies. Gender mainstreaming can work, but it requires high-level leadership as well as technical and budgetary resources—it is not cost free.

There are well-known policy tools available to promote gender equality. They include interventions that, if designed properly, do not need to be specifically targeted to women. Examples range from government policies to promote export-oriented manufacturing to those that seek to facilitate the operation of microfinance institutions. But they also include targeted interventions, especially for subgroups of women in the population that suffer multiple exclusions. A third policy lesson is that civil society and the private sector have key roles to play in promoting gender equality—the former by forming alliances with government and promoting government accountability, and the latter by expanding economic opportunities for women.

In the short run, there may be policy-level tradeoffs between equity and efficiency; in the long run, however, greater gender equality in access to opportunities, rights, and voice can lead to more efficient economic functioning and better institutions, with dynamic benefits for investment and growth. The business case for investing in MDG3 is strong—it is nothing more than smart economics.

Notes

1. This belief is formalized in several international conventions: the Convention to Eliminate All forms of Discrimination Against Women (CEDAW); the Inter-American Convention on the Prevention, Punishment, and Eradication of Violence against Women (Convention of Belem do Para); and the Protocol to the African Charter on Human and People's Rights on the Rights of Women in Africa.

2. See UN Millennium Project Task Force on Gender Equality 2005; Germain 2004; Burkhalter 2002; de Walque 2006; and van der Straten and others 1998.

3. For 73 countries, the correlation coefficient between the poverty headcount ratio using 1997 data or the closest year to 1997 with available data (US$2/day; 1993 PPP dollars) and the female-to-male ratio in HDIs (1997) is –0.67, with an R square = 0.43. For the relationship between poverty and other gender equality measures, see Klasen (2006).

4. For 103 countries, the correlation between the average annual GDP per capita growth rate 1997–2004 (in percent) and the female-to-male ratio in HDIs (1997) is 0.35, with an R square of 0.14.

5. Equality of opportunity in education has received particular attention for two simple reasons. First, education—and, more broadly,

human capital—are easily incorporated into two frequently used econometric models of economic growth: the augmented Solow model and the endogenous growth models. Second, educational inequalities are easily measurable, and these measures are widely available.

6. See Knowles and others (2002) and Lorgelly (2000) for careful reviews of this literature.

7. Klasen estimates the effect of the gender gap in years of total schooling in the adult population on per capita income growth, using cross-country and panel regressions for the 1960–92 period for 109 developed and developing countries. He uses a variety of techniques to deal with potential simultaneity between economic growth rates and educational attainment, including instrumental variables and the use of only initial levels of educational attainment, which are not affected by growth in the subsequent period.

8. For a cross-country analysis of the impact of increased gender equality in earnings on household savings and gross domestic savings, see Seguino and Sagrario (2003).

9. The countries in Deere and Leon's sample are Brazil, Chile, Colombia, Ecuador, Honduras, Mexico, Paraguay, and Peru. The gender difference in average farmland size is statistically significant in only two countries: Chile and Paraguay.

10. Direct evidence is largely lacking that women's disadvantage relative to men's with respect to land ownership translates into inferior outcomes for women in investment, productivity, and individual incomes. Much more research is needed to understand the efficiency and welfare effects of this disadvantage for women as farmers and as household heads.

11. An important exception is Latin America, where recent episodes of agrarian reforms and land titling programs recognized dual-headed households, conferred joint titles, and explicitly targeted female-headed households (Deere and Leon 2001).

12. When studies do examine how gender affects technology adoption, they typically do so by including a variable for female-headed households as an additional covariate in multiple regression analyses. The empirical evidence on the conditional relationship between the gender of the household head and technology adoption is decidedly mixed. Most studies find that, controlling for differing sets of relevant characteristics, female-headed households are either less likely than—or as likely as—male-headed households to adopt new technologies (Asfaw and Admassie 2002; Paolisso and others 2002; Wier and Knight 2000;

Chirwa 2003; Doss and Morris 2001). A much smaller number of studies find that female-headed households are more likely to adopt new technologies than male-headed households (Bandiera and Rasul 2005).

13. Unlike the studies of the impact of women's control over resources using household surveys, the studies of the impact of transfer programs are argued to be free from the potential simultaneity between unearned or earned income and control over household resources.

14. Following UNESCO (2004), parity is defined as a female-to-male ratio exceeding 0.97. A ratio below 0.97 indicates significant female disadvantage. In 35 countries (of the 83 that achieved the 2005 target), there was significant male disadvantage, with boys' gross enrollment rate lagging behind girls' (the female-to-male ratio exceeded 1.03). In these countries, mostly countries of East Asia and the Pacific, Europe and Central Asia, and Latin America and the Caribbean, boys' enrollment exceeds 90 percent. Thus a male disadvantage tends to occur in education systems with overall high participation in schooling.

15. Net enrollment rates.

16. In Cambodia the share of women in the nonagricultural sector is about 53 percent, but the sector as a whole represents only 30 percent of total (male and female) employment—so only 16 percent of all employed women are in nonagricultural employment. Compare this with Latvia, where women's share in nonagricultural employment is also 53 percent, but the sector accounts for 86 percent of total employment, implying that 46 percent of all employed women are in this sector.

17. The fourth indicator, the proportion of seats held by women in national parliaments, is expressed as a proportion, but it is actually a measure of empowerment. While there has been a lot written on women's empowerment, there is no single accepted definition of empowerment. However, there is significant overlap in the words used to define the term: options, choice, control, and power—most often in the context of the ability of women to make decisions and affect outcomes that are important to them and their families (Malhotra and others 2002). Self-efficacy is also frequently an element of empowerment; women should be capable of defining self-interest and choice and be able and entitled to make choices (Chen 1992; G. Sen 1993; Rowlands 1995; A. Sen 1999; Nussbaum 2000; and Kabeer 2001; cited in Malhotra 2002).

18. This should not be interpreted as an argument for enrolling girls at the expense of boys,

once gender equality in enrollments has been achieved; rather, it simply notes that in order to measure the economic empowerment of women, absolute values matter, not just parity ratios.

19. Although an MDG6 indicator does measure contraceptive prevalence rate, this is problematic because it includes all forms of contraception, not just modern forms.

20. This is clearly the case not just for the MDG3 indicators, but for all MDG indicators.

21. This list of proposed indicators was culled from nearly one hundred indicators of gender equality that are currently used or recommended for use by the UN and sister agencies. They cover education, health, employment, violence against women, legal rights, and political voice. Their wide scope underscores the multidimensionality of gender equality.

22. The UN Millennium Task Force recommends replacing the existing four MDG3 indicators with 12 indicators, of which only two are current indicators (gross enrollment rates in primary, secondary, and tertiary education and percentage of seats held by women in the national parliament). Of the remaining ten proposed indicators, only four currently have enough data availability to be serious candidates as indicators: (1) ratio of female-to-male completion rates in primary, secondary, and tertiary education; (2) adolescent fertility rate; (3) proportion of contraceptive demand satisfied; and (4) share of women in employment, both wage and self-employment, by type. The remaining six (gender gaps in earnings in wage and self-employment; hours per day, or year, women and men spend fetching water and collecting fuel; land ownership, by male, female, or jointly held; housing title, by male, female, or jointly held; percentage of seats held by women in local government bodies; and prevalence of domestic violence) do not currently have sufficient data availability. For more details on these recommendations, see UN Millennium Project 2005a.

23. Survival to grade 5 is another measure of primary school completion rate. This indicator is not suitable for monitoring gender parity regarding completion, because it is based on the population of children enrolled in primary school and thus potentially excludes a large group of girls who never enroll in school. Girls who do enroll in school are more likely to be from advantaged backgrounds, especially in countries where discrimination against females is prevalent. Indeed, survival rates tend to be higher for girls than for boys, in all regions (UNESCO 2004).

24. A better measure would express the number of pupils graduating from the last grade of primary school as a proportion of the total number of children at the typical graduation age. But countries often do not report the number of primary graduates. Another shortcoming of this measure is that the primary school cycle varies greatly across countries. Although primary school in most countries lasts five to six years, there is a large variation in the length of the primary school (3 to 10 years) (UN Millennium Project Task Force on Universal Primary Education). This affects the comparability of the indicator across countries. It remains a useful indicator to measure gender equality in education, because it captures both access and quality of schooling.

25. To be discussed at the March 2007 meeting of the Inter-Agency and Expert Group for MDGs.

26. The adolescent (15–19) fertility rate, a closely related indicator, is being considered for inclusion in MDG5.

27. In countries of Sub-Saharan Africa and Latin America and the Caribbean, however, teenage childbearing before marriage or union is common. For example, data from Kenya and Colombia in 2003 show that close to 20 percent of teenage mothers were unmarried.

28. Based on Demographic and Health Surveys data.

29. The UN Millennium Project Task Force has recommended the indicator "share of women in employment, both wage and self-employment, by type." This chapter does not recommend using this indicator, although it is a valuable descriptive tool, because it is difficult or impossible to interpret as a measure of job quality. First, the share of women in any particular sector or employment must be put in the context of the overall importance of the sector to the economy as a whole. Second, there is enormous heterogeneity of job quality in each of the categories of employment; some self-employment is well remunerated and stable, while other self-employment is low-paid, unstable, and with no employment benefits. An alternative indicator of "percentage of women (as a share of female population) in remunerative employment" was explored, but not chosen because it was highly correlated with the existing MDG3 indicator of share of women in wage employment in the non-agricultural sector.

30. The reference period of the survey and the depth of questions that are asked influence the estimates of women's labor force participation. In developing countries, activities related to agriculture

predominate in rural areas, and large informal markets predominate in urban areas, where production often is home-based and mostly unregulated. The standard mode of eliciting information appropriate to developed country settings, therefore, is likely to yield much poorer estimates of labor force participation, particularly for women. Sociocultural practices can also affect data gathering. In strongly sex-segregated societies like those of South Asia, surveys using female enumerators to elicit information from women are generally better able to gather data on a range of topics, including data on work performed by women. Female enumerators tend to have better access to women in the households selected for the survey. In a setting where female work—especially paid work—has negative connotations, a male respondent such as the household head is likely to under-report female participation in labor.

31. Exceptions in these regions are Bolivia, Brazil, Nepal, and Uruguay where the female labor force participation rate exceeds 60 percent.

32. During the 1990s a number of countries in East Asia (such as Cambodia, Mongolia, and Vietnam) and Europe and Central Asia underwent a transition from a centrally planned economy to a market-based one. This transition was expected to affect gender wage differentials, but there is no consistent evidence of a widening or narrowing of the gap.

33. If the ranking were basically identical, the principle of parsimony would argue for retaining the existing indicators.

34. Empirical analysis was also carried out for the official MDG3 indicators against four recommended indicators (female-to-male primary completion rate, under-five mortality, female-to-male labor force participation rate, and DALYs). Because the sample size shrinks to 37 countries when labor force participation and DALYs are incorporated, the text discusses the comparison between the official and two of the proposed indicators (the female-to-male ratio of primary completion rate and the under-five mortality rate), with a sample of 54 countries.

35. We include only two of the proposed indicators because of sample size issues; were all the proposed recommended indicators included in one scatter plot, the sample size would shrink significantly.

36. Underregistrations of births and deaths are perhaps some of the most telling indicators of societal exclusion.

37. Analytical work in support of this recommendation and indicator was carried out by Women in Informal Employment: Globalizing and Organizing and the ILO, and reported in UNIFEM (2005).

38. Collecting data on intimate partner violence presents both methodological and ethical challenges. Methodologically, there is a tradeoff between the higher cost and greater accuracy of stand-alone surveys on intimate partner violence (such as the recent WHO multicountry study) and the lower cost and lower accuracy (such as underestimation of prevalence rates) of modules incorporated in other surveys, such as Macro International's DHS surveys (Ellsberg and others 2001). The principal ethical challenge of collecting data on intimate partner violence is to ensure that women respondents and interviewers are protected from potential retaliatory violence from the perpetrators of violence. WHO has recognized this challenge and has adopted a set of ethical guidelines for conducting population-based surveys on intimate partner violence (Watts and others 2001).

39. Outliers are defined as countries that fall in the highest or lowest 20 percent of the distribution of scores on gender equality.

40. A global ranking cannot be done because over 100 countries lack comparable data for 2000–05.

41. For reasons of space, trends in secondary enrollment and literacy rates are not pictured. Although they are not pictured, progress was notable for Algeria, Malawi, Nepal, Pakistan, and Sudan re literacy rates, and for Algeria, Cambodia, Malawi, and Nepal re secondary enrollment parity.

42. For reasons of space, trends in women's political participation, as measured by women's share in the national parliament, are not pictured. The top-quintile countries started off at levels similar to those of some bottom-quintile countries—the shares of Argentina, Mongolia, and Namibia were about the same as Guatemala, India, and Nepal. Since then, however, the top-quintile countries achieved much larger improvements in this dimension of gender equality. Two exceptions are Honduras and Mongolia, which lost ground after about 1990 and ended the period with levels below those of countries in the bottom quintile. In the bottom quintile, Morocco and Pakistan stand out because they made more significant gains than all other bottom-quintile countries. Indeed, Pakistan compares favorably to many top-quintile countries.

43. Law on Ensuring Equal Opportunities for Women and Men, No. 5-XVI of February 9, 2006.

4

Aid, Debt Relief, and Trade: Making Commitments Work

Developed countries can help developing countries' progress toward the MDGs by delivering on commitments of more (and more effective) assistance and by improving market access for these countries. The chapter assesses donors' performance by monitoring recent trends in the overall volume, allocation, and delivery of aid; implementation of debt relief; and progress on global trade reform.

The expansion in global aid has stalled. After climbing to a record high in 2005, official development assistance (ODA) by members of the OECD's Development Assistance Committee (DAC) fell 5 percent in 2006. Most of the increase in ODA in 2005 reflected exceptional debt relief operations to two countries; less than a quarter represented net transfers of new resources. A winding down of debt relief operations and a decline in other forms of aid pulled ODA lower in 2006, and official assistance is projected to fall in 2007.

At the Group of Eight summit in 2005, DAC donors pledged to scale up their aid to Sub-Saharan Africa. Nearly two years later, there is little indication of actual increases. In fact, official assistance to the region—excluding Nigeria, one of the two recipients of exceptional debt relief—edged lower in 2005 and stagnated in 2006. Moreover, a survey of DAC members' planned future aid flows provides scant evidence of an intended scaling up of aid to Africa. DAC donors need to accelerate the provision of aid that they have promised, and provide reliable information on resource availability.

For scaling up, action is required of recipient countries as well. Although scale-up opportunities exist in a broad range of reforming countries, these countries face difficulties in developing sound, results-oriented development strategies. Scaling up requires strengthening development strategies; identifying and addressing absorptive capacity constraints; and establishing closer links between development strategies and policy making, planning, and budgeting processes. For their part, donors and international financial institutions need to be ready to support country efforts.

The Paris Declaration of March 2005 raised expectations and generated a momentum for change in aid delivery practices. The results of the 2006 Baseline Survey show that a number of challenges need to be addressed: ownership of the Declaration by operational staff; demonstration of tangible benefits from doing business differently; and deepening the harmonization and alignment of aid efforts at the country level. The rise of nontraditional donors, including private foundations, and a profusion of global vertical funds also heighten the need for alignment and harmonization among a wider donor community.

The past year saw major progress in extending and deepening debt relief to the poorest countries. The Multilateral Debt Relief Initiative (MDRI) has provided debt relief of about $38 billion (in nominal terms) to 22 countries. The MDRI commits donors to providing additional resources to International Development Assocation (IDA) and the African Development Fund (AfDF) to cover the losses to these organizations stemming from debt forgiveness; the upcoming 15th replenishment of IDA will be an important test of donors' intentions regarding their support of the MDRI and of IDA.

As the pace of global integration increases, harnessing the new opportunities and managing the risks places a premium for all countries on a trade strategy of greater openness, coupled with behind-the-border reforms to dismantle remaining barriers to trade. Donors need to honor their commitment to increasing their support of trade liberalization in developing countries, or "aid for trade." Aid for trade needs to be focused on bringing practical solutions to countries' trade needs.

The Doha Round of multilateral trade negotiations continued to struggle in 2006. A small window of opportunity remains open for a deal to be reached in 2007, and flexibility will be required from all sides. Concluding the round remains an important step in efforts to achieve the Millennium Development Goals (MDGs) by the target date of 2015. Even as multilateral efforts faltered, preferential trade agreements continued to proliferate, raising concerns about their impact on countries left out.

Aid

Trends in Aid Volumes and Instruments

Higher aid flows amid a changing aid landscape. Aid worldwide continued on an upward trend in 2005 as DAC members, non-DAC traditional donors, and nontradi-tional donors all expanded their assistance to developing countries. Total aid then edged lower in 2006 and is expected to decline slightly in 2007. DAC members continue to be the largest source of official assistance, but so far much of the increase in their aid flows has added little to total aid as measured by net transfers or by the availability of new resources for development. Moreover, these donors have been slow to translate their aid commitments—in particular, a promised doubling of assistance to Africa—into increases in aid volume and tangible action plans.

After climbing to a record $106.8 billion in 2005, DAC members' ODA pulled back to $103.9 billion (preliminary) in 2006 (figure 4.1). The 5.1 percent decline in real terms was the first drop in ODA in real terms since 1997. Over 70 percent of the $25 billion real increase in net ODA in 2005 was due to higher amounts of debt relief ($18 billion) resulting from implementation of the Paris Club agreements for Iraq and Nigeria. (See box 4.1 for a discussion of debt forgiveness in DAC statistics.) By contrast, the expansion in other bilateral ODA—that is, ODA minus special-purpose grants such as debt relief, humanitarian aid, and technical cooperation—was a moderate $5.6 billion, or less than a fourth of the total increase. The reduction in ODA in 2006 resulted from the winding down of these debt relief operations; other forms of ODA also contracted by nearly 2 percent in real terms.

The latest numbers show that 17 of the 22 DAC members met their Monterrey commitments on 2006 ODA targets. At 0.43 percent, ODA relative to DAC-EU donors' average gross national income was above the 0.39 percent target set in 2002. These countries now account for close to 60 percent of DAC assistance. Overall, the share of ODA in donor GNI was 0.3 percent, below the level of the early 1990s.

2007 could see a noticeable fall in ODA as debt relief continues to decline. Other forms of aid will have to expand very rapidly in 2008–10 for donor promises of an additional $50 billion in annual aid (over 2004 levels) to be met by 2010. Based on announced commitments,

FIGURE 4.1 Evolution of aid: 1990–2006 and prospects

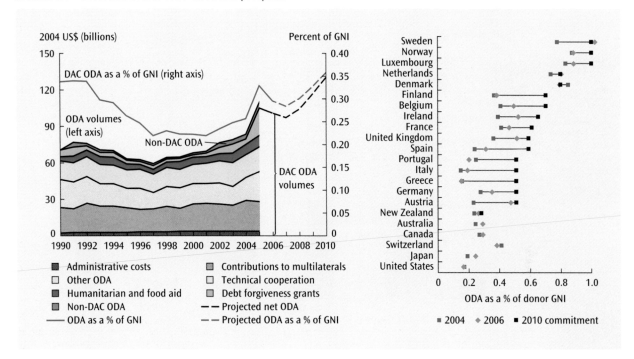

Source: OECD DAC Development Co-operation Report 2006 and DAC database.
Note: In the second panel, data for 2010 are shown only for DAC donors with announced ODA/GNI commitments. Prospects are for DAC donors only and are based on these donors' public announcements.

nearly a third of donors face an expansion in ODA/GNI of 50 percent or more (figure 4.1). This is prompting concerns that donors may fail to deliver on their commitments.

The continuing concentration of aid increases in a handful of recipient countries meant that aid to most countries rose very slowly, if at all. Despite a nearly 55 percent increase in real aid volumes in 2001–05, only 16 out of 81 IDA-eligible countries saw their ODA expand by 50 percent or more in this period (figure 4.2). The largest increases were in fragile states such as Afghanistan, Republic of Congo, Democratic Republic of Congo, Liberia, Nigeria, and Sudan. Indeed, 10 fragile states saw an expansion in ODA of over 50 percent. Just over half of low-income countries actually saw an outright decline in aid received during this period. Among lower-middle-income countries (that are not

IDA-eligible), Iraq saw the largest gain and 70 percent (24 out of 34) saw a decline.

Contributions to multilateral institutions dipped in 2005, both absolutely and as a share of total ODA as bilateral aid surged through exceptional debt relief. The share of these contributions in DAC members' ODA has averaged about 30 percent in recent years, but in 2005 this share dropped precipitously to 23 percent. Within this group, the share of IDA and regional development banks was sharply lower as well (at 6.5 percent), which could undermine these financial institutions' role in supporting poverty reduction. Donors have promised to provide IDA and the African Development Fund with additional resources to compensate them for debt service forgone under the MDRI, and this should translate into higher future contributions. However, it is important that

FIGURE 4.2 Expansion in ODA is concentrated in a few countries

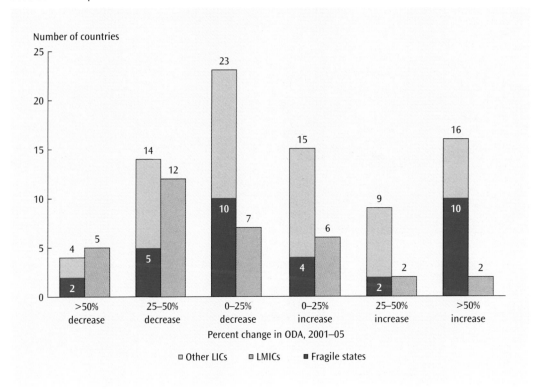

Source: OECD DAC database.
Note: Other LICs are IDA-eligible countries that are not fragile states; LMICs comprise lower-middle-income countries that are not IDA-eligible.

the pace of increase of contributions to these multilateral development banks not constrain the relative importance of these institutions in the future.

A wide range of other donors are increasing their aid to poor countries, and the amounts of this aid are set to rise. Non-DAC ODA was $5 billion in 2005, reflecting a threefold increase over 2001 amounts. Several non-DAC OECD countries—including the Republic of Korea, Mexico, and Turkey—have ambitious plans to scale up aid, as do some EU countries that are non-DAC members. ODA from these countries is likely to double by 2010, to over $2 billion (OECD 2007a). Other EU states that are not OECD members will also see their ODA increase because of EU commitments. Saudi Arabia (with an estimated $1 billion) and other Middle East countries

provided nearly $2 billion in assistance in 2005, and indications are that these amounts will continue to expand.

With their growing global economic prominence, countries such as Brazil, China, India, the Russian Federation and South Africa are also becoming more important providers of official support to poor countries.[1] For example, China was the third-largest food aid donor in the world in 2005, and it is fast becoming a leading foreign creditor to Africa. The Export-Import Bank of China, now one of the world's largest export credit agencies, is playing an important role in facilitating trade between China and countries in that region, as well as providing economic support. It has recently expanded operations in Africa: over the past two years the agency committed around $8 billion in loans and credits to

BOX 4.1   Accounting for debt forgiveness in ODA statistics[a]

A surge in debt forgiveness grants beginning in 2002 has drawn attention to their treatment in ODA statistics. The table below shows the amount (in nominal terms) of debt forgiveness grants provided in recent years. These grants (measured in gross terms) have ballooned from a modest $2.5 billion in 2001 to $25 billion in 2005. Depetris Chauvin and Kraay (2006, 2005) argue that the standard data do not provide a reliable estimate of the value of debt relief—that is, in present value terms—and they have developed PV estimates of debt relief. Another problem with DAC debt relief statistics is that forgiveness of outstanding amounts, debt service flows, and arrears is treated in the same way, even though the cash flow implications for borrowers' budgets is quite different. Despite these methodological issues, DAC debt forgiveness statistics are widely used.

Debt relief from the donors' perspective (budget effort) can be quite different from that of the recipients' perspective (availability of resources). One question that arises is whether ODA debt forgiveness grants represent additional flows (cross-border flows) to recipients.

ODA Bilateral Debt forgiveness grants: 2001–05 (in US$ billions)

	Debt forgiveness grants (A)	Offsetting entries for debt relief (B)	Net debt forgiveness grants (A)–(B)
2001	2.51	0.54	1.97
2002	5.33	0.81	4.52
2003	8.44	1.58	6.86
2004	7.11	2.92	4.19
2005	24.96	2.43	22.53

DAC statistical guidelines allow debt cancellation to be reported as debt forgiveness when the action on debt occurs within the "framework of a bilateral agreement and is implemented for the purpose of promoting the development or welfare of the recipient."[b] Thus, forgiveness of ODA, other official flows (OOF), and private claims—principal, interest, and arrears—is captured in DAC statistics under "Debt forgiveness grants."[c] Appropriate offsetting items (or counter entries) for principal and interest of each type of claim are reported, but not all are ODA flows—only forgiven principal on ODA loans is included under "Offsetting entry for debt forgiveness" in ODA flows.[d]

Most of the debt forgiveness grants in DAC statistics represent forgiveness of OOF and private claims typically under the framework of the Paris Club. The counter entries are not ODA flows, so there is concern that recent debt actions assign a large amount of flows to recipients, that do not represent any new transfer of resources. This point is well illustrated by the 2002 Paris Club debt relief agreement for the Democratic Republic of Congo. The country had an unbearable debt burden and under reasonable conditions was clearly unable to meet its obligations to external creditors. The Paris Club agreement restructured $8.98 billion of debt—$8.49 billion in principal and interest arrears and $490 million of future payments.[e] Approximately $1.4 billion in outstanding claims were ODA loans. The country received Naples Terms—67 percent of commercial credits were cancelled and the remaining 33 percent were rescheduled; and ODA credits were rescheduled.[f] The resulting DAC data for ODA disbursements in 2003 (when the bulk of relief granted under the Paris Club agreement was reported in the DAC statistics) show debt forgiveness grants of $4.441 billion and offsetting entries for debt relief of only $4.9 million. Together, these two items account for $4.44 billion of net ODA flows. Yet, the country did not receive additional resources anywhere near to this amount. However, the country's debt burden was substantially reduced and it was able to normalize relations with the international community, improving its prospects for growth.

Although debt cancellation may not deliver additional flows to borrowers, it does reflect government budget effort. The extent of the current budget effort will depend upon the terms of government guarantees for export/commercial credits and on the timing of write-offs for official loans—some may have been already written down.[g]

continued

BOX 4.1   Accounting for debt forgiveness in ODA statistics[a] *(continued)*

Because of differences in practices across donors, the extent of the budget effort for a particular debt action varies across countries.

a. A whole host of debt actions are presented in DAC statistics. The focus here is on debt forgiveness.

b. OECD DAC "Handbook for Reporting Debt Reorganization on the DAC Questionnaire" and "DAC Statistical Reporting Directives."

c. Reorganization of OOF and private claims within the framework of the Paris Club often involves concessionality in the form of debt reduction, debt service reduction, and capitalization of moratorium interest. The cancellation of part of the claims (or the amount equivalent to the reduction in net present value) is treated as debt forgiveness in ODA with no offsetting items in ODA flows. Amounts of OOF and private claims that are rescheduled are not part of ODA and are included as "Rescheduling" loans under OOF flows.

d. Forgiven OOF principal is reported under "Offsetting entries for debt relief" in OOF flows and forgiven private principal is accounted in "Offsetting entry for debt relief" under private flows. There are no offsets to forgiven interest in ODA, OOF, or private flows. Instead, appropriate counter entries "Offsetting entry for forgiven interest" are to be noted in memo items—the data for which are usually incomplete. The result is that the treatment of debt cancellation in ODA statistics assigns a larger amount of net flows to recipients than amounts actually received.

e. Paris Club Press Release of September 13, 2002.

f. In November 2003 the country received Cologne Terms from Paris Club donors.

g. Also see the OECD's Development Cooperation Report 2006.

such countries as Angola, Ghana, Mozambique, and Nigeria (Moss and Rose 2006). India's export credit agency, Exim India, has also issued lines of credit totaling $558 million to West African countries to enhance its commercial relations with the region. Little is known about the size and composition of flows from emerging donors, and better information is needed to facilitate monitoring and donor coordination.

Financing by emerging donors is targeting productive sectors and physical infrastructure, areas that traditional donors have largely exited. Not all of this financing is in the form of aid; rather it represents a mix of concessional and nonconcessional funds. There is a concern that access to large amounts of funds from these newer donors may strain recipients' capacity to use additional resources effectively. Low-income countries that have only recently received major debt reductions through the Heavily Indebted Poor Countries (HIPC) Initiative and the MDRI may see yet another buildup of debt (see the section on debt relief below).[2] This reinforces the need for good practices in accounting, reporting, and transparency on the part of all donors and the need for borrowers to adhere to established international reporting standards. Creditor and borrowing countries alike are urged to use the joint Bank-Fund framework for assessing debt sustainability in low-income countries, to appropriately manage the associated risks.

Private flows to developing countries have shown strong growth in recent years, but most low-income countries remain heavily dependent on grants and concessional finance (see chapter 5). Private giving through foundations, charities, and other nongovernmental organizations is on the rise as well. Reported aid flows from private citizens more than doubled over 2001–05, reaching $14.7 billion. Private sources have a significant role in mobilizing resources and setting policies for certain activities, including humanitarian and disaster relief and research into vaccines and tropical diseases. For example, the Bill and Melinda Gates Foundation has contributed over $6.6 billion for global health programs, $2 billion of which is for fighting malaria, tuberculosis, and HIV/AIDS and other sexually transmitted diseases. The growing role of private donors calls for closer coordination and exploitation of possible synergies between official and nonofficial donors.[3] [For a detailed discussion of private capital flows and remittances see *Global Development Finance 2007*.]

PROGRESS ON INNOVATIVE FINANCING

A number of innovative financing proposals for both the public and the private sector are being developed, and some are already in the pilot stage. Some of the proposed new mechanisms could contribute to expanding aid flows.

On the public sector side, new forms of taxation and securitized borrowing are being deployed. The International Finance Facility for Immunization (IFFIm) issued its first $1 billion bond last November, part of a plan to raise $4 billion over the next 10 years. The bond is backed by six donor countries—France, Italy, Norway, Spain, Sweden, and the United Kingdom—and will be repaid over 20 years. This new financing tool accelerates donor contributions to programs under the Global Alliance for Vaccines and Immunization, and it helps to lock in associated aid flows, which usually depend on annual budgets.

Air ticket levies could yield an estimated $1 billion to $1.5 billion a year, with France one of the largest contributors at $250 million a year. Views are mixed, however, on whether these levies add resources to what would otherwise have been provided. Meanwhile (in February) donors launched the first pilot Advance Market Commitment, to provide incentives for the development of vaccines of importance to developing countries.[4] Canada, Italy, Norway, Russia, the United Kingdom, and the Gates Foundation provided $1.5 billion in commitments to the pilot. Although AMCs do not increase aid flows to poor countries (especially not in the short run), by supporting the development of vaccines they could prove helpful in meeting the MDGs.

Blending, or the use of a combination of financing mechanisms toward a common objective, is seen as a way to augment MDB and donor resources aimed at accelerating progress on poverty and on social goals in middle-income countries. The World Bank is working with other MDBs to develop a menu of blending arrangements that would deploy part of current and future bilateral aid to middle-income countries so as to leverage the MDBs' nonconcessional lending.

Various private entities, meanwhile, have proposed a wide range of innovative financing measures. These include electronic billing-based fundraising; global development bonds, which would use financial engineering techniques to reduce the risk of developing-country investments; and results-based sequencing of funds, in which a country would receive additional funds only after specified targets have been met (de Ferranti 2006). Together these mechanisms are mobilizing new contributors to development finance in both the private and the public sector. Although this is surely a welcome development, it also heightens the need for stronger cooperation and collaboration among all actors so as to deliver resources more efficiently and effectively.

Progress on Scaling Up Aid to Africa: Actions Lag Commitments

At the 2005 Gleneagles summit, the Group of Eight leaders promised to double aid to Sub-Saharan Africa by 2010. Nearly two years later, that promise is not translating into actual increases: Sub-Saharan Africa is seeing little new aid beyond debt relief and certain special initiatives (figure 4.3). Indeed, DAC members' ODA to Sub-Saharan Africa—excluding Nigeria, the recipient of exceptional debt relief—actually declined by about 1 percent in real terms in 2005; preliminary data show that these flows stagnated in 2006. The prominence of debt relief in aid flows is evident during 2001–05: bilateral ODA to the region more than doubled over this period and the share of ODA allocated to Sub-Saharan Africa increased, but close to 70 percent of the expansion represented debt relief. The Bank's Africa Action Plan progress report aptly notes that "A typical 'well performing' African country has seen little or no increase in the resources available to support

FIGURE 4.3   Evolution of Net ODA to SSA, 1990–2005

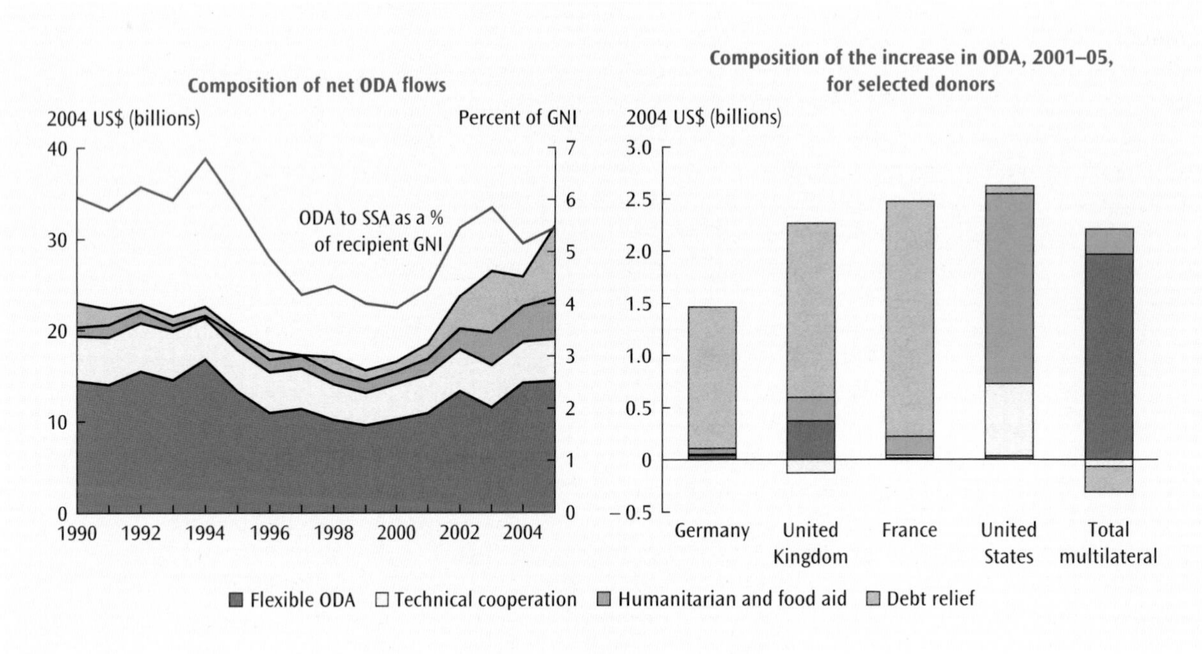

Composition of net ODA flows

2004 US$ (billions)   Percent of GNI

ODA to SSA as a % of recipient GNI

Composition of the increase in ODA, 2001–05, for selected donors

2004 US$ (billions)

Germany   United Kingdom   France   United States   Total multilateral

■ Flexible ODA   □ Technical cooperation   ■ Humanitarian and food aid   □ Debt relief

Source: OECD DAC database.

development projects and programs." ODA from several of the largest bilateral donors to the region shows a similar pattern—the exception is the United States where humanitarian assistance and technical cooperation account for the bulk of the expansion in ODA. Moreover, a partial survey of DAC members' planned future aid flows by country and region provides scant evidence of any substantial scaling up of aid on the horizon. Without concrete action to further boost aid, the Gleneagles promise risks going unfulfilled.

Action is needed on both sides of the aid relationship. Scaling up requires recipient countries to strengthen nationally owned poverty reduction strategies (PRSs), building upon the solid progress of recent years. Particular attention must be on enhancing analytic capacity to identify and assess absorptive capacity constraints—macroeconomic, sectoral, and institutional—and develop appropriate interventions to alleviate them. Previous Global

Monitoring Reports have addressed some of these issues and highlighted the importance of sequencing interventions across the range of constraints and of aligning public investments with these priorities.[5] As well, there is a need to establish closer links between the PRS and decision making processes in order to strengthen accountability to domestic stakeholders. One way of achieving this is by integrating the PRS and the budget process, thereby strengthening results orientation and domestic accountability.[6]

A range of reforming countries is well positioned to absorb scaled-up aid. The Bank teamed up with the OECD-DAC and UNDP to focus on six well-performing low-income countries in Africa which, because of their improved economic performance and better-developed aid alignment and harmonization mechanisms, were readier for scaled-up donor support. Within these countries, selected sector programs were costed to demonstrate that 15–30 percent of additional aid could be absorbed in these countries. Another recent World Bank study (2007b) draws on 12 country case studies to identify a variety of fiscal constraints to growth and to assess the financing options to achieve higher growth. Among countries with high aid access, such as Madagascar, Rwanda, and Uganda, the study finds that physical public infrastructure is both a critical constraint to growth and to achievement of the MDGs. Because of structural constraints (small size of the formal sector, high dependency ratios, etc.) the study assesses the scope for generating additional domestic revenue to be modest. Given the need to restrain new borrowing, and relatively limited scope to capture efficiency gains, these countries will have to rely substantially on scaled-up aid to finance growth-enhancing expenditure. The study finds that the situation is quite different in some other countries—Kenya could undertake limited borrowing for key investments but will need to address governance concerns to access greater aid flows; Tajikistan will need to improve the regulatory and governance environment to attract private investment and to access more aid. In other cases, such as India, increased revenue effort and changes in the composition of expenditure will be needed to address constraints to growth.

The challenge is to establish an effective mechanism for scaling up. Donors have come to see results and resources (R&R) processes as important to facilitating the scaling up of aid within the country-based development model. The R&R process builds and improves on the consultative group meetings that are the existing mechanism for donor coordination. It proposes linking funds to ambitious country-owned strategies and development results in a framework of mutual accountability. Although the underlying principles are common to the countries involved, the specific modalities may vary from country to country. Several African countries are in the process of preparing well-defined and well-costed-out programs for using the additional aid. The example of Ghana illustrates how one country is implementing the results and resources agenda (box 4.2).

The Africa Catalytic Growth Fund (ACGF) is also a possible vehicle for scaling up. The ACGF is a new mechanism to provide targeted support to help countries scale up to achieve economic growth and hard-to-reach MDGs. Within a country-based framework, the ACGF identifies opportunities where resources from multiple sources can fill funding gaps.[7]

Donor Support for Gender Equality: Toward a More Realistic Agenda

At the 1995 Beijing Women's Conference, donors made commitments to focus actions and resources on promoting gender equality in the developing world through mainstreaming of gender issues and women's empowerment. Gender inequalities in the areas of education and health were of particular concern. Efforts to redress this situation are apparent in the pattern of aid allocations for 2001–05: nearly three-fourths of aid with a gender equality focus is directed to the social sectors (figure 4.4). A quarter of all bilateral ODA allocated by sector—$5 billion out of $20 billion in average annual commitments—is focused on gender equality. Because aid for activities with no explicit gender equality focus, such as infrastructure, can also have a beneficial impact on girls and women, it is hard to say what the appropriate amount of financing for gender equality should be. What can be said is that the share allocated to gender equality is increasing.[8,9]

Despite donors' strong policy commitments to gender equality, implementation has been disappointing. Self-evaluations of nine donor agencies' performance reflect a gap between words and deeds.[10] One reason for the shortfall has been an unfortunate diffusion of responsibility, the result of initial decisions to spread responsibility for gender mainstreaming across all staff, with little accountability. Agency staff found themselves suddenly tasked with mainstreaming gender issues in the project portfolio, yet nobody was held specifically responsible for making it happen. A second reason was the broad, ambitious scope of the gender mainstreaming mandate itself, which

BOX 4.2 Country-based scaling up: The case of Ghana

Within the results and resources framework, work on the scaling-up agenda is now under way in the initial focus countries, with several R&R meetings planned in 2007. The first such meeting for Ghana took place in June 2006. Although the specific modalities of the R&R process will vary from country to country, the Ghana experience provides a good illustration of the key elements. Country ownership and leadership have been at the center of the process in Ghana. The R&R meeting was organized under the leadership of the Ghanaian government, closely assisted by the World Bank. An ambitious, country-led Growth and Poverty Reduction Strategy II (GPRS II), covering the period 2006–09, provided the strategic framework. The strategy is focused on raising economic growth from its recent 5 to 6 percent a year to between 8 and 8.5 percent, and it sets out clear development goals and identifies policies and programs to achieve them.

GPRS II encompasses an initial costing of the country's whole development strategy, linking development goals to an investment plan and a medium-term expenditure framework. This is complemented by a resource assessment, evaluating the macroeconomic and fiscal space for the scaled-up development strategy and outlining the planned mobilization of domestic resources and the amount and composition of resources to be raised externally. GPRS II also included an assessment of, and articulated a plan for strengthening, the country's institutional absorptive capacity, with particular attention to public resource management and the monitoring and evaluation system, to ensure value-for-money and efficiency of expenditure. GPRS II was supplemented by several key documents prepared specifically for the R&R meeting: these included a synthesis paper setting out Ghana's enhanced growth strategy, the macroeconomic context, and specific scale-up opportunities; a results matrix linking expected outcomes, resources, and indicators for monitoring progress; a financing matrix detailing recent and projected donor support; and a matrix on Ghana's Harmonization and Aid Effectiveness Action Plan. The World Bank worked closely with the government and with other development partners in preparing these documents.

Ghana's strategy for scaled-up development, with its emphasis on stronger economic growth, was well received by donors at the R&R meeting. Donors confirmed significantly increased and more predictable financial assistance, including $5 billion in new disbursements ($800 million more than had been projected six months earlier at a consultative group meeting) and $1.3 billion in debt relief under the HIPC Initiative and the MDRI, for a total of $6.3 billion in identified partner support for the four-year GPRS II period. The government noted that additional financing of about $2 billion ($500 million a year, or about 4 percent of the country's GDP) would be needed to fully fund the scaled-up investment plan, especially its infrastructure components, to achieve the GPRS II targets for accelerated growth. Donors committed to a full review of the financing requirements of GPRS II, based on further work to flesh out and assess the government's enhanced growth strategy and the associated investment plan. This work is now in progress, and the World Bank is contributing through a country economic report focused on the agenda for accelerated growth. In keeping with the Aid Effectiveness Action Plan, Ghana's development partners, including the Bank, have prepared a Joint Assistance Strategy that establishes a framework for support of GPRS II. The next R&R meeting on Ghana, scheduled for June 2007, will assess program implementation over the past year against the agreed results and progress indicators. It will also consider the financing requirements that remain unmet. Future R&R meetings are envisaged on an annual basis.

sought to encompass all actions throughout a given agency. This only reinforced inaction when the mandate was not translated into concrete priorities. Compounding these problems were inconsistent or limited support from senior management levels, and difficulty in tracking financial resources not specifically dedicated to or earmarked for gender equality objectives.

The evaluations did find some successes in mainstreaming gender issues in operations, although few projects systematically measured

FIGURE 4.4   Gender equality focus of bilateral ODA by sector (2001–05)

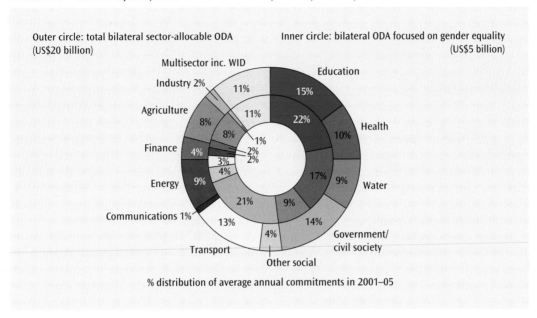

Outer circle: total bilateral sector-allocable ODA (US$20 billion)

Inner circle: bilateral ODA focused on gender equality (US$5 billion)

Multisector inc. WID

Industry 2%

Agriculture

Finance

Energy

Communications 1%

Transport

Other social

Education

Health

Water

Government/ civil society

11% 11% 8% 8% 1% 2% 2% 3% 4% 4% 9% 21% 13% 4% 9% 14% 17% 9% 10% 22% 15%

% distribution of average annual commitments in 2001–05

Source: OECD DAC.
Note: Not all donors report the gender focus of their bilateral aid.

the results and impacts. Examples include the embedding of gender issues in country dialogues and Poverty Reduction Strategy Papers (PRSPs) as well as in specific development projects, especially those where an enabling environment supported the gender equality agenda. In Tanzania, for instance, the United Kingdom through its development agency the Department for International Development supported the development of gender indicators in the poverty monitoring system. As a result, progress in gender equality is now systematically measured as part of Tanzania's overall poverty reduction performance assessment. In Nicaragua, the Swedish International Development Cooperation Agency and other donors were instrumental in helping mainstream gender issues in health sector projects.

These evaluation exercises, together with a more favorable political climate, have helped reenergize the commitment of donors to gender equality and women's empowerment. Several donors are in the process of fine-tuning or revamping their approaches, recognizing the importance of both gender mainstream-

ing and specific actions to reduce gender inequalities and empower women. Proposed changes include the following: much greater selectivity in targeting efforts at gender mainstreaming; adoption of a results orientation and strengthening of monitoring and accountability frameworks; stronger organizational arrangements for gender mainstreaming; and exploitation of synergies with the aid effectiveness agenda. This last change links gender equality instrumentally to the effectiveness of aid. It builds gender dimensions into the results and country ownership frameworks defined by the Paris Declaration, while recognizing the challenge of mainstreaming gender issues into programs and budgets.

Within this more realistic agenda, there is wide agreement that high-level leadership, technical expertise, and financial resources will be key to ensuring that donor agencies' gender policies are implemented. Financial resources, in particular, are needed up front, to enhance the capacity of donor and implementation agencies to mainstream gender issues. Beyond these internal challenges, success in implementing gender equality policies will depend largely on recipient countries' interest and institutional capacity.

Despite the challenge of estimating the financial resources needed to achieve gender equity goals, a few countries, such as Ethiopia, Gabon, Kenya, Mauritania, Niger, Senegal, Tajikistan, Togo, and Yemen have drafted a variety of innovative gender intervention proposals with corresponding cost estimates.[11] These countries' proposed gender mainstream interventions cover both traditional gender sectors such as health and education and nontraditional sectors such as energy and infrastructure.[12]

Gender mainstream intervention proposals vary across countries contingent on national needs, priorities, and sectoral development of gender action. For example, Kenya calculates $2.41 per capita per year to provide energy subsidies to female-headed households to facilitate income generation through biomass and renewable energy, petroleum, and electricity. In Niger, an intervention proposes providing vocational and skills training to facilitate secondary school female graduate entry into the workforce with a projected annual cost of $2.13 per capita. The Dominican Republic proposes transferring subsidies to mothers of children in pre-primary, primary, and secondary education at an annual per capita cost of $1.78. Outlining financial requirements is an important first step in targeting gender action priorities and costs to which national governments and donor agencies may respond. [See box 3.5 for progress on gender budgeting.]

Selectivity in Aid Allocations

A SHARPER FOCUS ON POLICY

Although aid is allocated on the basis of several criteria, donors are becoming more focused on policy performance. For example, the distribution of DAC bilateral aid by the quality of countries' policies and institutions (CPIA) shows that the best-performing third of recipients receive a modest 40 percent of all aid, while the worst-performing third receive only a little over a fifth (figure 4.5).[13] The analysis excludes Afghanistan because CPIA data are not available for the country and Iraq because it is not in the group of 81 IDA-eligible countries. Including these two countries could alter the results. There is some variation in the distribution by type of aid: nearly half of flexible ODA (ODA not in the form of special-purpose grants) is directed to the top third of recipients, whereas debt relief is concentrated in the middle third. Donors also focus on recipient-country governance, and here the data exhibit a somewhat similar pattern: flexible ODA tends to be allocated to countries with relatively better quality of governance, and debt relief to those with relatively weaker governance.

Where the relationship between aid allocation and policy performance and poverty has been studied empirically, bilateral donors are found to be increasingly focused on these criteria. Both policy and poverty selectivity indexes exhibit an improving trend over 2001–05 (figure 4.6). This is true for each of the various types of aid as well. The policy selectivity index in 2005 for non-humanitarian ODA shows that, on average, a 1 percent increase in a country's policy and institutional quality (CPIA) score is associated with a more than 1.5 percent increase in ODA (with bilateral donors showing less selectivity than multilateral ones; see chapter 5). Studies of the responsiveness of aid flows to improved governance report fairly similar results: a 1 percent improvement in the quality of governance is associated with about a 1.4 percent increase in aid. The results for disaggregated aid show that flexible ODA is the most selective, and technical cooperation the least selective, with respect to policy performance (and no significant relationship is found between CPIA scores and debt relief). The results for poverty selectivity are similar: flexible ODA is again the most selective with respect to poverty, and technical cooperation the least selective.

AID TO FRAGILE STATES: ADDRESSING THE CHALLENGES

The world's fragile states with their multitude of chronic problems pose a particular

FIGURE 4.5 Quality of policy matters: Distribution of 2004–05 DAC bilateral ODA

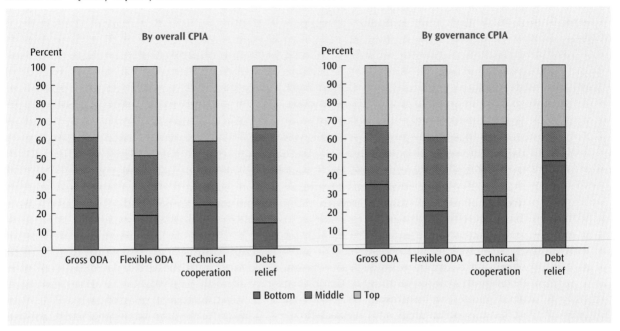

Source: ODA data from OECD DAC database; CPIA data from World Bank.
Note: IDA-eligible countries are divided into three groups—bottom, middle, and top—using the 33.3 and 66.7 percentiles of overall CPIA or governance-CPIA (quality of public sector management and institutions). Afghanistan is not included in the above charts because CPIA data are not available for the country; Iraq is not in the group of IDA-eligible and is not included.

FIGURE 4.6 Sharper donor focus on policy and need

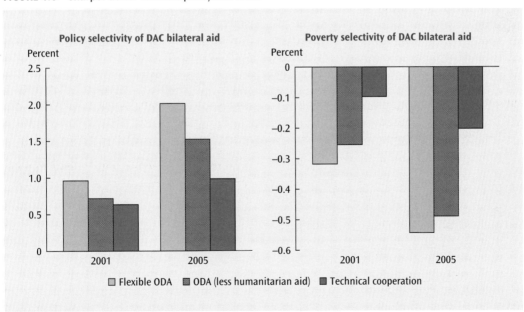

Source: Staff estimates, based on Dollar and Levin (2004).
Note: The quality of policies and institutions is measured by the overall CPIA. Policy selectivity shows the policy selectivity index, which measures the elasticity of aid with respect to the CPIA. Poverty selectivity shows the poverty elasticity index, which measures the elasticity of aid with respect to recipients' per capita income. The selectivity results do not include Afghanistan and Iraq because data on CPIA are not available.

challenge to the international community, but progress has been made in understanding and responding to these situations. In 2005 donors endorsed 12 principles for engagement in fragile states. Since then these principles have been piloted in nine countries, and their experiences have been fed back to allow the principles to be refined further (OECD DAC 2006b). The 12 principles emphasize the need to distinguish between country situations and to customize the mix and sequence of aid instruments accordingly. The central focus of international engagement in these countries should be on state building: supporting the legitimacy and accountability of the state and its capacity to foster development. The interdependence among political, security, and development objectives requires that donors devise coherent policies to deal with the multidimensional challenges these countries face. Where possible, donors should align their assistance with the recipient government's own priorities, and avoid actions that undermine long-term capacity building. The principles call for coordination among donors in making assessments, designing strategies, and assigning tasks. They also call on donors to act flexibly, to be prepared to engage over a longer horizon than they do with other low-income countries, and, specifically, to address the problem of aid orphans—those countries that for whatever reason get less assistance than their development indicators warrant.

Much remains to be done to improve development effectiveness of aid in fragile states. For one thing, application of the recently agreed principles needs to be extended beyond the few pilot programs to all fragile states. The principles also need to be mainstreamed with efforts to implement the Paris Declaration. International actors need to adopt "whole of government" approaches, fostering close collaboration across the economic, development, diplomatic, and security fields. The support provided by the international community to the creation of the United Nations Peace-Building Commission demonstrates the importance of this nexus, and work is now under way to consider how to make the hoped-for collaboration a reality. The principles also have organizational implications for donor agencies; for example, donors will have to create internal capacity to respond quickly to changing environments, build an appropriate local presence in fragile states, and attract skilled staff to work in these countries. Finally, appropriate performance indicators are needed so that progress can be monitored against the objective of building lasting peace among a more robust family of nations.

The focus on fragile states is beginning to translate into increased assistance, although aid flows to this group continue to be volatile. Overall aid to fragile states rose by more than two-thirds in 2005 alone, to nearly $20 billion (in 2004 dollars), and by 167 percent over 2001–05, just over half of which consisted of debt relief (figure 4.7). When debt relief and humanitarian assistance are excluded, aid to fragile states was around $10 billion in 2005.[14] Fragile states are also seeing an improving trend in aid received per capita. Although this group continues to receive less aid (excluding debt relief and humanitarian assistance) than the group of other low-income countries, the gap is narrowing (figure 4.8). Large increases in aid to Afghanistan, Sudan, and the Democratic Republic of Congo are behind this narrowing trend. Meanwhile, more than half of fragile states actually saw a decline in aid from 2001 to 2005 (figure 4.2). Aggregate trends mask the wide variation across different types of fragile states: those emerging from violent conflict typically receive much more aid than other fragile states, and more than other low-income countries. The DAC is therefore monitoring annual resource flows to fragile states to help identify those where international engagement seems imbalanced. The monitoring exercise conducted in June 2006 identified eight countries that appear to be underfunded and another three where aid is volatile and, on balance, falling (OECD DAC 2006c). The aim of the monitoring exercise is to use the findings on marginalized states to inform the consultative group meetings for these countries

FIGURE 4.7 Fragile states receive more of their aid in the form of debt relief and humanitarian assistance

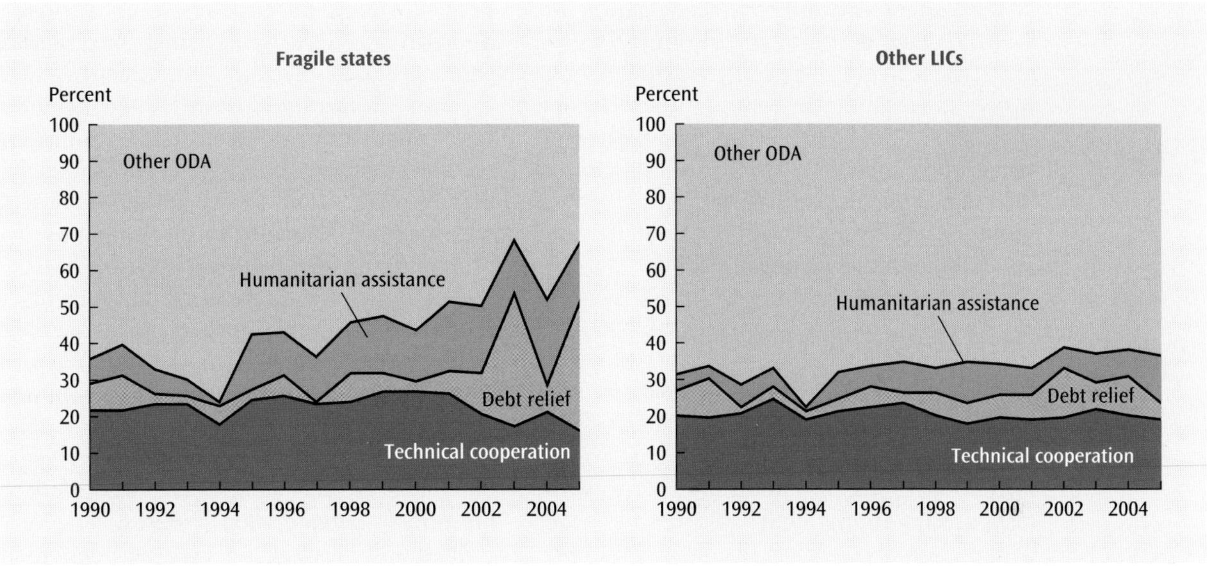

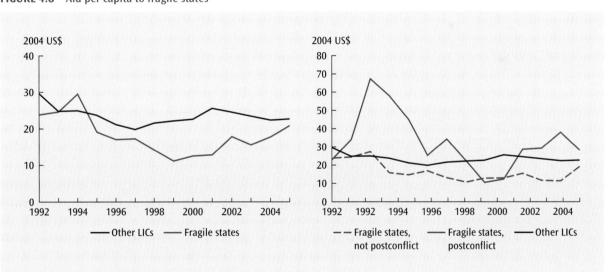

Source: OECD DAC database.
Note: Other LICs are IDA-eligible countries that are not fragile states.

FIGURE 4.8 Aid per capita to fragile states

Source: OECD DAC database and staff estimates.
Note: Data exclude India. Aid is net ODA less humanitarian aid and debt relief.

and address the local bottlenecks to greater engagement by donors.

Despite an overall increase in aid flows, empirical evidence shows that fragile states as a group continue to be underfunded compared to other countries with similar policy and poverty characteristics. However, the extent of underfunding (as measured by the coefficient on the fragile states dummy) appears to be declining in recent periods.[15] Evidence of underfunding is stronger for certain types of aid, especially flexible ODA. More important, the role of other factors such as regional and global spillovers and vulnerability has yet to be carefully examined in assessing the allocation of aid to this group of countries (Amprou, Guilliaumont, and Guilliaumont Jeanneney 2006).

Focus on Aid Effectiveness and Results

PROGRESS ON HARMONIZATION, ALIGNMENT, AND RESULTS

This section provides an update on the implementation of the harmonization and alignment actions at the global and country level in light of mutual commitments made by donors and partner countries in the Paris Declaration to improve aid effectiveness (actions by bilateral donors are reviewed here, while chapter 5 discusses implementation status of MDBs). Based on qualitative reviews and the Baseline Monitoring Survey of partner countries and donors,[16] it is evident that the international aid community is taking tangible actions toward meeting the Paris commitments but that results to date are modest. The Paris Declaration has raised expectations and generated a momentum for change in aid practices, but a number of challenges still need to be addressed by partners and donors if the targets of the Paris Declaration are to be met.

Following the adoption of the Paris framework in 2005, donors have taken a broad range of actions to disseminate the agreed commitments. Two-thirds of DAC donors have included the Paris Declaration as a strategic priority in official statements, indicating political ownership.[17] Many donors have also developed action plans for implementing the Paris framework. As of November 2006, 16 DAC members had adopted an action plan on implementing the Paris Declaration. An additional three members have adopted the principles of harmonization, alignment, and results in their aid strategies and policies, and four others have intentions of having an action plan. Along with the broad dissemination within donor agencies, a majority of DAC members have provided training courses on the commitments under the Paris Declaration to staff; some agencies have advanced training in budget support, sectorwide approaches, and public financial management. Donors have also collaborated with partner countries to disseminate Paris principles through regional workshops.

But implementing the Declaration involves a broad and complex process of change. In terms of organizing to strengthen internal processes, half of the donor agencies are focusing on mainstreaming responsibility for implementing the aid effectiveness agenda while the other half are relying on specialized units to promote implementation. Progress on decentralization is slower, however, with less than a third of DAC members reporting that field representatives are taking responsibility for advancing the Paris agenda on the ground.

At the country level, a growing number of partner countries are collaborating with donors on harmonization and alignment actions. Six countries—Burkina Faso, Ghana, Mozambique, Tanzania, Uganda, and Vietnam—are taking actions and making substantive progress across a broad range of areas.[18,19] An additional 13 countries are taking action and are making good progress. In the other countries, efforts are under way to implement harmonization and alignment actions but this progress is not as broad as in the more advanced countries.

Although the findings are preliminary, the qualitative and quantitative monitoring of the Paris Declaration[20] provides a useful assessment of the state of play on the basic trends in implementation of the commitments. The qualitative part of the 2006 baseline review finds that progress on ownership by partnership countries is uneven. While countries increasingly have developed comprehensive national strategies and improved the links to operational frameworks, as well as enhanced the functioning of country systems, there is significant room for improvement, even in the better-performing countries. According to the review, only 17 percent of the surveyed countries had developed operational national development strategies—strategies linked to fiscal policy and budget processes—that are considered "largely developed towards good practice," compared to a target of 75 percent of partner countries with largely or substantially developed strategies. Better use of the national budget to allocate resources in a more vigorous and consistent way to agreed policy priorities and activities is needed if countries are to close the gap on this target.

Furthermore, to align aid with country systems requires reliable country systems—for example those for public financial management (PFM) and public procurement systems. Nearly a third of countries have public financial systems that are moderately weak or worse—a CPIA-PFM quality score of 3 or less—and about a third have PFM systems that are moderately strong or better—a CPIA-PFM quality score of 4 or higher (figure 4.9). The Paris target for this indicator calls for half of the partner countries to move up at least half a point by 2010. Strengthening PFM and procurement systems is central to increasing

utilization of country systems by donors. Sustained technical assistance from donors, when coupled with adequate country ownership of PFM reforms, has led to improvements in PFM systems—for example, reform efforts in Mozambique and Tanzania have been well coordinated and owned by the countries, and have resulted in significant improvements in their PFM systems. The survey also finds that very few countries have a mechanism for mutual review of implementation of aid effectiveness commitments (those in the Paris Declaration and in local agreements). As more countries develop and adopt harmonization action plans, this is expected to change.

According to the 2006 Baseline Survey, the status of implementation against the Paris indicators for which donors have primary responsibility is mixed; the breadth and depth of actions vary among donors. Donor effort to align aid with country policies and processes is measured by several indicators including use of country systems, less reliance on creating parallel project implementation units, disbursing on time and on budget, and coordinating support to strengthen capacity.

FIGURE 4.9   Quality of country public financial system and use of PFM system for aid to government sectors

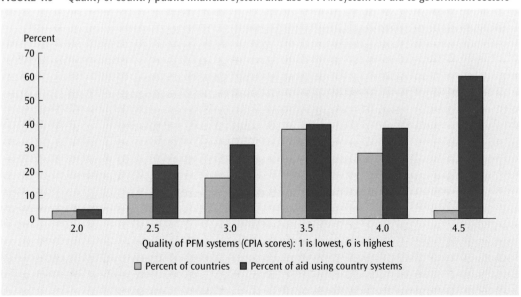

Source: Preliminary results from the 2006 Survey on Monitoring the Paris Declaration, OECD/DAC (March 1, 2007); CPIA scores from World Bank.

Table 4.1 shows the results from the survey for bilateral donors and all donors for each of these indicators.

Among bilateral donors, 39 percent of their disbursements use the partner country's public financial management system and 42 percent of disbursements use the country's procurement system. Better quality of PFM systems (as measured by the CPIA) do tend to be associated with a higher use of these systems for aid that is provided to the public sector—correlation of quality with use is just over 0.4 (figure 4.9). Nevertheless, there is wide variation among bilateral donors (DAC members) on the use of PFM systems for delivering aid to government sectors— from a low of 10 percent to a high of 90 percent.

According to the survey, 67 percent of bilateral aid is reported to be disbursed during the fiscal year in which it is scheduled, though with considerable variation at the country level in the shortfall between planned and actual disbursements. (Also see box 4.3.) For another indicator, bilateral donors report that 48 percent of their capacity-building support is coordinated with other donors, as compared to the Paris target for 2010 of 50 percent. This is one area where the definition of "coordinated" needs to be reviewed to ensure greater consistency or the target for this indicator might be more ambitious.

The survey finds that the bilateral donors provide 40 percent of their aid through program-based approaches such as budget support and sectorwide approaches, relative to the Paris target of 66 percent; there appears to be an increasing trend for sectorwide approaches and other similar programmatic arrangements, although reliance on such programmatic approaches outside the social sectors is not widespread. An area where greater attention is needed is with respect to project implementation units (PIUs); in the 34 countries surveyed 1,005 parallel PIUs are relied upon to implement projects, with a Paris target to reduce this number to 335 by 2010. In addition, the extent to which bilateral donors conduct joint missions is low—the survey found that 24 percent of missions

TABLE 4.1 Indicators pertaining to bilateral donors' implementation of the Paris Declaration

Indicator	Bilateral Donors	All Donors	2010 Target
Strengthen capacity by coordinated support	48%	47%	50%
Percentage of aid that is disbrused using country public financial management systems	39%	39%	Reduction of aid not using country PFM systems by a third or more
Percentage of aid that is disbursed using country procurement systems	42%	39%	Target under development
Number of Parallel Implementation Units (PIUs)	1,005	1,767	Reduction by 2/3
Percentage of aid that is disbursed on time	67%	66%	Reduction by 50% of aid not disbursed on time
Percentage of aid that is disbursed through program-based approaches	40%	43%	66%
Percentage of missions that is done jointly with other donors	24%	24%	40%
Percentage of country analytic work that is done jointly with other donors and/or partner government	48%	54%	66%

Source: Preliminary results from the 2006 Survey on Monitoring the Paris Declaration, OECD/DAC (March 1, 2007).
Note: The data reflect implementation as of 2005 for donors that provided a total of more than $100 million for the government sector. The data are undergoing final review by the OECD/DAC.

BOX 4.3 Predictability of budget aid: Experience in eight African countries

Aid predictability has become a central issue in the quest for enhanced effectiveness, particularly in the discussion on how best to deliver untied budget aid. For countries whose budgetary spending depends heavily on disbursements of untied aid, volatile and unpredictable disbursements are seen as undermining the credibility and reliability of short- and medium-term budget planning, by rendering original allocations obsolete and forcing expenditure adjustments during execution.[a] These adjustments, in turn, can hamper the attainment of government objectives, most importantly by disrupting the implementation of poverty reduction strategies. Worse still, when significant adjustments are simply not feasible during a given budget year, the result can be deviations from macroeconomic targets, with potentially significant consequences for macroeconomic stability.

A recent study of the predictability of budget aid in eight African countries—Benin, Burkina Faso, Ghana, Mali, Mozambique, Senegal, Tanzania, and Uganda—finds that both negative and positive errors in the International Monetary Fund (IMF) aid projections are large, imposing burdens on budget management (Celasun and Walliser 2005). While weak donor reporting is an issue in aid predictability, another likely reason for aid shortfalls is the failure by recipients to meet disbursement triggers. Moreover, the delayed disbursements may be shifted to the following year, once the conditions are met, accounting for aid overruns. On average, the mean absolute error in projecting budget aid on a year-by-year basis was about 1 percent of recipient-country GDP during 1993–2004, or about 30 percent of actual aid received.[b] Errors have declined only slightly over time, from 1.13 percent of GDP during 1993–99 to 0.95 percent of GDP during 2000–04. Closer donor coordination and information sharing is needed to help improve the predictability of aid. Also, providing more donor financing through the budget would strengthen monitoring and forecasting.

The bulk of adjustments to these unforeseen variations in aid take the form of domestic bank financing of government, arrears, and changes in domestically financed investment expenditure. Little of the adjustment burden falls on recurrent expenditure, amortization, or other financing. It is also apparent that, for whatever reason, aid shortfalls tend to be accompanied by tax revenue shortfalls, and aid windfalls by tax windfalls (also see Bulir and Hamann 2003, 2006).[c] This, of course, only deepens the recipient country's predicament. Finally, the study also found that periods of excess aid and tax revenue are seldom used to accelerate domestically financed investment spending, to potentially catch up with previous shortfalls. This finding is important, since it signifies that aid volatility may have permanent costs in terms of lost output. The country examples point to potential gains from a greater emphasis on regular annual budget support and on strong donor coordination frameworks. Intrayear predictability remains an important issue for countries facing external financing constraints. It appears that coordinated budget support frameworks are likely to also improve intra-annual disbursement patterns and avoid the typical "year-end rush" of disbursements. Reaping these gains, however, is predicated on creating the environment for a reliable medium-term engagement of budget support donors.

a. Gelb and Eifert (2005) argue that although predictability poses a special challenge for budget support, there are practical ways to address this issue. They show that performance-based allocation rules that have a flexible precommitment rule can allow for precommitment of aid in a multiyear framework, while avoiding drawn-out periods of misallocations.

b. Although budget aid disbursements remain difficult to predict on a year-by-year basis and carry large prediction errors, the authors do not find evidence that, in the aggregate and over time, aid disbursements fall short of aid projections by large amounts.

c. This procyclicality of aid hurts investment and public debt management.

---

were undertaken jointly, while 48 percent of country analytic work was prepared jointly with another donor, relative to the 2010 Paris targets of 40 percent joint missions and 66 percent joint analytical work.

TOWARD A MORE EFFECTIVE AID ARCHITECTURE?

Even as the Paris Declaration is beginning to change aid delivery practices among traditional donors, the rise of new aid sources, including new donors, private foundations, and a profusion of global vertical funds is increasing the complexity of the global "aid architecture." These changes increase total resources, but they also present the international community with the challenge of coherence—of forging an aid architecture with closer coordination of aid activities among a wider donor community, as well as greater harmonization, less fragmentation, and earmarking of aid toward specific applications. Such coherence is vital if aid is to be successfully scaled up to meet the MDGs.

Donor proliferation has seen a marked increase over time. The average number of official donors—bilateral and multilateral—per country has increased threefold since the 1960s; the number of countries with over 40 active bilateral and multilateral donors has ballooned from zero to over 30 since 1990 (World Bank 2007a). This has been accompanied more recently by an expansion in the number of emerging donors, many of which are gaining a substantial presence in the aid community. Non-DAC donors are a heterogeneous group; the degree to which DAC approaches and norms are applied varies from country to country. Insufficient data make it difficult to accurately assess aid volumes and prospects from these sources. The number of private foundations and charitable organizations has also mushroomed, as have global programs (which are discussed in the next section) and funds. Donor contributions to 20 major global programs have increased from almost zero in the mid-1970s to about $3 billion annually. The number of active trust funds administered by the World Bank alone in FY2006 was 929, up from 840 in the previous year (World Bank 2007f). At the same time, contributions to multilaterals, including to IDA and the major regional development banks, have dropped (see above). The proliferation of aid channels can overwhelm the often limited capacity of recipient countries to implement the recording, processing, auditing, monitoring, and assessment requirements of different donors. It can also complicate the management of aid, undermining its effectiveness.

Proliferation is particularly pronounced in the health sector, and the case of Rwanda, which is discussed in chapter 2, highlights many of the challenges that are faced by countries with weak capacity—the need for policy coherence at the sector level and for complementarity between national, regional, and global priorities and programs. The need for building country capacity to effectively handle scaled-up aid is abundantly clear as well. Indeed, countries with strong capacity—Tanzania and Uganda—have had some success in pulling together a myriad of health donors into coordinated sectorwide approaches. Nevertheless, the profusion of aid channels heightens the need for coordination, alignment, and harmonization among a wider donor community, particularly when engaging with poor countries that find it difficult to turn down offers of assistance.

The problem of a large number of aid channels is compounded by the trend toward the small average size of funded activities. Using the OECD's Creditor Reporting Database, World Bank (2007a) shows that between 1997 and 2004 the average size of aid activities (measured in 2004 prices) dropped by $1 million to about $1.5 million and the number of activities surged from 20,000 to 60,000. Moreover, countries with lower institutional capacity had higher aid fragmentation. Previous *Global Monitoring Reports* have noted the negative implications of higher fragmentation on aid quality, especially through higher transaction costs for recipients and donors and through a smaller donor stake in overall country outcomes. Excessive fragmentation is a serious problem and measures to reduce it, such as through donors limiting the number of countries in which they focus, providing a larger amount of funds through more efficient vehicles (including multilateral channels) and modalities, and committing to delegate authority to lead donors, could help to reduce transactions costs and to improve the effectiveness of aid.

Recent trends in proliferation and fragmentation are thus impacting the global aid architecture, and posing a challenge to the quality and effectiveness of aid. Although the Paris Principles address some of these challenges, more is needed to achieve coherence in the aid architecture.

MAKING GLOBAL PROGRAMS MORE EFFECTIVE

Programs and partnerships of global scope have grown rapidly, reflecting the increasing influence of global issues over the development agenda. The international donor community—including both official and private donors—is already channeling substantial resources through these vehicles. Global programs typically focus on delivering either targeted key services such as primary education or HIV/AIDS treatment, or global public goods such as peace and security, control of infectious diseases, knowledge generation and dissemination, protection of the global commons, a free and open trading system, international financial stability, and protection from borderless crime. Global programs vary widely in terms of size, funding sources, financing arrangements, governance structures, and modalities. Their importance in delivering global public goods is revealed in the fact that nearly $20 billion in ODA grant commitments by DAC members—over a quarter of the

total—is now allocated to such goods (figure 4.10). The United States is the largest source of funds for global public goods, financing nearly 40 percent of all DAC donors' ODA commitments of this type. Other important official contributors include the Germany, Japan, the Netherlands, the United Kingdom, and the European Union as a group.

Further evidence of the robust growth in global programs is seen in the activities of the various trust funds administered by the World Bank, many of which are global and regional in scope. Contributions to these trust funds have more than doubled in recent years, from $2.2 billion in 2001 to $5.2 billion in 2006. Contributions by bilateral donors and the European Commission accounted for nearly 90 percent of the 2006 figure, and those by private entities for 1 percent. Disbursements have shown remarkable growth as well, rising to a record high of $4.4 billion in 2006. Nearly half of all trust fund disbursements in 2005 were for global programs.

A key challenge for global programs is how best to integrate their mandates and priorities with country-based programs into coherent development strategies. Successful integration depends on aligning the objectives and design of the global program with

FIGURE 4.10   DAC members' and EC's ODA commitments forGPGs

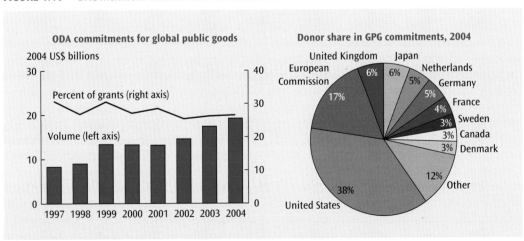

Source: OECD DAC database and staff estimates.
Note: GPGs include both global and regional public goods.

conditions at the country level. A 2006 World Bank report evaluates the alignment of global programs at the country level for seven countries. Focusing on the larger programs, such as the Global Fund to Fight AIDS, Tuberculosis, and Malaria, the Global Environment Facility, the Global Alliance for Vaccines and Immunization, the Education for All Fast Track Initiative, and the Consultative Group on International Agricultural Research, the study finds considerable variation among them. The Education for All Fast Track Initiative was found to be well aligned, and the Global Environment Facility reasonably well aligned, while other global programs, especially in health, were struggling to improve their alignment.[21] The study also finds that alignment is easier when the benefits of the global public good to the individual country are perceived to be high. Shared objectives and strategies strengthen local ownership, and this helps promote success. Establishing ownership and alignment is more complicated in countries with limited institutional capacity and greater donor fragmentation.

One way to improve the alignment of global programs is to anchor them in the Paris Principles. Also central to success are predictability and sustainability of funds, especially for recurrent expenditures, at the local level. Evaluations suggest that only a few global programs provide truly global public goods; many so-called global programs actually provide national or local goods (see also chapter 2 of this report). This suggests the need for selectivity in establishing global programs to avoid their uncoordinated proliferation. Another concern is that the funds raised by global programs may crowd out other funds rather than provide net additional resources; they may also compete with country and local programs for scarce resources and staff. Clearly a balance has to be struck between country-owned priorities and global program objectives. The MDBs are well placed to help reinforce the centrality of country strategies and ensure that global programs complement rather than compete with them. The convening power of MDBs can also help reduce the costs of donor fragmentation that a welter of global programs might otherwise foster.

Debt Relief

Progress on Implementing the MDRI

The past year saw major progress in extending and deepening debt relief to the poorest countries. Following a 2005 proposal by the G-8, three multilateral institutions—the AfDF, IDA, and the IMF—implemented the new Multilateral Debt Relief Initiative (MDRI), and agreed to provide 100 percent debt relief on their eligible claims to countries that have reached, or will eventually reach, the completion point under the HIPC Initiative. The MDRI was implemented at the beginning of 2006 by the IMF, in mid-2006 by IDA, and early 2007 by the AfDF (for the latter, delivery of debt relief will be provided retroactively to the beginning of 2006). To date, 22 postcompletion-point HIPCs have benefited from debt relief under this new initiative, which amounts to about $38 billion (in nominal terms)—two non-HIPCs, Cambodia and Tajikistan, have also received MDRI relief from the Fund. The remaining HIPCs that have not yet reached the completion point will automatically qualify for the MDRI once they do so.

The full cost of the MDRI for the three institutions is expected to be around $50 billion. The MDRI commits donors to providing additional resources to ensure that the reflow losses associated with debt forgiveness do not undermine these institutions' overall financial integrity or ability to provide financial support to low-income countries.[22] Last year's GMR presented the baselines established by IDA and the AfDF on which additionality of donor financing is to be assessed. Monitoring donors' commitments on financing the MDRI is important to ensuring actual additionality of donor financing over time. Chapter 5 presents the progress on donor financing of the MDRI; as of end-2006, IDA donors had provided firm financing commitments of $3.8 billion over the four decades of MDRI implementation, against a volume of irrevocable debt relief provided by IDA under the MDRI of currently $28.3 billion.[23] The upcoming IDA-15 replenishment will be an important test of donors' intentions regarding their support of the MDRI.

The proposal recently approved by the Inter-American Development Bank (IADB) to provide debt cancellation to postcompletion-point HIPCs (Guyana, Bolivia, Honduras, and Nicaragua) and to Haiti once it reaches completion point, in line with the MDRI, will provide debt relief of $4.4 billion—$3.4 billion in principal and $1 billion in interest—to these countries. Debt cancellation will be financed by the IADB out of internal sources, more specifically, from existing Funds for Special Operations (FSO). However, there is currently no consideration of an FSO replenishment linked to the above.

PROGRESS ON THE HIPC INITIATIVE

Overall, substantial progress has been made in the implementation of the HIPC Initiative. As of end-March 2007, 30 HIPCs have reached the decision point and are receiving debt relief. Progress toward reaching the com-

pletion point—when creditors provide the full amount of debt relief committed at the decision point on an irrevocable basis—continued in early 2007; four additional countries reached the completion point, bringing the total number of countries that have done so to 22. Several of the eight countries in the interim period between their decision point and completion point are on track with respect to their macroeconomic programs; others that experienced difficulties in program implementation are pursuing the necessary policy measures to bring their economic programs back on track (IMF-World Bank 2006b).[24]

Debt relief under the HIPC Initiative is projected to substantially lower debt and debt service ratios for most HIPCs that have reached the decision point. Net present value (NPV) of debt stocks in the 30 HIPCs that reached the decision point by end-March 2007 are projected to decline by about two-thirds once they reach their respective completion points, and by about 90 percent after the application of the MDRI (figure 4.11). The ratio of debt ser-

FIGURE 4.11   Reduction of debt stock (NPV terms) for the 30 decision-point countries

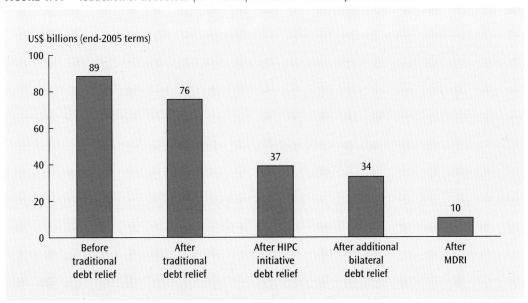

Sources: HIPC Initiative documents; IDA and IMF staff estimates.
Note: Based on decision-point debt stocks. (Updated compared to Progress Report to include Malawi, São Tomé and Principe, and Sierra Leone as completion-point countries and Haiti as interim country.)

vice to exports for these countries is estimated to have declined from an average of about 17 percent in 1998–99 to about 7 percent in 2005. These ratios are estimated to have declined further to about 4 percent in 2006.

For these 30 countries, poverty-reducing expenditures on average have risen from about 7 percent of GDP in 1999 to over 9 percent of GDP in 2005, a level more than five times that spent on debt service. In absolute terms, poverty-reducing spending is estimated to have increased from about $6 billion in 1999 to $15 billion in 2005, and is projected to have increased to $18 billion in 2006. Because of problems with cross-country consistency in the definition of poverty-related expenditures, it might be useful instead to review the trend in health and education expenditures (box 4.4).

THE CHALLENGE OF KEEPING DEBT BURDENS SUSTAINABLE

The challenge for countries receiving MDRI debt relief is to ensure that financial resources freed up by debt reduction are used for

---

BOX 4.4 Debt service savings and social expenditures: Is there a link?

Recent data suggest a relationship between cuts in debt service costs and increases in social expenditures for HIPCs. Using data on health and education expenditures for 110 countries for 1985–2003/04, Thomas (2006) finds that social expenditures in relation to output have risen gradually over time in both HIPC (an approximately 2 percentage point increase) and middle-income countries, whereas the ratio has fluctuated more widely for other low-income countries.[a] Debt service

Trends in social expenditures and debt service

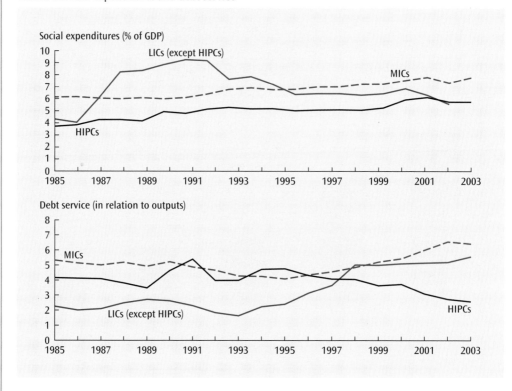

continued

BOX 4.4   Debt service savings and social expenditures: Is there a link?
(continued)

in relation to output has declined continuously among HIPC countries since the introduction of the HIPC initiative in 1996 while debt service costs have risen for middle-income and other low-income countries over this period. Econometric estimates confirm that the HIPC relationship is significant at the 10 percent level of significance. Moreover, social expenditures are protected from expenditure cuts among low-income countries but are boosted by expansionary budgets.

Over 2000–02, the social expenditure ratio among HIPCs rose rapidly by almost 1 percentage point and has subsequently stabilized at this level. The main factors associated with these changes include an expansionary budget policy in 2000 and lower debt service payments since then. Exports also appear to have played a contributing role in 2000, possibly because strong export growth is an indicator of a strong-performing economy.

Contribution to the change in social expenditures

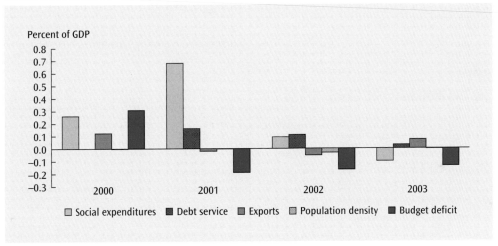

a. Some studies including Clements, Bhattacharya, and Nguyen (2003) find that the ratio of debt service to output is significantly negative relative to the public investment rate: with a coefficient of 0.2 they estimate that a decline in debt-service/GDP ratio from 10 percent to 5 percent would raise public investment/GDP by 1 percentage point. Kraay and Depetris Chauvin (2005) find that debt relief has not contributed to any significant change in health and education expenditures. One criticism is that they use imputed values of debt relief (PV terms). But one problem with using debt service is that debt service can change for reasons other than debt relief.

reaching the MDGs. Post debt relief, these countries are experiencing an increase in their perceived borrowing space as well as in the availability of financing from emerging official and private creditors and domestic sources. While these developments are welcome, they could raise new risks, if debt is built up too rapidly and abruptly. The debt sustainability framework for low-income countries, endorsed by the Boards of the IMF and IDA in 2005, can help countries design a financing strategy that will mitigate these risks without unnecessarily constraining access to resources for development.

The Boards of the IMF and IDA reviewed in late 2006 the application of this framework and have agreed to refinements aimed at improving the rigor and quality of the analyses in the post debt relief context. They concluded that ensuring long-term sustainability requires efforts by borrowers, lenders, and donors to promote prudent borrowing and a suitable mix of concessional and other finance. To this end, the broader use of the debt sustainability framework by creditors would help disseminate information between borrowers and creditors, as well as among creditors, and better inform financing decisions.[25] In addition, the capacity of borrowing countries to manage and monitor their debt must be strengthened so countries can develop their own medium-term strategy to support national development objectives, while containing the associated risks of debt distress and macroeconomic vulnerability. Improving the quality and availability of debt data—external and domestic debt—will be important to support monitoring and assessment of debt and associated risks.

Trade

Major Developments in Global Trade

World trade in 2006 continued its strong growth trend of recent years. Worldwide exports of merchandise reached $12 trillion in 2006, growing 16 percent in value, well above the average growth of 8 percent recorded in 1995–2004. Reflecting increases in fuel prices, fuel-exporting countries experienced the highest export growth, at 23 percent, but global non-oil exports also grew 15 percent. At 22

percent, developing-country export growth continued to outpace the global average. Turning to individual regions, higher energy prices contributed to export growth of 22 percent in Middle Eastern and North African countries. China continued its strong recent export performance, with a 27 percent increase in 2006. Exports from Sub-Saharan Africa continued to benefit from the healthy global economy, recording a 23 percent increase overall, while least-developed countries experienced a remarkable 25 percent growth. Industrialized countries expanded their exports at a more modest 4 percent rate.

In addition to favorable cyclical factors, last year's global trade performance reflects continuing unilateral trade reforms. Average tariffs in developing countries have fallen from 16.3 percent in 1997 to 11 percent in 2006. As the pace of global integration increases, the challenge of harnessing the new opportunities while managing the risks places a premium on a strategy of greater openness to trade, coupled with behind-the-border reforms. For example, a number of countries have proved able to compete with China following the phase-out of textile and clothing quotas, but central to their success have been reform of their tariffs and investment climate and support from the international community to overcome infrastructure constraints (box 4.5).

BOX 4.5   Developing-country clothing exports in a postquota world

The clothing sector has been at the forefront of export diversification in many developing countries, and employment in the sector has been an important source of income for many women. But trade in this sector is undergoing a profound change, as the system of quantitative restrictions that managed the industrial countries' imports of textiles and clothing for 30 years was finally dismantled at the end of 2004 as part of WTO Uruguay Round agreement. This change engendered widespread fears that global markets for textiles and clothing would be swamped by Chinese products, with adverse implications for other developing countries. Does this sector still serve today's low-income countries as the first rung on the ladder to higher-value-added exports?

Early signs suggest that adjustments in production patterns and trade flows following the removal of quotas have been less drastic than anticipated. Although China's total exports soared by 29 percent between 2004 and 2005, its share of global clothing exports has increased at a slower rate.[a] The substantial growth in the world market for clothing has allowed exports from many other countries, including Colombia, Egypt, India, Madagascar, Peru, Sri Lanka, and Turkey, to increase.

continued

BOX 4.5   Developing-country clothing exports in a postquota world *(continued)*

In Bangladesh, where the loss of 1 million jobs had been predicted (Oxfam 2004), exports to the European Union and the United States instead increased strongly between 2004 and 2006.

Nevertheless, some countries have seen substantial declines in exports of clothing. Exports to the European Union and the United States from Brazil, the Dominican Republic, and Swaziland have decreased by about 20 percent, and exports from Taiwan Province of China have fallen by nearly 30 percent. The clothing sectors in these economies face significant adjustment. Even in countries that have managed to increase exports, pressure for adjustment may be strong as the more efficient firms expand while those unable to compete in the global market decline. In the absence of other employment opportunities, especially for women, workers laid off from the textile and clothing sectors may fall back into poverty. Minimizing the costs incurred by these workers and their families and facilitating their shift to other productive activities will be a major challenge in a number of developing countries.

In Africa, where the end of the clothing sector had been predicted, exports have generally fallen (by 12.3 percent on a trade-weighted average), but some countries, such as Madagascar and Kenya, have managed to maintain or even increase exports. The slowdown in African clothing exports observed during 2005 has also started to reverse. Sub-Saharan African clothing exports to the European Union in the first eight months of 2006 were nearly 8 percent higher than in the same period in 2005 (but still 8 percent lower than in 2004). Exports to the United States, however, have continued to decline, falling 12.5 percent during 2006 after a 14 percent drop in 2005 (largely driven by Mauritius and South Africa). On the plus side, the downward trend in exports has reversed for 14 countries.[b]

The prospects for African exports of clothing to the United States have been enhanced by the recent extension, to 2012, of the nonrestrictive rules of origin under the African Growth and Opportunities Act (AGOA). These rules allow African producers to globally source the fabrics used in their garments and still receive U.S. trade preferences. In contrast, the European Union offers tariff preferences with restrictive rules that deny producers the ability to use the best and lowest-cost inputs wherever they may be found. The AGOA rules of origin were critical in the substantial increase of African clothing exports to the United States between 2000 and 2004, a period during which exports to the European Union stagnated.

The countries best able to expand clothing exports will be those that have a supportive business environment, low trade costs (efficient customs, ports, and other transport infrastructure), and competitive firms flexible enough to meet the changing demands of the global buyers that now dominate the industry. With these conditions in place, the clothing sector can still be a driver of industrial diversification in many poor countries, even in the face of unfettered competition from China.

a. Europe and the United States have introduced a number of temporary restrictions on imports from China under the special safeguards agreement included as part of China's WTO accession. It has been suggested that the very rapid surge in exports from China to both the European Union and the United States before the safeguard was imposed was partly a response to its anticipated use by increasing the base for quota calculations. The reimposition of limits on selected Chinese exports is likely also to have spillover effects on third parties.
b. Based on figures for January through October 2006. The United States and the European Union accounted for a large but declining share of global clothing imports, 23 and 35 percent, respectively, in 2005. Madagascar accounts for nearly two-thirds of the net increase in exports to the European Union between 2005 and 2006. At the same time, however, its exports to the United States have fallen.

UPDATE ON COUNTRY POLICIES

Trade policies and domestic welfare. Governments use a variety of instruments that have the effect of restraining trade, whether intentionally or as a side effect. For example, tariffs and antidumping actions have the restriction of imports as their explicit objective; regulatory policies motivated by public health or safety concerns do not, but may limit trade nonetheless. In fact, such policies may affect trade in a very product-specific way, with different effects on different countries. When quantifying the overall effects of a country's national trade policy, then, it is important to consider nontariff measures as well as tariffs. This report does so using two separate measures of trade-related policies. The first is a trade restrictiveness index (TRI), which is a measure of the impact of tariffs imposed by a country on itself. The second, called the Overall Trade Restrictiveness Index (OTRI), captures the impact of both tariffs and nontariff measures on a country's trading partners, that is, on the exporters that ship goods to the country.[26]

Assuming a country cannot affect its terms of trade, tariffs increase the relative price of imported goods in the country imposing them, thereby reducing national welfare. One way to quantify this loss of welfare is to calculate the deadweight loss due to the existing tariff structure. This can be done by comparing the welfare of the country given its TRI with what would obtain under zero tariffs.[27] The average TRI for all countries is 13 percent, with Bangladesh's the highest at 66 percent (see the annex to this chapter). The TRI is generally higher in developing than in industrial countries (table 4.2). Tariffs in Japan, however, generate the largest absolute deadweight loss of any single country ($28 billion in 2004), with Korea ($25 billion) a close second. Bangladesh and Korea suffer the highest losses in proportion to their economies, each

at more than 3 percent of GDP. By comparison, the average low-income country loses the equivalent of about 0.4 percent of its GDP as a result of its tariffs. The total deadweight loss that tariffs inflict on the world as a whole is on the order of $100 billion a year.[28]

Agricultural protection is the main source of these losses (table 4.2), particularly in high-income countries. Canada, Japan, Korea, Norway, Switzerland, and the European Union as a group all have TRIs for agriculture that exceed 40 percent (see the annex). The worldwide average TRI on agricultural goods, at about 22 percent, is twice that for manufactured goods.

Trade policies and trade flows. The last two columns of table 4.2 summarize the effect of all observed trade policies on trade flows of exporters, as measured by the OTRI, for high-, middle-, and low-income countries.[29] The OTRI includes the effects of regulatory measures such as product standards, as well as policies such as import licensing requirements and antidumping actions. As previous editions of *Global Monitoring Report* have stressed, the OTRI is a measure of trade restrictiveness, not protection. It measures the effect of included policies in limiting trade; it is not a measure of protectionist intent. As the table shows, the average OTRI for developing countries is 16 percent, and that for high-income countries about 8 percent. The effect of trade restrictions in the latter group of countries is to reduce annual imports by

TABLE 4.2 Trade restrictiveness and its impact on welfare and trade flows, by country income group, 2004

	Tariffs and impact on importing country							All trade restrictions and impact on trade flows	
	All goods			Agricultural goods		Manufactured goods			
		Welfare loss							
Country group	TRI	Billions of dollars	Percent of GDP	TRI	Welfare loss (billions of dollars)	TRI	Welfare loss (billions of dollars)	OTRI	Loss (billions of dollars)
High income	10	74.5	0.2	40	65.3	4	9.2	8	261.6
Middle income	15	13.3	0.2	30	3.8	12	9.5	16	180.3
Low income[a]	16	5.2	0.4	18	1.4	16	3.9	16	29.2

Source: World Bank staff calculations.
a. Data available for 22 countries only.

about $260 billion. The comparable figure for middle-income countries is about $180 billion, and that for the 22 low-income countries in the sample about $29 billion.

As with the TRI, the average OTRI for agriculture is much higher than that for manufacturing. Many developing countries impose similar levels of restrictiveness on agricultural imports as on manufactures, but for some developing nations the OTRI for agriculture is far higher than for goods. In India, for example, the ratio of agricultural to nonagricultural trade restrictiveness increased significantly following the recent liberalization of trade in industrial products. For developed countries this ratio tends to be much higher than in most developing countries, rising to 10 or more.

Changes in trade restrictiveness, 2000–06. Reflecting a steady reduction in tariffs, the global impact of policies in restricting trade has declined in recent years.[30] Except for a number of African countries, most economies have lower OTRIs than in 2000 (figure 4.12). Developing countries that have seen substantial falls in their OTRIs include India, Egypt, Nigeria, and Mauritius, as well as China and many Latin American nations. Among developed countries, overall trade restrictiveness in Japan and the United States has fallen somewhat, while it has remained largely unchanged in Canada and in the European Union.

Much of the decline in OTRIs pertains to manufacturing; much less has been achieved in agriculture. In a number of countries the agricultural sector is now more restrictive

FIGURE 4.12 Overall trade restrictiveness has declined (2000–06)

	Decrease (>5%)	Some Decrease (1–5%)	Small–No Change	Some Increase (1–5%)	Increase (>5%)
All Products	Burkina Faso, China, Côte d'Ivoire, Egypt, Ghana, India, Jordan, Kazakhstan, Lebanon, Mauritius, Morocco, Nigeria, Papua New Guinea, Paraguay, Peru, Philippines, Tunisia, Uruguay	Albania, Algeria, Argentina, Australia, Belarus, Bolivia, Brazil, Brunei, Chile, Colombia, El Salvador, Guatemala, Honduras, Indonesia, Japan, Kenya, Malaysia, Mali, Mexico, Moldova, Nicaragua, Russian Fed., Saudi Arabia, Senegal, Singapore, Switzerland, Tanzania, Thailand, Turkey, United States, Zambia	Bangladesh, Cameroon, Canada, Costa Rica, Ethiopia, European Union, Gabon, Hong Kong, China, Iceland, Korea, Rep. of, New Zealand, Norway, Oman, Romania, Sri Lanka, Trinidad and Tobago, Ukraine, Venezuela, R.B. de	Madagascar, Malawi, Uganda, South Africa	Sudan, Uganda
Agriculture	Argentina, Bangladesh, Burkina Faso, Chile, China, Côte d'Ivoire, Ghana, Guatemala, Lebanon, Mauritius, Nicaragua, Papua New Guinea, Peru, Thailand, Turkey, Ukraine, Zambia	Albania, Canada, Colombia, El Salvador, Ethiopia, Gabon, Iceland, Indonesia, Malaysia, Mexico, Paraguay, Russian Fed., Saudi Arabia, Senegal, Singapore, Sri Lanka, Uruguay, United States, Venezuela, R.B. de	Australia, Brazil, Brunei, Costa Rica, Egypt, European Union, Honduras, Hong Kong, China, Jordan, Kazakhstan, Korea, Rep. of, Mali, New Zealand, Nigeria, Philippines, Switzerland, Tanzania, Trinidad and Tobago	Algeria, Belarus, Bolivia, Cameroon, Japan, Madagascar, Malawi, Moldova, Morocco, Norway, Romania, Rwanda, South Africa, Sudan, Tunisia	India, Kenya, Oman, Uganda

Source: World Bank staff estimates.

than it was six years ago; the European Union has seen virtually no change, while Canada and the United States have registered a small decline in agricultural trade restrictiveness since 2000. A small number of countries, including Argentina, China, and Chile have achieved substantial reductions in the OTRI for agriculture since 2000.

Trade policies and market access. The effect of policies on exporters' access to markets differs across exporting regions (table 4.3).[31] These differences are partly the result of discriminatory application of trade policies (that is, trade preferences), but mostly they reflect differences in the product composition of exports. Agriculture generally faces much more restrictive market access conditions than manufacturing. Because of this, regions exporting mainly agricultural products generally face more restrictive markets than regions where manufacturing dominates the export sector. This is one reason why trade among developing countries is affected by high levels of trade restrictiveness. For example, Latin American exporters face

an average OTRI of 48 percent in the Middle East and North Africa, while products originating in Sub-Saharan Africa confront a 38 percent average OTRI in South Asia.

Table 4.3 reports both the OTRI including nontariff measures and a tariffs-only version of the OTRI. Nontariff measures (NTMs) have a substantial impact on the level of the OTRI, especially in countries with low tariffs. As mentioned previously, NTMs are not necessarily protectionist in intent, but they can represent a significant burden, especially for exports originating in developing countries. In practice, developing countries often benefit from tariff preferences in and enjoy duty- and quota-free access to many industrial-country markets, implying that NTMs, not tariffs, are the main factor restricting their access to these markets. The incidence of nontariff measures is highly product-specific. As the product composition of exports varies widely across exporters, there is often a wide range of OTRIs confronting different countries in the same market.

Antidumping. With the steady decline in tariff barriers, countries seeking to re-impose

TABLE 4.3 Market access (OTRI)

Importing Region	Exporting Region					
	Latin America & Caribbean	Europe & Central Asia	East Asia & Pacific	Middle East & North Africa	South Asia	Sub-Saharan Africa
Latin America	31	11	15	17	24	17
	5	*5*	*6*	*5*	*8*	*11*
Europe & Central Asia	39	21	18	6	40	18
	10	*8*	*7*	*4*	*9*	*14*
East Asia & Pacific	10	12	20	8	15	18
	4	*3*	*4*	*3*	*5*	*8*
Middle East & North Africa	48	25	26	24	28	23
	20	*11*	*12*	*4*	*7*	*6*
South Asia	39	25	29	11	35	38
	19	*15*	*15*	*9*	*7*	*32*
Sub-Saharan Africa	14	13	15	33	25	25
	5	*7*	*9*	*7*	*10*	*4*
All developing countries	27	20	21	13	27	19
	7	*8*	*7*	*5*	*9*	*12*
High-income countries	25	12	18	22	39	32
	6	*4*	*3*	*6*	*10*	*3*

Source: World Bank staff estimates.
Note: Values in *italics* are tariff-only OTRIs (i.e., excluding NTMs). Regions are developing country only.

protection often resort to so-called contingent protection measures, such as antidumping and safeguard actions. Major users of antidumping now include developing as well as industrial countries; indeed, India is now the most frequent user of this instrument. Worldwide, the number of antidumping investigations increased from about 1,200 in 1995–99 to almost 1,400 during 2000–04; the share of investigations started by developing countries rose from 43 percent to 48 percent. China is the leading target of such actions. Notwithstanding their much smaller share in world trade, middle-income countries as a group have surpassed the high-income countries as targets for investigations.

Given the small share of total imports hit by antidumping investigations, antidumping has a negligible effect on trade worldwide and little impact on overall trade restrictiveness. However, the protectionist effect of antidumping can be great for certain specific imports from targeted countries, and the threat of antidumping can have a chilling effect on the expansion and pricing of exports. The average effect of antidumping investigations imposed by India is estimated to be equal to a 44 percent ad-valorem tariff equivalent for the affected products. Antidumping investigations launched by China generate an ad valorem equivalent of 36 percent. In the industrial countries the effect of antidumping investigations tends to be smaller; in the case of the European Union the average ad valorem equivalent is about 13 percent.[32]

The Doha Round Negotiations

Despite intensive consultations throughout June and July, negotiations on the Doha Round were effectively suspended on July 23, 2006, amid disagreement over how ambitious an agreement to seek on agricultural market access and on greater reductions in trade-distorting domestic support in agriculture. Major players expressed their disappointment while uniformly reaffirming their commitment to a successful outcome.

The remaining months of 2006 saw efforts to relaunch the negotiations through intensive bilateral consultations and a series of ministerial meetings. These efforts culminated on February 7, 2007, in an agreement by World Trade Organization (WTO) members to restart the talks.

The general view is that there is now a narrow window of opportunity to reach agreement early in 2007 on the key elements of a preliminary package that could pave the way for a final deal and be sufficient to assist the extension of U.S. Trade Promotion Authority (TPA) by July 2007. (TPA allows the U.S. president to submit a negotiated trade agreement to Congress for an up-or-down vote, without amendment.) Even with the prospect of such a preliminary Doha deal, however, renewal of TPA is by no means certain. Moreover, notwithstanding some indications of new flexibility among the major players, it is unclear whether agreement on key elements of a preliminary package can be reached in the first half of this year.

The World Bank and the IMF will continue to advocate a timely conclusion to the Doha negotiations and to argue against backsliding on progress already made. While a deal at any price is not supported, many of the proposals reportedly under discussion, when combined with progress already made (such as offers to eliminate agricultural export subsidies by 2013 and to provide duty- and quota-free market access for at least 97 percent of exports from least developed countries), are sufficiently substantive to make a deal worthwhile. Significant gains for developing countries would also flow from services liberalization and trade facilitation, and from aid for trade accompanying the Doha Round.

Failure to conclude the Doha Round would send a strong negative signal to the world economy about the ability of countries to pursue multilateral solutions. It could weaken the multilateral trading system, which provides developing countries with guaranteed nondiscriminatory market access, rules-based settlement of disputes, and transparency of trade regimes. Trade disputes may also increase, feeding protectionist sentiment and overstraining the WTO dispute settlement system. The risk of trade diversion from the growing number of preferential trade agreements (PTAs; see the discussion below) will also increase in the absence of progress on multilateral liberalization, and PTAs will, in any case, continue to leave unaddressed the high levels of trade-distorting domestic support in agriculture.

But the biggest risk of failure in the Doha Round is to countries' own economic growth. Trade reform is fundamentally about self-interest: increasing global competition and domestic budgetary pressures both argue against delay in reforming costly domestic protection. Regardless of the outcome of the Doha talks, countries should continue to pursue unilateral trade reform, and the World Bank and the IMF will continue to work closely with developing countries to support efforts to integrate trade into national development strategies, and to advocate the reform of developed-country trade practices that hamper development efforts.

AID FOR TRADE

Further progress was made on aid for trade in 2006. Support for trade-related assistance continued to grow, while efforts continued to establish the necessary international architecture to ensure improved coordination and effectiveness of this aid. At 2004 constant prices and exchange rates, assistance for trade policy and regulations in 2005 reached $905 million, while trade development activities peaked at $2.17 billion (figure 4.13).[33] Additionally, an estimated $12.1 billion was spent to support the economic infrastructure essential for international trade.

World Bank lending for trade also continued on an upward trend, with 49 trade-related projects undertaken in fiscal 2005 valued at $1.08 billion, and 51 projects in fiscal 2006, valued at $1.61 billion, representing a threefold increase over 2003.[34] Expansion to date has been driven by trade-related infrastructure in support of regional integration in Africa, trade-related infrastructure in East Asia, and

FIGURE 4.13 Aid for trade is rising

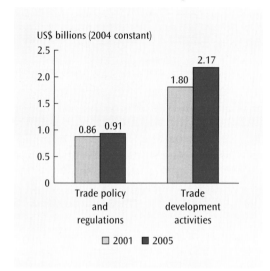

Source: WTO/OECD-DAC Trade Capacity Building database.

budget support to competitiveness reforms in Latin America and the Caribbean. From July to December 2006 (i.e., the first half of fiscal 2007), lending reached $0.8 billion, and this uptrend is expected to be sustained.

The IMF has provided financial support for trade-related adjustment, augmented by the Trade Integration Mechanism (TIM) and the option to use floating tranches of IMF lending to support trade reform in IMF-supported programs.[35] At present, three countries (Bangladesh, the Dominican Republic, and Madagascar) are availing themselves of support under the TIM. Total financing of up to $211 million is being made available to these three countries under the TIM, including amounts that could be drawn (under the TIM deviation feature) in the event the actual BOP effect of qualifying trade policy events turned out to be larger than anticipated.[36]

A focus of international activity on aid for trade in the past year was on establishing the necessary architecture to improve the coordination of such aid. Important elements of this work have taken place under the auspices of the WTO, given the general consensus that aid for trade is an essential complement to, and not a substitute for, a successful outcome to the Doha Round. The Task Force on Enhancing the Integrated Framework (IF)[37] issued its recommendations on July 5, 2006, which included the following: the creation of a new executive secretariat in Geneva; strengthening of country capacity; a funding target for the IF trust fund of $400 million over an initial five-year period; and creation of a monitoring and evaluation framework. The task force also agreed that an IF-type mechanism could be useful for low-income developing countries that are not among the least developed. Transition teams were subsequently established on institutional issues, in-country issues, and the trust fund, with a view to operationalizing the enhanced IF by January 2007. Although progress was made, this deadline was not met. The World Bank and the IMF continue to actively engage with other parties in Geneva to develop workable and effective administrative arrangements for the enhanced IF.

A further international effort to improve the coordination of aid for trade took place under the auspices of the WTO Task Force on Aid for Trade, which also delivered its report in July 2006.[38] The report provided a welcome clarification of the definition of aid for trade. Under that definition, aid for trade encompasses not only activities related to trade policy and regulation and trade development, but also those involving trade-related infrastructure, building productive capacity, and support for trade-related adjustment. The report also contained a series of proposals to improve monitoring and evaluation, including establishment of a monitoring body in the WTO, an annual discussion on aid for trade in the WTO General Council, and inclusion of an assessment of aid for trade, for donors and recipients, in WTO Trade Policy Reviews. The report put forward a range of proposals for strengthening both the supply and the demand sides of aid for trade (and for matching the two), although it stopped short of providing concrete operational recommendations.[39] The report proposed instead that the Director General of the WTO establish an ad hoc consultative group to follow up on its recommendations.

Aid for trade enjoys broad acceptance within the development community as part of the growth agenda, but a number of important challenges remain. Donors have indicated that they are prepared to offer large increases in aid for trade, but how much of this would be additional to existing aid remains unclear. Much also remains to be done to operationalize aid for trade, particularly with respect to supporting countries other than the least developed in the articulation of trade integration strategies, addressing the needs of the growing regional and cross-country agendas, and establishing systems to monitor and evaluate results. Establishing an effective enhanced IF will also be critical. Central to meeting these challenges will be implementation of aid for trade within the parameters of the Paris Principles, using existing development institutions and mechanisms with proven effectiveness.

PREFERENTIAL TRADE AGREEMENTS

PTAs continued to proliferate in 2006, both among developing countries and between developed and developing countries. Approximately 170 still-active PTAs have been notified to the WTO. However, given that many agreements have not been notified, the actual figure is estimated at around 250, with 20 more awaiting ratification and another 70 under negotiation.

In the past year, interest in PTAs has intensified in developing and developed countries alike. Asia has seen a renewed interest in regional integration, prompted in part by China's rapid growth, and meanwhile integration continues to deepen in Latin America. The United States completed negotiations toward a PTA with the Andean countries and is continuing negotiations with Korea, Malaysia, Thailand, and the United Arab Emirates. The European Union's new trade strategy also places a greater emphasis on PTAs (EU 2006). The Association of Southeast Asian Nations, Korea, and Mercosur are identified as priorities for PTAs,

> ## BOX 4.6   Economic Partnership Agreements
>
> The end of the Cotonou agreement in 2008,[a] along with the need to negotiate another WTO waiver for any further unilateral preferences (given that they have been found to be inconsistent with WTO rules), prompted the EU and ACP countries to launch negotiations on EPAs in 2000. EPAs are to be reciprocally negotiated PTAs, providing for mutual market access; some services liberalization; a regulatory agenda on investment, competition, and intellectual property rights; institutional provisions to facilitate trade; and new technical assistance for trade negotiation and development.
>
> The EPAs could spur trade—and raise incomes—in the African, Caribbean, and Pacific countries *if* they catalyze progress toward integration within regions, with other EPA groupings, and with the global market. However, their development impact will depend on their design, and here there are several concerns. First, the EPA regional groupings do not conform to existing common markets and PTAs. Coupled with the uneven progress in implementing existing regional agreements and the reluctance of the European Union to date to accept variable geometry,[b] this makes it difficult for countries to leverage the negotiations to promote effective intraregional liberalization. Second, preferential access for the EU countries and their neighbors behind currently high most-favored-nation (MFN) tariffs may displace more efficient sources of supply, underlining the need for MFN tariff reductions to precede backloaded preferential access for EU firms in EPA markets. Third, access to the EU market may be restricted if rules of origin, as yet undefined, require local value added greater than (say) 10 percent. Fourth, trade reforms, especially preferences to EU firms, may cut into public sector revenue when they are enacted, requiring compensatory tax reforms phased in to match any losses in tariff revenues. Finally, a key issue is the level of additional aid for trade on the table. Although there are benefits to keeping discussion of appropriate levels of aid for trade separate from the negotiations, this has eliminated one major incentive for the least-developed countries to join EPAs, since they already enjoy duty- and quota-free access to the EU countries under the Everything But Arms initiative. Appropriately designed, pro-development EPAs can help the ACP countries move forward on reforms to promote their competitiveness and regional integration.
>
> *Source:* Hinkle, Hoppe, and Newfarmer 2005.
> a. The Cotonou agreement covers unilateral trade preferences and development cooperation between member states of the European Union and their former colonies in the African, Caribbean, and Pacific regions.
> b. Variable geometry refers to arrangements under which not all countries in a regional grouping need to have a common external tariff on a most-favored-nation basis or toward the European Union.

with India, Russia, and the Gulf Cooperation Council members also of interest. The strategy also places emphasis on enhanced trade relations with Turkey, the Southern Mediterranean countries, and some countries of the former Soviet Union (under the New Neighborhood Policy).

The European Union is also due to finalize the ongoing negotiations with African, Caribbean, and Pacific (ACP) countries under the Economic Partnership Agreements (EPAs).[40] The EPAs offer an important opportunity for trade reform in many countries, notably in Africa, but have also highlighted the extent to which the design of agreements can influence their development impact (box 4.6). Properly designed PTAs can benefit their members, especially if combined with a nondiscriminatory reduction in external barriers. But if they are designed badly, the cost of such agreements, in terms of trade diversion, high information costs, and demands on limited institutional capacity, may well exceed the benefits. For example, as many as half of all PTAs may divert more trade than they create, and bilateral "hub and spoke" PTAs benefit the hub (the rich country) disproportionately more than the spokes (developing countries).[41]

Notes

1. The larger emerging economies are also playing a greater role in trade, investment, and private financial flows to poor countries. For example, both China and India doubled their annual growth rates of imports from Africa between 1990–94 and 1999–2004; these two countries account for 50 percent of Asia's exports to Africa (see Broadman 2006 for an analysis of Africa-Asia trade.) Foreign direct investment in Africa from emerging economies, particularly Brazil, China, India, Malaysia, and South Africa, is also growing rapidly.

2. Global Monitoring Report 2006 discussed the increased risk of situations where nonconcessional lenders may indirectly obtain financial gain from debt forgiveness, grants, and concessional financing by the international financial institutions. This could lead to an excessive buildup of debt if nonconcessional borrowing is not carefully managed.

3. In collaboration with Portugal and the European Foundation Centre, the DAC will cosponsor an international conference on the developmental role of philanthropic foundations in early 2007.

4. Under an AMC, donors guarantee a set envelope of funding at a given price for a new vaccine that meets specified target requirements.

5. Also see Heller and others (2006) for fiscal policy issues with scaled-up aid; Gupta, Powell, and Yang (2006) for macroeconomic management with scaling up aid; and Bourguignon and others (2004, 2005) for a general dynamic equilibrium model for analyzing MDG strategies.

6. Based on a review of the PRS-budget link in nine poor countries, Renzio, Wilhelm, and Williamson (2006) find that policy making, planning, and budgeting are typically fragmented processes. To strengthen the PRS-budget link, they recommend accessing high-level support for policies, targeting PRS and budget processes on the actual decision making, and harmonizing existing planning and budgeting processes.

7. The ACGF is a multidonor trust fund with initial capital of $379 million from the UK. The first tranche of $56.8 million was received in the fall of 2006, and five ACGF projects with total projected disbursements of $148 million are under preparation. The Bank's Africa region is actively seeking other contributors to the ACGF, and several donors have expressed interest in contributing to the fund in fiscal 2007.

8. See OECD (2005b) for an analysis of earlier trends in ODA for gender equality.

9. The financial cost of reducing gender inequality is difficult to calculate, both because gender inequality is multidimensional and multisectoral, and because efforts to reduce it must necessarily work through multiple channels, not just those focused on gender. The task of collecting adequate data alone is expensive and difficult, which poses a challenge to countries in estimating the financial resources needed to achieve gender equity goals.

10. The nine agencies are the Australian Agency for International Development, Finland's Ministry of Foreign Affairs, the Norwegian Agency for Development Cooperation, the Swedish International Development Agency, the United Kingdom's Department for International Development, the International Labour Organization, the United Nations Development Programme, UN Habitat, and the World Food Programme. See Gender Mainstreaming Evaluations: An Assessment report discussed at the DAC-WB sponsored OECD DAC Gendernet meeting of November 2006. This section was completed with information from a number of donor members' of DAC Gendernet, including from Canada and the United States.

11. See individual country needs assessments and Grown and others (2006).

12. Health interventions include upgrading clinics with comprehensive prenatal, antenatal, and emergency obstetric care; providing vitamin, mineral, and nutrition supplements for mothers and children; sensitizing men to risks of STDs and providing service; managing malaria and anemia in pregnancy. Education interventions include literacy programs for women and provision of separate bathrooms for girls. Interventions in agriculture, infrastructure, and urban development include subsidizing home energy costs for female-headed households and building day care centers, shelters, and community centers.

13. The World Bank's Country Policy and Institutional Assessment rates countries against a set of 16 criteria grouped in four clusters: (1) economic management; (2) structural policies; (3) policies for social inclusion and equity; and (4) public sector management and institutions. Individual countries are scored on a scale of 1–6, with 6 being the highest.

14. The special circumstances of fragile states could influence the composition of aid.

15. This follows the analysis in Levin and Dollar (2005). The coefficient on the fragile state dummy shows whether this group of countries

receives more (i.e., the coefficient is positive and significant) or less (i.e., the coefficient is negative and significant) aid than would be predicted by the other explanatory variables in the regression equation.

16. Data presented here are preliminary estimates (as of March 1, 2007) and are being reviewed by the OECD/DAC Joint Venture on Monitoring the Paris Declaration. The data reflect implementation as of 2005 for donors that provided a grand total of more than $100 million for the government sector. A final report by that group is expected to be published by early April 2007. The broad trends are, however, expected to remain stable.

17. OECD DAC 2006a.

18. Last year's GMR detailed the following areas: the harmonization road map; the joint/collaborative assistance strategy; the common performance assessment framework; coordinated budget support; sectorwide approaches; joint diagnostic/analytic work; use of common arrangement; and the independent monitoring process.

19. World Bank 2006b.

20. OECD DAC 2007b.

21. Most aid for health programs is targeted to a particular program or disease, often reflecting the priorities and interests of foreign donors, as opposed to local residents, and these programs are seldom integrated into general public health systems. Moreover, by drawing resources away from other public health funding recipients, they often fail to improve the overall health of the population (see Garrett 2007).

22. Chapter 5 of the report presents donors' MDRI financing commitments against targets.

23. Multilateral Debt Relief Initiative (MDRI): Update on debt relief by IDA and donor financing to date (February 2007).

24. In September 2006, the two Boards decided to let the sunset clause of the Initiative take effect at end-2006 and to grandfather the countries that meet the income and indebtedness criteria at end-2004.

25. IMF-World Bank 2006a.

26. One of the major advantages of the OTRI over the more commonly used indicators of trade restrictiveness is that the OTRI takes into account the effect of nontariff policies on trade. While the OTRI estimates have been very robust to recent improvements to the methodology—which is well-established and directly related to generally accepted concepts in trade policy analysis—it is important to note that the existing data on nontariff policy is generally of lower quality than data on tariffs (less timely and less comprehensive). Thus, underlying data weaknesses may affect the accuracy of the OTRI for some countries. Greater investment by governments in support of the activities of the international trade agencies that compile the data on tariffs and, especially, nontariff measures, that feed into the OTRI estimates would improve their quality.

27. A deadweight loss is the loss in economic efficiency (consumer surplus) caused by policies that prevent agents from equating marginal costs to marginal benefits. The TRI is the uniform tariff that would provide the same level of welfare in the importing country as the existing tariff structure. It is calculated on tariffs only, because certain nontariff measures may be welfare enhancing. For a detailed discussion of the methodology used to estimate this index, see Kee, Nicita, and Olarreaga (2006).

28. This figure is comparable to the results from general equilibrium models, which suggest annual global welfare losses from protection ranging from $78 billion to $128 billion.

29. The OTRI is defined as the uniform tariff-equivalent that will yield the observed level of aggregate imports, which is determined by the prevailing set of tariffs and nontariff measures in a country. In addition to tariffs and specific duties, the OTRI includes all the nontariff measures reported in the UNCTAD TRAINS database as well as data on product standards compiled by the World Bank. Only data from publicly available sources are used. It should be recognized that the quality of data on NTMs is below that for data on tariffs, in terms of both comprehensiveness of coverage and timeliness (NTM data may not be updated annually).

30. Because the OTRI is designed to take into account the value of imports and the import demand elasticities at the six-digit level of the Harmonized System of commodity classification, changes in the OTRI may reflect not only changes in observed trade-related policies but also changes in import composition and import prices.

31. Calculations are based on the Market Access version of the OTRI (MA-OTRI). This measures the average level of restrictiveness in all importing countries that receive an export product of a country, keeping the aggregate exports of that country constant. For a detailed discussion of the methodology used to estimate this index, see Kee, Nicita, and Olarreaga (2006).

32. These estimates are based on the impacts of antidumping investigations on bilateral trade in

the affected products, controlling for other determinants of trade in a product between the exporting and the importing (imposing) country. This methodology focuses on the effects of investigations, not their outcomes, and therefore captures the potential "chilling" effect of the mere launching of investigations on trade flows.

33. The definitions and figures used here come from the OECD-DAC/WTO database on trade-related assistance. Figures refer to commitments. Trade policy and regulations include support for participation in multilateral trade negotiations, analysis and implementation of multilateral trade agreements, trade policy mainstreaming and technical standards, trade facilitation including tariff structures and customs regimes, support to PTAs, and human resource development in trade. Trade development activities include business development, activities aimed at improving the business climate, access to trade finance, and trade promotion, including at the enterprise and institutional level.

34. For a broader overview of World Bank and IMF activities on aid for trade, see IMF-World Bank (2006c).

35. The TIM seeks to assist IMF member countries in meeting balance of payments shortfalls that might result from multilateral trade liberalization. In addition to its regular policy dialogue on trade with member countries in the context of Article IV consultations and IMF-supported programs, the IMF has provided diagnostic support and policy discussions to member countries, as well as an increased focus on trade and trade facilitation issues in technical assistance for customs and tax reform.

36. Several regular, ongoing IMF arrangements support adjustment in the context of domestic trade reform. Thus far there has been no request for the incorporation of floating tranches related to trade adjustment in Fund arrangements.

37. The Integrated Framework for Trade-Related Technical Assistance (IF) is a cooperative interagency effort (involving the IMF, the International Trade Centre, UNCTAD, the United Nations Development Programme, the World Bank, and the WTO) supported by bilateral donors aimed at facilitating coordination of trade-related technical assistance to the least-developed countries and mainstreaming trade into national development and poverty reduction strategies.

38. The task force included Barbados, Brazil, Canada, China, Colombia, the European Union, Japan, India, Thailand, the United States, and the coordinators of the ACP (Africa, Caribbean and Pacific), African, and least-developed-country groups.

39. The task force also highlighted the need to address regional or cross-country aid for trade issues, where cooperation on trade-related projects could help promote the competitiveness of low-income countries in ways that purely national interventions could only do inefficiently or not at all. This issue had also been highlighted by the World Bank and the IMF, which put forward a range of proposals to address these concerns at their 2006 annual meetings. The Development Committee agreed on the need to improve existing instruments to address cross-country and regional projects and to strengthen the monitoring of regional initiatives and funding.

40. Particular attention is given to the EPA agreements becausee they concern many of the world's poorest countries, which are facing particular challenges in meeting the MDGs. Furthermore, EPAs have implications for implementation of existing preferential trade arrangements in Africa. Development of PTAs in other regions, notably Asia, is generally among the higher-growth middle-income countries.

41. For a fuller discussion, see World Bank, Global Economic Prospects 2005.

Monitoring the Performance of International Financial Institutions

The environment in which the international financial institutions (IFIs)—the World Bank, the International Monetary Fund (IMF), and the regional development banks—operate today is different from that of just a few years ago. Globalization, a growing differentiation among developing countries, the availability of alternative financial resources, and the multiplication of actors on the development landscape—all these have forced IFIs to adapt their strategies for supporting developing countries' efforts to meet the Millennium Development Goals (MDGs). Through closer collaboration with one another and with development partners, and through reform of their own governance, these institutions are seeking greater legitimacy and relevance in a world of overlapping and increasingly complex development mandates. This chapter examines the responsibilities of the IFIs within the Monterrey compact and their recent performance in carrying out those responsibilities.

Evolving Roles

All IFIs are constantly adapting their strategies to respond to new demands and the changing external environment. The IMF recently conducted a broad-based review of its medium-term strategy (box 5.1).[1] The World Bank and the regional development banks have devoted considerable attention to clarifying roles and determining priorities. Although deliberations are still under way, and agreement has not yet been reached on all the trade-offs, discussions to date have highlighted five key challenges:

■ How best to support progress toward the MDGs in the poorest countries
■ How to strengthen and adapt the IFIs' engagement in middle-income countries
■ How to respond to the challenges of globalization and the need for global public goods
■ How to better promote coherence and collaboration among IFIs and between them and their development partners, and
■ How to strengthen the voice and representation of developing countries in the governance of the IFIs.

Accelerating Progress on MDGs in the Poorest Countries

Increased financing, advice, and capacity support from the IFIs is critical if low-income countries are to sustain recent progress in implementing the MDGs. Poverty reduction strategies provide a sound framework for countries to articulate development priorities and for IFIs to support countries' efforts.

BOX 5.1   The IMF's medium-term strategy

The IMF's medium-term strategy, published in September 2005, considered the future direction of the IMF in areas key to its lead mandate on international monetary cooperation and global financial stability.

Surveillance: The IMF is enhancing the effectiveness of surveillance through greater focus, candor, and even-handedness. The medium-term strategy is proceeding on two parallel tracks: implementation of surveillance and development of its legal basis. Steps to enhance the implementation of surveillance have included initiation of the first multilateral consultation, a new modality for discussing common problems; deeper analytical work on exchange rates, including extension of the existing multicountry framework to emerging market economies; strengthening of the IMF's analytical and advisory capacity on financial sector and capital market issues, with better integration of this work into surveillance; greater focus on cross-border spillovers, regional issues, and cross-country issues; and stronger outreach. The legal framework is being revisited through an ongoing review of the 1977 decision on surveillance over exchange rate policies and consideration of a possible remit-independence-accountability framework.

Emerging market economies: The IMF is strengthening its advice on financial sector and capital market issues and considering the adequacy of instruments to support members, as well as the possibility of a new contingent financing instrument for crisis prevention.

Low-income countries: The IMF is enhancing support for efforts to achieve the MDGs by sharpening its focus on issues critical for growth within its macroeconomic and financial areas of responsibility, providing assistance for capacity building in these areas, helping meet challenges of effective use of increased aid inflows and debt relief, and supporting the development of debt strategies and improved debt management.

Capacity building: The IMF is improving alignment with members' needs and its own strategic priorities, taking advantage of complementarities with other providers.

Governance: Work in the area of governance is currently focused on reform of quotas and voice; other priority issues include the management selection process and the role of the IMF Executive Board.

Efficient operations: The IMF is enhancing efficiency and prioritization in its operational work and support activities and strengthening its risk management systems. Efforts under way have resulted in a number of streamlining initiatives, as well as real reductions in the IMF's administrative budget in recent years. These efforts are being complemented by consideration of ways to strengthen the IMF's income base and the ongoing review of World Bank-IMF collaboration (see below).

Source: IMF 2006. "Managing Director's Report on the IMF's Medium Term Strategy." September SM/05/332.

Countries are now setting clear goals and targets linked to public actions, improving their budgeting and monitoring systems, and opening the public space to a more inclusive discussion of national priorities and policies. On the donor side, progress has been made to align and harmonize assistance with countries' priorities, and filling country-specific analytical gaps. Yet connecting results with resources remains a major challenge.

Increased attention is being devoted to coordinating aid at the country, regional, and global levels. Coordination has become paramount not only because of the increased number of players, but also because many of the new providers deliver aid in a more fragmented fashion and outside the established domestic process and framework. This includes ensuring that resources from vertical funds support country-specific development priorities, and that the delivery of aid reinforces rather than undermines domestic processes (including budget formulation and execution). As discussed in chapter 4, progress has been made in some of these areas, but scaling up has been limited. The upcoming 15th replenishment of the International Development Association (IDA) will be an important test of donors' intentions regarding not only their 2005 commitments (to support the Multilateral Debt Relief Initiative (MDRI) and scale up official development assistance), but also the role they see for the multilateral development banks (MDBs) in a changing aid landscape.

The Africa Action Plan (AAP) illustrates how the World Bank is working to promote country-led efforts in partnership with other donors (box 5.2).[2] The AAP is based on an outcome-oriented framework to guide the work of the Bank's Africa region in four pillars: accelerating shared growth, building capable states, sharpening the focus on results, and strengthening the development partnership. The AAP was designed to be dynamic and adaptive in order to concentrate on those areas that promise strong results and reflect the World Bank's evolving role in the development partnership.

IFIs are also paying greater attention to the special needs of states with weak policies and institutions, and to tailoring support to different groups of low-income countries with different needs. How they are strengthening countries' capacity to promote growth and deliver basic services to the citizens of fragile states is described in the final section of this chapter.

Strengthening and Adapting Engagement in Middle-Income Countries

The growing differentiation in development conditions across countries and the increased availability of alternative financial resources

---

BOX 5.2 The World Bank's Africa Action Plan

The first progress report on the AAP, to be presented to the World Bank's Board of Executive Directors in spring 2007, examines emerging regional and international trends and assesses progress against each of the four pillars on which the AAP is based. It also proposes changes to strengthen the World Bank's role in the development partnership in Africa. Specifically, the report recommends increasing efforts to accelerate economic growth by deploying resources in a concerted effort to overcome the most critical constraints to growth, supporting good governance and capacity development in resource-rich but slowly growing economies, using innovative instruments to mobilize development finance, and helping integrate vertical programs and new partners into sustainable country-based institutions.

Implementation progress in fiscal years 2005/06 and 2006/07 was broadly satisfactory:

- *Progress has been best in the shared growth pillar—supporting the drivers of growth and participating in growth.* The AAP is on track to deliver the results committed to in all but two (agricultural productivity and gender) of the pillar's nine thematic areas. It is ahead of projected progress in four areas. Private sector development, closing the infrastructure gap, and addressing HIV/AIDS and malaria have shown significant progress, both in increased Bank Group support and from evidence that countries are closer to delivering development outcomes. Good progress has been achieved in establishing the preconditions for an export push, in regional integration, and in primary education, including addressing gender discrimination. Progress is on track in supporting skills development, and the IFC has played a leading role in pushing business education. Accelerated progress will be needed to increase agricultural productivity and to connect the poor to markets. Despite some promising initiatives, substantially more work is needed to increase the economic empowerment of women.
- *The capable states pillar has supported African governments in improving the transparency, accountability, and provision of social services, but progress has been mixed.* Good progress

continued

BOX 5.2 The World Bank's Africa Action Plan *(continued)*

was made in improving public financial management and in rolling out the Extractive Industries Transparency Initiative. The Africa Region's Capacity Development Management Action Plan (CDMAP) supports countries in building capable states. More progress could have been made with an earlier launch of the program.

- *The results pillar is assisting countries in developing operational strategies to deliver development outcomes.* There has been good progress on the results framework, and the Bank Group is on track to deliver the priority actions. Some African countries, such as Burkina Faso, Ghana, Mozambique, and Tanzania, undertook substantial efforts to clarify their development goals and targets, based on a medium- to long-term vision, and to link these to public actions. They also developed action plans to improve monitoring and evaluation. Implementation of statistical capacity building and accelerated data programs have picked up pace; however, progress in building statistical capacity remains low throughout Africa and lags other regions. Progress on the Bank's results agenda has been sufficient to mainstream these efforts into the day-to-day management of the AAP.
- *The global development partnership pillar is leveraging IDA-14 for greater impact.* There has been considerable progress on the partnership pillar. Countries have taken the lead in developing baselines and action plans for the Paris Declaration with development partners. Progress on harmonization and alignment at the policy level—expressed through the working groups of the OECD Development Assistance Committee—has been encouraging. Progress includes work on selective scaling up of aid for Africa, the launch of resources and results processes, and improved alignment with development partners to the new generation of poverty reduction strategies. The Africa Catalytic Growth Fund received initial funding and has launched operations designed to crowd in substantial donor support.

The IFC and the Multilateral Investment Guarantee Agency (MIGA) have made substantial contributions to implementing the AAP. Much of the progress in the shared growth pillar is due to the joint efforts of IDA, the IFC, and MIGA in private sector development, infrastructure, and skills development. The IFC began its Strategic Initiative for Africa based on three objectives: improving investment climates, improving support for small and medium-size enterprises, and supporting project development for potential IFC projects.

Despite good progress, significant changes to the AAP are needed in light of the development picture in Africa, results achieved during early implementation, the World Bank Group's evolving role in the development partnership, and global priorities needing collective action. The AAP will focus more selectively on outcomes over the next three years, concentrating on areas that promise strong results and reflect the Bank's evolving role in the development partnership. It will also use a new country classification, based on economic performance and institutional capacity, to guide the implementation strategy. And it will strengthen the leverage of IDA by adapting its strategy for scaling up resources.

Source: World Bank 2007.

have important bearing on IFIs' support to middle-income countries. Traditional bundled lending and knowledge management products remain important for many middle-income countries, particularly those with credit ratings below investment grade, but many middle-income countries are also increasingly looking for more customized financial and advisory services, unbundled from financing itself. Global public goods is one area where the IFIs are expected to play a key role in supporting middle-income countries' needs for customized financial and advisory services (see below).

Despite real progress in many middle-income countries, the support of the IFIs remains critical to these countries, which are home to 70 percent of the world's poor and still face major challenges in attaining the MDGs. The IFIs retain comparative advantages in providing strategic policy advice, development finance and financial services, and technical assistance and knowledge services, but this support needs to be better tailored to specific country conditions. The dialogue between IFIs and their middle-income clients has also highlighted a number of impediments, such as the responsiveness of the institutions to countries' concerns and the cost of doing business with them. These impediments must be tackled if the IFIs are to provide the full measure of support of which they are capable.

The focus of discussion by the heads of MDBs and the Development Committee last September in Singapore was on how to adapt strategies, priorities, and instruments in an environment in which the IFIs provide a smaller share of financial flows to middle-income countries than they once did.[3] The Development Committee strongly endorsed the World Bank's corporate role and mission to eradicate poverty in its partnerships with middle-income countries, reviewing the Bank's proposals to strengthen the IBRD's value added and engagement in response to the evolving and diverse needs of middle-income countries. The heads of the MDBs agreed to move ahead on three fronts in the middle-income countries' agenda: holding joint consultations with middle-income countries; exploring the possibilities for blending bilateral grant and multilateral lending resources; and expanding ongoing joint analytical work, technical assistance, and advisory and operational work.

Increasing the Provision of Global Public Goods

Growing cross-country interactions and interdependence have also brought attention more generally to the inadequate provision of global public goods and to the increasing role middle-income countries are expected to play in their provision. The recent report of the International Task Force on Global Public Goods highlights the factors that constrain the provision of global public goods.[4] Here the IFIs can play a central role, among other things in enhancing international financial stability, strengthening the international trading system, addressing climate change, preventing the emergence and spread of infectious disease, and generating knowledge.

One vital area where IFIs can have a broader role is that of clean energy and climate change. The communiqué issued by the leaders of the Group of Eight countries at their July 2005 Gleneagles summit called on the World Bank to take a leadership role in creating a new framework for clean energy and development. This request was reaffirmed by the Development Committee in September 2005, and the World Bank presented a framework for clean energy at the Spring 2006 Meetings (box 5.3).[5] Also the Asian Development Bank (ADB) established the Asia Pacific Carbon Fund in November 2006, and the Water Financing Partnership Facility in December 2006.

Improving Coherence and Cooperation among Institutions

The Monterrey conference placed a high priority on improving coherence and cooperation among key multilateral players. This is especially important given the growing interconnectedness of the development agenda. Cooperation among MDBs has been improving in recent years, evolving from ad hoc consultations to systemic cooperation across a broad range of issues. The heads of MDBs have by now articulated and published joint positions on most major global development challenges.[6]

Thematic cooperation, often pursued through technical working groups endorsed by the heads of MDBs, has been central to these coherence-building efforts. It has encompassed

---

BOX 5.3   The World Bank's framework on clean energy

"Clean Energy and Development: Towards an Investment Framework," the World Bank's framework on clean energy, is structured around three pillars: access, mitigation, and adaptation. The strategy supports widening access to energy services, efforts to control greenhouse gas emissions, and assistance to developing countries in adapting to climate risks. The approach was broadly endorsed by the Bank's Development Committee in April 2006.

A second World Bank report was presented at the September 2006 Annual Meetings at the request of the Development Committee. That report, "An Investment Framework for Clean Energy and Development: A Progress Report," assessed the potential value of new and existing financial instruments for accelerating progress in each of these pillars. It argued that the current financing instruments for energy access and adaptation are adequate, but that financing needs far outstrip available funds. The Bank is currently working with donors to increase concessional financing for the access agenda in Sub-Saharan Africa and performing more detailed analyses of what financing is needed for the adaptation agenda.

In contrast to instruments for energy access and adaptation, current financing instruments and resources for designing and scaling up mitigation efforts are inadequate. The report suggested that a clean energy financing vehicle, with an initial capitalization of $10 billion, is needed. Such an instrument would blend concessional and carbon financing to fund the upfront capital costs of low-carbon technologies; it would be recapitalized through loan repayments and the sale of carbon credits. The Development Committee did not endorse the proposed financing vehicle, arguing that better use should be made of existing instruments.

A long-term, stable, global, and equitable regulatory framework is required to stimulate an international carbon market that could transfer tens of billions of dollars a year to developing countries in return for reducing their emissions. Without a significant increase in financing, progress on transitioning to a low-carbon economy is severely constrained, exacerbating climate changes and increasing the need for adaptation measures. The Bank and potential donors are discussing the concept of a carbon continuity fund that aims to ensure the carbon market does not collapse while governments negotiate a post-2012 regulatory framework.

In addition to developing an investment framework, the Bank is responding to other climate change–related mandates that emerged from the Gleneagles summit of the Group of Eight. It is working with the G8+5 countries to develop national action plans for a transition to a low-carbon economy. These plans would analyze which sectors and technologies provide the best opportunity for reducing greenhouse gas emissions, what policies would be needed, and what financing would be required. The lessons will be integrated in future country assistance strategies in order to promote growth options that are less intensive in greenhouse gas emissions but still meet developing-country priorities.

The Bank is also developing a screening tool that will provide the core tools for World Bank staff and client countries to assess the exposure of investments to risks from climate change and develop steps for dealing with them. Pilot adaptation studies are being prepared in several countries.

Finally, the IFC has responded to the mandate to develop local commercial capacity to develop and finance cost-effective energy efficiency and low-carbon energy projects by providing specialized credit lines and credit enhancement vehicles to local banks and leasing companies to establish self-sustaining lending products for sustainable energy.

Source: World Bank 2006. "Clean Energy and Development: Towards an Investment Framework."

---

all key aspects of the current development agenda, including the harmonization of procurement, financial management, environment and safeguard policies, investment climate surveys, and capacity development, governance, and anticorruption. MDBs that operate concessional windows have made considerable progress in harmonizing their performance-based allocation approaches, including related country and institutional assessments.

Memoranda of Understanding underpin much of this cooperation at the country level. All the regional development banks have such agreements with the World Bank, and the ADB has a similar agreement with the Inter-American Development Bank (IADB). More explicit and accountable cooperation frameworks at the country level would be however useful for addressing duplication and allowing MDBs to undertake operations on a larger scale.

Collaboration between the World Bank and the IMF and their division of responsibilities have also received considerable attention. In 2006 the managing director of the IMF and the president of the World Bank commissioned an external review on collaboration between the two institutions.[7] The report of the committee identifies scope for improvement and makes several recommendations. It calls on the institutions to develop a new "understanding on collaboration"; to strengthen cooperation on crisis management; to improve integration and harmonization of work on fiscal issues; to clarify the IMF's role in low-income countries; and to continue to improve collaboration on financial sector issues.

Increasing Voice and Participation by Developing Countries

At the Singapore meetings, the IMF's Board of Governors approved a package of reforms on quotas and voice aimed at better aligning the IMF's current governance regime with its members' relative positions in the world economy, and enhancing the voice and participation of developing countries within the IMF. These reforms are designed as an integrated two-year program to be completed no later than the 2008 annual meeting of the IMF Board of Governors. The first step in the program—increasing quotas for a small group of the most underrepresented countries, including China, the Republic of Korea, Mexico, and Turkey—was also approved at Singapore. These ad hoc quota changes would increase total IMF quotas by 1.8 percent and would raise the quota

share of the four countries from 5.4 percent to 7.1 percent (and their voting shares from 5.3 percent to 7.0 percent).

Work has since begun on additional measures. One of these is a new formula to guide the assessment of the adequacy of members' quotas in the IMF, in preparation for a second round of ad hoc quota increases. Another is a proposal to increase the "basic" votes allotted to each member, to ensure adequate voice for low-income countries. Reform will also involve steps to enhance the capacity of African Executive Directors' offices to participate effectively in the governance of the IMF. These reforms will include an increase in staffing resources and possible amendment of the Articles of Agreement to enable Executive Directors elected by a large number of members to appoint more than one alternate director.

The Development Committee in Singapore "welcomed the [IMF] Managing Director's report on progress made in the reform of IMF quotas and voice, acknowledging the measures already taken by the Bank to enhance capacity in Executive Directors' offices and capitals of developing and transition countries, [and] asked the Bank to work with its shareholders to consider enhancement in voice and participation in the governance of the Bank." A series of consultations with the World Bank executive directors is ongoing, building on the issues identified by the Development Committee in previous meetings.

How Well Are the IFIs Performing?

Measuring the contribution of the IFIs to development effectiveness is difficult, and the measures used are imperfect. This section reviews the measurement of performance and suggests ways of strengthening such evaluations.

The Challenge of Assessing Effectiveness

IFIs play a multitude of roles. Some of these, such as supporting macroeconomic stability, providing development finance, and reporting on country performance, are more tangible than others and thus more amenable to assessment. Others, such as generating knowledge to inform policy makers or convening donor support around country strategies, are more difficult.

Although traditional portfolio performance indicators such as financial disbursements are relatively easily tracked, they say little about the IFIs' contributions to development. As the ultimate objective of all the institutions' activities is to foster development outcomes on the ground, measurement strategies must capture changes—or the lack of changes—in the lives of households, the activities of firms, and organizations on the ground.

The difficulty in assessing performance is compounded by the long time it takes for many development initiatives to bear fruit, and by weaknesses in statistics and monitoring. But a central constraint is that of attribution: a reduction in child mortality, for example, may be due in part to aid-supported programs, but many other factors may also be at work. Clear attribution of credit or blame is often not possible. Moreover, because money is fungible, it may be hard to know exactly what a given package of aid is financing, even if it is earmarked.

The challenge of attribution is made more difficult by the complex chain of causality linking external financing to development outcomes. External assistance to policy makers may influence the policy debate, sometimes through conditionality that is attached while operating with imperfect knowledge and little control over implementation. National and local policy makers manage the external dialogue with donors, but their ability to set and implement policies often depends on politics and the quality and capacity of bureaucracies and institutions. All this is compounded by the uncertainty over how policies themselves influence final outcomes.

Although far from complete, a stock of knowledge does exist on the development impact of many policies. Economic research and evaluations can generate this knowledge through ex ante and ex post analysis

of national experiences, and through impact evaluations of specific interventions. Rigorous impact evaluation is indeed an important tool for generating knowledge and insight to help guide policy formulation.

IFIs and other groups, including independent evaluation agencies, international assessment initiatives, and interagency working groups, use various approaches to evaluate development effectiveness, as *Global Monitoring Report 2006* discussed. Each IFI has an independent evaluation agency that conducts evaluations at the project, country, and sector or institutionwide levels (box 5.4). While such assessments play an important evaluation role, some have asked that these evaluations be complemented by external evaluations.

Three aspects of IFIs' performance—financial support, efforts to strengthen results-based management, and progress toward harmonizing and aligning aid through the Paris Declaration—are discussed below.

Financial Resources for Development

IFIs provide a smaller share of financial flows to developing countries than they once did. Net official lending to developing countries has declined in recent years, while net private lending has significantly expanded. Private flows are estimated to have reached a record $643 billion in 2006, up from $551 billion in 2005 and about equally split between foreign direct investment ($325 billion), on the one hand, and private debt and portfolio equity ($318 billion), on the other (figure 5.1). Recorded private remittances also continued their upward trend, reaching almost $200 billion in 2006. The breakdown of private capital inflows underlying figure 5.1 reveals the sharp difference in their importance across country groups. The lion's share of flows is directed to middle-income and 'blend' countries (those countries eligible for both concessional and nonconcessional financing from IFIs, such as India and Indonesia). By contrast, only 1.6 percent of private debt and portfolio equity

---

BOX 5.4   How well does the World Bank contribute to development effectiveness?

Evaluations in 2006 by the World Bank's Independent Evaluation Group (IEG) shed light on how well the institution is reducing poverty, working with fragile states, implementing sectoral programs in education, infrastructure, and the environment, and responding to natural disasters.

Reducing poverty: The *Annual Review of Development Effectiveness 2006* identified three key areas where the Bank can strengthen its effectiveness in helping countries reduce poverty:

- Ensure that growth leads to jobs for the poor and productivity increases in poorer regions and sectors where the poor earn their incomes.
- Clearly articulate results chains so that Bank country assistance programs and individual projects set realistic objectives, consider key cross-sectoral constraints to achieving them, and pay adequate attention to building capacity.
- Tailor efforts to increase the accountability of public sector institutions to local conditions.

Working with fragile states: The Bank has contributed to macroeconomic stability and to the delivery of significant amounts of physical infrastructure, especially in postconflict situations. However, reforms in some fragile states have lacked selectivity and prioritization, and while the Bank has generally been effective in the immediate postconflict phase, its effectiveness needs to be improved following this phase, when structural change is needed.

Implementing sectoral programs: Bank projects in education have helped raise enrollment rates, but have paid less attention to learning outcomes. Best practice appears to be doing both simultaneously. Infrastructure investments have contributed to growth and poverty alleviation, but often have imposed environmental burdens. Opportunities to mitigate these burdens require broader assessments of environmental impact, and sound national environmental strategies in designing and implementing infrastructure programs, setting environmental standards, and coordinating programs across sectors over a reasonably long time horizon. IEG also examined the Bank's work in looking at natural disasters. The Bank is the largest funding agency for disaster recovery and reconstruction in developing countries. Since 1984, the Bank has financed a total of $26 billion in disaster relief activities. The more than 500 projects involved represent almost 10 percent of all Bank loan commitments during this period. Over 80 percent of Bank disaster relief financing has addressed rapid onset disasters—floods, earthquakes, tropical storms, and fires. Within disaster relief projects, the Bank did better at reconstructing damaged infrastructure and housing than it did in reducing vulnerabilities and addressing their root causes. It is possible to anticipate where many natural disasters will strike, yet the Bank's disaster assistance efforts are underutilizing these vital lifesaving forecasts.

---

inflows are received by the 63 low-income countries, and only 4.7 percent of foreign direct investment. Remittances, however, are relatively important, with low-income countries receiving nearly 15 percent of total estimated inflows.

Despite the increasing share of private sources of financing, the IFIs' role remains important. In 2006, the five MDBs disbursed about $43 billion, a 20 percent increase over 2005. Although it is too early to assess whether it represents a temporary fluctuation or a permanent departure from recent trends, two occurrences stand out: a sustained increase in nonconcessional lending by the International Finance Corporation (IFC) and the European Bank for Reconstruction and Development (EBRD), mainly to the private sector; and a slight decline in concessional lending and overall disbursements to Africa.

Nonconcessional flows. Net official lending declined in the first part of this decade, particularly because of net repayments to the IMF of

FIGURE 5.1 Net private capital flows to developing countries

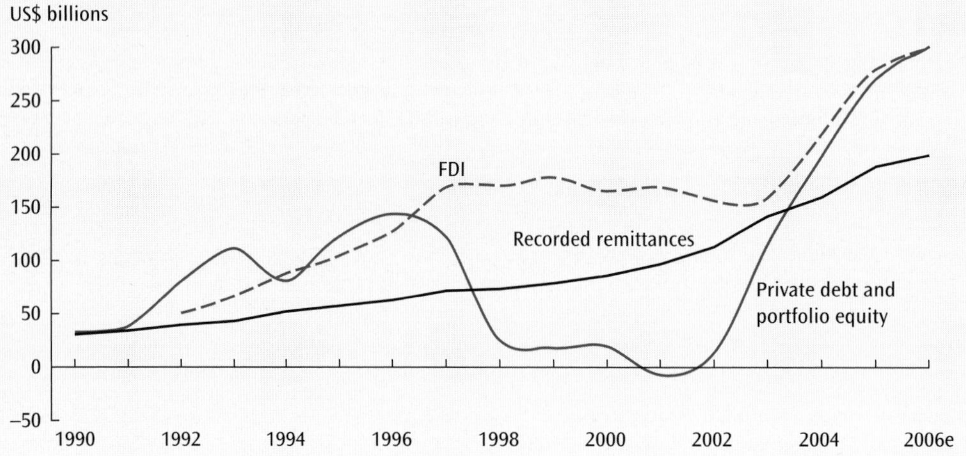

	1998	1999	2000	2001	2002	2003	2004	2005	2006
Private debt and portfolio equity (net inflows)	24.7	17.7	20.6	-6.5	12.1	113.7	194.6	270.6	318
IBRD and blend countries	26.2	18.0	21.5	−4.2	13.5	114.4	191.2	266.2	
IDA oil-exporters	−1.2	0.6	−0.5	−0.6	0.7	−0.3	0.1	0.4	
Other IDA countries	−0.4	-0.9	−0.4	−1.8	−2.1	−0.4	3.3	4.0	
Foreign direct investment (net inflows)	170.0	178.0	166.5	171.0	157.1	160.0	217.8	280.8	325
IBRD and blend countries	161.1	167.1	157.9	161.2	145.4	144.8	203.9	267.6	
IDA oil-exporters	4.7	5.4	4.6	4.3	4.9	6.5	7.4	7.7	
Other IDA countries	4.2	5.5	4.0	5.5	6.7	8.8	6.6	5.5	
Recorded Remittances (received)	70.7	76.6	83.8	95.3	116.2	143.8	163.7	189.5	200
IBRD and blend countries	61.3	66.7	73.1	82.1	100.0	125.1	140.9	161.9	
IDA oil-exporters	5.9	6.8	7.4	8.0	10.0	12.4	14.6	17.9	
Other IDA countries	3.4	3.2	3.3	5.2	6.2	6.3	8.2	9.7	

Source: Work Bank Debt Reporting System and staff estimates.
Note: e = estimate.

large disbursements of emergency assistance (box 5.5) as well as early repayments of World Bank loans by some middle-income countries. However, gross disbursements—a proxy for new demand—suggest that nonconcessional lending by MDBs to middle-income countries remains strong (figure 5.2). Non-concessional gross disbursements increased by 29 percent to about $32 billion, in 2006. This represents the first significant increase in non-concessional lending that was not preceded by a financial crisis. By far the greatest share of the 2006 increase came from the EBRD,

which increased its lending in dollar terms by 80 percent,[8] followed by the IBRD, and the IFC, which increased their lending by 31 percent and 38 percent respectively. Most of the recent increase went to Europe (figure 5.3).

Concessional flows. Growth in concessional lending in previous years had been driven by IDA's contribution, with support for Sub-Saharan Africa growing sharply between 2000 and 2004 and support for East and South Asia rising in 2004. This support fell in 2005–06 (figure 5.4), with lending by IDA declining but lending by other MDBs continuing to

BOX 5.5 Lending by the IMF

The IMF's General Resources Account (GRA) provides nonconcessional financial support to member countries experiencing temporary balance of payments difficulties. The IMF also provides financial support through special GRA facilities and policies (including emergency assistance for natural disasters and postconflict emergency assistance) and concessional loans to low-income countries under the Poverty Reduction and Growth Facility (PRGF). GRA net flows depend largely on the needs of large middle-income countries facing economic crises; they are consequently erratic on a year-to-year basis. Following early repayments of large loans by Argentina, Brazil, and Indonesia, the IMF's GRA credit outstanding declined to SDR 9.8 billion ($15 billion) at end-2006, its lowest level in 25 years, and well below its all-time peak of SDR 70 billion ($105 billion) in 2003. Net PRGF lending is less erratic but also substantially affected by the needs of larger low-income member countries and the provision of debt relief.

Net flows from the IMF to developing countries, 2000–06 (in millions of U.S. dollars)

	2000	2001	2002	2003	2004	2005	2006
Net Concessional Fund Assistance[a]	**−148**	**106**	**567**	**9**	**−179**	**−715**	**−3,587**
Disbursements	650	1,111	1,741	1,187	1,204	597	744
Repayments [b]	798	1,005	1,174	1,178	1,383	1,312	4,332
Net Nonconcessional (GRA) Fund Assistance [c]	**−10,644**	**19,031**	**13,109**	**2,002**	**−14,314**	**−39,802**	**−27,382**
Disbursements	9,466	30,249	32,678	28,429	6,181	3,381	3,486
Repayments	20,111	11,219	19,569	26,427	20,495	43,183	30,868
Total Net Flows	**−10,793**	**19,137**	**13,676**	**2,010**	**−14,493**	**−40,517**	**−30,970**
Of which: Sub-Saharan Africa	−22	−178	165	−394	−318	−739	−3,053
Memo: Gross Emergency Assistance	184	0	35	18	453	189	10

Source: IMF Finance Department.
a. Includes disbursements and repayments of PRGF, SAF and Trust Fund loans.
b. The sharp increase in repayments in 2006 reflects the provision of MDRI debt relief.
c. Korea is classified as a high-income country and so their GRA repurchase of SDR 4,462.5 million in 2001 is excluded.

increase. The dwindling relevance of the MDBs in leveraging external resources—due to a possible decline of contributions to IDA and the regional development banks (RDBs) as a share of total official development assistance—may further affect their role in supporting achievement of the MDGs in low-income countries. Among multilateral organizations, IDA's role as main channel for multilateral ODA has been surpassed by the European Commission and the United Nations since the 1990s. The amounts of core contributions channeled through IDA and, on a smaller scale, through regional banks, peaked in the 1980s and have declined thereafter. IDA's share in total multilateral ODA declined from 42 percent in the 1970s to an average of 20 percent in the 2001–05 period.

An additional factor that may affect the future ability of IDA and the RDBs to support low-income countries could result from the impact of debt relief provided under the Heavily Indebted Poor Countries (HIPC) and Multilateral Debt Relief Initiative (MDRI). Through both of these initiatives, IFIs are providing large amounts of debt relief to poor countries.[9] Recognizing this, donors have specified that additional contributions are to be calculated relative to a baseline that maintains current contribution levels in real terms.

FIGURE 5.2 Concessional and nonconcessional lending by MDBs, 1999–2006

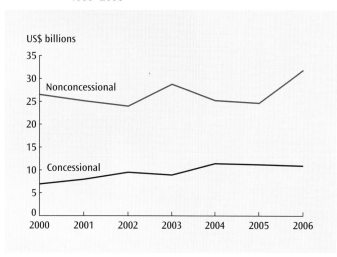

Source: Staff of the big five multilateral development banks.

Although donors have agreed on the need to have firm MDRI financing commitments backing the 10-year disbursement period of each future IDA replenishment, their actions do not yet reflect these commitments (figure 5.5). Monitoring donors' commitments on financing the MDRI is important to ensuring the additionality of donor financing over time. Of the 34 donor countries that have pledged to contribute to the MDRI replenishment of IDA, 28 had provided their Instruments of Commitment (IoC) as of end-December 2006.[10] IoC provide firm or unqualified financing commitments of $3.8 billion (representing 10 percent of the original projected cost of the MDRI) and qualified financing commitments of $20.5 billion (56 percent of total MDRI costs).[11] This leaves a gap between total costs and commitments of $12.4 billion (34 percent of total MDRI costs). Regarding forgone credit reflows resulting from the HIPC Initiative, donors have provided firm financing commitments to cover $1.4 billion in HIPC costs occurring under IDA's 14th replenishment (IDA-14). Beyond that, donor commitments will be needed to cover HIPC and

FIGURE 5.3 Nonconcessional lending by MDBs to different regions (gross disbursements), 1999–2006

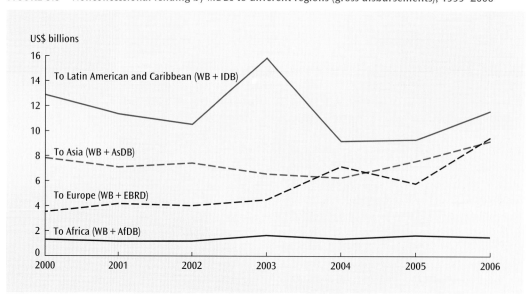

Source: Staff of the big five multilateral development banks.

MDRI financing over the next two decades or so. Donors need to be mindful that any short-fall between targeted and actual commitments undermines IDA's long-term financial capabil-ity. The upcoming replenishments of the MDBs' concessional windows will be an important test of donor's intentions regarding their support for the MDRI and the future role they see for MDBs in a changing aid environment.

Selectivity of Financial Resources in Support of the Development Agenda

As part of the Monterrey compact, MDBs com-mitted themselves to using more transparent and incentive-improving resource allocation systems aimed at maximizing aid effectiveness and encouraging stronger policies and insti-tutions in recipient countries. At present, the foundation of each of these systems is a for-mula that calculates the share of the resources that will be allocated to individual countries on the basis of their financial need (proxied by population and income per capita) and per-formance. Each MDB combines these factors somewhat differently in its performance allo-cation formula and uses different methods to

FIGURE 5.4 Gross disbursements of concessional lending by MDBs, 1999–2006

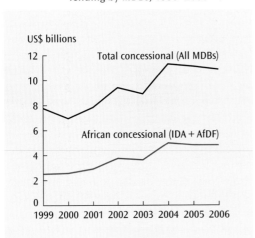

Source: Staff of the big five multilateral development banks.

FIGURE 5.5 Donor financing commitments to IDA under the Multilateral Debt Relief Initiative, as of December 31, 2006 ($ million equivalent)

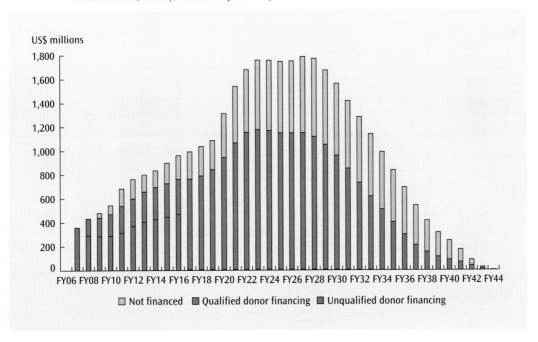

Source: World Bank 2007. "MDRI: Update on Debt Relief by IDA and Donor Financing to Date."

accommodate exceptional circumstances, such as countries in postconflict situations. In the past, however, MDBs have taken significant steps to harmonize their performance-based allocation (PBA) systems and country performance and institutional assessment (CPIA) questionnaires. Because of their performance-based allocation formula and the use of per capita income ceilings to determine countries' eligibility for MDBs' concessional resources, MDBs continue to exhibit higher policy and poverty selectivity than bilateral aid agencies (See figure 5.6.).[12]

As described in the final section of this chapter, the MDBs recognize fragile states' special needs and circumstances and their difficulties in making investments that promise sufficient returns to enable repayment even of concessional loans. In response, MDBs have increasingly offered support in the form of grants, which now make up a much larger percentage of disbursements to them (31 percent) than among other low-income countries (9 percent; figure 5.7). Also, both the AfDB and the World Bank have developed exceptional allocation frameworks for postconflict countries to allow countries to benefit from

additional resources over and above their performance-based allocation for a limited period.

Progress in Results Management

The Third Roundtable on Managing for Development, held in Hanoi in February 2007, built on the findings of the 2004 Marrakech Roundtable. It provided a venue and format for each of the 43 country delegations to summarize their experiences and to initiate a country action planning process, with targets for steps to be completed in advance of the Ghana High-Level Forum on Aid Effectiveness to be held in September 2008. The Hanoi Roundtable provided compelling evidence that country partners are keenly interested in improving the effectiveness of development assistance and domestic resources by strengthening systems that enable information on expected and actual results to be used in decision making.

The agenda for the Hanoi meeting was based on the recommendations of country practitioners and development partners made through an 18-month Mutual Learning Initiative supported by the Joint Venture on Manag-

FIGURE 5.6   Policy and poverty selectivity of concessional assistance by MDBs

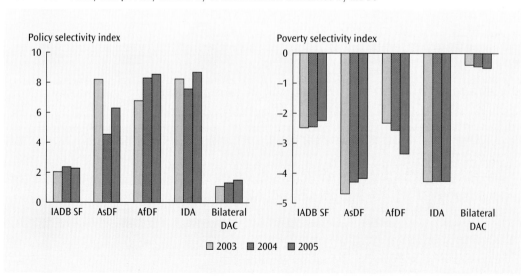

Source: World Bank staff calculation based on Dollar and Levin (2004).

ing for Results (one of four subgroups working on behalf of the Working Party on Aid Effectiveness of the OECD-DAC). Representatives of 22 countries and bilateral and multilateral agencies met in a series of workshops (in Burkina Faso, Singapore, Uganda, and Uruguay) leading up to the Roundtable.[13]

This process, as well as country experience with poverty monitoring, suggests that building country capacity to manage for development results needs to focus on five thematic areas:[14]

- Leadership and political will
- Strong links from results to planning and budgeting processes, to strengthen incentives to use information on expected and actual results in decision making
- Evaluation and monitoring tools necessary to generate feedback on the performance of policies and programs
- Mechanisms established by donors and country partners that encourage mutual accountability
- Statistical capacity in developing countries and systems for applied data use in government, both to supply and help generate greater demand for managing for development results in developing countries (box 5.6).[15]

Several observations that emerged from the Roundtable relate to the progress that country and donor partners are making as they work to achieve greater development effectiveness through managing for results:

- *Progress and opportunities at the country level*. A key achievement of the Roundtable is that each of the country delegations worked to initiate a country action planning process, to identify ways that they could work to strengthen their own capacity to manage for results, applying lessons learned along each of the five thematic elements of capacity. Many countries recognized that, despite real progress toward articulating a poverty-monitoring framework at the national level, its implemen-

FIGURE 5.7 Grants and loans as shares of MBD concessional disbursements in 2006

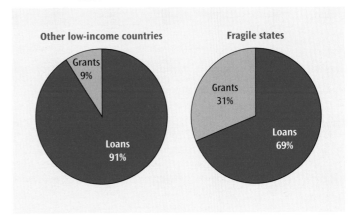

Source: Staff of four MDBs: World Bank, AfDB, IADB, and ADB.

tation is constrained by fragmentation at the line ministry and agency level. Country partners are thus keen to develop results frameworks at the sectoral level. These frameworks could then serve as a basis for harmonizing donor efforts to monitor and evaluate specific interventions and overcome the obstacles presented by the presence of multiple, partial and donor-driven, monitoring systems. Countries also expressed an interest in exploring the use of performance-based management tools, including output- and outcome-based disbursement principles, and they identified the need to engage key stakeholders such as legislators in both defining and monitoring the achievement of results. A particularly strong common theme running through the planning discussions was the importance of grounding results-based management systems in stronger accountability to citizens. Many country action plans proposed to strengthen participatory approaches and to ensure that results were communicated transparently to the public. Many countries were keen to explore better methods for assessing and tracking citizen satisfaction. All of the country delegations stressed the need to strengthen statistical capacity to ensure that the information nec-

> ### BOX 5.6 The Marrakech Action Plan for Statistics and the Accelerated Data Program
>
> To address short-term data needs, a pilot Accelerated Data Program (ADP) was launched in 2006. Its goal is to produce relevant data for policy design, monitoring, and evaluation by implementing a coordinated program of data collection, analysis, and dissemination. The program focuses on sample household surveys, because they provide estimates of many indicators relating to the MDGs and other key outcomes, as well as data needed for research and impact evaluation.
>
> The pilot ADP is being implemented in selected countries in Africa, Asia, and Latin America by the World Bank and the PARIS21 Secretariat of the OECD, in cooperation with multiple partners (UN agencies and others). Two million dollars a year has been allocated for the pilot ADP through the Development Grant Facility for the Marrakech Action Plan for Statistics (MAPS) for 2006–08.
>
> The MAPS and the ADP provide robust frameworks, but a stronger commitment from donor agencies is still needed. The PARIS21 Secretariat estimates that development partners are spending about $70 million a year on statistical capacity improvement in Sub-Saharan Africa. Implementation of the MAPS in IDA countries in Sub-Saharan Africa, including the scaling up of the pilot ADP, is estimated to require an additional $60 million a year.
>
> *Source:* World Bank. "Better Data for Better Results: An Action Plan for Improving Development Statistics."

essary for an effective results management system is made available. Countries put a high priority on finding ways to learn from countries that have done more to build up their systems (Chile, China, Thailand, Vietnam, and others). They recognized the value of peer learning between countries and were keen to participate in the communities of practice that are developing to facilitate country-country learning. The Roundtable included a meeting of a community of practice in the Asia region (supported initially by the ADB, in which practitioners among 11 Asian countries are networking with each other to share practices and experience), and the launching of a similar community of practice in the Africa region.

■ *Progress and opportunities at the donor level.* Donors recognized that managing for results should not be seen mainly as a set of measuring and monitoring tools, although statistics and monitoring and evaluation are essential components. Donors as well as country partners agreed that it was useful to unpack the notion of capacity to manage for results along the five themes of the Roundtable

so as to think of results management as a country system, which, along with those for procurement and financial management, permits greater accountability and more credible feedback on performance. The issue of donor agency effectiveness was also prominent in the discussions. In particular, the question was raised of how to strengthen the focus on managing for results, bearing in mind the Paris Declaration provisions on results-based frameworks and mutual accountability. Donors will be pursuing ways to support country-to-country learning and the further development of communities of practice, as well as finding ways to follow up on the action planning process in individual countries. The strongest conclusion to emerge from the donor discussions, however, was the urgent need to scale up resources to support stronger statistical systems at the country level, through finding ways to support, financially and with technical know-how, the further development of statistical capacity. This should serve the need for monitoring sectoral performance as well as that of central agencies, while accelerating the progress made through the Marrakech Action Plan on Statistics.

The Common Performance Assessment System

The Common Performance Assessment System (COMPAS) is an interagency effort to develop a common system that all MDBs can use to monitor their results orientation. COMPAS focuses on processes and results within the control of the institutions themselves. Its intent is not to compare performance across different MDBs—such comparisons are exceedingly difficult, given that the institutions themselves are so diverse—but rather to provide baseline data against which each institution can measure its own progress over time.

The three pillars of COMPAS—actions to support country capacity for managing for development results, actions to improve the results orientation of internal systems, and actions to improve interagency cooperation for results—are described in *Global Monitoring Report 2006*. In 2006 a new COMPAS report was prepared under the leadership of the IADB (chairmanship of the COMPAS group rotates among members).[16] The report examines the seven performance categories developed for the 2005 report, adjusted to reflect the feedback received on the first COMPAS report. Broadly speaking, the changes give greater specificity to the indicators used, reduce the room for discretion in the provision of answers, and increase the objectivity and credibility of the COMPAS itself.[17] As a result of these changes, few comparisons are possible between this year's and last year's COMPAS, but this year's COMPAS should provide a sound basis for tracking future progress (Box 5.7).

The 2006 COMPAS report illustrates the MDBs' commitment to self-assessment. It also indicates their willingness to disclose information about the way they conduct business and the way they organize themselves to meet their strategic development objectives. The annual *Global Monitoring Report* provides a vehicle for communicating these results to the broad development community, but greater effort is needed in communicating and sharing the results of this exercise within each institution. Review and discussion by both management and staff are critical to ensure that the findings permeate the institutions and do not simply gather dust in institutional files.

The 2006 COMPAS identifies two new opportunities. First, the similarities between the private sector windows of the four MDBs and the EBRD may militate in favor of their merging their efforts under a more coherent performance assessment reporting format. Second, other multilateral organizations have expressed an interest in joining the COMPAS effort. In particular, the MDB Working Group on Managing for Results will be discussing proposals from International Fund for Agricultural Development and the Islamic Development Bank (IsDB) in the COMPAS in the spring of 2007.

Improving Harmonization and Alignment: MDBs and the Paris Declaration

All the MDBs (together with the OECD DAC and the UNDP) cosponsored the 2005 High-Level Forum, which adopted the Paris Declaration on Aid Effectiveness. The cosponsorship by the MDBs reflects their commitment to improving the effectiveness with which aid is planned, delivered, and managed.

Country-level monitoring of the implementation of the mutual commitments in that declaration, including through 12 quantitative indicators of actions, took place for the first time in 2006 (table 5.1). Along with bilateral and other donors, the ADB, the African Development Bank (AfDB), the IADB, and the World Bank participated in exercises to measure performance in 34 countries in which partner country and donor performance had been surveyed. Results of this 2006 monitoring round will serve as a baseline for reviewing progress in 2008 and against the agreed 2010 targets

BOX 5.7   Are the MDBs focusing on results?

Several important findings emerge from the 2006 COMPAS report.

Support for country capacity to manage for development results is increasing. MDBs use various approaches to assess country capacity to manage for results. The ADB and the AfDB produce diagnoses for a growing number of countries as part of their country strategy formulation. The IADB carries out capacity diagnostics through a specific program (PRODEV) that covers 69 percent of countries in the region. MDBs also support the strengthening of capacity through a variety of means, including World Bank–funded broad public sector management projects. Eighteen of 29 EBRD member countries received technical assistance through its Legal Transition program.

Country Strategies are being put in place, but implementation weaknesses remain. Guidelines for preparing country strategies require sound results frameworks—clearly defined monitoring indicators, with baseline data and targets to be reached at the end of the strategy implementation period. There is significant room for improving the results focus of country strategies against these criteria.

Concessional resources are being allocated on the basis of performance. All of the MDBs (except the EBRD, which does not provide concessional financing) allocate concessional resources on the basis of performance, as reflected in policies, institutions, and portfolio performance, among other criteria. Allocation criteria also typically include a "needs" factor.

Project performance could be improved. More than half of all projects reviewed received overall quality-at-entry ratings of satisfactory or better. However, there is significant room for improvement in terms of monitoring frameworks and implementation: 3–25 percent of projects suffered from unsatisfactory implementation progress, were unlikely to achieve their development objectives, or both. Moreover, implementation delays affected 34–69 percent of operations. Completion reports prepared as a percentage of number due ranged from 57 to 100 percent across the MDBs. Some 51–94 percent of reports indicated satisfactory or better use of outcome indicators. Development objectives were achieved in 61–78 percent of projects. EBRD disbursed 55 percent of its commitments annually; the disbursement ratios at other MDBs were just 20–30 percent.

Application of institutional learning from operational experience is not sufficiently systematic. All of the MDBs have formal devices for drawing lessons from operational experience and disseminating them to staff members and member countries. It is not clear how well the lessons are applied, however. Independent evaluation offices in all MDBs help promote the learning of lessons and accountability through evaluations of individual operations, sectors, themes, and country strategies and programs. On the whole their recommendations appear to influence the way MDBs conduct their business, but only the World Bank has a formal mechanism to keep track of and measure management's adoption of independent evaluation recommendations.

Salary increases are related to results. All of the MDBs have programs in place to strengthen the results-related skills of their operational staff; in recent years they have provided training on such topics as results-oriented planning, budgeting and monitoring, and evaluation. Although specific approaches vary across institutions, all MDBs link salary increases to the accomplishment of agreed upon objectives.

Sources: AfDB, ADB, EBRD, IADB, and World Bank. *2006 COMPAS: Multilateral Development Banks Common Performance Assessment System: Steering for Results.* January 26, 2007.

for collective action. Preliminary results of the survey were presented in the 2006 Asian Regional Forum on Aid Effectiveness held at ADB to discuss best practices, and measures to enhance implementation of the Paris Declaration in the Asia and the Pacific region.

For the Paris Declaration to achieve results at the country level, MDBs and other donors will need to bolster the capacity of partner

TABLE 5.1 Indicators pertaining to MDB implementation of the Paris Declaration
(preliminary data based on 2006 Round of Monitoring)

Indicator	MDBs	Other donors	2010 Target
4: Strengthen capacity by coordinated support	47%	47%	50%
5a: Percentage of aid that is disbursed using country public financial management systems	44%	36%	Reduction of aid not using country PFM systems by a third or more
5b: Percentage of aid that is disbursed using country procurement systems	40%	38%	Target under development
6: Number of Parallel Implementation Units (PIUs)	444	1,323	Reduction by 2/3
7: Percentage of aid that is disbursed on time	72%	62%	Reduction by 50% of aid not disbursed on time
9: Percentage of aid that is disbursed through program-based approaches	52%	40%	66%
10a: Percentage of missions that is done jointly with other donors	21%	26%	40%
10b: Percentage of country analytic work donors that is done jointly with other donors and/or partner government	52%	55%	66%

Source: Preliminary results from the 2006 Survey on Monitoring the Paris Declaration, OECD/DAC (March 1, 2007).
Note: The data reflect implementation as of 2005 for donors that provided a grand total of more than $100 million for the government sector. The data are undergoing final review by the OECD/DAC. More reliable data will be presented in OECD/DAC reporting in April 2007.

countries to lead the effort, take action in their own programs, and push for greater collective implementation throughout the donor community. Substantial actions are being taken. The MDBs are continuing to harmonize their procedures, to strengthen country systems, and to align their own activities with these systems where possible. Country financial management systems are currently being used for 44 percent of all lending by MDBs.

One key commitment in the Paris Declaration is to increase the proportion of aid delivered through program-based approaches that are closely aligned with a country's sector or subsector priorities and strategies, using country systems and procedures to the extent possible, harmonized among donors, with close attention paid to capacity building (indicator 9 of the Paris Declaration). Such program-based approaches are typically delivered through sectorwide approaches, development policy operations, and projects with joint financing—

all key means of encouraging collaboration among financing institutions and promoting the alignment of programs with country priorities, strategies, and systems.

Joint analytic work can lever a more harmonized delivery of aid. Not only does joint analytic work lay a cost effective basis for forging a common understanding of issues and providing more consistent advice on strategy, it also provides the basis for future collaboration and donors on projects and programs, drawing on common performance assessment frameworks and conditionality. Data from the monitoring survey show that the MDBs now undertake 52 percent of their analytic work jointly, and further attention will be needed to meet the target of 66 percent for this indicator by 2010.

Decreasing reliance on use of project implementation units (PIUs) that are parallel to government administrative structures and institutions and in many cases undermine capacity building is a common challenge facing all donors. The monitoring data indicate that MDB-supported programs account for one quarter of all these parallel PIUs. To meet the ambitious 2010 Paris target of a two-thirds reduction of these units will require a substantial change in how MDBs organize for project management and implementation, and work more closely with integrated PIUs.

MDBs are finding new ways to help achieve the objectives of the Paris Declaration. Of particular note has been the increasing use of joint or collaborative country assistance strategies to harmonize country diagnostics, align efforts with country priorities, and prepare a coordinated portfolio of activities. Such exercises have recently been completed in Bangladesh and Cambodia (by the ADB and the World Bank), Nigeria (the World Bank), and Uganda (the AfDB and the World Bank) and are virtually complete in Tanzania (the AfDB and the World Bank). Similar work is under way or planned in Ghana, the Kyrgyz Republic, Malawi, Mozambique, Nicaragua, Vietnam, and Zambia and is being discussed in a number of other countries.

MDBs also have a role to play in helping ensure the integration of vertical programs into sector strategies by drawing them into strategy development and planning their own programs to ensure complementarity. They have begun to discuss the coordination of governance and anticorruption actions, and planning is under way to better harmonize legal documentation.

Special Topics for IFIs

This section describes actions by the IFIs in the two areas highlighted by this year's *Global Monitoring Report:* gender equality and fragile states.

Promoting Gender Equality

Following the 1995 United Nations World Conference on Women in Beijing, the IFIs realigned their commitment to gender equality and women's advancement by main-

streaming gender policies and strengthening institutional arrangements to achieve gender-related objectives. In 1998 the ADB adopted a policy on gender and development that marked a shift from targeted interventions in the social sectors to identification of gender equity as a cross-cutting issue in all areas of operation. The AfDB adopted a gender policy in 2002. The IADB expanded the scope of its Women in Development Policy (1987) to pursue a dual strategy of mainstreaming gender equality in its lending portfolio and addressing critical themes of women's empowerment. Acting on a commitment made in Beijing to address domestic violence, the IADB mainstreamed its initiative to reduce domestic violence against women into a broader initiative to enhance citizen security throughout Latin America and the Caribbean.[18] The World Bank had already adopted a gender policy in 1990, but its emphasis on mainstreaming increased markedly after Beijing. Its Board of Executive Directors adopted a gender mainstreaming strategy in 2001.[19]

Progress toward mainstreaming gender policies has been modest but steady. The share of gender-responsive loans at the ADB increased from 15 percent in 1998 to 38 percent in 2004.[20] At the IADB, lending operations that mainstreamed equal opportunities for women and men represented 37 percent of the total investment of the loan portfolio between 2002 and 2005, up from just 24 percent in 1998–2001.[21] The World Bank increased its share of projects incorporating gender issues in the design stage from 68 percent in 2001 to 87 percent in 2004–05.[22]

The AfDB, the IADB, and the World Bank all recently adopted gender action plans to make their gender mainstreaming policies more strategic and operationally effective. The ADB, which adopted a focus on gender as an important cross-cutting theme in the 1990s, has been effectively using project-level gender action plans for some years.[23] It is also developing an institutionwide three-year plan of action.[24] The AfDB adopted a gender plan of action in 2004 and included gender among 14 key indicators of development effectiveness.[25] The gender mainstreaming action plan at the IADB, adopted in 2003, has helped target activities, develop sounder actions, and monitor these actions more effectively.[26] "Gender Equality as Smart Economics," the World Bank's gender action plan crafted in 2006, focuses on previously neglected economic sectors. It highlights key upstream and downstream actions, linking them to outcomes and indicators of success.[27]

Despite these improvements, significant gaps remain, particularly in the areas of economic growth, agriculture, competitiveness, infrastructure, and private sector development, where progress has been slower than in the health and education sectors. Greater attention has been paid to gender in project design than in implementation; very little has been paid in monitoring and evaluation. Institutions have generally been slow to develop and adopt measurable indicators of progress in gender equality. The IFIs' internal rating systems have primarily measured good intentions (whether gender has been incorporated into project design) rather than results or financial commitments to gender issues.[28] Regarding the latter, an inherent problem arises in assessing the amount of resources allocated to an objective that by definition is fully mainstreamed. Since budget tracking is an important tool for accountability, the more the IFIs mainstream gender, the harder it is to hold them accountable.

The IFIs should use their comparative advantages to significantly scale up the MDG3 agenda. Specifically, they could:

- Invest dedicated resources in including gender equality and women's empowerment in results frameworks and the results agenda, and the associated impact evaluation work, to both strengthen gender equality interventions and increase accountability for their own performance
- Play a leadership role in strengthening the monitoring of MDG3 at the international level
- Assist client countries in significantly scaling up MDG3 interventions by using analytical, policy, and research instruments to

help them assess the advantages of investing in gender equality; translating gender objectives into specific actions that can have a measurable impact on women's lives; budgeting adequate financial and technical resources to implement projects at scale and measure results; and aligning investments on gender equality with needed policy and institutional changes.

Supporting Fragile States

IFIs have been working closely together toward strengthening their support to fragile states by harmonizing their approaches along four main areas of specialized response: strategy, policy, and procedural frameworks; exceptional financial instruments; customized organizational and staffing approaches; and partnership work. Progress varies among international organizations, but all are committed to more effective and rapid responses to fragility (table 5.2).[29] At their meeting in London in March 2007, the heads of MDBs agreed to set up a working group on fragile states to identify common operating principles for engagement in fragile situations, enhance partnerships, and coordinate the division of labor within the MDBs and other partner agencies.

Strategies. The ADB's strategy for engaging weakly performing countries is designed to increase the effectiveness of existing and planned operations in countries characterized by weak governance, ineffective public administration, and civil unrest. Its framework for guiding operational planning and implementation includes a methodology for classifying such countries and alternative interventions that may be modified depending on the country context. The ADB emphasizes country ownership, bolstered by systematic capacity development.

The AfDB identifies 25 countries in its region as fragile. Of those, 16 have been designated "core fragile states." The AfDB is in the process of enhancing its assistance to these countries by strengthening its operational response and enhancing resource

TABLE 5.2 IFI reforms to strengthen response in fragile states

	IMF	WB	ADB	AfDB	IADB
Strategy	Under way	Yes	Under way	Under way	Yes
Business Procedures	No	Yes	Under way	Under way	Yes
Financing	Under way	Yes	Under way	Under way	Yes
Staffing	No	Under way	Under way	Under way	Yes
Partnerships	No	Yes	Yes	Yes	Yes

Source: Staff of the of the IMF, WB, ADB, AfDB, and IADB.
Note: Yes = Comprehensive specialized framework adopted and implemented;
Under way = Specialized framework under development or some specialized response implemented;
No = No specialized framework implemented.

mobilization capacity. The AfDB's envisaged strategy focuses on the following categories of engagement: (1) catalytic role; (2) strategic partnership; and (3) areas of minimal engagement. Where the AfDB undertakes a catalytic role, it proposes to engage in rebuilding state capacity and accountability and in rehabilitating and reconstructing basic infrastructure. Where it builds strategic partnerships, the AfDB intends to support economic and structural reforms and economic integration and regional projects. The AfDB will also step up its efforts in generating knowledge with respect to fragile states and situations in Africa. The proposed strategy also identifies a need to streamline and simplify the AfDB's procedures in these states.

Although it has not formally defined fragile states for separate strategic engagement, the Islamic Development Bank (IsDB) has developed policy notes on assistance to regional member countries experiencing fragility.[30] It also utilizes simple and flexible procurement and disbursement procedures for its work in fragile states, in line with procedures proposed for emergency response. Similarly, the IADB utilized special measures for its engagement in Haiti, which included simplified start-up requirements, broader eligible expenditure categories, and elimination of counterpart financing requirements.

The IMF is actively engaged in assisting almost all fragile states, although it also does not define them formally for such purposes. This engagement focuses in the IMF's core macroeconomic and financial areas of responsibility. Assistance takes the form of policy advice on fiscal, monetary, exchange rate, and financial issues; help in identifying gaps in the related institutional and legal frameworks; and technical cooperation to follow up much of this advice—all essential elements of statebuilding. In cooperation with the World Bank, the IMF assists countries seeking to qualify for debt relief under the enhanced HIPC Initiative and the MDRI, and also seeks to help them avoid the reemergence of debt problems afterward. While the IMF's direct financial assistance is generally not a major element of financing packages, for some countries its lending—most often through postconflict emergency assistance or the Poverty Reduction and Growth Facility (PRGF)—can also be important. IMF staff are currently preparing a report that reviews support to postconflict countries and other fragile states, and examines the adequacy of existing instruments in terms of policy flexibility and their capacity-building component.

Since the inception of the Low-Income Countries under Stress (LICUS) initiative, the World Bank has underlined the importance of supporting efforts that contribute to peace-building and state-building goals, highlighting the need for institutional flexibility and close international coordination. The World Bank has developed specific guidance on assistance strategies and transitional results frameworks in fragile states; they distinguish among countries that are facing deteriorating governance, those in postconflict or political transition, those currently in conflict or crisis, and those transiting from fragility. In February 2007, the World Bank's Board also approved a "New Framework for Rapid Bank Response to Crises and Emergencies," which provides quicker and more effective responses to emergencies and crises through accelerated and streamlined review and implementation procedures; it gives the World Bank the flexibility to respond to a wider range of fragile situations and clarifies the objective of its engagement to include adequate focus on the social aspects of recovery and peace-building.

Financing instruments and allocation. Both the AfDB and the World Bank have developed an exceptional allocation framework for postconflict countries. Like IDA's special postconflict assistance, the African Development Fund's postconflict enhancement factor allows countries to benefit from additional resources over and above their performance-based allocation for a limited period after they are designated postconflict countries. IDA extended the duration of exceptional assistance under the postconflict framework in IDA-14 to correspond with the results of research on the pattern of aid and absorptive capacity for countries emerging from conflict.[31]

Many fragile states face difficulties from the build-up of large and protracted arrears on their debt. The AfDB has established the Post-Conflict Country Facility (PCCF) to help countries emerging from conflict to clear these arrears. The IADB can grant limited grant financing to conflict-affected countries with large overdue debt payments, before arrears clearance. Recognizing the need to maintain positive financial flows, the IADB has introduced innovations in Haiti; ongoing IADB interventions combining investment and policy loans are complemented with a program of nonreimbursable technical assistance and nonfinancial products to underpin program and policy implementation and increase country knowledge. IDA can provide pre-arrears grants to postconflict countries if certain conditions are met. Under IDA-14 it can also provide exceptional support to countries that are re-engaging with IDA after a prolonged period of disengagement.

Organizational capacity. All of the IFIs recognize the importance of increasing their field presence in fragile states, where low capacity and volatile conditions require sustained assistance on the ground and empowerment of staff in the field. Until recently, the AfDB had limited field presence in African fragile states, and two-thirds of the World Bank's field offices in fragile states had no or just one international staff member in 2005. Both institutions are taking steps to increase their field presence. Under its decentralization strategy, which is currently being implemented, the AfDB is strengthening its field presence in fragile states by opening field offices in Chad, the Democratic Republic of Congo, Sierra Leone, and Sudan. The IADB has posted additional staff to Haiti, aligned with areas of portfolio focus, and delegated additional responsibilities to its representative in Port-au-Prince. The World Bank has proposed an increase of at least 50 percent in its field positions in fragile states over the next two years.

Partnerships. The IFIs have worked with one another and participated in wider initiatives to develop international consensus on shared approaches and tools in fragile states. The World Bank co-chairs the Fragile States Group within the OECD DAC; this group includes the ADB and the AfDB. There is a general shift toward joint assistance strategies and cofinancing with other donors: the World Bank has four joint country assistance strategies in place in fragile states and two others under way; the ADB and the AfDB emphasize cofinancing with other partners.

Future priorities. All the IFIs recognize the need to strengthen approaches to fragile states by focusing on strategy, financing instruments, organization and staffing, and partnerships. Specific priorities going forward include the following:

- Support efforts under the Paris Declaration to implement the Principles for Good International Engagement in Fragile States.
- Strengthen exchanges among the IFIs on strategic assistance models, strengthening and harmonizing business policy and procedures, financing instruments, and organization and staffing issues.
- Strengthen common approaches with other international partners, in particular through efforts to improve both coordination and division of labor with organizations leading peace-building efforts, such as the United Nations and regional institutions.
- Review the types of financial assistance provided to different kinds of fragile states along with the effectiveness of resource use in these countries.

The IFIs have been supportive of strengthening coherence across the diplomatic, security, and development spheres as they engage in fragile states, as demonstrated by their support of the United Nations Peace-Building Commission. A number of other international actors, including the above-mentioned Fragile States Group, now have work under way to consider how to better integrate approaches among diplomatic, security, financial, and development actors in fragile states. The World Bank also coordinates with the UNDG in making postconflict needs assessments: these are joint planning tools that cover the political, security, social, and economic spheres; they are currently undergoing a revision to strengthen their focus on peace building, institution building, and the monitoring of implementation and results. The regional development banks participate in these joint assessment and planning missions for countries in their regions.

Notes

1. IMF (2006).
2. World Bank (2007).
3. World Bank (2006).
4. International Task Force on Global Public Goods (2006).
5. World Bank (2006).
6. MDBs Report (2006).
7. "Report of the External Review Committee on Bank-Fund Collaboration" (2007).
8. The doubling of EBRD lending in USD terms is a combination of actual growth and exchange rate movements. In terms of Euros, growth has been about 15 percent—from €4.3bn to €4.9bn.
9. The full cost to IDA, the AfDF, and the IMF of the MDRI was estimated to be around $50 billion in July 2006. IDA (2006).
10. The other six donors—Hungary, the Republic of Korea, Kuwait, Saudi Arabia, South Africa, and Switzerland—are in the process of securing required approvals to issue their instruments of commitment.
11. Firm financing commitments for the MDRI are backed by necessary legislative and parliamentary approvals in the donor country. Qualified financing commitments are not backed by such approvals and are subject to a donor's future capacity and willingness to provide funding.
12. Dollar and Levin (2004).
13. These workshops and reviews of experience are summarized in the OECD's Sourcebook on Emerging Good Practices in Managing for Development Results (2006).
14. Bedi, Coudouel, Cox, Goldstein, and Thornton (2006).
15. World Bank (2004).
16. AfDB, AsDB, EBRD, IADB, and World Bank (2007).
17. A good example corresponds to the subcategory relating to the timely implementation of projects. The 2006 COMPAS offers a single metric for the disbursement ratio and for actual, versus planned, execution period.
18. Buvinic (2004).
19. World Bank (2001).
20. ADB (2006).
21. IADB (2006).

22. Gender and Development Group, World Bank (2006). Whereas the IADB and the ADB use as a denominator or comparator the totality of projects in the loan portfolio, the World Bank excludes from the exercise roughly 20 percent of projects that potentially have no gender-relevant dimensions.

23. ADB (2006).

24. ADB (2006).

25. Response to informal questionnaire, January 2007.

26. IADB (2006).

27. World Bank (2006).

28. How much is spent on gender issues is difficult to determine, especially as these issues are increasingly mainstreamed.

29. Although the Bank has approved a new policy framework and business procedures for its response in fragile situations and it provides special financing to fragile countries through the LICUS Trust Fund, it continues to work on strengthening its support to this fragile group of countries. The IADB experience is based on the single fragile country in the region (Haiti), for which interim country assistance strategies were formulated and regularly updated. EBRD does not have programs targeted to fragile states, but does have two special programs for their least advanced members (the Early Transition Countries and the Western Balkans countries).

30. Unlike that from other MDBs, the IsDB's assistance to fragile states includes a substantial element of humanitarian assistance. The primary focus is on emergency relief, followed by basic social and economic infrastructure and long-term rehabilitation and reconstruction.

31. The ADB invests in technical assistance and capacity building in fragile states, usually in the form of grants. The AfDB continues to provide emergency relief assistance in the form of grants to affected countries, many of them fragile states. The IsDB has a special assistance account, the Waqf Fund, to provide humanitarian relief to member countries and Muslim communities affected by natural disasters and calamities. The World Bank established the LICUS Trust Fund from a series of grants from the IBRD surplus, to support peace building and capacity building in fragile states, with a focus on countries in nonaccrual status.

References

Chapter 1

Abu-Ghaida, Dina, and Stephan Klasen. 2004. "The Costs of Missing the Millennium Development Goal on Gender Equality." *World Development* 32 (7): 1075–107.

Auty, Richard M., and Alan H. Gelb. 2001. "Political Economy of Resource-Abundant States." In Resource *Abundance and Economic Development*, ed. R. M. Auty. New York: Oxford University Press.

Barwell, Ian. 1996. "Transport and the Village: Findings from African Village-Level Travel and Transport Surveys and Related Studies." World Bank Discussion Paper No. 344, Africa Region Series, World Bank, Washington, DC.

Caplan, B. 2001. "How Does War Shock the Economy?" *Journal of International Money and Finance* 21.

Chauvet, Lisa, and Paul Collier. 2004. "Development Effectiveness in Fragile Stated: Spillovers and Turnarounds." Centre for the Study of African Economies, Oxford University.

Chen, Shaohua, and Martin Ravallion. Forthcoming. "Absolute Poverty Measures for the Developing World."

Collier, Paul. 1999. "On the Economic Consequences of Civil War." *Oxford Economic Papers* 51 (1).

DFID (U.K. Department for International Development). 2005. "Why We Need to Work More Effectively with Fragile States." DFID, London.

Dollar, David, and Roberta Gatti. 1999. "Gender Inequality, Income and Growth: Are Good Times Good for Women?" Policy Research Report on Gender and Development, Working Paper Series No. 1, World Bank, Washington, DC.

Ezzati, Saleh, and Daniel M. Kammen. 2000. "The Contributions of Emissions and Spatial Microenvironments to Exposure to Indoor Air Pollution from Biomass Combustion in Kenya." *Environmental Health Perspectives* 108 (9): 833–40.

———. 2001. "Indoor Air Pollution from Biomass Combustion and Acute Respiratory Infections in Kenya: An Exposure-Response Study." *The Lancet* 358.

Hallward-Driemeier, Mary. 2006. "The Impact of Improvements in the Investment Climate: Evidence from Panel Surveys in Bangladesh." World Bank, Washington, DC.

Kaufmann, Daniel, Aart Kraay, and Massimo Mastruzzi. 2006. "Governance Matters V: Governance Indicators for 1996–2005." World Bank, Washington, DC.

Klasen, Stephan. 2002. "Low Schooling for Girls, Slower Growth for All? Cross-country Evidence on the Effect of Gender Inequality in Education on Economic Development." *World Bank Economic Review* 16 (3): 345–73.

Knight, M., N. Loaza, and D. Villaneuva. 1996. "The Peace Dividend: Military Spending Cuts and Economic Growth." IMF Staff Papers (43) 1. International Monetary Fund, Washington, DC.

Marshall, Monty, and Keith Jaggers. 2002. "POLITY IV Project: Political Regime Characteristics and Transitions, 1800–2002." Dataset Users' Manual, Center for International Development and Conflict Management, University of Maryland.

Moreno Torres, Magui, and Michael Anderson. 2004. "Fragile States: Defining Difficult Environment for Poverty Reduction." PRDE Working Paper 1, Poverty Reduction in Difficult Environments. DFID, London.

Nankhuni, F. 2004. "Environmental Degradation, Resource Scarcity and Children's Welfare in Malawi: School Attendance, School Progress, and Children's Health." PhD thesis, Agricultural Economics and Demography, Pennsylvania State University.

OECD/DAC (Organisation for Economic Development and Co-operation/Development Co-operation Directorate). 2005. "Principles for Good International Engagement in Fragile States." OECD, Paris.

———. 2006. "Monitoring Resource Flows to Fragile States—2005 Report." OECD, Paris.

Staines, Nicholas. 2004. "Economic Performance over the Conflict Cycle." IMF Working Paper WP/04/95, International Monetary Fund, Washington, DC.

Stotsky, Janet. 2006. "Gender and Its Relevance to Macroeconomic Policy: A Survey." IMF Working Paper WP/06/233, International Monetary Fund, Washington, DC.

World Bank. 2005. "Low-Income Countries Under Stress: Update." Operations Policy and Country Services, World Bank, Washington, DC.

———. 2006a. *Where Is the Wealth of Nations: Measuring Capital for the XXI Century.* Washington, DC: World Bank.

———. 2006b. *World Development Indicators.* Washington, DC: World Bank.

Chapter 2

Bloom, Erik, Indu Bushan, David Clingingsmith, Rathavuth Hong, Elizabeth King, Michael Kremer, Benjamin Loevinsohn, and Brad Schwartz. 2006. "Contracting for Health: Evidence from Cambodia." Informal paper.

Buckland, Peter. 2005. *Reshaping the Future: Education and Post-Conflict Reconstruction.* Washington, DC: World Bank.

Bustreo, Flavia, Eleonora Genovese, Elio Omobono, Henrik Axelsson, and Ian Bannon. 2005. "Improving Child Health in Post-Conflict Countries: Can the World Bank Contribute?" Children and Youth, HDNCY No. 3. World Bank, Washington, DC.

Chaudhury, Nazmul, Jeffrey Hammer, Michael Kremer, Karthik Muralidharan, and F. Halsey Rogers. 2006. "Missing in Action: Teacher and Health Worker Absence in Developing Countries." *Journal of Economic Perspectives* 20 (1): 91–116.

Clemens, M. 2004. "The Long Walk to School: International Education Goals in Historical Perspective." Center for Global Development, Washington, DC.

Cohen, Joel E., David E. Bloom, and Martin B. Malin. 2006. *Educating All Children: A Global Agenda.* American Academy of Arts and Sciences, Cambridge, MA.

Collier, P., S. Dercon, and J. Mackinnon. 2003. "Density versus Quality in Health Care Provision: Using Household Data to Make Budgetary Choices in Ethiopia." *World Bank Economic Review* 16 (3): 425–48.

Cotlear, Daniel. 2006. *A New Social Contract for Peru*. Washington, DC: World Bank.

Crouch, Louis, and Tazeen Fasih. 2004. "Patterns in Educational Development: Implications for Further Efficiency Analysis." Informal paper, World Bank, Washington, DC.

Danel, I. 1999. "Maternal Mortality Reduction, Honduras, 1990–1997: A Case Study." World Bank, Washington, DC.

Das, Jishnu, and Paul Gertler. 2007. "Practice-Quality Variation in Five Low-Income Countries: A Conceptual Overview." Informal paper, World Bank, Washington, DC.

Das, Jishnu, and Jeffrey Hammer. 2004. "Strained Mercy: The Quality of Medical Care in Delhi." *Economic and Political Weekly* 39 (9): 951–65.

Duflo, Esther. 2001. "Schooling and Labor Market Consequences of School Construction in Indonesia: Evidence from an Unusual Policy Experiment." *American Economic Review* 91 (September): 795–813.

Duflo, Esther, Pascaline Dupas, Michael Kremer, and Samuel Simei. 2006. "Education and HIV/AIDS Prevention: Evidence from a Randomized Evaluation in Western Kenya." Informal paper, Harvard University, Cambridge, MA.

Dupas, P. 2005. "Relative Risks and the Market for Sex: Teenagers, Sugar Daddies and HIV in Kenya." Informal paper, Dartmouth College, Hanover, NH.

Fewtrell, L., R.B. Kaufmann, D. Kay, W. Enanoria, L. Haller, and J. M. Colford, Jr. 2005. "Water, Sanitation, and Hygiene Interventions to Reduce Diarrhea in Less Developed Countries: A Systematic Review and Meta-analysis." *The Lancet Infectious Diseases* 5 (1): 42–52.

Filmer, Deon, Amer Hasan, and Lant Pritchett. 2006. "A Millennium Learning Goal: Measuring Real Progress in Education." Center for Global Development, Washington, DC.

Greaney, V., and Robert Prouty. 2007. "National and International Assessments of Student Achievement." Informal paper, World Bank, Washington, DC.

Hanushek, Eric A., and D. D. Kimko. 2000. "Schooling, Labor-Force Quality, and the Growth of Nations." *American Economic Review* 90 (5): 1184–208.

Hanushek, Eric A., and Javier A. Luque. 2003. "Efficiency and Equity in Schools around the World." *Economics of Education Review* 22 (August): 481–502.

Hanushek, Eric A., and Ludger Woessmann. 2007."The Role of School Improvement in Economic Development." NBER Working Paper No. 12832, National Bureau of Economic Research, Cambridge, MA.

Hoeffler, A., and M. Reynal-Querol. 2003. "Measuring the Cost of Conflict." Oxford University Press, Oxford.

Jones, G., R. Steketee, R. Black, Z. Bhutta, S. Morris, and the Bellagio Child Survival Study Group. 2003. "How Many Child Deaths Can We Prevent This Year?" *The Lancet* 362 (9377): 65–71.

Lavy, Victor, and Jean-Marc Germain. 1994. "Quality and Cost in Health Care Choice in Developing Countries." Working Paper No. 105, Living Standards Measurement Study, World Bank, Washington, DC.

Leonard, Kenneth, Melkiory C. Masatu, and A. Vialou. 2005. "Getting Doctors To Do Their Best: Ability, Altruism and Incentives." University of Maryland, College Park, MD.

Lewis, Maureen, and Marlaine Lockheed. 2006. *Inexcusable Absence*. Washington, DC: The Center for Global Development.

Loevinsohn, B., and A. Harding. 2005. "Buying results? Contracting for Health Services Delivery in Developing Countries." *The Lancet* 366 (9486): 676–81.

Manor, James, ed. 2007. *Aid That Works: Successful Development in Fragile States*. Washington, DC: World Bank.

Mills, E.J., J.B. Nachega, I. Buchan, J. Orbinski, and A. Attaran. 2006. "Adherence to Antiretroviral Therapy in Sub-Saharan Africa and North America: A Meta-analysis." *Journal of the American Medical Association* 296 (6): 679–90.

Mills, Samuel, Eduard Bos, Elizabeth Lule, G.N.V. Ramana, and Rodolfo Bulatao. 2007. "Preventable Maternal Deaths: Emergency Obstetric Care Is Lacking or Late in Ghana, Kenya, and India." Informal paper, World Bank, Washington, DC.

Mizala, A., and P. Romaguera. 2002. "Equity and Educational Performance," *Economía, Journal of the Latin America and the Caribbean Economic Association* 2 (2): 219–62.

Murthy, K.J.R., T.R. Frieden, A. Yazdani, and P. Hreshikesh. 2001. "Public Private Partnership in Tuberculosis Control: Experience in Hyderabad, India." *International Journal of Tuberculosis Lung Disease* 5 (4): 354–59.

Nickell, Stephen. 2004. "Poverty and Worklessness in Britain." *Economic Journal* 114 (March): C1–C25.

Pratham. 2005. "Annual Status of Education Report (ASER)." Mumbai, India. Available at http://www.pratham.org/aserrep.php.

Pritchett, Lant. 2004. "Access to Education." In *Global Crises, Global Solutions*, ed. Björn Lomborg, 175–234. Cambridge U.K.: Cambridge University Press.

Ransom, E., and N. Yinger. 2002. "Making Motherhood Safer: Overcoming Obstacles on the Pathways to Care." Population Reference Bureau, Washington, DC.

Republic of Rwanda. 2006. "Scaling Up to Achieve the Health MDGs in Rwanda." A Background Study for the High-Level Forum Meeting in Tunis, June 12–13, 2006.

Stover, John, Stefano Bertozzi, Juan-Pablo Gutierrez, Neff Walker, Karen A. Stanecki, Robert Greener, Eleanor Gouws, Catherine Hankins, Geoff P. Garnett, Joshua A. Salomon, J. Ties Boerma, Paul De Lay, and Peter D. Ghys. 2006. "The Global Impact of Scaling Up HIV/AIDS Prevention Programs in Low- and Middle-Income Countries." *Science* 311 (5766): 1474–76.

Stover, John, and M. Fahnenstock. 2006. "Coverage of Selected Services for HIV/AIDS Prevention and Care in Low- and Middle-Income Countries in 2005." Funded by United Nations Programme on HIV/AIDS, U.S. Agency for International Development, and United National Population Fund. Futures Group/POLICY Project, Washington, DC.

Stringer, J.S., I. Zulu, J. Levy J, et al. 2006. "Rapid Scale-up of Antiretroviral Therapy at Primary Care Sites in Zambia: Feasibility and Early Outcomes." *Journal of the American Medical Association* 296: 782–93.

Thaddeus, S., and D. Maine. 1994. "Too Far to Walk: Maternal Mortality in Context." *Social Science and Medicine* 38: 1091–10.

Thirumurthy, H., J. Graff-Zivin, and M. Goldstein. 2005. "The Economic Impact of AIDS Treatment: Labor Supply in Western Kenya." NBER Working Paper No. 11871, National Bureau of Economic Research, Cambridge, MA.

Thornton, Rebecca. 2005. "The Demand for and Impact of Learning HIV Status: Evidence from a Field Experiment." Informal paper, Harvard University, Cambridge, MA.

Umansky, Ilana, and Luis Crouch. 2006. *Fast Track Initiative: Initial Evidence of Impact.* Washington, DC: World Bank.

UNAIDS (United Nations Programme on HIV/AIDS). 2006. "Report on the Global AIDS Epidemic." UNAIDS, Washington, DC.

UNAIDS (United Nations Programme on HIV/AIDS) and WHO (World Health Organization). 2005. "AIDS Epidemic Update. Special Report on HIV Prevention." UNAIDS, Washington, DC.

UNESCO (United Nations Educational, Scientific and Cultural Organization). 2005. *EFA Global Monitoring Report 2005—The Quality Imperative.* Paris: UNESCO.

———. 2007. *EFA Global Monitoring Report 2007—Early Childhood Care and Education.* Paris: UNESCO.

Vegas, Emiliana, and Jenny Petrow. 2007. *Raising Student Learning in Latin America: The Challenge for the 21st Century.* Washington, DC: World Bank.

Walker, Dilys, Juan Pablo Gutierrez, Pilar Torres, and Stefano M. Bertozzi. 2006. "HIV Prevention in Mexican Schools: Prospective Randomised Evaluation of Intervention." *British Medical Journal* 332 (May 20): 1189–194.

Walter, Steven. 2007. "Preliminary Report of Some Findings on Primary Education in Boyo Division." Informal paper, World Bank, Washington, DC.

WHO (World Health Organization). 2006. "Stop TB Partnership: The Global Plan to Stop TB, 2006–2015." WHO, Geneva, Switzerland.

Woessmann, Ludger. 2003. "Schooling Resources, Educational Institutions, and Student Performance: The International Evidence." *Oxford Bulletin of Economics and Statistics* 65 (2): 117–70.

World Bank. 1999. "Safe Motherhood and the World Bank: Lessons from 10 Years of Experience." World Bank, Washington, DC.

———. 2006. "Progress Report for the Education for All–Fast Track Initiative." World Bank, Development Committee Meeting, Washington, DC.

———. 2007. "Aid Architecture and the Main Trends in Official Development Assistance Flows." World Bank, Washington, DC.

Chapter 3

Abu-Ghaida, Dina, and Stephan Klasen. 2004. "The Costs of Missing the Millennium Development Goal on Gender Equity." *World Development* 32 (7): 1075–107.

Agarwal, Bina. 1994. "Gender and Command over Property: A Critical Gap in Economic Analysis and Policy in South Asia." *World Development* 22 (10): 1455–478.

Alderman, H., J. Hoddinott, and B. Kinsey. 2002. "Long Term Consequences of Early Childhood Malnutrition." *Oxford Economic Papers* 58 (3): 450–74.

Anderson, Kathryn, Elizabeth M. King, and Yan Wang. 2003. "Market Returns, Transfers and Demand for Schooling in Malaysia, 1976–89." *Journal of Development Studies* 39 (3): 1–28.

Asfaw, Abay, and Assefa Admassie. 2004. "The Role of Education on the Adoption of Chemical Fertiliser under Different Socioeconomic Environments in Ethiopia." *Agricultural Economics* 30: 215–28.

Ballington, Judith, and Azza Karam, eds. 2005. *Women in Parliament: Beyond Numbers*. Stockholm: International Institute for Democracy and Electoral Assistance.

Bandiera, Oriana, and Imran Rasul. 2006. "Social Networks and Technology Adoption in Northern Mozambique." *Economic Journal* 116: 862–902.

Barwell, Ian. 1996. "Transport and the Village: Findings from African Village-Level Travel and Transport Surveys and Related Studies." World Bank Discussion Paper No. 344, Africa Region Series, World Bank, Washington, DC.

Baydas, Mayada M., Richard L. Meyer, and Nelson Aguilera-Alfred. 1994. "Discrimination Against Women in Formal Credit Markets: Reality or Rhetoric?" *World Development* 22 (7): 1073–082.

Behrman, Jere, and Mark Rosenzweig. 2004. "Returns to Birthweight." *Review of Economics and Statistics* 86 (2): 586–601.

Brown, Philip H. 2006. "Parental Education and Investment in Children's Human Capital in Rural China." *Economic Development and Cultural Change* 54 (4): 759–89.

Burkhalter, H.J. 2002. *The Violent Transmission of HIV/AIDS*. Washington, DC: CSIS HIV/AIDS Task Force.

Buvinic, Mayra, and Marguerite Berger. 1990. "Sex Differences in Access to a Small Enterprise Development Fund in Peru." *World Development* 18 (5): 695–705.

Caldwell, J.C. 1979. "Education as a Factor in Mortality Decline: An Examination of Nigerian Data." *Population Studies* 33 (3): 395–413.

Carr, Marilyn, and Martha Chen. 2004. "Globalization, Social Exclusion and Gender." *International Labour Review* 143 (1–2): 25–26.

Cebu Study Team. 1991. "Underlying and Proximate Determinants of Child Health: The CEBU Longitudinal Health and Nutrition Study." *American Journal of Epidemiology* 133 (2): 185–201.

Chirwa, Ephraim. 2005. "Fertilizer and Hybrid Seeds Adoption among Smallholder Maize Farmers in Southern Malawi." *Development Southern Africa* 22 (1): 1–12.

Chung, Woojin, and Monica Das Gupta. 2007. "Why Is Son Preference Declining in Korea?" Paper prepared for the Population Association of America meeting, New York, March 29–31.

Croppenstedt, Andre, Mulat Demeke, and Meloria M. Meschi. 2003. "Technology Adoption in the Presence of Constraints: The Case of Fertilizer Demand in Ethiopia." *Review of Development Economics* 7: 58–70.

Das Gupta, Monica, Jiang Zhenghua, Xie Zhenming, Li Bohua, Woojin Chung, and Bae Hwa-Ok. 2003. "Why Is Son Preference so Persistent in East and South Asia?" Journal of Development *Studies* 40 (2): 153–87.

Deere, Carmen Diana, and Magdalena Leon. 2001. *Empowering Women: Land and Property Rights in Latin America.* Pittsburgh: University of Pittsburgh Press.

Deere, Carmen Diana, and Magdalena Leon. 2003. "The Gender Asset Gap: Land in Latin America." *World Development* 31: 925–47.

De Walque, Damien. 2006. "Discordant Couples: HIV Infection Among Couples in Burkina Faso, Cameroon, Ghana, Kenya, and Tanzania." Policy Research Working Paper No. 3956, World Bank, Washington, DC.

Diagne, Aliou, Manfred Zeller, and Manohar Sharma. 2000. "Empirical Measurements of Households' Access to Credit and Credit Constraints in Developing Countries: Methodological Issues and Evidence." IFPRI FCND Discussion Paper No. 90, International Food Policy Research Institute, Washington, DC.

Doss, Cheryl. 1996. "Women's Bargaining Power in Household Economic Decisions: Evidence from Ghana." Staff Paper Series P96-11. University of Minnesota, College of Agricultural, Food and Environmental Sciences, Department of Applied Economics.

Doss, Cheryl. 2005. "The Effects of Intrahousehold Property Ownership on Expenditure Patterns in Ghana." *Journal of African Economies* 15: 149–80.

Doss, Cheryl, and Michael L. Morris. 2001. "How Does Gender Affect the Adoption of Agricultural Technologies? The Case of Improved Maize Technology in Ghana." *Agricultural Economics* 25: 27–39.

Duflo, Esther. 2003. "Grandmothers and Granddaughters: Old Age Pension and Intra-Household Allocation in South Africa." *World Bank Economic Review* 17 (1): 1–25.

Duflo, Esther, and Christopher Udry. 2004. "Intrahousehold Resource Allocation in Côte d'Ivoire: Social Norms, Separate Accounts and Consumption Choices." NBER Working Paper No. 10498, National Bureau of Economic Research, Cambridge, MA.

Duryea, Suzanne, Alejandra Cox Edwards, and Manuelita Ureta. 2004. "Women in the Latin America Labor Market: The Remarkable 1990s." In *Women at Work: Challenges for Latin America*, ed. Claudia Piras, 27–60. Washington, DC: Inter-American Development Bank.

Duryea, Suzanne, Sebastian Galiani, Hugo Nopo, and Claudia Piras. 2006. "Education Gender Gap in Latin America and the Caribbean." Research Department Working Paper, Inter-American Development Bank, Washington, DC.

Duryea, Suzanne, and Maria Eugenia Genoni. 2004. "Ethnicity, Race and Gender in Latin American Labor Markets." In *Social Inclusion and Economic Devel-*

opment in Latin America, ed. Mayra Buvinic and Jacqueline Mazza, with Ruthanne Deutsch, 247–60. Washington, DC: Inter-American Development Bank.

Galloway, Rae, and Mary Ann Anderson. 1994. "Prepregnancy Nutritional Status and Its Impact on Birthweight." *SCN News* 11: 6–10.

Germain, Adrienne. 2004. "Reproductive Health and Human Rights." *The Lancet* 363 (9402): 65–66.

Glewwe, Paul, Hanan G. Jacoby, and Elizabeth M. King. 2001. "Early Childhood Nutrition and Academic Achievement: A Longitudinal Analysis." *Journal of Public Economics* 81 (3): 345–68.

Goodkind, Daniel. 1996. "On Substituting Sex Preference Strategies in East Asia: Does Prenatal Sex Selection Reduce Postnatal Discrimination?" *Population and Development Review* 22 (1): 111–25.

Grown, Karen. 2006. "Indicators and Indices of Gender Inequality: What Do They Measure and What Do They Miss?" Background paper for *Global Monitoring Report 2007.* World Bank, Washington, DC.

Hoddinott, John, and Lawrence Haddad. 1995. "Does Female Income Share Influence Household Expenditures? Evidence from Côte d'Ivoire." *Oxford Bulletin of Economics and Statistics* 57 (1): 77–96.

INSTRAW (United Nations International Research and Training Institute for the Advancement of Women). 2005. "Institutional Mechanisms for the Advancement of Women: New Challenges." INSTRAW progress report. Available at www.un-instraw.org/en/images/stories/Beijing/institutionalmechanisms.pdf (accessed January 2007).

Jacobs, Susie. 2002. "Land Reform: Still a Goal Worth Pursuing for Rural Women?" *Journal of International Development* 14: 887–98.

Kabeer, Naila. 1999. "Resources, Agency, Achievements: Reflections on the Measurement of Women's Empowerment." *Development and Change* 30 (3): 435–64.

Kabeer, Naila, and Simeen Mahmud. 2004. "Rags, Riches and Women Workers: Export-oriented Garment Manufacturing in Bangladesh." In *Chains of Fortune: Linking Women Producers and Workers with Global Markets*, ed. Marilyn Carr, 133–62. London: Commonwealth Secretariat.

Kishor, Sunita, and Kiersten Johnson. 2004. "Profiling Domestic Violence: A Multi-country Study." ORC Macro, Calverton, MD.

Klasen, Stephan. 2002. "Low Schooling for Girls, Slower Growth for All? Cross-country Evidence on the Effect of Gender Inequality in Education on Economic Development." *World Bank Economic Review* 16: 345–73.

———. 2006. Guest editor's introduction, Special Issue on Revisiting the Gender-related Development Index (GDI) and Gender Empowerment Measure (GEM). *Journal of Human Development* 7 (2): 145–59.

Knowles, Stephen, A. K. Lorgelly, and Dorian Owen. 2002. "Are Educational Gender Gaps a Brake on Economic Development? Some Cross-country Empirical Evidence." *Oxford Economic Papers* 54 (1): 118–49.

Lastarria-Cornheil, Susana. 1997. "Impact of Privatization on Gender and Property Rights in Africa." *World Development* 25 (8): 1317–333.

Lewis, Maureen, and Marlaine Lockheed. 2006. *Inexcusable Absence: Why 60 Million Girls Still Aren't in School and What to Do About It.* Washington, DC: Center for Global Development.

Lorgelly, Paula. 2000. "Are There Gender-Separate Human Capital Effects on Growth? A Review of the Recent Empirical Evidence." University of Nottingham GREIT Research Paper 00/12, University of Nottingham.

Malhotra, A., S. Schuler, and C. Boender. 2002. "Measuring Women's Empowerment as a Variable in International Development." World Bank Gender and

Development Group Background paper. World Bank, Washington, DC. Available at www.icrw.org/docs/MeasuringEmpowerment_workingpaper_802.doc.

Morrison, Andrew, and Francesca Lamana. 2006. "Gender Issues in the Kyrgyz Labor Market." Background paper for Kyrgyz Poverty Assessment, World Bank, Washington, DC.

Morrison, Andrew, Dhushyanth Raju, and Nistha Sinha. 2007. "Gender Equality, Poverty, and Economic Growth." Background paper for *Global Monitoring Report 2007*. World Bank, Washington, DC.

Narayan, Deepa. 2006. *Measuring Empowerment: Cross-disciplinary Perspectives*. Washington, DC: World Bank.

Paolisso, Michael J., Kelly Hallman, Lawrence Haddad, and Sibesh Regmi. 2002. "Does Cash Crop Adoption Detract from Child Care Provision? Evidence from Rural Nepal." *Economic Development and Cultural Change* 50: 313–37.

Pham, T. Hung, and Barry Reilly. 2006. "The Gender Pay Gap in Vietnam, 1993–2002: A Quantile Regression Approach." PRUS Working Paper Number 34, Poverty Research Unit at Sussex, University of Sussex.

Phavi, Ing Kantha, and Cheryl Urashima. 2006. "Policies to Promote Women's Economic Opportunities in Cambodia." Presented at High Level Consultation on MDG3, "Gender Equality and Women's Empowerment," World Bank, Washington, DC, February 16.

Pitt, Mark M., and Shahidur R. Khandker. 1998. "The Impact of Group-Based Credit Programs on Poor Households in Bangladesh: Does the Gender of Participants Matter?" *Journal of Political Economy* 106: 958–96.

Quisumbing, Agnes R., Jonna P. Estudillo, and Keijiro Otsuka. 2004. *Land and Schooling: Transferring Wealth Across Generations*. Baltimore, MD: John Hopkins University Press.

Ratusi, Mayank, and Anand V. Swamy. 1999. "Explaining Ethnic Differentials in

Credit Market Outcomes in Zimbabwe." *Economic Development and Cultural Change* 47: 585–604.

Rubalcava, Luis, Graciela Teruel, and Duncan Thomas. 2004. "Spending, Saving and Public Transfers Paid to Women." Working Paper 024-04, California Center for Population Research, University of California, Los Angeles.

Schultz, T.P. 1997. "The Demand for Children in Low Income Countries." In *Handbook of Population and Family Economics*, ed. M. R. Rosenzweig and O. Stark, 349–430. Amsterdam: North-Holland.

———. 2002. "Why Governments Should Invest More to Educate Girls." *World Development* 30 (2): 207–25.

Seguino, Stephanie, and Marla Sagrario Floro. 2003. "Does Gender Have Any Effect on Aggregate Savings? An Empirical Analysis." *International Review of Applied Economics* 17 (2): 147–66.

Semu, Linda. 2003. "Kamuzu's Mbumba: Malawi Women's Embeddedness to Culture in the Face of International Political Pressure and Internal Legal Change." *Africa Today* 49 (2): 76–99.

Storey, D. J. 2004. "Racial and Gender Discrimination in the Micro Firms Credit Market? Evidence from Trinidad and Tobago." *Small Business Economics* 23 (5): 401–22.

Thomas, Duncan, and John Strauss. 1992. "Prices, Infrastructure, Household Characteristics and Child Height." *Journal of Development Economics* 39 (2): 301–31.

Thomas, Duncan, John Strauss, and Maria-Helena Henriques. 1991. "How Does Mother's Education Affect Child Height?" *Journal of Human Resources* 26 (2): 183–211.

Udry, Christopher. 1996. "Gender, Agricultural Production, and the Theory of the Household." *Journal of Political Economy* 104: 1010–046.

United Nations. 2003. *The UN Handbook on Indicators for Monitoring Millennium Development Goals*. New York: United Nations.

UNDAW (United Nations Division for the Advancement of Women). 2004. "The Role of National Mechanisms in Promoting Gender Equality and the Empowerment of Women." Report of the Expert Group Meeting. Rome, Italy, November 29–December 2, 2004.

UNESCO (United Nations Educational, Scientific and Cultural Organization). 2004. *EFA Global Monitoring Report 2005. Education for All: The Quality Imperative.* Paris: UNESCO.

UNESCO (United Nations Educational, Scientific and Cultural Organization) Institute for Statistics. 2005. *Children out of School: Measuring Exclusion from Primary Education.* Montreal: UNESCO.

UNIFEM (United Nations Development Fund for Women). 2005. *Progress of the World's Women 2005.* New York: UNIFEM.

UN Millennium Project. 2005a. *Taking Action: Achieving Gender Equality and Empowering Women.* New York: Task Force on Education and Gender Equality.

———. 2005b. *Toward Universal Primary Education: Investments, Incentives, and Institutions.* New York: Task Force on Education and Gender Equality.

Van der Straten, Ariane, Rachel King, Olga Grinstead, Eric Vittinghoff, Antoine Serufilira, and Susan Allen. 1998. "Sexual Coercion, Physical Violence, and HIV Infection Among Women in Steady Relationships in Kigali, Rwanda." *AIDS and Behavior* 2 (1): 61–73.

Webb, P., and S. Block. 2004. "Nutrition Information and Formal Schooling as Inputs to Child Nutrition." *Economic Development and Cultural Change* 52 (4): 801–20.

WHO (World Health Organization). 2005. *WHO Multi-country Study on Women's Health and Domestic Violence Against Women.* Geneva, Switzerland: WHO.

Wier, Sharada, and John Knight. 2000. "Adoption and Diffusion of Agricultural Innovations in Ethiopia: The Role of Education." Centre for the Study of African Economies Working Paper 2000-5, Oxford University.

World Bank. 2001. *World Bank Policy Research Report 2001: Engendering Development: Through Gender Equality in Rights, Resources, and Voice.* New York: Oxford University Press.

———. 2002. *Gender in Transition.* Washington, DC: World Bank.

———. 2003. "Country Gender Assessment for Turkey." World Bank, Washington, DC.

———. 2005. *World Development Report 2006.* Washington, DC: World Bank.

———. 2006. *World Development Report 2007.* Washington, DC: World Bank.

Xinhua. 2005. "Imbalanced Sex Ratio in China Not Owed to Family Planning." *China Daily.* Available at http://www.chinadaily.com.cn/english/doc/2005-08/24/content_471890.htm (accessed January 2007).

Yuan, Xin, and Edward Jow-Ching Tu. 2005. "High Sex Ratio at Birth and its Implications in China." Paper presented at the IUSSP International Population Conference, Tours, France, July 18–23.

Zabin, Laurie Schwab, and Karungari Kiragu. 1998. "The Health Consequences of Adolescent Sexual and Fertility Behavior in Sub-Saharan Africa." *Studies in Family Planning* 29 (2): 210–32.

Zeng Yi, Tu Ping, Gu Baochang, Xu Yi, Li Bohua, and Li Yongping. 1993. "Causes and Implications of the Recent Increase in the Reported Sex Ratio at Birth in China." *Population and Development Review* 19 (2): 283–302.

Chapter 4

Alesina, Alberto, and David Dollar. 2000. "Who Gives Aid to Whom and Why? *Journal of Economic Growth* 5 (1): 33–64.

Amprou, Jacky, Patrick Guillaumont, and Sylviane Guillaumont Jeanneney. 2006. "Aid Selectivity According to Augmented Criteria." Working Paper No. 9. Agence Française de Dévelopment, Paris.

Arslanalp, Serkan, and Peter Blair Henry. 2003. "The World's Poorest Countries: Debt Relief or Aid?" Stanford Research Paper Series 1809, Stanford University.

Berthelemy, J.C., and A. Tichit. 2004. "Bilateral Donors' Aid Allocation Decisions. A Three Dimensional Panel Analysis."

Bourguignon, François, Mark Sundberg, and Hans Lofgren. 2005. "Building Absorptive Capacity to Meet the MDGs." Manuscript, presented at the Seminar on Foreign Aid and Macroeconomic Management, Maputo, Mozambique, March 14–15.

Broadman, Harry G. 2006. *Africa's Silk Road: China and India's New Economic Frontier.* Washington, DC: World Bank.

Bulir, Ales, and A. Javier Hamann. 2003. "Aid Volatility: An Empirical Assessment." IMF Working Paper 01/50, International Monetary Fund, Washington, DC.

———. 2006. "Volatility of Development Aid: From the Frying Pan onto the Fire?" IMF Working Paper 06/65, International Monetary Fund, Washington, DC.

Celasun, Oya, and Jan Walliser. 2005. "Predictability of Budget Aid: Experiences in Eight Africa Countries." Paper presented at World Bank practitioners forum on budget support, Cape Town, South Africa, May 5–6.

Clements, Benedict, Rina Bhattacharya, and Toan Quoc Nguyen. 2003. "External Debt, Public Investment, and Growth in Low-Income Countries." IMF Working Paper 03/249, International Monetary Fund, Washington, DC.

de Ferranti, David. 2006. "Innovative Financing Options and the Fight Against Global Poverty: What's New and What's Next." In *Transforming the Development Landscape,* ed. Lael Brainard, Washington, DC: Brookings Institution Press.

Depetris Chauvin, Nicolas, and Aart Kraay. 2005. "What Has 100 Billion Dollars Worth of Debt Relief Done for Low-Income Countries." Manuscript.

———. 2006. "Who Gets Debt Relief?" Policy Research Working Paper No. 4000, World Bank, Washington, DC.

Dollar, David, and Victoria Levin. 2004. "The Increasing Selectivity of Foreign Aid." Policy Research Working Paper 3299, World Bank, Washington, DC.

EU (European Union). 2006. "Global Europe: Competing in the World. A Contribution to the EU's Growth and Jobs Strategy." Communication of the EU Commission, October.

Garrett, Laurie. 2007. "The Challenge of Global Health." *Foreign Affairs* Jan./Feb.

Gelb, Alan, and Ben Eifert. 2005. "Improving the Dynamics of Aid." Policy Research Working Paper No. 3732, World Bank, Washington, DC.

Grown, Caren, Chadrika Bahadur, Jessie Handbury, and Diane Elson. 2006. The Financial Requirements of Achieving Gender Equality and Women's Empowerment. Levy Economics Institute Working Paper No. 467, Bard College, Blithewood, NY.

Heller, Peter S., Menachem Katz, Xavier Debrun, Theo Thomas, Taline Koranchelian, and Isabelle Adenauer. 2006. "Making Fiscal Space Happen: Managing Fiscal Policy in a World of Scaled-Up Aid." IMF Working Paper 06/270, International Monetary Fund, Washington, DC.

IMF (International Monetary Fund) and World Bank. 2006a. "Applying the Debt Sustainability Framework for Low-Income Countries Post Debt Relief." IMF and World Bank, Washington, DC.

———. 2006b. "Heavily Indebted Poor Countries (HIPC)-Status of Implementation." IMF and World Bank, Washington, DC.

———. 2006c. "Doha Development Agenda and Aid for Trade." IMF and World Bank, Washington, DC.

Kee, Hiau Looi, Alessandro Nicita, and Marcelo Olarreaga. 2006. "Estimating Trade Restrictiveness Indices." Available at http://econ.worldbank.org/WBSITE/EXTERNAL/EXTDEC/EXTRESEARCH/0,,contentMDK:21085342~pagePK:64214825~piPK:64214943~theSitePK:469382,00.html.

Lele, Uma, Nafis Sadik, and Adele Simmons. 2006. "The Changing Aid Architecture: Can Global Initiatives Eradicate Poverty?" Draft.

Levin, Victoria, and David Dollar. 2005. "The Forgotten States: Aid Volumes and Volatility in Difficult 'Partnership Countries (1992–2002)." Draft.

McGillivray, Mark. 1989. "The Allocation of Aid Among Developing Countries: A Multi-Donor Analysis Using a Per Capita Aid Index." *World Development* 17 (4): 561–68.

Moss, Todd, and Sarah Rose. 2006. "China's Export-Import Bank and Africa: New Lending, New Challenges." Center for Global Development, Washington, DC.

OECD (Organisation for Economic Development and Co-operation). 2000. "Handbook for Reporting Debt Reorganization on the DAC Questionnaire." OECD, Paris.

———. 2005a. "Directives for Reporting to the Creditor Reporting System." OECD, Paris.

———. 2005b. *Aid Activities in Support of Gender Equality: 1999–2003*. Paris: OECD.

———. 2006a. "Donor Reporting on Dissemination of the Paris Declaration." DAC Meeting, Development Co-operation Directorate, Paris, November 15.

———. 2006b. "Fragile States: Policy Commitment and Principles for Good International Engagement in Fragile States and Situations." Development Co-operation Directorate, Paris.

———. 2006c. "Monitoring Resource Flows to Fragile States 2005 Report." Development Co-operation Directorate, Paris.

———. 2006d. "Whole of Government Approaches to Fragile States." OECD, Paris.

———. 2007a. "Development Co-operation Report 2006." OECD, Paris.

———. 2007b. "Progress Report on the 2006 Survey on Monitoring the Paris Declaration." Development Co-operation Directorate, Paris.

Oxfam. 2004. "Stitched Up: How Rich-Country Protectionism in Textiles and Clothing Trade Prevents Poverty Alleviation." Briefing Paper 60, Oxford, London.

Reisen, Helmut, Marcelo Soto, and Thomas Weithoner. 2004. "Financing Global and Regional Public Goods Through ODA: Analysis and Evidence from the OECD Creditor Reporting System." OECD Development Centre Working Paper 232, OECD, Paris.

Renzio, Paolo, Vera Wilhelm, and Tim Williamson. 2006. "Minding the Gaps: Integrating Reporting on Poverty Reduction Strategy and Budget Implementation for Domestic Accountability." Draft.

Strategic Partnership with Africa. 2006. "Strategic Partnership with Africa: Survey of Budget Support, 2006." Draft. Report by the Budget Support Working Group, Strategic Partnership with Africa, Washington, DC.

Thomas, Alun. 2006. "Do Debt-Service Savings and Grants Boost Social Expenditures?" IMF Working Paper 06/180, International Monetary Fund, Washington, DC.

World Bank. 2005a. "A Strategic Framework for the World Bank's Global Programs and Partnerships." World Bank, Washington, DC.

———. 2005b. *Global Economic Prospects 2005*. Washington, DC: World Bank.

———. 2006a. *Global Development Finance 2006*. Washington, DC: World Bank.

———. 2006b. "Harmonization and Alignment for Greater Aid Effectiveness: An Update on Global Implementation and the Bank's Commitments." World Bank, Washington, DC.

———. 2006c. "Integrating Global Partnership Programs with Country-Led National Programs: Synthesis of findings and Recommendations." World Bank, Washington, DC.

———. 2007a. "Aid Architecture and the Main Trends in Official Development Assistance Flows." World Bank, Washington, DC.

———. 2007b. "Fiscal Space Policy for Growth and Development." Draft. World Bank, Washington, DC.

———. 2007c. "IDA's Long-Term Financial Capacity." Draft. World Bank, Washington, DC.

———. 2007d. "Multilateral Debt Relief Initiative (MDRI): Debt Relief by IDA and Donor Financing to Date." Draft. World Bank, Washington, DC.

———. 2007e. "The World Bank's Africa Action Plan: Progress in Implementation." Draft. World Bank, Washington, DC.

———. 2007f. "The World Bank Group 2006 Trust Funds Annual Report." World Bank, Washington, DC.

World Food Program. 2006. Available at http://www.wfp.org/english/?ModuleID=137&Key=2166).

Chapter 5

ADB (Asian Development Bank). 2006a. "Enhancing ADB Support to Middle-Income Countries and Borrowers from Ordinary Capital Resources (OCR).

———. 2006b. "Implementation Review of the Policy on Gender and Development." ADB, Manila.

AfDB (African Development Bank), ADB (Asian Development Bank), EBRD (European Bank for Reconstruction and Development), IADB (Inter-American Development Bank), and World Bank. 2006. "Cooperation among Multilateral Development Banks." Update. Washington, DC.

———. 2007. "The 2006 Multilateral Development Bank Common Performance Assessment System (COMPAS) Report." Washington, DC.

Bedi, Tara, A. Coudouel, M. Cox, M. Goldstein, and Nigel Thornton. 2006. "Beyond the Numbers: Understanding the Institutions for Monitoring Poverty Reduction Strategies." Washington, DC.

Buvinic, Mayra. 2004. "Mainstreaming Attention to Domestic Violence in Lending Operations: Six Elements of Inter-American Bank Success." Washington, DC.

Dollar, David, and Victoria Levin. 2004. "The Increasing Selectivity of Foreign Aid, 1984–2002." Policy Research Working Paper No. 3299, World Bank, Washington, DC.

IADB (Inter-American Development Bank). 2006. "A Report to the Board of Executive Directors." IADB, Washington, DC.

IMF (International Monetary Fund). 2006. "Managing Director's Report on the IMF's Medium-Term Strategy." SM/05/332, IMF, Washington, DC.

International Task Force on Global Public Goods. 2006. "Meeting Global Challenges: International Cooperation in the National Interest." ITF, Stockholm.

Malan, Pedro, Michael Callaghan, Caio Koch-Weser, William McDonough, Sri Mulyani Indrawati, and Ngozi Okonjo-Iweala. 2007. "Report of the External Review Committee on Bank-Fund Collaboration." Washington, DC.

World Bank. 2001. "Integrating Gender into the World Bank's Work: A Strategy for Action." World Bank, Washington, DC.

———. 2004. "Better Data for Better Results: An Action Plan for Improving Development Statistics." World Bank, Washington, DC.

———. 2006a. "Clean Energy and Development: Towards an Investment Framework." World Bank, Washington, DC.

———. 2006b. "Gender Equality as Smart Economics: A World Bank Group Gender Action Plan (Fiscal Years 2007–10)." World Bank, Washington, DC.

———. 2006c. "Implementing the World Bank's Gender Mainstreaming Strategy." World Bank, Washington, DC.

———. 2006d. "Strengthening the World Bank's Engagement with IBRD Partner Countries." World Bank, Washington, DC.

———. 2007. "Accelerating Development Outcome in Africa: Progress and Change in the Africa Action Plan." World Bank, Washington, DC.

Statistical Appendix

CPIA: Country Policy and Institutional Assessment; ICS: Investment Climate Surveys; KK: Kaufmann and Kraay; OTRI: Overall Trade Restrictiveness Index; TI: Transparency International; TRI: Trade Restrictiveness Index.

TABLE A.1 Millennium Development Goals

	Goal 1 Eradicate extreme poverty		Goal 2 Achieve universal primary education		Goal 3 Promote gender equality		Goal 4 Reduce child mortality	
	Poverty (US$1 a day headcount ratio,%)	Share of revenue to poorest quintile (%)	Primary education completion (gross intake to final primary grade,%)	Secondary enrollment (gross,%)	Ratio of girls to boys in primary and secondary school(%)	Women in nonagricultural sector (% of total nonagricultural employment)	Child mortality (under-5 mortality rate per 1,000)	Measles immunization (% of children age 12–13 months)
	1998–2005[a]	1998–2005[a]	2001–2005[a]	2005	2005	2004	2005	2005
Afghanistan	..	..	32	16	55	..	257	64
Albania	<2	8.2	97	78	99	31.7	18	97
Algeria	<2	7.0	96	83	102	17.0	39	83
Angola	..	0.0	..	17	..	..	260	45
Argentina	6.6	..	101	86	111	45.5	18	99
Armenia	<2	..	91	88	108	46.5	29	94
Australia	..	5.9	..	149	102	48.6	6	94
Austria	..	8.6	..	101	102	46.2	5	75
Azerbaijan	3.7	7.4	94	83	98	48.8	89	98
Bangladesh	36.0	9.1	77	46	101	23.1	73	81
Belarus	<2	..	100	95	105	56.0	12	99
Belgium	..	8.5	..	109	103	44.8	5	88
Benin	30.9	7.4	65	33	73	..	150	85
Bhutan	..	..	..	..	..	..	75	93
Bolivia	23.2	1.5	101	89	93	36.5	65	64
Bosnia and Herzegovina	..	9.5	..	..	..	..	15	90
Botswana	28.1	3.2	92	75	102	43.0	120	90
Brazil	7.5	2.8	108	102	105	46.7	33	99
Bulgaria	<2	..	98	102	100	53.0	15	96
Burkina Faso	27.2	6.9	31	14	77	14.6	191	84
Burundi	54.6	5.1	36	14	83	..	190	75
Cambodia	34.1	6.8	92	29	87	51.3	87	79
Cameroon	17.1	5.6	62	44	83	21.6	149	68
Canada	..	7.2	..	109	106	49.4	6	94
Central African Republic	66.6	2.0	23	12	65	..	193	35
Chad	..	..	32	16	60	12.8	208	23
Chile	<2	3.8	95	89	98	38.1	10	90
China	9.9	4.3	98	73	98	40.9	27	86
Hong Kong, China	..	..	110	87	93	47.3	..	81
Colombia	7.0	2.5	98	79	104	48.3	21	89
Comoros	..	..	51	35	84	..	71	80
Congo, Dem. Rep. of	..	..	39	22	73	20.1	205	70
Congo, Rep. of	..	..	58	39	89	..	108	56
Costa Rica	3.3	3.5	92	79	104	38.5	12	89
Côte d'Ivoire	..	..	43	25	67	..	195	51
Croatia	<2	8.3	91	88	104	46.2	7	96
Cuba	..	..	94	94	110	37.7	7	98
Czech Republic	<2	10.3	104	96	101	47.1	4	97
Denmark	..	8.3	99	124	109	48.8	5	95
Djibouti	..	..	32	24	75	..	133	65
Dominican Republic	2.8	4.0	92	71	111	38.2	31	99
Ecuador	17.7	3.3	101	61	..	42.7	25	93
Egypt, Arab Rep. of	3.1	8.6	95	87	..	20.6	33	98
El Salvador	19.0	2.7	87	63	100	34.8	27	99

Goal 5 Improve maternal health		Goal 6 Combat HIV/AIDS and other diseases		Goal 7 Ensure environmental sustainability		Goal 8 Develop a global partnership for development	
Maternal mortality ratio (modeled estimate per 100,000 live births)	Births attended by skilled health staff (% of total)	HIV prevalence (% of population ages 15–49)	Incidence of tuberculosis (per 100,000 people)	Access to an improved water source (% of population)	Access to improved sanitation facilities (% of population)	Fixed-line and mobile phone suscribers (per 1,000 people)	Internet users (per 1,000 people)
2000	2000–2005[a]	2005	2005	2004	2004	2005	2005
..	14	0.1	168	39	34	44	1
55	98	..	20	96	91	493	60
140	96	0.1	55	85	92	494	58
1700	45	3.7	269	53	31	75	11
82	95	0.6	41	96	91	798	177
55	98	0.1	71	92	83	260	53
8	99	0.1	6	100	100	1470	698
4	..	0.3	12	100	100	1441	486
94	88	0.1	76	77	54	397	81
380	13	0.1	227	74	39	71	3
35	100	0.3	62	100	84	755	347
10	..	0.3	13	100	100	1337	458
850	75	1.8	88	67	33	98	50
420	51	0.1	103	62	70	111	39
420	67	0.1	211	85	46	334	52
31	100	0.1	52	97	95	656	206
100	94	24.1	655	95	42	541	34
260	97	0.5	60	90	75	587	195
32	99	0.1	39	99	99	1128	206
1000	38	2.0	223	61	13	51	5
1000	25	3.3	334	79	36	18	5
450	44	1.6	506	41	17	40	3
730	62	5.4	174	66	51	102	15
6	98	0.3	5	100	100	1080	520
1100	44	10.7	314	75	27	27	3
1100	14	3.5	272	42	9	14	4
31	100	0.3	15	95	91	860	172
56	97	0.1	100	77	44	570	85
..	100	..	75	..	..	1799	508
130	96	0.6	45	93	86	648	104
480	62	0.1	45	86	33	55	33
990	61	3.2	356	46	30	48	2
510	86	5.3	367	58	27	102	13
43	99	0.3	14	97	92	575	254
690	68	7.1	382	84	37	108	11
8	100	0.1	41	100	100	1097	327
33	100	0.1	9	91	98	87	17
9	100	0.1	10	100	98	1465	270
5	..	0.2	8	100	100	1628	527
730	61	3.1	762	73	82	69	13
150	99	1.1	91	95	78	508	169
130	75	0.3	131	94	89	601	47
84	74	0.1	25	98	70	325	68
150	92	0.9	51	84	62	492	93

(continued)

TABLE A.1   Millennium Development Goals *(continued)*

	Goal 1 Eradicate extreme poverty		Goal 2 Achieve universal primary education		Goal 3 Promote gender equality		Goal 4 Reduce child mortality	
	Poverty (US$1 a day headcount ratio,%)	Share of revenue to poorest quintile (%)	Primary education completion (gross intake to final primary grade,%)	Secondary enrollment (gross,%)	Ratio of girls to boys in primary and secondary school(%)	Women in nonagricultural sector (% of total nonagricultural employment)	Child mortality (under-5 mortality rate per 1,000)	Measles immunization (% of children age 12–13 months)
	1998–2005[a]	1998–2005[a]	2001–2005[a]	2005	2005	2004	2005	2005
Eritrea	..	..	51	31	*70*	..	78	84
Estonia	<2	6.7	102	*98*	*114*	52.2	7	96
Ethiopia	23.0	9.1	55	31	76	40.6	127	59
Finland	..	9.6	100	*109*	*107*	50.7	4	97
France	..	7.2	..	*111*	*105*	47.2	5	87
Gabon	..	..	66	*50*	*94*	..	91	55
Gambia, The	59.3	4.8	..	*47*	*97*	..	137	84
Georgia	6.5	..	87	83	103	50.3	45	92
Germany	..	8.5	96	*100*	..	46.6	5	93
Ghana	44.8	5.6	72	44	91	..	112	83
Greece	..	6.7	102	*96*	*105*	40.7	5	88
Guatemala	13.5	2.9	74	51	91	38.8	43	77
Guinea	..	7.0	55	31	74	..	160	59
Guinea-Bissau	..	5.2	27	*18*	65	..	200	80
Guyana	<2	4.5	96	*102*	*100*	39.9	63	92
Haiti	53.9	2.4	..	..	..	..	120	54
Honduras	14.9	3.4	79	*66*	*109*	46.8	40	92
Hungary	<2	..	95	*97*	*107*	47.0	8	99
India	33.5	8.1	89	*54*	*87*	17.3	74	58
Indonesia	7.5	8.4	102	*64*	*97*	31.1	36	72
Iran, Islamic Rep. of	<2	5.1	96	81	99	13.7	36	94
Iraq	..	..	74	45	76	..	125	90
Ireland	..	7.4	101	*112*	*103*	47.6	6	84
Israel	..	5.7	105	*93*	*105*	49.6	6	95
Italy	..	6.5	101	*99*	*106*	41.3	4	87
Jamaica	<2	5.3	84	*88*	*104*	47.0	20	84
Japan	..	10.6	..	*102*	*98*	41.2	4	99
Jordan	<2	6.7	97	*87*	*102*	25.0	26	95
Kazakhstan	<2	7.4	114	99	106	49.4	73	99
Kenya	22.8	6.0	95	49	*94*	38.7	120	69
Korea, Dem. Rep. of	..	..	..	..	..	..	55	96
Korea, Rep. of	<2	7.9	104	93	87	41.6	5	99
Kuwait	..	..	101	95	110	25.2	11	99
Kyrgyz Republic	<2	..	98	86	105	43.8	67	99
Lao PDR	27.0	8.1	76	47	84	..	79	41
Latvia	<2	6.6	92	*97*	*115*	53.2	11	95
Lebanon	..	..	90	89	104	..	30	96
Lesotho	36.4	1.5	67	39	103	..	132	85
Liberia	..	..	..	*32*	73	..	235	94
Libya	..	..	..	*104*	106	..	19	97
Lithuania	<2	..	98	*102*	*110*	52.2	9	97
Macedonia, FYR	<2	..	96	*84*	*103*	42.3	17	96
Madagascar	61.0	4.9	58	..	96	..	119	59
Malawi	20.8	7.0	61	28	*98*	12.4	125	82

Goal 5 Improve maternal health		Goal 6 Combat HIV/AIDS and other diseases		Goal 7 Ensure environmental sustainability		Goal 8 Develop a global partnership for development	
Maternal mortality ratio (modeled estimate per 100,000 live births)	Births attended by skilled health staff (% of total)	HIV prevalence (% of population ages 15–49)	Incidence of tuberculosis (per 100,000 people)	Access to an improved water source (% of population)	Access to improved sanitation facilities (% of population)	Fixed-line and mobile phone suscribers (per 1,000 people)	Internet users (per 1,000 people)
2000	2000–2005[a]	2005	2005	2004	2004	2005	2005
630	28	2.4	282	60	9	18	16
63	100	1.3	43	100	97	1402	513
850	6	1.4	344	22	13	14	2
6	100	0.1	6	100	100	1401	534
17	..	0.4	13	100	..	1376	430
420	86	7.9	308	88	36	498	48
540	55	2.4	242	82	53	192	33
32	92	0.2	83	82	94	337	39
8	..	0.1	7	100	100	1628	455
540	47	2.3	205	75	18	143	18
9	..	0.2	17	..	..	1472	180
240	41	0.9	78	95	86	457	79
740	56	1.5	236	50	18	20	5
1100	35	3.8	206	59	35	8	20
170	86	2.4	149	83	70	521	213
680	24	3.8	306	54	30	64	70
110	56	1.5	78	87	69	247	36
16	100	0.1	22	99	95	1257	297
540	43	0.9	168	86	33	128	55
230	72	0.1	239	77	55	271	73
76	90	0.2	24	94	..	384	103
..	72	..	56	81	79	57	1
5	100	0.2	12	..	..	1501	276
17	..	..	8	100	..	1545	470
5	..	0.5	7	..	..	1659	478
87	97	1.5	7	93	80	1146	404
10	..	0.1	28	100	100	1202	668
41	100	..	5	97	93	423	118
210	..	0.1	144	86	72	350	27
1000	42	6.1	641	61	43	143	32
67	97	..	178	100	59	41	0
20	100	0.1	96	92	..	1286	684
5	100	..	24	..	..	1140	276
110	99	0.1	121	77	59	191	54
650	19	0.1	155	51	30	120	4
42	100	0.8	63	99	78	1131	448
150	93	0.1	11	100	98	554	196
550	55	23.2	696	79	37	163	24
760	51	..	301	61	27	3	0
97	..	..	18	..	97	156	36
13	100	0.2	63	..	..	1510	358
23	99	0.1	30	..	..	882	79
550	51	0.5	234	46	32	31	5
1800	56	14.1	409	73	61	41	4

(continued)

TABLE A.1   Millennium Development Goals *(continued)*

	Goal 1 Eradicate extreme poverty		Goal 2 Achieve universal primary education		Goal 3 Promote gender equality		Goal 4 Reduce child mortality	
	Poverty (US$1 a day headcount ratio,%)	Share of revenue to poorest quintile (%)	Primary education completion (gross intake to final primary grade,%)	Secondary enrollment (gross,%)	Ratio of girls to boys in primary and secondary school(%)	Women in nonagricultural sector (% of total nonagricultural employment)	Child mortality (under-5 mortality rate per 1,000)	Measles immunization (% of children age 12–13 months)
	1998–2005[a]	1998–2005[a]	2001–2005[a]	2005	2005	2004	2005	2005
Malaysia	<2	4.4	94	*76*	*109*	36.9	12	90
Mali	36.1	6.1	38	24	75	..	218	86
Mauritania	25.9	6.2	45	21	96	..	125	61
Mauritius	..	..	98	89	98	37.5	15	98
Mexico	3.0	4.3	99	*80*	*101*	37.4	27	96
Moldova	<2	..	92	82	109	54.6	16	97
Mongolia	10.8	7.5	97	94	116	50.3	49	99
Morocco	<2	6.5	80	50	88	21.8	40	97
Mozambique	36.2	5.4	42	14	*82*	..	145	77
Myanmar	..	..	79	40	105	..	105	72
Namibia	34.9	1.4	75	61	*101*	48.8	62	73
Nepal	24.1	6.0	75	46	88	17.4	74	74
Netherlands	..	7.6	100	*119*	99	45.4	5	96
New Zealand	..	6.4	..	*118*	*113*	50.5	6	82
Nicaragua	45.1	5.6	76	66	103	..	37	96
Niger	60.6	2.6	28	9	72	7.8	256	83
Nigeria	70.8	5.1	82	34	*82*	..	194	35
Norway	..	9.6	101	*116*	109	49.2	4	90
Oman	..	..	93	87	99	25.7	12	98
Pakistan	17.0	9.3	63	27	76	8.6	99	78
Panama	7.4	2.5	97	70	110	43.5	24	99
Papua New Guinea	..	4.5	54	*26*	*87*	35.4	74	60
Paraguay	13.6	2.4	91	*63*	*101*	43.9	23	90
Peru	10.5	3.7	100	*92*	*103*	34.6	27	80
Philippines	14.8	5.4	97	86	106	40.4	33	80
Poland	<2	..	100	*97*	109	47.2	7	98
Portugal	<2	5.8	104	*97*	108	46.6	5	93
Puerto Rico	..	..	..	..	..	39.3	..	..
Romania	<2	8.1	93	*85*	105	46.5	19	97
Russian Federation	<2	..	94	*93*	110	50.9	18	99
Rwanda	60.3	5.3	39	14	99	..	203	89
São Tomé and Principe	..	..	77	45	99	..	118	88
Saudi Arabia	..	..	85	88	101	13.5	26	96
Senegal	17.0	6.6	52	26	90	..	119	74
Serbia and Montenegro	..	8.3	96	*89*	103	45.4	15	96
Sierra Leone	57.0	1.1	..	30	*71*	..	282	67
Singapore	..	5.0	..	..	..	47.0	3	96
Slovak Republic	<2	8.8	99	*94*	104	52.0	8	98
Slovenia	<2	9.1	102	*100*	109	47.6	4	94
Solomon Islands	..	..	..	30	*91*	..	29	72
Somalia	..	..	..	..	..	..	225	35
South Africa	10.7	3.5	99	*93*	*101*	45.9	68	82
Spain	..	7.0	109	*119*	*107*	42.0	5	97
Sri Lanka	5.6	7.0	..	*83*	*102*	43.2	14	99

Goal 5 Improve maternal health		Goal 6 Combat HIV/AIDS and other diseases		Goal 7 Ensure environmental sustainability		Goal 8 Develop a global partnership for development	
Maternal mortality ratio (modeled estimate per 100,000 live births)	Births attended by skilled health staff (% of total)	HIV prevalence (% of population ages 15–49)	Incidence of tuberculosis (per 100,000 people)	Access to an improved water source (% of population)	Access to improved sanitation facilities (% of population)	Fixed-line and mobile phone suscribers (per 1,000 people)	Internet users (per 1,000 people)
2000	2000–2005[a]	2005	2005	2004	2004	2005	2005
41	97	0.5	102	99	94	943	435
1200	41	1.7	278	50	46	70	4
1000	57	0.7	298	53	34	256	7
24	99	0.6	62	100	94	863	146
83	83	0.3	23	97	79	650	181
36	100	1.1	138	92	68	480	96
110	97	0.1	191	62	59	279	105
220	63	0.1	89	81	73	455	153
1000	48	16.1	447	43	32	40	7
360	57	1.3	171	78	77	13	2
300	76	19.6	697	87	25	206	37
740	15	0.5	180	90	35	26	4
16	..	0.2	7	100	100	1436	739
7	..	0.1	9	..	..	1283	672
230	67	0.2	58	79	47	260	27
1600	16	1.1	164	46	13	23	2
800	35	3.9	283	48	44	151	38
16	..	0.1	5	100	100	1489	735
87	95	..	11	..	..	623	111
500	31	0.1	181	91	59	116	67
160	93	0.9	45	90	73	555	64
300	41	1.8	250	39	44	15	23
170	77	0.4	68	86	80	374	34
410	73	0.6	172	83	63	280	165
200	60	0.1	291	85	72	459	54
13	100	0.1	26	..	..	1074	262
5	100	0.4	33	..	..	1487	279
25	100	..	5	..	..	974	221
49	99	0.1	134	57	..	820	208
67	99	1.1	119	97	87	1119	152
1400	39	3.0	361	74	42	18	6
..	76	..	105	79	25	97	131
23	93	..	41	..	..	740	70
690	58	0.9	255	76	57	171	46
11	92	0.2	34	93	87	917	148
2000	42	1.6	475	57	39	19	2
30	100	0.3	29	100	100	1435	571
3	99	0.1	17	100	99	1065	464
17	100	0.1	15	..	..	1288	545
130	..	..	142	70	31	28	8
1100	25	0.9	224	29	26	73	11
230	92	18.8	600	88	65	825	109
4	..	0.6	28	100	100	1375	348
92	96	0.1	61	79	91	235	14

(continued)

TABLE A.1 Millennium Development Goals *(continued)*

	Goal 1 Eradicate extreme poverty		Goal 2 Achieve universal primary education		Goal 3 Promote gender equality		Goal 4 Reduce child mortality	
	Poverty (US$1 a day headcount ratio,%)	Share of revenue to poorest quintile (%)	Primary education completion (gross intake to final primary grade,%)	Secondary enrollment (gross,%)	Ratio of girls to boys in primary and secondary school(%)	Women in nonagricultural sector (% of total nonagricultural employment)	Child mortality (under-5 mortality rate per 1,000)	Measles immunization (% of children age 12–13 months)
	1998–2005[a]	1998–2005[a]	2001–2005[a]	2005	2005	2004	2005	2005
Sudan	..	..	50	34	89	16.8	90	60
Swaziland	..	4.3	64	*45*	*94*	29.9	160	60
Sweden	..	9.1	..	*103*	*112*	50.9	4	94
Switzerland	..	7.6	97	*93*	*94*	47.1	5	82
Syrian Arab Republic	..	..	111	68	94	18.2	15	98
Tajikistan	7.4	7.9	102	82	84	53.3	71	84
Tanzania	57.8	7.3	54	..	95	45.4	122	91
Thailand	<2	6.3	82	73	101	46.4	21	96
Togo	..	..	65	40	72	..	139	70
Trinidad and Tobago	12.4	5.9	99	88	104	41.1	19	93
Tunisia	<2	6.0	97	*81*	*105*	25.0	24	96
Turkey	3.4	..	88	*79*	84	19.9	29	91
Turkmenistan	..	6.1	..	..	..	..	104	99
Uganda	..	5.7	57	16	*96*	..	136	86
Ukraine	<2	9.2	114	89	102	55.1	17	96
United Arab Emirates	..	..	77	64	*126*	14.5	9	92
United Kingdom	..	6.1	..	*105*	*107*	49.4	6	82
United States	..	5.4	..	*95*	*109*	48.5	7	93
Uruguay	<2	..	91	*108*	*114*	46.8	15	95
Uzbekistan	<2	7.2	97	*95*	*96*	39.5	68	99
Venezuela, R. B. de	18.5	3.3	92	75	*104*	41.5	21	76
Vietnam	..	9.0	94	76	94	49.1	19	95
West Bank and Gaza	..	..	98	99	104	17.9	23	99
Yemen, Rep. of	15.7	7.4	62	48	61	..	102	76
Zambia	63.8	3.6	78	28	92	..	182	84
Zimbabwe	56.1	4.6	80	*36*	95	21.8	132	85
World	**18.3**	..	**85**	**65**	**94**	**38.1**	**75**	**77**
Fragile States	..	..	65	*38*	82	..	178	56
Low income	..	..	74	*45*	87	23.4	114	65
Middle income	..	..	96	*77*	99	40.9	37	87
Lower middle income	..	..	97	*76*	99	40.2	39	86
Upper middle income	..	..	95	*86*	99	44.2	27	93
Low & middle income	..	..	84	*61*	93	36.2	82	75
East Asia & Pacific	9.1	..	98	*71*	99	40.6	33	83
Europe & Central Asia	0.9	..	92	*91*	96	47.6	32	96
Latin America & Caribbean	8.6	..	98	*86*	102	43.3	31	92
Middle East & North Africa	1.5	..	89	*73*	90	17.7	53	92
South Asia	31.7	..	82	*50*	88	17.8	83	64
Sub-Saharan Africa	41.1	..	58	*31*	86	..	163	64
High income	..	..	97	*100*	*100*	46.0	7	93
European Monetary Union	..	..	101	*106*	*105*	45.1	5	90

Source: 2007 World Development Indicators database.
Figures in italics refer to periods other than those specified.
a. Data are for the most recent year available.
.. Not available

Goal 5 Improve maternal health		Goal 6 Combat HIV/AIDS and other diseases		Goal 7 Ensure environmental sustainability		Goal 8 Develop a global partnership for development	
Maternal mortality ratio (modeled estimate per 100,000 live births)	Births attended by skilled health staff (% of total)	HIV prevalence (% of population ages 15–49)	Incidence of tuberculosis (per 100,000 people)	Access to an improved water source (% of population)	Access to improved sanitation facilities (% of population)	Fixed-line and mobile phone suscribers (per 1,000 people)	Internet users (per 1,000 people)
2000	2000–2005[a]	2005	2005	2004	2004	2005	2005
590	87	1.6	228	70	34	69	77
370	74	33.4	1262	62	48	208	32
2	..	0.2	6	100	100	1804	764
7	..	0.4	7	100	100	1610	498
160	70	..	37	93	90	307	58
100	71	0.1	198	59	51	46	1
1500	43	6.5	342	62	47	56	9
44	99	1.4	142	99	99	537	110
570	61	3.2	373	52	35	82	49
160	96	2.6	9	91	100	861	123
120	90	0.1	24	93	85	692	95
70	83	..	29	96	88	869	222
31	97	0.1	70	72	62	82	8
880	39	6.4	369	60	43	56	17
35	100	1.4	99	96	96	546	97
54	100	..	16	100	98	1273	308
13	..	..	14	100	..	1616	474
17	99	0.6	5	100	100	1227	630
27	99	0.5	28	100	100	624	193
24	96	0.2	114	82	67	80	34
96	95	0.7	42	83	68	606	125
130	90	0.5	175	85	61	306	129
..	97	..	21	92	73	398	67
570	27	..	82	67	43	92	9
750	43	17.0	600	58	55	89	20
1100	..	20.1	601	81	53	79	77
410	63	1.0	136	83	57	523	137
886	..	3.1	278	58	42	85	26
684	41	1.7	220	75	38	114	44
150	88	0.6	111	84	62	590	115
163	87	0.3	113	82	57	511	95
91	92	2.2	104	94	84	901	196
450	61	1.1	158	80	52	382	85
117	87	0.2	137	79	51	496	89
58	94	0.7	84	92	85	898	190
194	87	0.6	61	91	77	496	156
183	74	0.1	43	90	76	389	89
564	37	0.7	174	84	37	119	49
921	45	5.8	348	56	37	142	29
14	..	0.4	17	100	100	1338	527
10	..	0.3	13	100	..	1511	439

TABLE A.2 Measures of Governance Performance

	Overall governance performance[a]			Bureaucratic capability[a]		Checks-and-balances institutions[a]			
	Control of corruption			Budget and financial management	Public administration	Voice and accountability		Justice and rule of law	
	TI Corruption Perceptions Index[b]		ICS—unofficial payments for time to get things done (% of sales)[c]	CPIA 13[d]	CPIA 15[d]	KK Voice and Accountability[e]		KK Rule of Law[e]	
	Est. 2006	S.E.	2006	2005	2005	Est. 2005	S.E.	Est. 2005	S.E.
Afghanistan	..	..	..	..	..	−1.28	0.15	−1.68	0.21
Albania	2.6	0.3	1.6	4	3	0.08	0.12	−0.84	0.16
Algeria	3.1	0.9	6.0	..	..	−0.92	0.12	−0.71	0.14
Angola	2.2	0.5	..	2.5	2.5	−1.15	0.12	−1.28	0.15
Argentina	2.9	0.5	0.7	..	..	0.43	0.14	−0.56	0.13
Armenia	2.9	0.3	0.7	4	4	−0.64	0.12	−0.46	0.14
Australia	8.7	0.7	..	..	..	1.32	0.16	1.80	0.14
Austria	8.6	0.7	..	..	..	1.24	0.16	1.87	0.14
Azerbaijan	2.4	0.4	2.7	4	3	−1.16	0.11	−0.84	0.13
Bangladesh	2	0.5	2.1	3	3	−0.50	0.12	−0.87	0.14
Belarus	2.1	0.3	0.5	..	..	−1.68	0.12	−1.04	0.16
Belgium	7.3	1.3	..	..	..	1.31	0.16	1.47	0.14
Benin	2.5	0.8	4.6	4	3	0.34	0.15	−0.59	0.17
Bhutan	6	3.2	..	3.5	4	−1.05	0.15	0.52	0.24
Bolivia	2.7	0.6	2.1	3.5	3.5	−0.09	0.12	−0.78	0.14
Bosnia and Herzegovina	2.9	0.4	0.3	3.5	3	−0.11	0.12	−0.74	0.15
Botswana	5.6	1.8	1.0	..	..	0.68	0.14	0.70	0.14
Brazil	3.3	0.5	..	..	..	0.36	0.14	−0.41	0.13
Bulgaria	4	1.4	1.0	..	..	0.59	0.11	−0.19	0.13
Burkina Faso	3.2	0.8	5.7	4	3.5	−0.37	0.13	−0.54	0.19
Burundi	2.4	0.4	2.9	2.5	2.5	−1.15	0.16	−1.17	0.19
Cambodia	2.1	0.5	4.6	2.5	2.5	−0.94	0.16	−1.13	0.16
Cameroon	2.3	0.4	2.6	3.5	3	−1.19	0.14	−1.02	0.15
Canada	8.5	0.9	..	..	..	1.32	0.16	1.81	0.14
Cape Verde	..	..	0.0	3.5	4	0.83	0.18	0.21	0.21
Central African Republic	2.4	0.3	..	2	2	−1.15	0.16	−1.29	0.19
Chad	2	0.5	..	3	2.5	−1.25	0.16	−1.23	0.18
Chile	7.3	1	0.3	..	..	1.04	0.14	1.20	0.13
China	3.3	0.6	1.6	..	..	−1.66	0.12	−0.47	0.13
Colombia	3.9	1.2	0.7	..	..	−0.32	0.12	−0.71	0.13
Comoros	..	..	..	2	2	−0.28	0.19	−0.96	0.26
Congo, Dem. Rep. of	2.2	0.1	..	2.5	2.5	−1.64	0.14	−1.76	0.16
Congo, Rep. of	2	0.4	..	3	2.5	−0.71	0.18	−1.42	0.17
Costa Rica	4.1	1.5	2.3	..	..	0.99	0.14	0.54	0.14
Côte d'Ivoire	2.1	0.2	..	2.5	2	−1.50	0.14	−1.47	0.16
Croatia	3.4	0.6	0.3	..	..	0.51	0.11	0.00	0.13
Cuba	3.5	2.9	..	..	..	−1.87	0.14	−1.14	0.16
Czech Republic	4.8	0.8	0.4	..	..	1.01	0.11	0.70	0.12
Denmark	9.5	0.2	..	..	..	1.51	0.16	1.99	0.14
Djibouti	..	..	..	3	2.5	−0.84	0.19	−0.87	0.21
Dominican Republic	2.8	0.8	..	..	..	0.20	0.14	−0.66	0.14
Ecuador	2.3	0.3	2.8	..	..	−0.16	0.12	−0.84	0.14
Egypt, Arab Rep. of	3.3	0.7	1.3	..	..	−1.15	0.12	0.02	0.13

(continued)

TABLE A.2 Measures of Governance Performance *(continued)*

	Overall governance performance[a]			Bureaucratic capability[a]		Checks-and-balances institutions[a]			
	Control of corruption			Budget and financial management	Public administration	Voice and accountability		Justice and rule of law	
	TI Corruption Perceptions Index[b]		ICS—unofficial payments for time to get things done (% of sales)[c]	CPIA 13[d]	CPIA 15[d]	KK Voice and Accountability[e]		KK Rule of Law[e]	
	Est. 2006	S.E.	2006	2005	2005	Est. 2005	S.E.	Est. 2005	S.E.
El Salvador	4	1.6	1.1	..	..	0.26	0.14	−0.37	0.15
Equatorial Guinea	2.1	0.5	..	..	..	−1.71	0.19	−1.33	0.20
Eritrea	2.9	1.3	0.2	2.5	3	−1.83	0.13	−0.81	0.22
Estonia	6.7	1.3	0.2	..	..	1.05	0.12	0.82	0.12
Ethiopia	2.4	0.4	..	3.5	3	−1.10	0.12	−0.77	0.15
Finland	9.6	0.3	..	..	..	1.49	0.16	1.96	0.14
France	7.4	1.1	..	..	..	1.28	0.16	1.35	0.14
Gabon	3	0.9	..	..	..	−0.71	0.16	−0.48	0.15
Gambia, The	2.5	0.5	..	2.5	3	−0.72	0.18	−0.29	0.18
Georgia	2.8	0.5	0.2	3.5	3.5	−0.27	0.12	−0.82	0.14
Germany	8	0.6	0.3	..	..	1.31	0.16	1.76	0.14
Ghana	3.3	0.6	..	3.5	3.5	0.41	0.14	−0.23	0.14
Greece	4.4	1.1	0.2	..	..	0.95	0.16	0.66	0.14
Guatemala	2.6	0.7	2.6	..	..	−0.37	0.14	−1.04	0.14
Guinea	1.9	0.4	..	3	3	−1.18	0.15	−1.11	0.19
Guinea–Bissau	..	..	..	2.5	2.5	−0.31	0.18	−1.33	0.21
Guyana	2.5	0.4	0.4	3.5	2.5	0.49	0.18	−0.80	0.18
Haiti	1.8	0.1	..	2.5	2.5	−1.41	0.15	−1.62	0.20
Honduras	2.5	0.3	1.7	4	3	−0.14	0.12	−0.78	0.14
Hong Kong, China	8.3	1.1	..	..	..	0.26	0.17	1.50	0.14
Hungary	5.2	0.4	0.5	..	..	1.01	0.12	0.70	0.12
India	3.3	0.5	4.2	4	3.5	0.35	0.14	0.09	0.13
Indonesia	2.4	0.4	1.1	3.5	3.5	−0.21	0.14	−0.87	0.13
Iran, Islamic Rep. of	2.7	0.8	..	..	..	−1.43	0.12	−0.76	0.14
Iraq	1.9	0.5	..	..	..	−1.47	0.14	−1.81	0.17
Ireland	7.4	1.2	0.1	..	..	1.41	0.16	1.63	0.14
Isle of Man	..	..	..	..	..	..	..	..	..
Israel	5.9	1.3	..	..	..	0.61	0.16	0.76	0.14
Italy	4.9	1	..	..	..	1.00	0.16	0.51	0.14
Jamaica	3.7	0.6	0.3	..	..	0.57	0.14	−0.55	0.14
Japan	7.6	1.1	..	..	..	0.94	0.16	1.33	0.14
Jordan	5.3	1.2	..	..	..	−0.74	0.14	0.43	0.13
Kazakhstan	2.6	0.5	0.7	..	..	−1.19	0.11	−0.79	0.12
Kenya	2.2	0.4	2.9	3.5	3	−0.12	0.14	−0.94	0.14
Korea, Dem. Rep. of	..	..	..	..	..	−2.06	0.14	−1.15	0.18
Korea, Rep. of	5.1	0.8	0.0	..	..	0.74	0.14	0.73	0.13
Kuwait	4.8	1.4	..	..	..	−0.47	0.15	0.67	0.15
Kyrgyz Republic	2.2	0.6	2.4	3	2.5	−1.03	0.12	−1.07	0.14
Lao PDR	2.6	1.1	..	2.5	2.5	−1.54	0.13	−1.12	0.17
Latvia	4.7	1.5	0.5	..	..	0.89	0.12	0.43	0.13
Lebanon	3.6	0.6	2.5	..	..	−0.72	0.14	−0.36	0.15
Lesotho	3.2	0.7	0.2	3	3	0.28	0.18	−0.19	0.19
Liberia	..	..	..	..	..	−0.92	0.15	−1.60	0.26

(continued)

TABLE A.2   Measures of Governance Performance *(continued)*

	Overall governance performance[a]				Bureaucratic capability[a]		Checks-and-balances institutions[a]			
	Control of corruption				Budget and financial management	Public administration	Voice and accountability		Justice and rule of law	
	TI Corruption Perceptions Index[b]		ICS—unofficial payments for time to get things done (% of sales)[c]		CPIA 13[d]	CPIA 15[d]	KK Voice and Accountability[e]		KK Rule of Law[e]	
	Est. 2006	S.E.	2006		2005	2005	Est. 2005	S.E.	Est. 2005	S.E.
Libya	2.7	0.8	..		..	..	−1.93	0.12	−0.73	0.16
Lithuania	4.8	1.4	0.8		..	..	0.90	0.11	0.46	0.13
Macedonia, FYR	2.7	0.3	0.4		..	..	0.03	0.11	−0.38	0.14
Madagascar	3.1	1.4	0.9		3	3.5	−0.01	0.15	−0.15	0.17
Malawi	2.7	0.5	1.2		3	3.5	−0.45	0.14	−0.35	0.14
Malaysia	5	1	..		..	..	−0.41	0.14	0.58	0.13
Mali	2.8	0.8	2.9		4	3	0.47	0.15	−0.12	0.17
Mauritania	3.1	1.6	4.6		2	3	−1.09	0.15	−0.54	0.20
Mauritius	5.1	2.2	0.6		..	..	0.92	0.15	0.79	0.15
Mexico	3.3	0.3	0.5		..	..	0.29	0.14	−0.48	0.13
Moldova	3.2	1.1	0.8		3.5	3	−0.49	0.11	−0.59	0.13
Mongolia	2.8	1.1	..		4	3.5	0.36	0.15	−0.26	0.17
Morocco	3.2	0.7	..		..	..	−0.76	0.14	−0.10	0.14
Mozambique	2.8	0.5	..		3.5	3	−0.06	0.13	−0.72	0.15
Myanmar	1.9	0.5	..		..	..	−2.16	0.14	−1.56	0.17
Namibia	4.1	1.3	0.8		..	..	0.36	0.14	−0.01	0.14
Nepal	2.5	0.6	..		3.5	3	−1.19	0.15	−0.81	0.15
Netherlands	8.7	0.7	..		..	..	1.45	0.16	1.78	0.14
New Zealand	9.6	0.2	..		..	..	1.39	0.16	1.95	0.14
Nicaragua	2.6	0.5	1.8		3.5	3.5	−0.01	0.14	−0.70	0.15
Niger	2.3	0.5	4.7		3.5	3	−0.06	0.15	−0.82	0.19
Nigeria	2.2	0.3	..		3	2.5	−0.69	0.14	−1.38	0.14
Norway	8.8	0.7	..		..	..	1.45	0.16	1.99	0.14
Oman	5.4	2.1	1.0		..	..	−0.94	0.17	0.72	0.16
Pakistan	2.2	0.4	1.6		3.5	3.5	−1.23	0.14	−0.81	0.13
Panama	3.1	0.5	2.6		..	..	0.52	0.14	−0.11	0.14
Papua New Guinea	2.4	0.3	..		3.5	3	−0.05	0.15	−0.92	0.16
Paraguay	2.6	1.1	5.3		..	..	−0.19	0.12	−1.00	0.14
Peru	3.3	1	0.1		..	..	0.04	0.12	−0.77	0.13
Philippines	2.5	0.5	1.2		..	..	0.01	0.12	−0.52	0.13
Poland	3.7	1.2	0.4		..	..	1.04	0.11	0.32	0.12
Portugal	6.6	1.4	0.1		..	..	1.32	0.16	1.01	0.14
Puerto Rico	..	..	..		..	..	1.03	0.21	0.62	0.28
Romania	3.1	0.2	0.6		..	..	0.36	0.11	−0.29	0.12
Russian Federation	2.5	0.4	1.0		..	..	−0.85	0.10	−0.84	0.12
Rwanda	2.5	0.3	..		3.5	3.5	−1.32	0.13	−1.00	0.20
Saudi Arabia	3.3	1.5	..		..	..	−1.72	0.14	0.20	0.15
Senegal	3.3	0.9	0.2		3.5	3.5	0.30	0.14	−0.26	0.15
Serbia and Montenegro	3	0.6	0.6		3.5	4	0.12	0.11	−0.81	0.15
Sierra Leone	2.2	0.1	..		3.5	3	−0.38	0.15	−1.12	0.20
Singapore	9.4	0.3	..		..	..	−0.29	0.14	1.83	0.13
Slovak Republic	4.7	0.9	0.4		..	..	1.04	0.12	0.41	0.12
Slovenia	6.4	1.3	0.1		..	..	1.08	0.12	0.79	0.13

(continued)

TABLE A.2 Measures of Governance Performance *(continued)*

	Overall governance performance[a]			Bureaucratic capability[a]		Checks-and-balances institutions[a]			
				Budget and financial management	Public administration	Voice and accountability		Justice and rule of law	
	Control of corruption								
	TI Corruption Perceptions Index[b]		ICS—unofficial payments for time to get things done (% of sales)[c]	CPIA 13[d]	CPIA 15[d]	KK Voice and Accountability[e]		KK Rule of Law[e]	
	Est. 2006	S.E.	2006	2005	2005	Est. 2005	S.E.	Est. 2005	S.E.
Somalia	..	..	..	..	..	−1.89	0.15	−2.36	0.26
South Africa	4.6	1	0.1	..	..	0.82	0.14	0.19	0.12
Spain	6.8	0.9	0.0	..	..	1.12	0.16	1.13	0.14
Sri Lanka	3.1	0.8	0.1	4	3	−0.26	0.14	0.00	0.14
Sudan	2	0.4	..	2.5	2.5	−1.84	0.14	−1.48	0.17
Swaziland	2.5	0.5	0.5	..	..	−1.28	0.15	−0.75	0.19
Sweden	9.2	0.3	..	..	..	1.41	0.16	1.84	0.14
Switzerland	9.1	0.3	..	..	..	1.43	0.16	2.02	0.14
Syrian Arab Republic	2.9	0.9	..	..	..	−1.67	0.12	−0.42	0.16
Taiwan, China	5.9	0.6	..	..	..	0.79	0.14	0.83	0.13
Tajikistan	2.2	0.4	1.0	3	2.5	−1.17	0.11	−0.99	0.15
Tanzania	2.9	0.4	0.2	4.5	3.5	−0.31	0.14	−0.47	0.14
Thailand	3.6	0.7	..	..	..	0.07	0.12	0.10	0.13
Timor–Leste	2.6	0.7	..	..	..	0.18	0.18	−0.55	0.26
Togo	2.4	0.7	..	2	2	−1.23	0.15	−1.07	0.19
Trinidad and Tobago	3.2	0.8	..	..	..	0.44	0.16	−0.07	0.15
Tunisia	4.6	1.7	..	..	..	−1.13	0.12	0.21	0.14
Turkey	3.8	0.9	0.4	..	..	−0.04	0.12	0.07	0.13
Turkmenistan	2.2	0.6	..	..	..	−1.95	0.12	−1.41	0.15
Uganda	2.7	0.6	1.3	4	3	−0.59	0.14	−0.74	0.14
Ukraine	2.8	0.5	1.4	..	..	−0.26	0.11	−0.60	0.12
United Arab Emirates	6.2	1.3	..	..	..	−1.08	0.14	0.58	0.15
United Kingdom	8.6	0.7	..	..	..	1.30	0.16	1.69	0.14
United States	7.3	1.2	..	..	..	1.19	0.16	1.59	0.14
Uruguay	6.4	1.1	0.1	..	..	0.99	0.14	0.43	0.14
Uzbekistan	2.1	0.4	0.6	3	2.5	−1.76	0.11	−1.31	0.14
Venezuela, R. B. de	2.3	0.2	..	..	..	−0.50	0.14	−1.22	0.13
Vietnam	2.6	0.5	0.5	4	3.5	−1.60	0.14	−0.45	0.13
West Bank and Gaza	..	..	..	..	..	−1.22	0.20	−0.52	0.31
Yemen, Rep. of	2.6	0.3	..	3	3	−1.07	0.14	−1.01	0.15
Zambia	2.6	0.9	1.1	3	3	−0.35	0.12	−0.62	0.14
Zimbabwe	2.4	0.8	..	2.5	2	−1.65	0.14	−1.47	0.14

Sources: Various indicators as labeled for individual columns.
a. Though shown only for KK and TI, all indicators have margins of error
b. Transparency International's Corruption Perceptions Index (CPI) score relates to perceptions of the degree of corruption as seen by businesspeople and country analysts and ranges between 10 (highly clean) and 0 (highly corrupt) (http://www.transparency.org/policy_research/surveys_indices/cpi/2006)
c.http://www.enterprisesurveys.org
d. The CPIA 2005 data are grouped from strong (1) to weak (5)
e. KK Governance indicators lie between −2.5 amd 2.5, with higher scores corresponding to better ourcomes (www.worldbank.org/wbi/governance/data)
.. Not available

TABLE A.3a Trade Restrictiveness Index (TRI) and deadweight loss (US$, millions)

	TRI	DWL	DWL/GDP	TRI Agric.	DWL Agric.	TRI Mfg.	DWL Mfg.
Albania	9	9	0.1%	8	1	9	8
Algeria	15	219	0.2%	14	42	15	176
Argentina	16	432	0.2%	11	6	16	426
Australia	7	284	0.0%	5	8	7	275
Bangladesh	66	2,103	3.5%	11	11	74	2,091
Belarus	10	71	0.2%	11	9	9	62
Bolivia	8	7	0.1%	10	1	8	6
Brazil	11	496	0.1%	9	24	11	472
Brunei	8	4	0.1%	0	0	8	4
Burkina Faso	13	10	0.2%	14	1	12	9
Cameroon	16	34	0.2%	18	8	15	27
Canada	14	2,867	0.3%	54	2,555	5	312
Chile	6	40	0.0%	6	3	6	36
China	9	1,991	0.1%	14	258	8	1,733
Colombia	14	186	0.2%	16	32	14	154
Costa Rica	8	20	0.1%	13	6	7	14
Côte d'Ivoire	11	22	0.1%	12	4	11	18
Egypt, Arab Rep. of	34	677	0.8%	41	235	32	442
El Salvador	9	19	0.1%	17	9	7	10
Ethiopia	16	28	0.3%	14	4	17	24
European Union	14	13,672	0.1%	49	12,045	5	1,626
Gabon	18	16	0.2%	21	4	18	12
Ghana	17	61	0.6%	13	8	18	54
Guatemala	8	32	0.1%	12	8	7	24
Honduras	7	9	0.1%	11	4	6	5
Hong Kong, China	0	0	0.0%	0	0	0	0
Iceland	6	7	0.0%	13	3	4	4
India	21	2,321	0.3%	78	1,196	15	1,125
Indonesia	8	198	0.1%	7	18	8	181
Japan	33	27,567	0.6%	85	24,321	12	3,246
Jordan	15	95	0.7%	16	17	14	78
Kazakhstan	3	3	0.0%	3	0	3	2
Kenya	15	49	0.3%	35	31	10	18
Korea, Rep. of	48	24,873	3.2%	183	24,374	7	500
Lebanon	9	38	0.2%	17	19	7	19
Madagascar	11	8	0.2%	11	1	11	7
Malawi	14	10	0.5%	12	1	14	9
Malaysia	10	432	0.3%	5	7	10	425
Mali	11	7	0.1%	14	1	10	5
Mauritius	6	6	0.1%	8	2	6	4
Mexico	21	4,428	0.6%	52	2,111	16	2,317
Morocco	25	594	1.1%	43	194	21	400
Moldova	6	3	0.1%	11	1	5	2
New Zealand	8	85	0.0%	13	15	8	69
Nicaragua	8	7	0.1%	13	2	7	5
Nigeria	13	118	0.1%	24	49	10	69
Norway	14	561	0.2%	45	462	6	99
Oman	5	10	0.0%	4	1	5	9
Papua N. Guinea	7	3	0.1%	12	2	6	2
Paraguay	11	16	0.2%	12	1	11	15
Peru	10	58	0.1%	11	11	9	47

continued

TABLE A.3a Trade Restrictiveness Index (TRI) and deadweight loss (US$, millions) *(continued)*

	TRI	DWL	DWL/GDP	TRI Agric.	DWL Agric.	TRI Mfg.	DWL Mfg.
Philippines	6	93	0.1%	17	41	5	52
Romania	18	605	0.6%	26	75	17	530
Russian Fed.	12	575	0.1%	17	169	10	406
Rwanda	23	5	0.3%	22	1	23	4
Saudi Arabia	5	70	0.0%	7	15	5	55
Senegal	11	17	0.2%	12	6	10	11
Singapore	0	0	0.0%	0	0	0	0
South Africa	12	408	0.2%	9	10	13	398
Sri Lanka	10	41	0.2%	17	14	9	28
Sudan	20	74	0.3%	20	9	20	65
Switzerland	10	559	0.2%	39	513	3	46
Tanzania	15	32	0.3%	30	17	11	15
Thailand	11	628	0.4%	15	62	11	567
Trinidad and Tobago	10	30	0.2%	21	10	9	20
Tunisia	26	387	1.3%	53	110	23	276
Turkey	9	452	0.1%	37	265	6	187
Uganda	19	36	0.4%	32	20	14	16
Ukraine	7	85	0.1%	7	6	7	80
Uruguay	10	15	0.1%	13	2	10	13
USA	7	3,770	0.0%	13	714	6	3,055
Venezuela, R. B. de	14	110	0.1%	16	20	13	90
Zambia	12	19	0.3%	17	3	12	16
High income	10	74,537	0.2%	40	65,299	4	9,237
Middle income	15	13,320	0.2%	30	3,800	12	9,520
Low income	16	5,249	0.4%	18	1,398	16	3,852

Source: World Bank staff estimates.
Note: TRI is estimated using the most recent available tariff schedules (2005–2006). These data originates from the UNCTAD TRAINS and World Bank WITS databases. TRI is the uniform tariffs that would provide the same level of welfare in the importing country as the existing tariff structure. Deadweight loss (DWL) is measured by comparing the existing TRI to zero tariff. Deadweight loss is in million USD. For a detailed discussion of the methodology used to estimate the TRI see Kee, Nicita, and Olarreaga (2006).

TABLE A.3b Overall Trade Restrictiveness Index (OTRI) and import loss (US$, millions)

	All Products			Agriculture		Manufacturing	
	OTRI	Import Loss (US$, millions)	Import Loss (Percent of Total Imports)	OTRI	Import Loss (US$, millions)	OTRI	Import Loss (US$, millions)
Albania	7	−165	−6%	9	−37	7	−129
Algeria	38	−4,567	−25%	54	−1,235	34	−3,332
Argentina	16	−4,237	−15%	19	−155	16	−4,083
Australia	10	−8,239	−7%	41	−1,454	8	−6,785
Bangladesh	28	−1,327	−12%	30	−313	27	−1,014
Belarus	16	−1,721	−10%	34	−337	13	−1,384
Bolivia	15	−209	−9%	35	−51	12	−158
Brazil	22	−11,185	−15%	35	−1,045	21	−10,140
Brunei	9	−77	−6%	19	−20	7	−57
Burkina Faso	13	−126	−10%	36	−34	10	−93
Cameroon	16	−341	−12%	22	−75	14	−266
Canada	7	−14,302	−5%	34	−3,306	5	−10,996
Chile	9	−1,746	−6%	29	−355	7	−1,392
China	11	−43,411	−7%	19	−3,377	11	−40,034
Colombia	22	−2,936	−14%	46	−709	19	−2,227
Costa Rica	5	−301	−3%	11	−67	4	−233
Côte d'Ivoire	29	−700	−12%	53	−309	20	−391
Egypt, Arab Rep. of	32	−2,211	−17%	39	−614	30	−1,597
El Salvador	12	−369	−8%	16	−89	11	−281
Ethiopia	14	−228	−8%	11	−40	14	−189
European Union	9	−73,084	−2%	56	−26,901	5	−46,183
Gabon	16	−127	−13%	19	−36	15	−92
Ghana	14	−468	−11%	23	−156	12	−312
Guatemala	13	−900	−9%	48	−328	9	−572
Honduras	5	−159	−3%	19	−81	3	−79
Hong Kong, China	2	−2,104	−1%	17	−749	1	−1,355
Iceland	5	−171	−3%	19	−45	4	−126
India	20	−15,092	−10%	99	−1,849	17	−13,243
Indonesia	6	−2,706	−5%	16	−652	4	−2,054
Japan	16	−38,760	−8%	75	−24,447	5	−14,313
Jordan	23	−1,327	−13%	27	−228	22	−1,099
Kazakhstan	10	−474	−3%	43	−147	7	−327
Kenya	9	−277	−6%	29	−99	5	−178
Korea, Rep. of	10	−12,078	−5%	86	−3,741	4	−8,337
Lebanon	17	−939	−10%	64	−483	8	−456
Madagascar	9	−104	−9%	9	−13	9	−91
Malawi	16	−141	−12%	31	−44	13	−97
Malaysia	22	−12,191	−11%	47	−1,704	20	−10,487
Mali	12	−108	−11%	27	−29	10	−79
Mauritius	14	−235	−7%	33	−94	10	−141
Mexico	27	−34,405	−15%	63	−5,051	24	−29,354
Moldova	5	−74	−3%	7	−15	5	−59
Morocco	39	−4,484	−22%	80	−910	33	−3,574
New Zealand	14	−2,249	−8%	36	−432	12	−1,817
Nicaragua	12	−195	−8%	43	−86	7	−109
Nigeria	26	−2,295	−15%	63	−598	20	−1,697
Norway	6	−1,513	−3%	46	−1,023	2	−490
Oman	10	−657	−7%	47	−291	5	−366

continued

TABLE A.3b Overall Trade Restrictiveness Index (OTRI) and import loss (US$, millions) *(continued)*

	All Products			Agriculture		Manufacturing	
	OTRI	Import Loss (US$, millions)	Import Loss (Percent of Total Imports)	OTRI	Import Loss (US$, millions)	OTRI	Import Loss (US$, millions)
Papua N. Guinea	9	−66	−5%	31	−39	4	−27
Paraguay	14	−272	−9%	48	−65	11	−207
Peru	18	−1,483	−12%	56	−540	11	−942
Philippines	14	−3,891	−8%	48	−800	12	−3,091
Romania	17	−4,984	−12%	42	−638	16	−4,346
Russian Fed.	26	−14,221	−14%	44	−3,472	22	−10,749
Rwanda	24	−39	−15%	20	−7	25	−31
Saudi Arabia	8	−3,078	−5%	19	−621	6	−2,458
Senegal	33	−610	−17%	47	−242	28	−368
Singapore	14	−12,906	−6%	54	−1,570	13	−11,336
South Africa	7	−3,174	−6%	12	−289	7	−2,885
Sri Lanka	6	−419	−5%	16	−126	5	−293
Sudan	47	−998	−14%	47	−126	47	−873
Switzerland	6	−4,160	−3%	42	−1,968	3	−2,192
Tanzania	40	−640	−23%	50	−107	38	−533
Thailand	8	−6,112	−5%	44	−1,407	6	−4,705
Trinidad and Tobago	7	−306	−5%	25	−82	5	−224
Tunisia	30	−2,155	−16%	81	−338	26	−1,818
Turkey	11	−9,022	−8%	23	−639	11	−8,383
Uganda	10	−159	−8%	19	−51	8	−109
Ukraine	10	−2,381	−7%	10	−175	10	−2,206
Uruguay	16	−310	−8%	50	−66	13	−244
USA	9	−91,807	−5%	26	−14,745	8	−77,062
Venezuela, R. B. de	23	−1,822	−8%	58	−541	16	−1,281
Zambia	10	−205	−8%	31	−36	8	−169
High income	8	261,605		46	80,557	6	181,048
Middle income	16	180,270		37	27,083	13	153,186
Low income	16	29,214		30	5,053	13	24,161

Source: World Bank staff estimates.
Note: OTRI is estimated using the most recent available tariff schedules (2005–2006) and nontariff measures (about 2001). These data originate from the UNCTAD TRAINS and World Bank WITS databases. The OTRI measures the restrictiveness of a country's own trade policies. It is defined as the uniform tariff that would keep aggregate imports at their observed level. Import loss is calculated by comparing the existing OTRI to zero tariff. Import Loss is in million USD. For a detailed methodology on the estimation of the OTRI see Kee, Nicita, and Olarreaga (2006). The OTRI published here is not directly comparable with the OTRI published in previous Global Monitoring Reports, as the underlining data have been improved. There are 21 fewer countries due to consolidation in the European Union (8) and elimination of 13 countries estimated out of sample (basically without their own data).

TABLE A.3c Market Access-Overall Trade Restrictiveness Index (MA-OTRI)

	MA-OTRI	MA-OTRI Ag.	MA-OTRI Mfg.		MA-OTRI	MA-OTRI Ag.	MA-OTRI Mfg.
Albania	40	34	41	Mali	10	19	10
Algeria	1		1	Mauritius	51	101	34
Argentina	35	54	7	Mexico	13	35	10
Australia	21	57	6	Moldova	32	45	24
Bangladesh	44	16	46	Morocco	28	49	20
Belarus	10	34	9	New Zealand	45	66	7
Bolivia	12	34	4	Nicaragua	29	30	29
Brazil	18	44	6	Nigeria	12	61	0
Brunei	16		16	Norway	8	36	4
Burkina Faso	23	55	14	Oman	2	12	2
Cameroon	18	54	2	Papua N. Guinea	21	46	4
Canada	6	33	2	Paraguay	13	18	5
Chile	20	35	7	Peru	14	28	9
China	15	23	14	Philippines	13	15	13
Colombia	15	29	5	Romania	22	41	22
Costa Rica	21	26	14	Russian Fed.	8	30	5
Côte d'Ivoire	26	30	3	Rwanda	37	65	4
Egypt, Arab Rep. of	14	30	11	Saudi Arabia	4		4
El Salvador	47	37	48	Senegal	31	37	12
Ethiopia	46	56	10	Singapore	9		9
European Union	25	40	18	South Africa	10	48	3
Gabon	2	0	2	Sri Lanka	34	32	35
Ghana	32	45	2	Sudan	38	72	4
Guatemala	34	25	42	Switzerland	9	91	6
Honduras	41	27	45	Tanzania	29	43	5
Hong Kong, China	24	38	24	Thailand	26	71	15
Iceland	28	40	5	Trinidad and Tobago	3	80	2
India	23	32	21	Tunisia	24	27	24
Indonesia	18	30	16	Turkey	23	38	22
Japan	10		10	Uganda	35	39	7
Jordan	28	38	28	Ukraine	11	34	7
Kazakhstan	9	23	8	Uruguay	36	66	8
Kenya	39	50	13	USA	11	42	8
Korea, Rep. of	14		14	Venezuela, R. B. de	3	9	3
Lebanon	12	26	9	Zambia	23	43	18
Madagascar	22	14	36	High income	15	53	9
Malawi	34	36	11	Middle income	21	39	16
Malaysia	14	24	12	Low income	30	39	19

Source: World Bank staff estimates.
Note: MA-OTRI is estimated using the most recent available tariff schedules (2005–2006) and non tariff measures (about 2001). These data originate from the UNCTAD TRAINS and World Bank WITS databases. The MA-OTRI is calculated accounting for tariff preferences. The MA-OTRI measures the restrictiveness of other countries' trade policies on the export bundle of each country. For a detailed methodology on the estimation of the MA-OTRI see Kee, Nicita, and Olarreaga (2006). The MA-OTRI published here is not directly comparable with the MA-OTRI published in previous Global Monitoring Reports, as the underlining data have been improved. There are 21 fewer countries due to consolidation in the European Union (8) and elimination of 13 countries estimated out of sample (basically without their own data). MA-OTRI Ag. was not estimated for Algeria, Brunei, Indonesia, Rep. of Korea, Saudia Arabia, and Singapore owing to their limited agricultural exports.

TABLE A.4a Net Official Development Assistance (ODA) by DAC and non-DAC Countries

| | 2001 | | 2005 | | | | | | |
| | | | | of which: | | | | | |
	ODA (current US$ millions)	ODA (percent of GNI)	ODA (current US$ millions)	Technical Co-operation Grants	Humanitarian and Food Aid Grants	Debt Forgiveness Grants[a]	Other Bilateral ODA[b]	Contributions to Multilaterals	ODA (percent of GNI)
DAC Donors									
Austria	633	0.34	1573	150	89	904	57	341	0.52
Belgium	867	0.37	1963	500	124	472	166	655	0.53
Denmark	1634	1.03	2109	115	225	0	901	751	0.81
Finland	389	0.32	902	98	91	150	224	305	0.46
France	4198	0.31	10026	2364	652	3211	678	2787	0.47
Germany	4990	0.27	10082	2865	357	3441	578	2635	0.36
Greece	202	0.17	384	77	27	0	73	178	0.17
Ireland	287	0.33	719	13	85	0	354	237	0.42
Italy	1627	0.15	5091	121	79	1670	360	2821	0.29
Luxembourg	139	0.76	256	4	25	0	147	69	0.82
Netherlands	3173	0.82	5115	609	503	324	2002	1432	0.82
Portugal	268	0.25	377	115	13	3	72	159	0.21
Spain	1737	0.3	3018	483	145	473	658	1155	0.27
Sweden	1666	0.77	3362	140	405	53	1532	1106	0.94
United Kingdom	4579	0.32	10767	845	628	3506	2758	2603	0.47
DAC EU Members, Total	**26388**	**0.33**	**55745**	**8498**	**3448**	**14207**	**10559**	**17236**	**0.45**
Australia	873	0.25	1680	740	324	19	290	231	0.25
Canada	1533	0.22	3756	335	344	455	1450	924	0.34
Japan	9847	0.23	13147	1873	574	3553	3704	2740	0.28
New Zealand	112	0.25	274	41	66	0	102	50	0.27
Norway	1346	0.8	2786	320	412	0	1164	754	0.94
Switzerland	908	0.34	1767	154	329	224	664	367	0.44
United States	11429	0.11	27623	8966	4111	4076	7071	2343	0.22
DAC Members, Total	**52435**	**0.22**	**106777**	**20926**	**9607**	**22533**	**25003**	**24644**	**0.33**
Non-DAC Donors									
Czech Republic	27	0.05	135	15	19	10	17	71	0.11
Hungary			100				40	61	0.11
Iceland	10	0.13	27				20	7	0.18
Korea, Rep. of	265	0.06	752	80	27		337	289	0.1
Poland	36	0.02	205				48	157	0.07
Saudi Arabia*	490		1700						
Other Arab Countries	200		689				633	56	
Slovak Republic	8	0.04	56				31	25	0.12
Turkey	64	0.04	601	163	179		134	69	0.17
Other Bilateral Donors	95		665				568	98	
Non-DAC Countries, Total	**1194**		**4931**	**258**	**225**	**10**	**1827**	**832**	

a. Debt forgiveness grants are offset in order to avoid double-counting of Debt forgiveness of loans previously counted as ODA.
b. Other Bilateral ODA is Bilateral ODA - special purpose grants (technical cooperation, debt forgiveness, food and emergency aid) and administrative costs (not shown).
* Saudi Arabia has not yet reported to the DAC. No breakdown by instrument is available. $1700 is an estimate from the DAC.

TABLE A.4b   Net Official Development Assistance (ODA) Receipts

| | 2001 | 2005 | | | | | | |
| | | | of which: | | | | | |
	ODA (current US$ millions)	ODA (current US$ millions)	Technical Co–operation Grants	Debt Forgiveness Grants	Food and Emergency Aid Grants	Other ODA	ODA per capita (in current US$)	ODA (percent of GNI)
Afghanistan	405	2775	1132	0	296	1348		38.5
Albania	270	319	98	0	8	214	101.82	3.7
Algeria	224	371	199	38	41	93	11.28	0.4
Angola	283	442	80	0	122	240	27.72	1.7
Argentina	146	100	61	0	1	38	2.57	0.1
Armenia	198	193	85	0	46	62	64.07	3.9
Azerbaijan	232	223	76	0	38	110	26.64	2.0
Bangladesh	1025	1321	191	5	86	1039	9.31	2.1
Belarus	39	54	28	0	5	21	5.50	0.0
Benin	272	349	94	2	10	244	41.36	8.2
Bhutan	61	90	23	0	0	67	98.06	11.0
Bolivia	734	583	193	4	36	351	63.48	6.5
Bosnia and Herzegovina	639	546	135	4	48	360	139.77	5.7
Botswana	29	71	53	1	0	17	40.17	0.8
Brazil	229	192	192	0	2	−2	1.03	0.0
Burkina Faso	390	660	97	4	25	534	49.86	12.8
Burundi	137	365	40	4	151	170	48.36	46.8
Cambodia	418	538	181	0	20	336	38.22	10.4
Cameroon	486	414	152	148	13	100	25.35	2.5
Cape Verde	77	161	44	0	10	107	316.88	17.1
Central African Republic	66	95	39	2	6	50	23.60	7.0
Chad	185	380	47	2	111	220	38.96	8.6
Chile	57	152	60	0	2	89	9.31	0.1
China	1473	1757	859	0	37	861	1.35	0.1
Colombia	380	511	448	0	53	11	11.21	0.4
Comoros	27	25	13	0	3	9	42.02	6.6
Congo, Dem. Rep. of	243	1828	189	143	332	1164	31.76	27.5
Congo, Rep. of	74	1449	32	1234	26	156	362.31	36.8
Costa Rica	2	30	29	0	1	−0	6.82	0.2
Côte d'Ivoire	169	119	77	11	58	−27	6.56	0.8
Croatia	113	125	52	0	8	66	28.22	0.3
Cuba	54	88	33	0	9	46	7.79	
Djibouti	58	79	32	0	5	41	99.11	10.1
Dominican Republic	107	77	65	0	2	11	8.66	0.3
Ecuador	173	210	139	−42	8	104	15.84	0.6
Egypt, Arab Rep. of	1256	926	386	148	2	390	12.51	1.0
El Salvador	237	199	86	0	52	61	28.98	1.2
Equatorial Guinea	13	39	17	3	0	20	77.45	0.0
Eritrea	281	355	26	0	171	158	80.69	36.3
Ethiopia	1104	1937	217	34	678	1008	27.19	17.4
Fiji	26	64	29	0	0	35	75.45	2.3
Gabon	9	54	46	0	1	8	38.93	0.7
Gambia, The	54	58	10	0	3	45	38.33	13.1
Georgia	300	310	132	0	49	129	69.23	4.7
Ghana	641	1120	129	66	22	903	50.65	10.6
Guatemala	227	254	97	0	62	95	20.13	0.8
Guinea	281	182	63	5	35	79	19.37	6.9
Guinea-Bissau	59	79	16	1	17	45	49.88	27.3

(continued)

TABLE A.4b Net Official Development Assistance (ODA) Receipts *(continued)*

	2001	2005						
			of which:					
	ODA (current US$ millions)	ODA (current US$ millions)	Technical Co–operation Grants	Debt Forgiveness Grants	Food and Emergency Aid Grants	Other ODA	ODA per capita (in current US$)	ODA (percent of GNI)
Guyana	97	137	28	1	3	105	182.08	18.6
Haiti	171	515	143	0	152	220	60.39	12.1
Honduras	679	681	108	158	48	367	94.50	8.2
India	1701	1724	363	0	104	1258	1.58	0.2
Indonesia	1467	2524	476	10	667	1371	11.44	0.9
Iran, Islamic Rep. of	114	104	75	0	24	5	1.54	0.1
Iraq	121	21654	1646	13920	484	5603		
Jamaica	54	36	44	9	10	−27	13.45	0.4
Jordan	449	622	126	0	2	494	114.95	4.7
Kazakhstan	148	229	95	0	7	128	15.13	0.5
Kenya	462	768	206	3	76	483	22.43	4.3
Korea, Dem. Rep. of	118	81	10	0	46	26	3.61	
Kyrgyz Republic	189	268	93	4	15	156	52.07	11.4
Lao PDR	245	296	82	0	7	207	49.92	11.2
Lebanon	243	243	105	0	35	103	67.93	1.2
Lesotho	56	69	14	0	6	49	38.34	3.8
Liberia	38	236	55	0	130	52	71.93	54.1
Libya	7	24	11	0	1	13	4.18	0.0
Macedonia, FYR	247	230	101	0	3	127	113.23	4.0
Madagascar	374	929	96	294	41	498	49.94	18.7
Malawi	404	575	101	5	68	401	44.66	28.4
Malaysia	27	32	53	0	2	−23	1.25	0.0
Mali	351	692	130	5	28	529	51.15	14.1
Mauritania	267	190	44	1	45	101	62.04	10.4
Mauritius	21	32	24	0	0	8	25.58	0.5
Mexico	73	189	149	0	1	39	1.84	0.0
Moldova	122	192	60	0	57	75	45.59	5.8
Mongolia	211	212	86	0	15	111	82.95	11.6
Morocco	518	652	386	0	6	260	21.61	1.3
Mozambique	931	1286	205	4	39	1038	64.97	20.8
Myanmar	126	145	41	1	33	70	2.86	
Namibia	109	123	66	0	0	57	60.73	2.0
Nepal	391	428	128	5	34	261	15.77	5.8
Nicaragua	930	740	111	131	44	454	134.88	15.2
Niger	256	515	65	23	78	350	36.93	15.2
Nigeria	168	6437	234	5548	25	631	48.94	7.4
Oman	1	31	11	0	0	20	11.95	0.0
Pakistan	1942	1667	201	0	698	767	10.70	1.5
Panama	28	20	27	0	0	−7	6.05	0.1
Papua New Guinea	203	266	161	0	4	102	45.21	6.6
Paraguay	61	51	46	0	0	5	8.30	0.6
Peru	449	398	228	7	12	152	14.22	0.5
Philippines	572	562	247	0	36	279	6.76	0.5
Rwanda	299	576	114	11	51	400	63.73	27.4
São Tomé and Principe	38	32	11	0	1	20	203.81	58.6
Senegal	413	689	224	85	11	370	59.12	8.4
Serbia and Montenegro	1306	1132	326	201	81	524	138.54	4.3

(continued)

TABLE A.4b Net Official Development Assistance (ODA) Receipts *(continued)*

| | 2001 | 2005 | | | | | | |
| | | | of which: | | | | | |
	ODA (current US$ millions)	ODA (current US$ millions)	Technical Co–operation Grants	Debt Forgiveness Grants	Food and Emergency Aid Grants	Other ODA	ODA per capita (in current US$)	ODA (percent of GNI)
Sierra Leone	343	343	31	4	46	262	62.15	29.6
Solomon Islands	59	198	143	0	1	54	414.95	70.5
Somalia	148	236	9	0	165	62	28.73	
South Africa	428	700	270	0	2	428	15.49	0.3
Sri Lanka	313	1189	97	0	400	692	60.73	5.1
Sudan	181	1829	131	0	1267	431	50.47	7.1
Swaziland	29	46	5	0	4	37	40.70	1.7
Syrian Arab Republic	153	78	77	0	7	−7	4.09	0.3
Tajikistan	169	241	57	0	45	139	37.09	10.8
Tanzania	1269	1505	196	1	47	1261	39.27	12.5
Thailand	281	−171	149	0	45	−364	−2.66	−0.1
Timor-Leste	194	185	74	0	5	105	189.37	26.7
Togo	43	87	34	2	5	47	14.11	4.0
Tunisia	377	377	146	0	2	229	37.57	1.4
Turkey	169	464	177	0	76	212	6.39	0.1
Turkmenistan	72	28	24	0	0	4	5.84	0.0
Uganda	790	1198	235	1	187	775	41.58	14.0
Ukraine	519	410	228	0	12	170	8.69	0.0
Uruguay	15	15	15	−9	0	8	4.22	0.1
Uzbekistan	153	172	76	0	3	94	6.48	1.3
Venezuela, R. B. de	44	49	36	0	14	−0	1.83	0.0
Vietnam	1450	1905	316	1	13	1575	22.96	3.7
West Bank and Gaza	869	1102	208	0	153	740	303.81	
Yemen, Rep. of	458	336	59	1	15	261	16.02	2.6
Zambia	349	945	181	340	37	388	80.99	14.2
Zimbabwe	162	368	61	0	84	223	28.26	11.6
East Asia & Pacific	7390	9497	3198	12	1147	5140		
Europe & Central Asia	5230	5732	2036	209	584	2902		
Latin America & Caribbean	5868	6309	2783	268	632	2626		
Middle East & North Africa	4905	26947	3550	14108	817	8472		
South Asia	5861	9261	2144	9	1655	5452		
Sub-Saharan Africa	13981	32620	4863	7985	4731	15041		
Unspecified by Region	8758	16008	4140	0	1848	10021		
Fragile States	6198	21477	3555	6957	3483	7482		
Low-income Countries	20878	40353	6979	6615	5643	21115		
Lower-Middle-income Countries	18322	43146	8879	15971	2823	15473		
Upper-Middle-income Countries	1746	2776	1353	−5	150	1278		
Middle-income Countries	20580	46913	10612	15966	3082	17254		
Unallocated	10535	19106	5123	10	2690	11284		
Developing Countries, Total	**51993**	**106372**	**22714**	**22591**	**11415**	**49653**		

Source: OECD DAC Database
Regional totals do not include ODA that is unspecufied by region. The total for developing countries includes ODA that is unallocated by country or income group.
Income group totals reflect the classifications used in the World Development Indicators which are different than the classifications used elsewhere in this report.

TABLE A.5 Measures of Gender Performance

	Primary Education[a]		Child Mortality[b]		Labor Force Participation[c]			
					Between 20 to 24 years old		Between 25 to 49 years old	
	Female primary completion rate	Female-to-male ratio: Primary completion rate	Female under-5 mortality rate	Female-to-male ratio: under-5 mortality rate	Female labor force participation	Female-to-male ratio: Labor force participation	Female labor force participation	Female-to-male ratio: Labor force participation
	2001–2004[d]	2001–2004[d]	2000–2005[d]	2000–2005[d]	2000–2005[d]	2000–2005[a]	2000–2005[d]	2000–2005[d]
Afghanistan	..	..	255	1.02	21.0	0.27	24.5	0.27
Albania	99.2	1.00	31.3	0.86	47.4	0.99	64.7	0.83
Algeria	94.5	1.01	39.6	0.95	..	..	..	..
Angola	..	..	230.8	0.89	61.4	..	81.7	..
Argentina	103.1	1.05	15.1	0.77	44.7	0.63	60.9	0.64
Armenia	107.6	1.02	32.5	0.87	40.1	0.71	57.3	0.71
Azerbaijan	95.2	0.98	86.5	0.92	44.3	0.66	62.4	0.69
Bangladesh	78.8	1.06	79.5	1.01	6.9	0.01	10.4	0.11
Belarus	98.7	0.96	14.6	0.71	62.3	1.03	90.3	0.97
Benin	38.3	0.65	158.8	0.97	73.6	1.19	88.8	0.93
Bhutan	..	..	81.7	0.96	69.3	0.96	77.3	0.83
Bolivia	97.9	0.96	67.4	0.88	59.2	0.76	77.7	0.80
Bosnia and Herzegovina	..	..	14	0.81	54.0	0.65	52.5	0.56
Botswana	94.1	1.05	100.2	0.90	..	..	..	..
Brazil	111.4	1.01	30.5	0.76	63.0	0.72	66.7	0.71
Bulgaria	97.4	0.98	14.9	0.81	63.8	0.82	83.0	0.93
Burkina Faso	25.3	0.76	190.7	0.95	79.0	0.89	85.9	0.88
Burundi	26.9	0.68	175.8	0.89	80.9	..	96.3	..
Cambodia	77.8	0.91	134.4	0.92	79.9	0.92	81.9	0.86
Cameroon	57.6	0.84	155.3	0.91	57.5	0.82	78.1	0.83
Cape Verde	95.3	1.00	25.2	0.54	62.8	0.76	70.3	0.75
Central African Republic	..	..	159.3	0.83	..	..	..	..
Chad	18.4	0.45	191.3	0.89	..	..	..	..
Chile	94.6	0.98	8.5	0.78	47.2	0.69	56.5	0.60
China	..	..	47.1	1.36	..	..	..	..
Colombia	96.4	1.04	30.1	0.85	64.2	0.75	68.3	0.71
Comoros	49.0	0.95	68.3	0.80	..	..	..	..
Congo, Dem. Rep. of	..	..	200.7	0.90	..	..	..	..
Congo, Rep. of	63.2	0.91	96.5	0.81	..	..	..	..
Costa Rica	93.5	1.03	10.7	0.79	53.8	0.63	54.0	0.56
Côte d'Ivoire	33.7	0.65	180.1	0.91	50.7	0.76	65.0	0.70
Croatia	90.8	0.99	7.6	0.88	51.3	0.84	78.2	0.90
Cuba	92.1	0.99	6.9	0.81	..	..	..	..
Czech Republic	104.0	1.00	5.7	0.93	..	..	..	..
Djibouti	25.0	0.75	131.2	0.88	61.3	..	42.2	..
Dominican Republic	93.4	1.06	45.5	0.82	49.5	0.57	60.3	0.64
Ecuador	101.1	1.01	25.1	0.73	48.5	0.61	59.0	0.62
Egypt, Arab Rep. of	92.8	0.96	38.9	0.83	52.2	..	53.9	..
El Salvador	86.2	1.01	31.2	0.82	45.3	0.57	59.8	0.64
Equatorial Guinea	47.0	0.87	172.6	0.91	..	..	..	..
Eritrea	34.4	0.68	89.5	0.91	..	..	..	..
Estonia	100.2	0.98	9.2	0.65	56.6	0.73	84.9	0.89
Ethiopia	48.8	0.80	163.7	0.91	56.5	0.64	59.9	0.62
Gabon	67.6	1.04	90.1	0.90	..	..	..	..
Gambia, The	..	..	121.8	0.90	47.0	..	66.0	..

(continued)

TABLE A.5   Measures of Gender Performance *(continued)*

	Primary Education[a]		Child Mortality[b]		Labor Force Participation[c]			
					Between 20 to 24 years old		Between 25 to 49 years old	
	Female primary completion rate	Female-to-male ratio: Primary completion rate	Female under-5 mortality rate	Female-to-male ratio: under-5 mortality rate	Female labor force participation	Female-to-male ratio: Labor force participation	Female labor force participation	Female-to-male ratio: Labor force participation
	2001–2004[d]	2001–2004[d]	2000–2005[d]	2000–2005[d]	2000–2005[d]	2000–2005[a]	2000–2005[d]	2000–2005[d]
Georgia	87.5	1.04	38.6	0.81	*35.9*	..	*70.1*	..
Germany	..	..	..	..	..	..	..	..
Ghana	68.7	0.91	100.2	0.97	*67.2*	..	*93.0*	..
Guatemala	65.4	0.87	45.5	0.79	34.2	0.40	36.9	0.39
Guinea	38.8	0.67	167.2	1.02	*79.5*	..	*89.3*	..
Guinea-Bissau	19.3	0.56	199.5	0.90	..	..	..	..
Guyana	91.5	0.92	57.2	0.73	*42.8*	..	*51.2*	..
Haiti	..	..	102	0.87	48.7	0.81	70.6	0.82
Honduras	81.8	1.06	43	0.81	42.4	0.48	51.0	0.54
Hungary	95.9	1.01	9.4	0.80	61.8	0.94	86.2	0.98
India	83.9	0.90	102	1.07	28.1	0.34	37.1	0.38
Indonesia	102.1	1.01	47.2	0.78	49.3	0.60	51.0	0.52
Iran, Islamic Rep. of	96.9	1.05	39.4	1.01	..	..	..	..
Iraq	62.7	0.74	118.4	0.92	..	..	..	..
Jamaica	85.7	1.03	19.5	0.89	39.4	0.69	50.4	0.76
Jordan	96.3	0.99	25.6	0.93	28.4	0.37	24.3	0.26
Kazakhstan	109.5	0.99	62.8	0.69	65.6	0.86	88.2	0.93
Kenya	90.3	0.97	110	0.88	*48.8*	..	*57.0*	..
Korea, Dem. Rep. of	..	..	54.9	0.87	..	..	..	..
Kyrgyz Republic	93.4	1.01	60.3	0.84	55.5	0.81	84.3	0.92
Lao PDR	69.6	0.89	137.1	0.95	..	..	..	..
Latvia	92.0	0.99	12.9	0.90	48.6	0.72	85.5	0.96
Lebanon	96.5	1.05	21.2	0.67	..	..	..	..
Lesotho	82.0	1.37	116.2	0.90	64.6	0.94	73.0	0.81
Liberia	..	..	214.8	0.92	..	..	..	..
Libya	..	..	21.1	1.00	..	..	..	..
Lithuania	97.2	0.99	9.5	0.69	94.2	0.94	97.1	0.97
Macedonia, FYR	97.3	1.02	17.1	0.88	..	..	..	..
Madagascar	46.0	1.03	125.8	0.92	54.3	0.81	54.0	0.90
Malawi	57.2	0.96	179.1	0.94	16.2	0.67	18.0	0.52
Malaysia	91.1	1.00	11.4	0.78	..	..	..	..
Mali	29.6	0.51	217.2	0.97	..	..	..	..
Mauritania	41.0	0.91	149.6	0.92	22.4	0.52	27.8	0.44
Mauritius	99.4	1.04	15.3	0.76	..	..	..	..
Mexico	99.6	1.02	21.8	0.80	42.4	0.53	53.0	0.56
Moldova	91.5	1.01	28.5	0.83	75.7	0.98	79.2	1.01
Mongolia	96.3	1.02	83.2	0.95	47.7	0.84	75.9	0.95
Morocco	72.0	0.91	38.6	0.72	*30.3*	..	*35.3*	..
Mozambique	23.4	0.68	173	0.91	*77.8*	..	*86.6*	..
Myanmar	79.1	1.03	102.3	0.84	..	..	..	..
Namibia	85.3	1.12	74.5	0.92	*48.6*	..	*66.2*	..
Nepal	69.5	0.87	91	1.07	*70.9*	..	*82.8*	..
Nicaragua	77.0	1.01	35.2	0.79	38.6	0.47	53.2	0.58
Niger	20.0	0.67	266.5	1.02	30.9	0.51	47.4	0.54
Nigeria	68.2	0.83	196.6	0.96	33.0	1.03	63.7	0.72

(continued)

TABLE A.5 Measures of Gender Performance *(continued)*

	Primary Education[a]		Child Mortality[b]		Labor Force Participation[c]			
					Between 20 to 24 years old		Between 25 to 49 years old	
	Female primary completion rate	Female-to-male ratio: Primary completion rate	Female under-5 mortality rate	Female-to-male ratio: under-5 mortality rate	Female labor force participation	Female-to-male ratio: Labor force participation	Female labor force participation	Female-to-male ratio: Labor force participation
	2001–2004[d]	2001–2004[d]	2000–2005[d]	2000–2005[d]	2000–2005[d]	2000–2005[a]	2000–2005[d]	2000–2005[d]
Oman	89.6	0.97	16.5	0.87	..	..	..	..
Pakistan	..	..	118.6	1.08	26.6	0.33	30.4	0.33
Panama	96.9	1.01	22.9	0.75	46.4	0.55	57.3	0.60
Papua New Guinea	49.5	0.86	103	1.01	..	..	..	..
Paraguay	91.1	1.01	39.5	0.78	58.2	0.68	64.1	0.67
Peru	98.9	0.99	46.9	0.82	62.1	0.78	74.1	0.78
Philippines	99.9	1.07	28	0.71	..	..	..	..
Poland	..	..	9.7	0.87	60.2	0.95	65.2	0.99
Romania	92.8	0.99	18.7	0.73	65.8	0.99	71.3	0.98
Russian Federation	..	..	18.7	0.77	72.2	0.94	100.0	1.00
Rwanda	36.8	0.97	178.4	0.89	*85.3*	..	*95.1*	..
Senegal	41.7	0.85	129.7	0.96	*28.2*	..	*52.6*	..
Serbia and Montenegro	95.9	0.99	13.8	0.82	49.2	0.81	74.5	0.82
Sierra Leone	..	..	277.4	0.92	57.4	1.19	78.4	0.95
Slovak Republic	99.6	1.00	9.4	0.90	..	..	..	..
Somalia	..	..	205.8	0.95	..	..	..	..
South Africa	97.5	1.04	69.3	0.89	46.1	0.87	67.9	0.80
Spain	..	..	..	..	..	..	..	..
Sri Lanka	..	..	14.8	0.60	55.3	0.64	47.6	0.50
Sudan	44.5	0.84	112.7	0.90	..	..	..	..
Swaziland	64.2	1.10	134.1	0.88	47.1	0.75	55.2	0.67
Syrian Arab Republic	104.3	0.96	17.8	0.74	..	..	..	..
Tajikistan	89.6	0.95	109.7	0.90	44.1	0.77	54.3	0.71
Tanzania	53.1	0.96	155.7	0.91	74.2	0.85	79.6	0.82
Thailand	..	..	18.7	0.62	70.6	0.87	86.2	0.88
Timor-Leste	..	..	130.2	0.94	42.0	0.55	40.8	0.43
Togo	55.0	0.71	128.7	0.88	..	..	..	..
Trinidad and Tobago	95.3	1.02	15.9	0.74	*41.3*	..	*46.8*	..
Tunisia	97.5	1.01	23	0.85	..	..	..	..
Turkey	82.3	0.88	43.7	0.80	40.7	0.50	38.8	0.41
Turkmenistan	..	..	88.7	0.81	..	..	..	..
Uganda	53.3	0.88	133	0.92	82.5	1.06	92.8	0.96
Ukraine	..	..	14.8	0.72	52.3	0.74	81.8	0.88
Uruguay	92.9	1.04	12.6	0.70	66.6	0.79	77.8	0.81
Uzbekistan	96.5	1.00	63.5	0.84	..	..	..	..
Venezuela, R. B. de	92.0	1.06	26.8	0.85	46.9	0.58	61.7	0.65
Vietnam	97.6	0.94	33	0.75	79.8	0.97	94.0	0.96
West Bank and Gaza	98.7	1.01	21.8	0.81	..	..	..	..
Yemen, Rep. of	45.6	0.58	91	0.92	*13.5*	..	*19.3*	..
Zambia	61.5	0.87	164.9	0.91	54.3	0.97	68.6	0.75
Zimbabwe	78.6	0.96	110.1	0.89	..	..	..	..

Sources: a. 2006 World Development Indicators database.
b. 2004 World Population Prospects.
c. Household surveys various year.
d. Data are for the most recent year available.
Figures in italics refer to periods other than those specified.
.. Not available